Advances in Delay Differential Equations

Advances in Delay Differential Equations

Advances in Delay Differential Equations

Editor

Alexandra Kashchenko

MDPI • Basel • Beijing • Wuhan • Barcelona • Belgrade • Manchester • Tokyo • Cluj • Tianjin

Editor
Alexandra Kashchenko
P.G. Demidov Yaroslavl State
University
Yaroslavl, Russia

Editorial Office
MDPI
St. Alban-Anlage 66
4052 Basel, Switzerland

This is a reprint of articles from the Special Issue published online in the open access journal *Mathematics* (ISSN 2227-7390) (available at: https://www.mdpi.com/si/mathematics/Delay_Differ_Equ).

For citation purposes, cite each article independently as indicated on the article page online and as indicated below:

LastName, A.A.; LastName, B.B.; LastName, C.C. Article Title. *Journal Name* **Year**, *Volume Number*, Page Range.

ISBN 978-3-0365-8286-3 (Hbk)
ISBN 978-3-0365-8287-0 (PDF)

Contents

About the Editor

Alexandra Kashchenko

Alexandra Kashchenko is Assistant Professor and Senior Researcher at the P. G. Demidov Yaroslavl State University. She is the co-author of a monograph on the dynamics of mathematical models of lasers, and an author of a number of the papers on nonlinear dynamics. Her research interests include local and nonlocal dynamics, theory of differential equations with delay, and nonlinear oscillations.

Preface

Differential equations naturally arise when modeling a large number of phenomena in optics, radiophysics, biology, medicine, economics, and sociology.

It is well known that, for the adequate mathematical modeling of the dynamics of many processes in various areas of science, it is crucial to take into account the influence of lags. That is why delay differential equations play an important role in mathematical modeling. For example, they are able to model gene networks, information transmission systems, population size, and infectious diseases.

Qualitative properties of solutions to equations with delay are also of great interest.

The present book contains the 11 articles accepted for publication out of the 31 manuscripts submitted to the Special Issue "Advances in Delay Differential Equations" of the MDPI journal *Mathematics*.

The 11 articles cover a wide range of topics connected to the theory of differential equations with delay. These topics include, among others, the construction of solutions and analytical and numerical methods for; dynamical properties of; and applications of DDE to the mathematical modeling of various phenomena and processes in physics, biology, ecology, and medicine.

It is hoped that the book will be interesting and useful for those working in the area of differential equations with delays and nonlinear dynamics, as well as for those with the proper mathematical background who are willing to become familiar with recent advances in mathematical modelling.

As the Guest Editor of the Special Issue, I am grateful to the authors of the papers for their quality contributions, to the reviewers for their valuable comments towards the improvement of the submitted manuscripts, and to the administrative staff of MDPI for the support needed to complete this project. Special thanks are due to the Managing Editor of the Special Issue, Dr. Syna Mu, for excellent collaboration and valuable assistance.

Alexandra Kashchenko
Editor

mathematics MDPI

Article

On a Coupled System of Random and Stochastic Nonlinear Differential Equations with Coupled Nonlocal Random and Stochastic Nonlinear Integral Conditions

Ahmed M. A. El-Sayed * and Hoda A. Fouad *

Faculty of Science, Alexandria University, Alexandria 21568, Egypt
* Correspondence: amasayed@alexu.edu.eg (A.M.A.E.-S.); hoda.fouad@alexu.edu.eg (H.A.F.)

Abstract: It is well known that Stochastic equations had many useful applications in describing numerous events and problems of real world, and the nonlocal integral condition is important in physics, finance and engineering. Here we are concerned with two problems of a coupled system of random and stochastic nonlinear differential equations with two coupled systems of nonlinear nonlocal random and stochastic integral conditions. The existence of solutions will be studied. The sufficient condition for the uniqueness of the solution will be given. The continuous dependence of the unique solution on the nonlocal conditions will be proved.

Keywords: stochastic processes; stochastic differential equation; coupled system; nonlocal stochastic integral conditions

MSC: 34A12; 34A30; 34D20; 34F05; 60H10

Citation: El-Sayed, A.M.A.; Fouad, H.A. On a Coupled System of Random and Stochastic Nonlinear Differential Equations with Coupled Nonlocal Random and Stochastic Nonlinear Integral Conditions. *Mathematics* **2021**, *9*, 2111. https://doi.org/10.3390/math9172111

Academic Editor: Alexandra Kashchenko

Received: 3 July 2021
Accepted: 27 August 2021
Published: 1 September 2021

1. Introduction

Let (Ω, F, P) be a fixed probability space, where Ω is a sample space, F is a σ-algebra and P is a probability measure.

The aim of this article is to extend the results of A.M.A. El-Sayed [1,2] on the stochastic fractional calculus operators defined on $C([0,T], L_2(\Omega))$ and the solution of stochastic differential equations subject to nonlocal integral conditions which have been considered in [3,4].

Moreover, we motivate the coupled system of integral equations in reflexive Banach space by A.M.A. El-Sayed and H.H.G.Hashem [5] to the coupled systems with random memory on the space of all second order stochastic process.

The continuous dependence of a unique solution has been studied on the random initial data and the random function which ensures the stability of the solution.

Nonlocal problem of differential equation have been studied by many authors (see for example [6–8]).

Let $Z(t;\omega) = Z(t)$, $t \in [0,T]$, $\omega \in \Omega$ be a second order stochastic process, i.e., $E(Z^2(t)) < \infty$, $t \in [0,T]$.

Let $C = C([0,T], L_2(\Omega))$ be the space of all second order stochastic processes which is mean square (m.s) continuous on $[0,T]$. The norm of $Z \in C([0,T], L_2(\Omega))$ is given by

$$\|Z\|_C = \sup_{t\in[0,T]} \|Z(t)\|_2, \qquad \|Z(t)\|_2 = \sqrt{E(Z^2(t))}.$$

Let $T \geq 1$. In this paper we study the existence of solutions $(x,y) \in C([0,T], L_2(\Omega))$ of the problem of the coupled system of random and stochastic differential equations

$$\frac{dx(t)}{dt} = f_1(t, y(\phi_1(t))), \quad t \in (0,T], \tag{1}$$
$$dy(t) = f_2(t, x(\phi_2(t)))dW(t), \quad t \in (0,T] \tag{2}$$

subject to each one of the two nonlinear nonlocal stochastic integral conditions

$$x(0) + \int_0^\tau h_1(s, y(s))dW(s) = x_0, \quad y(0) + \int_0^\eta h_2(s, x(s))ds = y_0 \tag{3}$$

and

$$x(0) + \int_0^\tau h_1(s, x(s))dW(s) = x_0, \quad y(0) + \int_0^\eta h_2(s, y(s))ds = y_0 \tag{4}$$

where x_0 and y_0 are two second order random variables.

Let $X = C([0,T], L_2(\Omega)) \times C([0,T], L_2(\Omega))$ be the class of all ordered pairs (x,y), $x, y \in C$ with the norm

$$\|(x,y)\|_X = \max\{\|x\|_C, \|y\|_C\} = \max\{\sup_{t\in[0,T]} \|x(t)\|_2, \sup_{t\in[0,T]} \|y(t)\|_2\}. \tag{5}$$

Let $\phi_i : [0,T] \to [0,T]$ be continuous functions such that $\phi_i(t) \le t$ and consider the following assumptions

Assumption 1. *$f_i : [0,T] \times L_2(\Omega) \to L_2(\Omega)$, $i = 1,2$ are measurable in $t \in [0,T]$ for all $x \in L_2(\Omega)$ and continuous in $x \in L_2(\Omega)$ for all $t \in [0,T]$. There exist two bounded measurable functions $m_i : [0,T] \to R$ and two positive constants b_i such that*

$$\|f_i(t,x)\|_2 \le |m_i(t)| + b_i\|x(t)\|_2, \quad i = 1,2. \tag{6}$$

Assumption 2. *$h_i : [0,T] \times L_2(\Omega) \to L_2(\Omega)$, $i = 1,2$ are measurable in $t \in [0,T]$ for all $x \in L_2(\Omega)$ and continuous in $x \in L_2(\Omega)$ for all $t \in [0,T]$. There exist two bounded measurable functions $k_i : [0,T] \to R$ and two positive constants c_i such that*

$$\|h_i(t,x)\|_2 \le |k_i(t)| + c_i\|x(t)\|_2, \quad i = 1,2. \tag{7}$$

Assumption 3. $M = \max\{\sup_{t\in[0,T]} |m_1(t)|, \sup_{t\in[0,T]} |m_2(t)|\}$, $b = \max\{b_1, b_2\}$.

Assumption 4. $K = \max\{\sup_{t\in[0,T]} |k_1(t)|, \sup_{t\in[0,T]} |k_2(t)|\}$, $c = \max\{c_1, c_2\}$.

Assumption 5. $(b + c)T < 1$.

Now, integrating the two random and stochastic differential Equations (1) and (2) (see [1,2,9–14]) and using the nonlocal conditions (3) and (4) the following Lemma can be proven.

Lemma 1. *The integral representations of the solutions of the nonlocal problems (1) and (2) with conditions (3) and (1) and (2) with conditions (4) are given by*

$$x(t) = x_0 - \int_0^\tau h_1(s, y(s))dW(s) + \int_0^t f_1(s, y(\phi_1(s)))ds, \tag{8}$$
$$y(t) = y_0 - \int_0^\eta h_2(s, x(s))ds + \int_0^t f_2(s, x(\phi_2(s)))dW(s). \tag{9}$$

and

$$x(t) = x_0 - \int_0^\tau h_1(s, x(s))dW(s) + \int_0^t f_1(s, y(\phi_1(s)))ds, \tag{10}$$
$$y(t) = y_0 - \int_0^\eta h_2(s, y(s))ds + \int_0^t f_2(s, x(\phi_2(s)))dW(s). \tag{11}$$

respectively.

2. Solutions of the Problem (1)–(3)

Define the mapping $(F(x,y))(t) = (F_1y, F_2x)(t), \quad t \in [0,T]$ where $(F_1y)(t)$, $(F_2x)(t)$ are given by the following stochastic integral equations

$$(F_1y)(t) = x_0 - \int_0^\tau h_1(s,y(s))dW(s) + \int_0^t f_1(s,y(\phi_1(s)))ds, \tag{12}$$

$$(F_2x)(t) = y_0 - \int_0^\eta h_2(s,x(s))ds + \int_0^t f_2(s,x(\phi_2(s)))dW(s). \tag{13}$$

Consider the set Q such that

$$Q = \{x,y \in C([0,T],L_2(\Omega)), (x,y) \in X : ||(x,y)||_X = \max\{||x(t)||_2, ||y(t)||_2\} \le r.\}$$

Now, we have the following two lemmas

Lemma 2. $F : Q \to Q.$

Proof. Let $y \in Q$, $\|y(t)\|_2 \le r_1$, then

$$\begin{aligned}
\|(F_1y)(t)\|_2 &\le \|x_0\|_2 + \|\int_0^\tau h_1(s,y(s))dW(s)\|_2 + \|\int_0^t f_1(s,y(\phi_1(s)))ds\|_2 \\
&\le \|x_0\|_2 + \sqrt{\int_0^\tau \|h_1(s,y(s))\|_2^2 ds} + \int_0^t \|f_1(s,y(\phi_1(s)))\|_2 ds \\
&\le \|x_0\|_2 + \sqrt{\int_0^\tau (|k_1(s)| + c_1\|y(s)\|_2)^2 ds} + \int_0^t (|m_1(S)| + b_1\|y(s)\|_2)ds \\
&\le \|x_0\|_2 + (K + cr_1)\sqrt{T} + (M + br_1)T < \|x_0\|_2 + (K + cr_1)T + (M + br_1)T = r_1
\end{aligned}$$

where

$$r_1 = \frac{\|x_0\|_2 + KT + MT}{1 - (b+c)T} > 0.$$

Let $x \in Q$, $\|x(t)\|_2 \le r_2$, then

$$\begin{aligned}
\|(F_2x)(t)\|_2 &\le \|y_0\|_2 + \|\int_0^\eta h_2(s,x(s))ds\|_2 + \|\int_0^t f_2(s,x(\phi_2(s)))dW(s)\|_2 \\
&\le \|y_0\|_2 + \int_0^\eta \|h_2(s,x(s))\|_2 ds + \sqrt{\int_0^t \|f_2(s,x(\phi_2(s)))\|_2^2 ds} \\
&\le \|y_0\|_2 + \int_0^\eta (|k_2(s)| + c_2\|x(s)\|_2)ds + \sqrt{\int_0^t (|m_2(t)| + b_2\|x\|_2)^2 ds} \\
&\le \|y_0\|_2 + (K + cr_2)T + (M + br_2)T < \|y_0\|_2 + (K + cr_2)T + (M + br_2)T = r_2
\end{aligned}$$

where

$$r_2 = \frac{\|y_0\|_2 + KT + MT}{1 - (b+c)T} > 0.$$

Let $r = \max\{r_1, r_2\}$, $(x,y) \in Q$, then

$$\begin{aligned}
\|F(x,y)\|_X &= \|(F_1y, F_2x)\|_X \\
&= \max\{\|(F_1y)\|_C, \|(F_2x)\|_C\} < r.
\end{aligned}$$

This proves that $F : Q \to Q$ and the class of functions $\{F(x,y)\}$ is uniformly bounded on Q. □

Lemma 3. *The class of functions* $\{F(x,y)\}$ *is equicontinuous on* Q.

Proof. Let $x, y \in Q$, $t_1, t_2 \in [0,T]$ such that $|t_2 - t_1| < \delta$, then

$$\begin{aligned}
\|(F_1y)(t_2) - (F_1y)(t_1)\|_2 &= \| \int_0^{t_2} f_1(s, y(\phi_1(s)))ds - \int_0^{t_1} f_1(s, y(\phi_1(s)))ds\|_2 \\
&\leq \int_{t_1}^{t_2} \|f_1(s, y(\phi_1(s)))\|_2 \\
&\leq (M + b\|y\|_C)(t_2 - t_1)
\end{aligned} \tag{14}$$

This proves the equicontinuity of the class $\{F_1y\}$ and

$$\begin{aligned}
\|(F_2x)(t_2) - (F_2x)(t_1)\|_2 &= \| \int_0^{t_2} f_2(s, x(\phi_2(s)))dW(s) - \int_0^{t_1} f_2(s, x(\phi_2(s)))dW(s)\|_2 \\
&\leq \sqrt{\int_{t_1}^{t_2} \|f_2(s, x(\phi_2(s)))\|_2^2 ds} \\
&\leq (M + b\|x\|_C)\sqrt{(t_2 - t_1)}.
\end{aligned} \tag{15}$$

This proves the equicontinuity of the class $\{F_1x\}$.
Now

$$\begin{aligned}
(F(x,y))(t_2) - F(x,y))(t_1)) &= ((F_1y)(t_2), (F_2x)(t_2)) - ((F_1y)(t_1), (F_2x)(t_1)) \\
&= ((F_1y)(t_2) - (F_1y)(t_1)), ((F_2x)(t_2) - (F_2x)(t_1))),
\end{aligned}$$

then from (14) and (15), we can deduce the equicontinuity of the class $\{F(x,y)\}$ on Q.
□

2.1. Existence Theorem

Now, we have the following existence theorem

Theorem 1. *Let the Assumptions 1–5 be satisfied, then there exists at least one solution* $(x,y) \in X$ *of the problem (1)–(3).*

Proof. Firstly, from the results of Lemmas 2 and 3 and Arzela–Ascoli Theorem [9] we deduce that the closure of FQ is a compact subset.

Let $(x_n, y_n) \in Q$ be such that

$$L.i.m_{n\to\infty}(x_n, y_n) = (x,y) \qquad w.p.1.$$

where $L.i.m$ denotes the limit in the mean square sense of the continuous second order process ([1,2,9]).

Now,

$$\begin{aligned}
L.i.m_{n\to\infty}F(x_n, y_n) &= (L.i.m_{n\to\infty}F_1y_n, L.i.m_{n\to\infty}F_2x_n) \\
&= (L.i.m_{n\to\infty}\{x_0 - \int_0^{\tau} h_1(s, y_n(s))dW(s) + \int_0^t f_1(s, y_n(\phi_1(s)))ds\}, \\
&\quad L.i.m_{n\to\infty}\{y_0 - \int_0^{\eta} h_2(s, x_n(s))ds + \int_0^t f_2(s, x_n(\phi_2(s)))dW(s)\}) \\
&= (x_0 - \int_0^{\tau} h_1(s, L.i.m_{n\to\infty}y_n(s))dW(s) + \int_0^t f_1(s, L.i.m_{n\to\infty}y_n(\phi_1(s)))ds, \\
&\quad y_0 - \int_0^{\eta} h_2(s, L.i.m_{n\to\infty}x_n(s))ds + \int_0^t f_2(s, L.i.m_{n\to\infty}x_n(\phi_2(s)))dW(s))
\end{aligned}$$

$$\begin{aligned} &= \left(x_0 - \int_0^\tau h_1(s,y(s))dW(s) + \int_0^t f_1(s,y(\phi_1(s)))ds,\right. \\ &\quad \left. y_0 - \int_0^\eta h_2(s,x(s))ds + \int_0^t f_2(s,x(\phi_2(s)))dW(s)\right) \\ &= (F_1 y, F_2 x) \;=\; F(x,y). \end{aligned}$$

Applying stochastic Lebesgue dominated convergence Theorem the operator $F : Q \to Q$ is continuous.

Finally, applying Schauder Fixed Point Theorem [9], we can deduce that there exists at least one solution $(x,y) \in Q$ of the problem (1)–(3) such that $x, y \in C([0,T], L_2(\Omega))$. □

2.2. Uniqueness Theorem

Replace the assumptions $(A1)$ and $(A2)$ by (A^*1) and (A^*2), respectively, such that

(A^*1) The functions $f_i : [0,T] \times L_2(\Omega) \to L_2(\Omega)$, $\quad i = 1,2$ are measurable in $t \in [0,T]$ for all $x \in L_2(\Omega)$ and satisfy the Lipschitz condition with respect to the second argument

$$\|f_i(t,u) - f_i(t,v)\|_2 \leq b\|u - v\|_2.$$

(A^*2) The functions $h_i : [0,T] \times L_2(\Omega) \to L_2(\Omega)$, $\quad i = 1,2$ are measurable in $t \in [0,T]$ for all $x \in L_2(\Omega)$ and satisfy the Lipschitz condition with respect to the second argument

$$\|h_i(t,u) - h_i(t,v)\|_2 \leq c\|u - v\|_2.$$

Remark 1. *Let the assumptions (A^*1) and (A^*2) be satisfied, then we can obtain*

$$\|f_i(t,u)\|_2 - \|f_i(t,0)\|_2 \leq \|f_i(t,u) - f_i(t,0)\|_2 \leq b\|u\|_2,$$

$$\|f_i(t,u)\|_2 \leq \|f_i(t,0)\|_2 + b\|u\|_2 \leq M + b\|u\|_2$$

and

$$\|h_i(t,u)\|_2 \leq \|h_i(t,0)\|_2 + c\|u\|_2 \leq K + c\|u\|_2.$$

Theorem 2. *Let the assumptions $(A^*1) - (A^*2)$ and $(A3) - (A5)$ be satisfied, then the solution of problem (1)–(3) is unique.*

Proof. Let (x_1, y_1) and (x_2, y_2) be two solutions of the problem (1)–(3), then

$$\begin{aligned} (x_i(t), y_i(t)) = (x_0 &- \int_0^\tau h_1(s,y(s))dW(s) + \int_0^t f_1(s,y(\phi_1(s)))ds, \\ y_0 &- \int_0^\eta h_2(s,x(s))ds + \int_0^t f_2(s,x(\phi_2(s)))dW(s)), \quad i = 1,2 \end{aligned} \tag{16}$$

where

$$\begin{aligned} \|x_1(t) - x_2(t)\|_2 &\leq \|\int_0^\tau [h_1(s,y_2(s)) - h_1(s,y_1(s))]dW(s)\|_2 + \|\int_0^t (f_1(s,y_1) - f_1(s,y_2))ds\|_2 \\ &\leq \sqrt{\int_0^\tau c^2\|y_2 - y_1\|_C^2 ds} + Tb\|y_1 - y_2\|_C \leq T\sqrt{c}\|y_1 - y_2\|_C + Tb\|y_1 - y_2\|_C \\ &\leq T(b+c)\|y_1 - y_2\|_C, \\ &\leq T(b+c)\max\{\|x_1 - x_2\|_C, \|y_1 - y_2\|_C\} \end{aligned}$$

and

$$\begin{aligned}\|y_1(t)-y_2(t)\|_2 &\le \int_0^\eta \|h_2(s,x_2(s))-h_2(s,x_1(s))\|_2 ds+\sqrt{\int_0^t b^2\|x_1(s))-x_2(s)))\|_2^2 ds}\\ &\le \sqrt{T}b\|x_1-x_2\|_C+cT\|x_2-x_1\|_C\\ &\le T(b+c)\|x_1-x_2\|_C,\\ &\le T(b+c)\max\{\|x_1-x_2\|_C,\|y_1-y_2\|_C\}.\end{aligned}$$

Hence,

$$\begin{aligned}\|(x_1,y_1)-(x_2,y_2)\|_X &= \|(x_1-x_2),(y_1,y_2)\|_X\\ &= \max\{\|(x_1-x_2)\|_C,\|(y_1,y_2)\|_C\}\\ &\le T(b+c)\max\{\|x_1-x_2\|_C,\|y_2-y_1\|_C\}\\ &\le T(b+c)\|(x_1,y_1)-(x_2,y_2)\|_X.\end{aligned}$$

This implies that

$$(1-T(b+c))\|(x_1,y_1)-(x_2,y_2)\|_X\le 0$$

and

$$\|(x_1,y_1)-(x_2,y_2)\|_X=0,$$

then $(x_1,y_1)=(x_2,y_2)$ and the solution of the problem (1)–(3) is unique. □

2.3. Continuous Dependence

Theorem 3. *Let the assumptions of Theorem 2 be satisfied. Then the solution (16) of the problem (1)–(3) depends continuously on the two random data (x_0,y_0).*

Proof. Let $(\hat{x},\hat{y})$ be the solution of the coupled system

$$\begin{aligned}\hat{x}(t) &= \hat{x}_0-\int_0^\tau h_1(s,\hat{y}(s))dW(s)+\int_0^t f_1(s,\hat{y}(\phi_1(s)))ds\\ \hat{y}(t) &= \hat{y}_0-\int_0^\eta h_2(s,\hat{x}(s))ds+\int_0^t f_2(s,\hat{x}(\phi_2(s)))dW(s),\end{aligned}$$

such that $\|(x_0,y_0)-(\hat{x_0},\hat{y_0})\|_X<\delta_1$, then

$$\begin{aligned}\|x-\hat{x}\|_C &\le \|x_0-\hat{x_0}\|_C+T(b+c)\|y-\hat{y}\|_C\\ &\le \delta_1+T(b+c)\|y-\hat{y}\|_C\\ &\le \delta_1+T(b+c)\max\{\|x-\hat{x}\|_C,\|y-\hat{y}\|_C\}\\ \|y-\hat{y}\|_C &\le \|y_0-\hat{y_0}\|_C+T(b+c)\|x-\hat{x}\|_C,\\ &\le \delta_1+T(b+c)\|x-\hat{x}\|_C\\ &\le \delta_1+T(b+c)\max\{\|x-\hat{x}\|_C,\|y-\hat{y}\|_C\}.\end{aligned}$$

Then

$$\begin{aligned}\|(x,y)-(\hat{x},\hat{y})\|_X &= \|(x-\hat{x},y-\hat{y})\|_X\\ &= \max\{\|x-\hat{x}\|_C,\|y-\hat{y}\|_C\}\\ &\le \delta_1+T(b+c)\max\{\|x-\hat{x}\|_C,\|y-\hat{y}\|_C\}\\ &\le \delta_1+T(b+c)\|(x,y)-(\hat{x},\hat{y})\|_X.\end{aligned}$$

This implies that

$$\|(x,y)-(\hat{x},\hat{y})\|_X \leq \frac{\delta_1}{1-T(b+c)} = \epsilon$$

which completes the proof. □

Theorem 4. *The solution (16) of the problem (1)–(3) depends continuously on the two random functions h_1 and h_2.*

Proof. Let $(\hat{x},\hat{y})$ be the solutions of the coupled system

$$\begin{aligned}
\hat{x}(t) &= x_0 - \int_0^\tau h_1^*(s,\hat{y}(s))dW(s) + \int_0^t f_1(s,\hat{y}(\phi_1(s)))ds, \\
\hat{y}(t) &= y_0 - \int_0^\eta h_2^*(s,\hat{x}(s))ds + \int_0^t f_2(s,\hat{x}(\phi_2(s)))dW(s)
\end{aligned}$$

such that $\|h_i^*(s,.)-h(s,.)\|_2 \leq \delta_2, \quad i=1,2,$ then

$$\begin{aligned}
\|x(t)-\hat{x}(t)\|_2 &= \|\int_0^\tau [h_1^*(s,\hat{y}(s))-h_1(s,y(s))]dW(s) + \int_0^t [f_1(s,y(\phi_1(s)))-f_1(s,\hat{y}(\phi_1(s)))]ds\|_2 \\
&\leq \sqrt{\int_0^\tau \|h_1^*(s,\hat{y}(s))-h_1(s,y(s))\|_2^2 ds} + \int_0^t \|f_1(s,y(\phi_1(s)))-f_1(s,\hat{y}(\phi_1(s)))\|_2 ds \\
&\leq \sqrt{\int_0^\tau [\|h_1^*(s,\hat{y}(s))-h_1^*(s,y(s))\|_2 + \|h_1^*(s,y(s))-h_1(s,y(s))\|_2]^2 ds} \\
&+ \int_0^t \|f_1(s,y(\phi_1(s)))-f_1(s,\hat{y}(\phi_1(s)))\|_2 ds \\
&\leq \sqrt{\int_0^\tau (c\|y(s)-\hat{y}(s)\|_2+\delta_2)^2 ds} + \int_0^t b\|y(s)-\hat{y}(s)\|_2 ds \\
&\leq (c\sqrt{T} + bT)\|y-\hat{y}\|_C + \delta_2\sqrt{T} \\
&\leq T(b+c)\max\{\|x-\hat{x}\|_C, \|y-\hat{y}\|_C\} + \delta_2 T
\end{aligned}$$

Similarly we can obtain

$$\begin{aligned}
\|y(t)-\hat{y}(t)\|_2 &= \|\int_0^\eta [h_2^*(s,\hat{x}(s))-h_2(s,x(s))]ds + \int_0^t [f_2(s,x(\phi_2(s)))-f_2(s,\hat{x}(\phi_2(s)))]dW(s)\|_2 \\
&\leq (cT + b\sqrt{T})\|x-\hat{x}\|_C + \delta_2 T \\
&\leq T(b+c)\|x-\hat{x}\|_C + \delta_2 T \\
&\leq T(b+c)\max\{\|x-\hat{x}\|_C, \|y-\hat{y}\|_C\} + \delta_2 T \\
&\leq T(b+c)\max\{\|x-\hat{x}\|_C, \|y-\hat{y}\|_C\} + \delta_2 T.
\end{aligned}$$

Now

$$\begin{aligned}
\|(x,y)-(\hat{x},\hat{y})\|_X &= \max\{\|x-\hat{x}\|_C, \|y-\hat{y}\|_C \\
&\leq T(b+c)\max\{(\|x-\hat{x}\|_C, \|y-\hat{y}\|_C\} + \delta_2 T \\
&\leq T(c+b)\|(x,y)-(\hat{x},\hat{y})\|_X + \delta_2 T.
\end{aligned}$$

This implies that

$$\|(x,y)-(\hat{x},\hat{y})\|_X \leq \frac{\delta_2 T}{1-T(b+c)} = \epsilon$$

which completes the proof. □

3. Solutions of the Problem (1), (2) and (4)

Define the mapping $L(x,y) = (L_1x, L_2y)$ where $L_1x,\ L_2y$ are given by the following stochastic integral equations

$$L_1x(t) = x_0 - \int_0^\tau h_1(s,x(s))dW(s) + \int_0^t f_1(s,y(\phi_1(s)))ds, \tag{17}$$

$$L_2y(t) = y_0 - \int_0^\eta h_2(s,y(s))ds + \int_0^t f_2(s,x(\phi_2(s)))dW(s). \tag{18}$$

Lemma 4. $L : Q \to Q$.

Proof. Let $x,\ y \in Q,$, then we obtain

$$\begin{aligned}
\|L_1x(t)\|_2 &\le \|x_0\|_2 + \|\int_0^\tau h_1(s,x(s))dW(s)\|_2 + \|\int_0^t f_1(s,y(\phi_1(s)))ds\|_2 \\
&\le \|x_0\|_2 + \sqrt{\int_0^\tau \|h_1(s,x(s))\|_2^2 ds} + \int_0^t \|f_1(s,y(\phi_1(s)))\|_2 ds \\
&\le \|x_0\|_2 + \sqrt{\int_0^\tau (|k_1(s)| + c_1\|x(s)\|_2)^2} \int_0^t (|m_1(s)| + b_1\|y(s)\|_2)ds \\
&\le \|x_0\|_2 + K\sqrt{T} + MT + c\sqrt{T}\|x\|_C + bT\|y\|_C) \\
&\le \|x_0\|_2 + \|y_0\|_2 + (K+M)T + 2rT(b+c)
\end{aligned}$$

and

$$\begin{aligned}
\|L_2y(t)\|_2 &\le \|y_0\|_2 + \|\int_0^\eta h_2(s,y(s))ds\|_2\|\int_0^t f_2(s,x(\phi_2(s)))dW(s)\|_2 \\
&\le \|y_0\|_2 = \int_0^\eta \|h_2(s,y(s))\|_2 ds + \sqrt{\int_0^t \|f_2(s,x(\phi_2(s)))\|_2^2 ds} \\
&\le \|y_0\|_2 + \int_0^\eta (|k_2(s)| + c_2\|y(s)\|_2)ds + \sqrt{\int_0^t (|m_2(t)| + b_2\|x\|_2)^2 ds} \\
&\le \|y_0\|_2 + KT + M\sqrt{T} + cT\|y\|_C + b\sqrt{T}\|x\|_C \\
&\le \|y_0\|_2 + (K+M)T + T(b+c)\|y\|_C + T(b+c)\|x\|_C \\
&\le \|x_0\|_2 + \|y_0\|_2 + (K+M)T + 2rT(b+c).
\end{aligned}$$

This implies that

$$\begin{aligned}
\|L(x,y)\|_X &= \|(L_1x, L_2y)\|_X \\
&= \max\{\|L_1x(t)\|_C, \|L_2y(t)\|_C\} \\
&\le \|x_0\|_2 + \|y_0\|_2 + (K+M)T + 2rT(b+c) = r
\end{aligned}$$

where

$$r = \frac{\|x_0\|_2 + \|y_0\|_2 + (K+M)T}{1 - T(b+c)},$$

then the class $\{L(x,y)\}$ is uniformly bounded and $L(x,y) : Q \to Q$. □

Lemma 5. *The class of function* $\{L(x,y)(t)\}$ *,* $t \in [0,T]$ *is equicontinuous.*

Proof. Let $x,\ y \in Q,\quad t_1, t_2 \in [0,T]$ such that $|t_2 - t_1| < \delta,$ then

$$\begin{aligned}\|L_1x(t_2) - L_1y(t_1)\|_2 &= \|\int_0^{t_2} f_1(s, y(\phi_1(s)))ds - \int_0^{t_1} f_1(s, y(\phi_1(s)))ds\|_2 \\ &\leq \int_{t_1}^{t_2} \|f_1(s, y(\phi_1(s)))\|_2 ds \\ &\leq (M + b\|y\|_C)(t_2 - t_1) \end{aligned} \tag{19}$$

and

$$\begin{aligned}\|L_2x(t_2) - L_2x(t_1)\|_2 &= \|\int_0^{t_2} f_2(s, x(\phi_2(s)))dW(s) - \int_0^{t_1} f_2(s, x(\phi_2(s)))dW(s)\|_2 \\ &\leq \sqrt{\int_{t_1}^{t_2} \|f_2(s, x(\phi_2(s)))\|_2^2 ds} \\ &\leq (M + b\|x\|_C)\sqrt{(t_2 - t_1)}. \end{aligned} \tag{20}$$

However,

$$\begin{aligned} L(x(t_2), y(t_2)) - L(x(t_1), y(t_1)) &= (L_1x(t_2), L_2y(t_2)) - (L_1x(t_1), L_2y(t_1)) \\ &= ((L_1x(t_2) - L_1x(t_1)), (L_2y(t_2) - L_2y(t_1))), \end{aligned}$$

then from (19) and (20), we deduce the equicontinuity of the class $\{L(x,y)(t)\}$ on Q. □

3.1. Existence Theorem

Now, we have the following existence theorem

Theorem 5. *Let the Assumptions (A1)–(A5) be satisfied, then there exists at least one solution $(x,y) \in X$ of the problem (1), (2) and (4).*

Proof. Let $\{(x_n, y_n)\} \in Q$ be such that

$$(x_n, y_n) \to (x,y) \qquad w.p.1.$$

Using Lemmas 1–3, then applying stochastic Lebesgue dominated convergence Theorem [9], we can obtain

$$\begin{aligned} L.i.m_{n\to\infty} L(x_n, y_n) &= (L.i.m_{n\to\infty} L_1 x_n, L.i.m_{n\to\infty} L_2 y_n) \\ &= (L.i.m_{n\to\infty}\{x_0 - \int_0^\tau h_1(s, x_n(s))dW(s) + \int_0^t f_1(s, y_n(\phi_1(s)))ds\}, \\ &\quad L.i.m_{n\to\infty}\{y_0 - \int_0^\eta h_2(s, y_n(s))ds + \int_0^t f_2(s, x_n(\phi_2(s)))dW(s)\}) \\ &= (x_0 - \int_0^\tau h_1(s, L.i.m_{n\to\infty} x_n(s))dW(s) + \int_0^t f_1(s, L.i.m_{n\to\infty} y_n(\phi_1(s)))ds, \\ &\quad y_0 - \int_0^\eta h_2(s, L.i.m_{n\to\infty} y_n(s))ds + \int_0^t f_2(s, L.i.m_{n\to\infty} x_n(\phi_2(s)))dW(s)) \\ &= (x_0 - \int_0^\tau h_1(s, x(s))dW(s) + \int_0^t f_1(s, y(\phi_1(s)))ds, \\ &\quad y_0 - \int_0^\eta h_2(s, y(s))ds + \int_0^t f_2(s, x(\phi_2(s)))dW(s)) \\ &= (L_1x, L_2y) \ = \ L(x,y). \end{aligned}$$

This proves that the operator $L : Q \to Q$ is continuous. □

Then by the Arzela–Ascoli Theorem [9], the closure of LQ is a compact subset of X, then applying Schauder Fixed Point Theorem [9], there exists at least one solution $(x,y) \in X$ of the problem (1), (2) and (4) such that $x, y \in C([0,T], L_2(\Omega))$.

3.2. Uniqueness Theorem

Theorem 6. *Let the assumptions* (A^*1)–(A^*2) *and* $(A3)$–$(A5)$ *be satisfied then the solution of problem (1), (2) and (4) is unique.*

Proof. Let (x_1, y_1) and (x_2, y_2) be two solutions of the problem (1), (2) and (4) on the form

$$\begin{aligned}(x(t), y(t)) = (x_0 &- \int_0^\tau h_1(s, x(s))dW(s) + \int_0^t f_1(s, y(\phi_1(s)))ds, \\ y_0 &- \int_0^\eta h_2(s, y(s))ds + \int_0^t f_2(s, x(\phi_2(s)))dW(s)), \end{aligned} \tag{21}$$

then we can obtain

$$\begin{aligned}\|x_1(t) - x_2(t)\|_2 &\le c\sqrt{T}\|x_1 - x_2\|_C + bT\|y_1 - y_2\|_C < cT\|x_1 - x_2\|_C + bT\|y_1 - y_2\|_C \\ &\le (b+c)T\|x_1 - x_2\|_C + (b+c)T\|y_1 - y_2\|_C \\ &\le (b+c)T\, max\{\|x_1 - x_2\|_C,\ \|y_1 - y_2\|_C\}. \end{aligned} \tag{22}$$

Similarly, we can obtain

$$\|y_1(t) - y_2(t)\|_2 \le (b+c)T\, max\{\|x_1 - x_2\|_C,\ \|y_1 - y_2\|_C\}. \tag{23}$$

Hence from (22) and (23)

$$\begin{aligned}\|(x_1, y_1) - (x_2, y_2)\|_X &= \|(x_1 - x_2), (y_1 - y_2)\|_X \\ &\le \max\{\|x_1 - x_2\|_C, \|y_1 - y_2\|_C\} \\ &\le (b+c)T\, max\{\|x_1 - x_2\|_C,\ \|y_1 - y_2\|_C\}. \end{aligned}$$

This implies that

$$(1 - (b+c)T)\|(x_1, y_1) - (x_2, y_2)\|_X \le 0.$$

Then

$$\|(x_1, y_1) - (x_2, y_2)\|_X = 0$$

and $(x_1, y_1) = (x_2, y_2)$ which proves that the solution of the problem (1), (2) and (4) is unique. □

3.3. Continuous Dependence

Theorem 7. *The solution (16) of the problem (1)–(2) and (4) depends continuously on the two random data* (x_0, y_0).

Proof. Let $(\hat{x}, \hat{y})$ be the solution of the coupled system

$$\begin{aligned}\hat{x}(t) &= \hat{x}_0 - \int_0^\tau h_1(s, \hat{x}(s))dW(s) + \int_0^t f_1(s, \hat{y}(\phi_1(s)))ds \\ \hat{y}(t) &= \hat{y}_0 - \int_0^\eta h_2(s, \hat{y}(s))ds + \int_0^t f_2(s, \hat{x}(\phi_2(s)))dW(s), \end{aligned}$$

such that $\|(x_0, y_0) - (\hat{x_0}, \hat{y_0})\|_X < \delta_3$. Then we have

$$\begin{aligned} x(t) - \hat{x}(t) &= x_0 - \hat{x_0} - \int_0^{\tau} [h_1(s, \hat{x}(s)) - h_1(s, x(s))] dW(s) \\ &+ \int_0^t [f_1(s, y(\phi_1(s))) - f_1(s, \hat{y}(\phi_1(s)))] ds \end{aligned}$$

and

$$\begin{aligned} \|x(t) - \hat{x}(t)\|_2 &\leq \|x_0 - \hat{x_0}\|_C + c\sqrt{T}\|x - \hat{x}\|_C + bT\|y - \hat{y}\|_C \\ &\leq \|x_0 - \hat{x_0}\|_C + cT\|x - \hat{x}\|_C + bT\|y - \hat{y}\|_C \\ &\leq \|x_0 - \hat{x_0}\|_2 + cTmax\{\|x - \hat{x}\|_C, \|y - \hat{y}\|_C\} + bTmax\{\|x - \hat{x}\|_C, \|y - \hat{y}\|_C\} \\ &\leq max\{\|x_0 - \hat{x_0}\|_2, \|y_0 - \hat{y_0}\|_2\} + (b + c)Tmax\{\|x - \hat{x}\|_C, \|y - \hat{y}\|_C\}. \end{aligned}$$

By the same way we can obtain

$$\|y(t) - \hat{y}(t)\|_2 \leq max\{\|x_0 - \hat{x_0}\|_2, \|y_0 - \hat{y_0}\|_2\} + (b + c)Tmax\{\|x - \hat{x}\|_C, \|y - \hat{y}\|_C\}$$

and

$$\begin{aligned} \|(x, y) - (\hat{x}, \hat{y})\|_X &= \max\{\|(x - \hat{x}\|_C, \|(y - \hat{y}\|_C\} \\ &\leq max\{\|x_0 - \hat{x_0}\|_2, \|y_0 - \hat{y_0}\|_2\} + (b + c)Tmax\{\|x - \hat{x}\|_C, \|y - \hat{y}\|_C\} \\ &\leq \delta_3 + (b + c)Tmax\{\|x - \hat{x}\|_C, \|y - \hat{y}\|_C\} \end{aligned}$$

which gives our result

$$\|(x, y) - (\hat{x}, \hat{y})\|_X \leq \frac{\delta_3}{1 - T(b + c)} = \epsilon$$

and completes the proof. □

Theorem 8. *The solution (16) of the problem (1), (2) and (4) depends continuously on the two random functions h_1 and h_2.*

Proof. Let $(\hat{x}, \hat{y})$ be the solutions of the coupled system of stochastic integral Equations (1), (2) and (4) such that

$$\begin{aligned} \hat{x}(t) &= x_0 - \int_0^{\tau} h_1^*(s, \hat{x}(s)) dW(s) + \int_0^t f_1(s, \hat{y}(\phi_1(s))) ds \\ \hat{y}(t) &= y_0 - \int_0^{\eta} h_2^*(s, \hat{y}(s)) ds + \int_0^t f_2(s, \hat{x}(\phi_2(s))) dW(s). \end{aligned}$$

Let $\|h_i^*(t, u(t)) - h(t, u(t))\|_2 \leq \delta_4, \quad i = 1, 2$ then

$$\begin{aligned} \|x(t) - \hat{x}(t)\|_2 &= \| \int_0^{\tau} [h_1^*(s, \hat{x}(s)) - h_1(s, x(s))] dW(s) + \int_0^t [f_1(s, y(\phi_1(s))) - f_1(s, \hat{y}(\phi_1(s)))] ds\|_2 \\ &\leq \sqrt{\int_0^{\tau} \|h_1^*(s, \hat{x}(s)) - h_1(s, x(s))\|_2^2 ds} + \int_0^t \|f_1(s, y(\phi_1(s))) - f_1(s, \hat{y}(\phi_1(s)))\|_2 ds \\ &\leq \sqrt{\int_0^{\tau} [\|h_1^*(s, \hat{x}(s)) - h_1^*(s, x(s))\|_2 + \|h_1^*(s, x(s)) - h_1(s, x(s))\|_2]^2 ds} \\ &+ \int_0^t \|f_1(s, y(\phi_1(s))) - f_1(s, \hat{y}(\phi_1(s)))\|_2 ds \\ &\leq \sqrt{\int_0^{\tau} (c\|x(s) - \hat{x}(s)\|_2 + \delta_4)^2 ds} + \int_0^t b\|y(s) - \hat{y}(s)\|_2 ds \end{aligned}$$

$$
\begin{aligned}
&\leq c\sqrt{T}\|x-\hat{x}\|_C + bT\|y-\hat{y}\|_C + \delta_4\sqrt{T}) \\
&\leq cT\|x-\hat{x}\|_C + bT\|y-\hat{y}\|_C + \delta_4 T. \\
&\leq cT\ max\{\|x-\hat{x}\|_C, \|y-\hat{y}\|_C\} + bT\ max\{\|x-\hat{x}\|_C, \|y-\hat{y}\|_C\} + \delta_4 T \\
&\leq (b+c)T\ max\{\|x-\hat{x}\|_C, \|y-\hat{y}\|_C\} + \delta_4 T.
\end{aligned}
$$

Similarly we can obtain

$$\|y-\hat{y}\|_C \leq (b+c)T\ max\{\|x-\hat{x}\|_C, \|y-\hat{y}\|_C\} + \delta_4 T$$

and

$$\|(x,y)-(\hat{x},\hat{y})\|_X = \max\{\|x-\hat{x}\|_C, \|y-\hat{y}\|_C\} \leq (b+c)T\ max\{\|x-\hat{x}\|_C, \|y-\hat{y}\|_C\} + \delta_4 T.$$

This implies that

$$\|(x,y)-(\hat{x},\hat{y})\|_X \leq \frac{\delta_4 T}{1-T(b+c)} = \epsilon$$

which completes the proof. □

Example 1. *Consider the coupled system*

$$
\begin{aligned}
\frac{dx}{dt}(t) &= \frac{a(t)+y(t)}{5(1+\|y(t)\|_2)}, \quad t \in (0,1] \\
dy(t) &= \frac{tx(t)}{2(1+\|x\|_2)} dW(t), \quad t \in (0,1]
\end{aligned}
\tag{24}
$$

subject to

$$x_0 = \int_0^\tau \frac{e^{-s}y(s)}{120+s^2} dW(s), \quad y_0 = \int_0^\eta \frac{x(s)}{\sqrt{s+36}} ds \tag{25}$$

where

$$\|f_1(t,y(t))\|_2 \leq \frac{1}{5}[|a(t)| + \|y(t)\|_2], \quad \|f_2(t,x(t))\|_2 \leq \frac{1}{2\|x(t)\|_2}$$

and

$$\|h_1(t,y(t)\|_2 \leq \frac{\|y(t)\|_2}{120}, \quad \|h_2(t,x(t)\|_2 \leq \frac{\|x(t)\|_2}{6}.$$

Easily, the coupled system (24) with nonlocal integral conditions (25) satisfies all the Assumptions 1–5 of Theorem 1. with $b = \frac{1}{2}$, $c = \frac{1}{6}$, *then there exists at least one solution of the system (24) on* $[0,1]$.

4. Conclusions

Here, we proved the existence of solutions of a coupled system of random and stochastic nonlinear differential equations with coupled nonlocal random and stochastic nonlinear integral conditions. The sufficient conditions for the uniqueness of the solution have been given. The continuous dependence of the unique solution has been studied.

Author Contributions: Conceptualization, A.M.A.E.-S. and H.A.F. Both authors have read and agreed to the published version of the manuscript.

Funding: This research received no external funding.

Institutional Review Board Statement: Not applicable.

Informed Consent Statement: Not applicable.

Data Availability Statement: Not applicable.

Acknowledgments: The authors would like to thank the referee and the editor for their valuable comments which led to improvement of this work.

Conflicts of Interest: The authors declare no conflict of interest.

References

1. El-Sayed, A.M.A. On the stochastic fractional calculus operators. *J. Fract. Calc. Appl.* **2015**, *6*, 101–109.
2. El-Sayed, A.M.A.; El-Tawil, M.A.; Saif, M.S.M.; Hafez, F.M. The mean square Riemann-Liouville stochastic fractional derivative and stochastic fractional order differential equation. *Math. Sci. Res. J.* **2005**, *9*, 142–150.
3. El-Sayed, A.M.A.; Gaafar, F.; El-Gendy, M. Continuous dependence of the solution of Ito stochastic differential equation with nonlocal conditions. *Appl. Math. Sci.* **2016**, *10*, 1971–1982. [CrossRef]
4. El-Sayed, A.M.A.; Gaafar, F.; El-Gendy, M. Continuous dependence of the solution of random fractional-order differential equation with nonlocal condition. *Fract. Differ. Calc.* **2017**, *7*, 135–149. [CrossRef]
5. El-Sayed, A.M.A.; Hashem, H.H.G. A coupled System of integral equations in reflexive Banach spaces. *Acta Math. Sci.* **2012**, *32B*, 2021–2028. [CrossRef]
6. Ahmad, B.; Ntouyas, S.K.; Alsaedi, A. On a coupled system of fractional differential equations with coupled nonlocal and integral boundary conditions. *Chaos Solitons Fractals* **2016**, *83*, 234–241. [CrossRef]
7. Yin, W.; Cao, J. Nonlocal stochastic differential equations with time-varying delay driven by G-Brownian motion. *Math. Meth. Appl. Sci.* **2020**, *43*, 600–612. [CrossRef]
8. Tsokos, C.P.; Padgett, W.J. *Stochastic Integral Equations in Life Sciences and Engineering*; International Statistical Institute: Voorburg, The Netherlands, 1973; Volume 41, pp. 15–38.
9. Curtain, R.F.; Pritchard, A.J. *Functional Analysis in Modern Applied Mathematics*; Academic Press: Cambridge, MA, USA, 1977.
10. Hafez, F.M.; El-Sayed, A.M.A.; El-Tawil, M.A. On a stochastic fractional calculus. *Fractional Calculus Appl. Anal.* **2001**, *4*, 81–90.
11. Hafez, F.M. The Fractional calculus for some stochastic processes. *Stoch. Anal. Appl.* **2004**, *22*, 507–523. [CrossRef]
12. Soong, T.T. *Random Differential Equations in Science and Engineering*; Academic Press: New York, NY, USA, 1973.
13. Wong, E. *Stochastic Processes, Informations and Dynamical Systems*; McGraw-Hill: New York, NY, USA, 1971.
14. Wong, E. *Introduction to Random Processes*; Springer: Berlin, Germany, 1980.

mathematics

Article

Ulam Stability of n-th Order Delay Integro-Differential Equations

Shuyi Wang * and Fanwei Meng

School of Mathematical Sciences, Qufu Normal University, Qufu 273165, China; fwmeng@qfnu.edu.cn
* Correspondence: sywang_math@126.com

Abstract: In this paper, the Ulam stability of an n-th order delay integro-differential equation is given. Firstly, the existence and uniqueness theorem of a solution for the delay integro-differential equation is obtained using a Lipschitz condition and the Banach contraction principle. Then, the expression of the solution for delay integro-differential equation is derived by mathematical induction. On this basis, we obtain the Ulam stability of the delay integro-differential equation via Gronwall–Bellman inequality. Finally, two examples of delay integro-differential equations are given to explain our main results.

Keywords: Ulam stability; delay integro-differential equation; Gronwall–Bellman inequality

Citation: Wang, S.; Meng, F. Ulam Stability of an n-th Order Delay Integro-Differential Equations. *Mathematics* **2021**, *9*, 3029. https://doi.org/10.3390/math9233029

Academic Editor: Alberto Cabada

Received: 20 October 2021
Accepted: 19 November 2021
Published: 26 November 2021

1. Introduction

In the year 1940, Ulam [1] put forward an abstract problem: under what conditions is the exact solution of an equation closed to the approximate solution? In the year 1941, in order to solve the problem raised by Ulam, Hyers [2] studied the functional equation in Banach space and gave the definition of Hyers–Ulam stability. In the year 1978, based on the work of Hyers, Rassias [3] gave the definition of Hyers–Ulam–Rassias stability. These two kinds of stability are called Ulam stability. After that, scholars began to study the Ulam stability of some solvable equations. See [4–7] and the references therein. Recently, the Ulam stability of delay differential equations and delay integro-differential equations has been discussed. See [8–13]. There are many results about the Ulam stability of delay differential equations. However, there are a few results about the Ulam stability of delay integro-differential equations.

In fact, delay integro-differential equations are usually used to describe many natural phenomena in the fields of thermodynamics, mechanics, mechanical engineering and control. See [14–17]. Mechanical processes, such as rigid heat conduction process [18] and the motion of charged particles with a delayed interaction [19], can be modeled by delay integro-differential equations. Furthermore, the delay integro-differential equation is an appropriate model for studying the effect of tire dynamics on a vehicle shimmy [20] and the optimal control of a size-structured population [21], which is one of its important applications. The mathematical model related to the delay integro-differential equation is an interesting memory effect model. However, new difficulties may arise when delay and integro-differential equations are introduced simultaneously. Some topics about delay integro-differential equations, such as the existence and uniqueness of solutions and Ulam stability, have attracted the attention of many scholars. See [12,14,15,22].

In [23], Otrocol studied Ulam stability of a first-order delay differential equation:

$$u'(t) = g(t, u(t), u(\tau(t))),\ t \in [t_0, t_1],$$

where $g \in C([t_0, t_1] \times \mathbb{R}^2, \mathbb{R})$; delay function $\tau(t) \le t$, $\tau \in C([t_0, t_1], [t_0 - l, t_1])$, $l > 0$.

In 2015, Kendre [24] discussed the existence of a solution for an integro-differential equation:

$$\begin{cases} u'(t) = g\left(t, u(u(t)), \int_{t_0}^{t} k(t,s)u(u(s))ds\right), \ t \in [t_0, t_1], \\ u(t_0) = u_0, \end{cases} \tag{1}$$

where $G = [t_0, t_1], g \in C(G^3, G); k \in C(G^2, G); t_0, u_0 \in G$.

In 2016, Sevgin [25] investigated the Ulam stability of the Volterra integro-differential equation:

$$u'(t) = f(t, u(t)) + \int_0^t g(t, s, u(s))ds, \ t \in [0, t_0],$$

where $f \in C([0, t_0] \times \mathbb{R}, \mathbb{R}); g \in C([0, t_0] \times [0, t_0] \times \mathbb{R}, \mathbb{R})$.

In 2018, Kishor [26] established the Ulam stability of the semilinear Volterra integro-differential equation:

$$u'(t) = Tu(t) + g\left(t, u(t), \int_0^t z(t, s, u(s))ds\right), \ t \in [0, t_0],$$

where $T\colon U \to U$ is the infinitesimal generator; U is Banach space; $g \in C([0, t_0] \times \mathbb{R}^2, \mathbb{R})$; $z \in C([0, t_0] \times \mathbb{R}^2, \mathbb{R})$.

In 2019, Zada [27] obtained the Ulam stability for the following n-th order delay differential equation:

$$\begin{cases} u^{(n)}(s) = z(s, \{u^{(0)}\}, \{u^{(1)}\}, \dots, \{u^{(n-1)}\}), \ s \in [s_0, s_0 + \eta], \\ u(s) = \chi(s), \ \ s \in [s_0 - \zeta, s_0], \end{cases} \tag{2}$$

where $\{u^{(j)}\} = \{u^{(j)}(s), u^{(j)}(\lambda_1(s)), u^{(j)}(\lambda_2(s)), \dots, u^{(j)}(\lambda_k(s))\}, j = 0, 1, \dots, n-1$; delay functions $\lambda_k \in C([s_0, s_0 + \eta], [s_0 - \zeta, s_0 + \eta]), \lambda_k(s) \le s, k \in \mathbb{Z}_+; \zeta > 0, \eta > 0, s_0$ are constants; $z \in C(\tilde{B}, \mathbb{R}), \tilde{B} \subset [s_0, s_0 + \eta] \times \mathbb{R}^{n(k+1)}$ is closed set; $\chi\colon [s_0 - \zeta, s_0] \to \mathbb{R}$.

However, the existence and uniqueness of solutions and Ulam stability for n-th delay integro-differential equations have not been studied hitherto. Inspired by [24,25,27], we study Ulam stability for the following n-th order delay integro-differential equation:

$$\begin{cases} u^{(n)}(s) = z\left(s, u^{(0)}, \dots, u^{(n-1)}, u^{(0)}(\lambda), \dots, u^{(n-1)}(\lambda), \int_{s_0}^{s} g(\tau, u^{(0)}, \dots, u^{(n-1)})d\tau\right), \\ u(s) = \chi(s), \ s \in [s_0 - \zeta, s_0], \\ u^{(j)}(s_0) = \chi^{(j)}(s_0), \ j = 1, \dots, n-1, \end{cases} \tag{3}$$

where the definition domain of the first formula of Equation (3) is $[s_0, s_0 + \eta]$, where $u^{(j)} = u^{(j)}(s), u^{(j)}(\lambda) = u^{(j)}(\lambda(s)), j = 0, \dots, n-1$; delay function $\lambda(s) \le s, \lambda \in C([s_0, s_0 + \eta], [s_0 - \zeta, s_0 + \eta]); z \in C(B, \mathbb{R}), B \subset [s_0, s_0 + \eta] \times \mathbb{R}^{2n+1}$ is closed set; $g \in C(H, \mathbb{R}), H \subset [s_0, s_0 + \eta] \times \mathbb{R}^n$ is closed set; $\chi \in C^n([s_0 - \zeta, s_0], \mathbb{R})$.

The aim of our paper is to study the Ulam stability and the existence and uniqueness of solutions for Equation (3). The main tools used in this paper are Lipschitz conditions and Gronwall–Bellman inequality.

The remainder of the paper is organized as follows: In Section 2, we give definitions and lemmas, which are essential for Section 3. In Section 3, we state some Lipschitz conditions, which will be helpful to prove the existence and uniqueness results for a delay integro-differential equation; then the Ulam stability for the delay integro-differential equation is given. In Section 4, we give two examples to illustrate main results.

2. Preliminaries

In this paper, we denote $\mathbb{R}^+ := [0, \infty)$, $J_1 := [s_0 - \zeta, s_0 + \eta]$, $J_2 := [s_0, s_0 + \eta]$, $J_3 := [s_0 - \zeta, s_0]$. Let $C(J_1, \mathbb{R})$ be real Banach space of all continuous functions with norm:

$$\|u\| = \sup\{|u(s)|;\ s \in J_1\}.$$

Definition 1. *Equation (3) is Hyers–Ulam stable on J_1 if there exists $C > 0$ such that for $\theta > 0$ and each solution $v(s)$ of the inequality*

$$\begin{cases} \left|v^{(n)}(s) - z\left(s, v^{(0)}, \ldots, v^{(n-1)}(\lambda), \int_{s_0}^{s} g(\tau, v^{(0)}, \ldots, v^{(n-1)})d\tau\right)\right| \le \theta,\ s \in J_2, \\ |v(s) - \chi(s)| \le \theta,\ s \in J_3, \end{cases} \tag{4}$$

there exists a solution $u(s) \in C(J_1, \mathbb{R}) \bigcap C^n(J_2, \mathbb{R})$ of Equation (3) with

$$|v(s) - u(s)| \le C \cdot \theta,\ s \in J_1.$$

Definition 2. *Equation (3) is Hyers–Ulam–Rassias stable with respect to $\sigma(s)$ on J_1 if there exists $K_{z,g,\sigma} > 0$ such that for each solution $v(s)$ of the inequality*

$$\begin{cases} \left|v^{(n)}(s) - z\left(s, v^{(0)}, \ldots, v^{(n-1)}(\lambda), \int_{s_0}^{s} g(\tau, v^{(0)}, \ldots, v^{(n-1)})d\tau\right)\right| \le \sigma(s),\ s \in J_2, \\ |v(s) - \chi(s)| \le \sigma(s),\ s \in J_3, \end{cases} \tag{5}$$

there exists a solution $u(s) \in C(J_1, \mathbb{R}) \bigcap C^n(J_2, \mathbb{R})$ of Equation (3) with

$$|v(s) - u(s)| \le K_{z,g,\sigma} \cdot \sigma(s),\ s \in J_1.$$

Lemma 1 (see [28]). *Assume that $f \in C(\mathbb{R}, Q)$, then n-th repeated integrable of f based at s_0,*

$$f^{(-n)}(s) = \int_{s_0}^{s} \int_{s_0}^{s_1} \int_{s_0}^{s_2} \int_{s_0}^{s_3} \cdots \int_{s_0}^{s_{n-1}} f(s_n) ds_n ds_{n-1} \ldots ds_2 ds_1,$$

is given by

$$f^{(-n)}(s) = \frac{1}{(n-1)!} \int_{s_0}^{s} (s - \tau)^{n-1} f(\tau) d\tau.$$

Theorem 1. *A function $u(s) \in C(J_1, \mathbb{R}) \bigcap C^n(J_2, \mathbb{R})$ is a solution of the delay integro-differential equation*

$$\begin{cases} u^{(n)}(s) = z\left(s, u^{(0)}, \ldots, u^{(0)}(\lambda), \ldots, u^{(n-1)}(\lambda), \int_{s_0}^{s} g(\tau, u^{(0)}, \ldots, u^{(n-1)})d\tau\right),\ s \in J_2, \\ u(s) = \chi(s),\ s \in J_3, \\ u^{(j)}(s_0) = \chi^{(j)}(s_0),\ j = 1, \ldots, n-1, \end{cases} \tag{6}$$

if and only if $u(s)$ is a solution of the integral equation

$$u(s) = \begin{cases} \sum\limits_{j=0}^{n-1} \frac{(s-s_0)^j \chi^{(j)}(s_0)}{j!} + \frac{1}{(n-1)!} \int_{s_0}^{s} (s - \tau)^{n-1} \\ \cdot z\left(\tau, u^{(0)}, \ldots, u^{(0)}(\lambda), \ldots, u^{(n-1)}(\lambda), \int_{s_0}^{\tau} g(r, u^{(0)}, \ldots, u^{(n-1)})dr\right) d\tau,\ s \in J_2, \\ \chi(s),\ s \in J_3. \end{cases} \tag{7}$$

Proof. For $n = 1$, from (6), we have

$$u^{(1)}(s) = z\left(s, u^{(0)}, u^{(0)}(\lambda), \int_{s_0}^{s} g(\tau, u^{(0)})d\tau\right),$$
$$u(s_0) = \chi(s_0),$$

then by integral formula, we have

$$u(s) = \chi(s_0) + \int_{s_0}^{s} z\left(\tau, u^{(0)}, u^{(0)}(\lambda), \int_{s_0}^{\tau} g(r, u^{(0)})dr\right)d\tau,\ s \in J_2.$$

This means that (7) holds for $n = 1$.
For $n = k$, from (6), we have

$$u^{(k)}(s) = z\left(s, u^{(0)}, \ldots, u^{(0)}(\lambda), \ldots, u^{(k-1)}(\lambda), \int_{s_0}^{s} g(\tau, u^{(0)}, \ldots, u^{(k-1)})d\tau\right),$$
$$u^{(j)}(s_0) = \chi^{(j)}(s_0),\ j = 1, \ldots, k-1.$$

Assume for $n = k$, (7) holds; that is,

$$u(s) = \sum_{j=0}^{k-1} \frac{(s-s_0)^j \chi^{(j)}(s_0)}{j!} + \frac{1}{(k-1)!}\int_{s_0}^{s} (s-\tau)^{k-1} \cdot z\Big(\tau, u^{(0)}, \ldots, u^{(0)}(\lambda), \ldots,$$
$$u^{(k-1)}(\lambda), \int_{s_0}^{\tau} g(r, u^{(0)}, \ldots, u^{(k-1)})dr\Big)d\tau,\ s \in J_2.$$

Hence, for $n = k+1$, from (6), we have

$$u^{(k+1)}(s) = z\left(s, u^{(0)}, \ldots, u^{(0)}(\lambda), \ldots, u^{(k)}(\lambda), \int_{s_0}^{s} g(\tau, u^{(0)}, \ldots, u^{(k)})d\tau\right),$$

then by the integral formula, we have

$$u^{(k)}(s) = \chi^{(j)}(s_0) + \int_{s_0}^{s} z\left(\tau, u^{(0)}, \ldots, u^{(0)}(\lambda), \ldots, u^{(k)}(\lambda), \int_{s_0}^{\tau} g(r, u^{(0)}, \ldots, u^{(k)})dr\right)d\tau.$$

From the inductive hypothesis and Lemma 1, we have

$$u(s) = \sum_{j=0}^{k-1} \frac{(s-s_0)^j \chi^{(j)}(s_0)}{j!} + \frac{1}{(k-1)!}\int_{s_0}^{s} (s-\tau)^{k-1} \cdot \chi^{(j)}(s_0)d\tau$$
$$+ \frac{1}{(k-1)!}\int_{s_0}^{s} (s-\tau)^{k-1} \int_{s_0}^{\tau} z\Big(r, u^{(0)}, \ldots, u^{(0)}(\lambda), \ldots, u^{(k)}(\lambda),$$
$$\int_{s_0}^{r} g(t, u^{(0)}, \ldots, u^{(k)})dt\Big)drd\tau$$
$$= \sum_{j=0}^{k} \frac{(s-s_0)^j \chi^{(j)}(s_0)}{j!} + \frac{1}{k!}\int_{s_0}^{s} (s-\tau)^{k} \cdot z\Big(\tau, u^{(0)}, \ldots, u^{(0)}(\lambda), \ldots,$$
$$u^{(k)}(\lambda), \int_{s_0}^{\tau} g(r, u^{(0)}, \ldots, u^{(k)})dr\Big)d\tau.$$

Hence, by mathematical induction, the conclusion is estabilished. □

Lemma 2 (see [23]). *(abstract Gronwall lemma) Let (Y, d) be an ordered metric space and $A\colon Y \longrightarrow Y$ be an increasing Picard operator ($F_A = \{x_A{}^*\}$). Then, for $x \in Y$, $x \leq A(x)$ implies $x \leq x_A{}^*$ and $x \geq A(x)$ implies $x \geq x_A{}^*$.*

Lemma 3 (see [29]). *(Gronwall lemma) Assume that* $u(s), b(s) \in C([a,+\infty), \mathbb{R}^+)$, $T > 0$ *is constant. If* $u(s) \in C([a,+\infty), \mathbb{R}^+)$ *satisfies*

$$u(s) \leq T + \int_a^s b(\tau)u(\tau)d\tau, \; s \in [a,+\infty),$$

then

$$u(s) \leq T \exp\left(\int_a^s b(\tau)d\tau\right), \; s \in [a,+\infty).$$

Lemma 4 (see [30]). *Assume that* $w(s), d(s), l(s), m(s), n(s) \in C(\mathbb{R}^+, \mathbb{R}^+)$ *and* $d(s), l(s)$ *are nondecreasing functions on* $\mathbb{R}^+$. *If* $w(s)$ *satisfies the delay integral inequality*

$$w^h(s) \leq d(s) + l(s)\int_0^s \left[m(\tau)w^a(\sigma(\tau)) + n(\tau)w^b(\tau) + \int_0^\tau z(r)w^c(r)dr\right]d\tau, \; s \in \mathbb{R}^+,$$

with initial conditions

$$w(s) = r(s), \; s \in [\alpha, 0]; r(\sigma(s)) \leq d(s)^{\frac{1}{h}}, \; s \in \mathbb{R}^+ \text{and } \sigma(s) \leq 0,$$

where $h \neq 0, h \geq a \geq 0, h \geq b \geq 0, h \geq c \geq 0$ *and* h, a, b, c *are constants;* $\sigma(s) \in C(\mathbb{R}^+, \mathbb{R})$ *and* $\sigma(s) \leq s$; $-\infty < \alpha = \inf\{\sigma(s), s \in \mathbb{R}^+\} \leq 0$ *and* $r(s) \in C([\alpha, 0], \mathbb{R}^+)$, *then*

$$w(s) \leq \left[d(s) + l(s)U(s)\exp\left(\int_0^s V(\tau)d\tau\right)\right]^{\frac{1}{h}},$$

where, for any $H > 0$, $s \in \mathbb{R}^+$,

$$\begin{aligned} U(s) = & \int_0^s m(\tau)\left[\left(\frac{a}{h}H^{\frac{a-h}{h}}d(\tau) + \frac{h-a}{h}H^{\frac{a}{h}}\right) + g(\tau,s)\left(\frac{b}{h}H^{\frac{b-h}{h}}d(\tau) + \frac{h-b}{h}H^{\frac{b}{h}}\right)\right. \\ & \left. + \int_0^\tau z(r)\left(\frac{c}{h}H^{\frac{c-h}{h}}d(r) + \frac{h-c}{h}H^{\frac{c}{h}}\right)dr\right]d\tau, \\ V(s) = & \left(\frac{a}{h}H^{\frac{a-h}{h}}m(s) + \frac{b}{h}H^{\frac{b-h}{h}}n(s)\right)l(s) + \int_0^s z(\tau)l(\tau)\frac{c}{h}H^{\frac{c-h}{h}}d\tau. \end{aligned}$$

3. Existence and Stability Results for the Delay Integro-Differential Equation

Before stating the main theorems, we give the following Lipschitz conditions:
(S_1):

$$\begin{aligned} & |z(s, u^{(0)}, \ldots, u^{(n-1)}, \overline{u}^{(0)}, \ldots, \overline{u}^{(n-1)}, \tilde{u}) - z(s, v^{(0)}, \ldots, v^{(n-1)}, \overline{v}^{(0)}, \ldots, \overline{v}^{(n-1)}, \tilde{v})| \\ & \leq K_z \sum_{j=0}^{n-1} [|u^{(j)} - v^{(j)}| + |\overline{u}^{(j)} - \overline{v}^{(j)}|] + M|\tilde{u} - \tilde{v}|, \end{aligned}$$

where $K_z > 0$, $M > 0$, $\overline{u}^{(j)} = u^{(j)}(\lambda)$, $\overline{v}^{(j)} = v^{(j)}(\lambda)$.
(S_2):

$$|g(s, u^{(0)}, \ldots, u^{(n-1)}) - g(s, v^{(0)}, \ldots, v^{(n-1)})| \leq N \sum_{j=0}^{n-1} |u^{(j)} - v^{(j)}|,$$

where $N > 0$.
(S_3):

$$\begin{aligned} & |z(s, u^{(0)}, \ldots, u^{(n-1)}, \overline{u}^{(0)}, \ldots, \overline{u}^{(n-1)}, \tilde{u}) - z(s, v^{(0)}, \ldots, v^{(n-1)}, \overline{v}^{(0)}, \ldots, \overline{v}^{(n-1)}, \tilde{v})| \\ & \leq e(s)|u^{(0)} - v^{(0)}|^l + k(s)|\overline{u}^{(0)} - \overline{v}^{(0)}|^m + M(s)|\tilde{u} - \tilde{v}|, \end{aligned}$$

where $e(s), k(s), M(s) > 0$, $s \in J_1$; $l, m \in (0,1]$; $\overline{u}^{(0)} = u^{(0)}(\lambda)$, $\overline{v}^{(0)} = v^{(0)}(\lambda)$.

(S_4):

$$|g(s, u^{(0)}, \ldots, u^{(n-1)}) - g(s, v^{(0)}, \ldots, v^{(n-1)})| \leq N(s)|u^{(0)} - v^{(0)}|^n,$$

where $N(s) > 0$, $s \in J_1$; $n \in (0,1]$.

(S_5):

Assume $\sigma(s)$ is a function from J_2 to $\mathbb{R}^+$ and there exists $L_\sigma > 0$ such that

$$\int_\tau^s \sigma(r)dr \leq L_\sigma \cdot \sigma(s),\ s \in J_2.$$

Firstly, we give the existence and uniqueness of a solution for (3).

Theorem 2. *Assume that (S_1) and (S_2) hold. If $\frac{\eta^n}{(n-1)!}(2K_z + MN\eta) < 1$, then Equation (3) has a unique solution.*

Proof. (i) We define the operator γ as follows:

$$(\gamma u)(s) = \begin{cases} \sum_{j=0}^{n-1} \frac{(s-s_0)^j \chi^{(j)}(s_0)}{j!} + \frac{1}{(n-1)!}\int_{s_0}^s (s-\tau)^{n-1} \\ \cdot z\left(\tau, u^{(0)}, \ldots, u^{(n-1)}(\lambda), \int_{s_0}^\tau g(r, u^{(0)}, \ldots, u^{(n-1)})dr\right)d\tau,\ s \in J_2, \\ \chi(s),\ s \in J_3. \end{cases} \tag{8}$$

Since $z \in C(B, \mathbb{R})$, γ is well defined. Let $u_1(s), u_2(s) \in C(J_1, \mathbb{R}) \bigcap C^n(J_2, \mathbb{R})$, for any $s \in J_3$. Then we have

$$|(\gamma u_1)(s) - (\gamma u_2)(s)| = 0.$$

For all $s \in J_2$, by condition (S_1) and (S_2), we have

$$\begin{aligned}
&|(\gamma u_1)(s) - (\gamma u_2)(s)| \\
=&\left|\frac{1}{(n-1)!}\int_{s_0}^s (s-\tau)^{n-1}\left[z\left(\tau, u_1^{(0)}, \ldots, u_1^{(n-1)}(\lambda), \int_{s_0}^\tau g(r, u_1^{(0)}, \quad, u_1^{(n-1)})dr\right)\right.\right. \\
&\left.\left. - z\left(\tau, u_2^{(0)}, \ldots, u_2^{(n-1)}, u_2^{(0)}(\lambda), \ldots, u_2^{(n-1)}(\lambda), \int_{s_0}^\tau g(r, u_2^{(0)}, \ldots, u_2^{(n-1)})dr\right)\right]d\tau\right| \\
\leq&\frac{1}{(n-1)!}\left|\int_{s_0}^s (s-\tau)^{n-1}\left[K_z \sum_{j=0}^{n-1}\left(|u_1^{(j)} - u_2^{(j)}| + |\overline{u_1}^{(j)} - \overline{u_2}^{(j)}|\right)\right.\right. \\
&\left.\left. + MN\int_{s_0}^\tau \sum_{j=0}^{n-1} |u_1^{(j)} - u_2^{(j)}|dr\right]d\tau\right| \\
\leq&\left|\int_{s_0}^s \frac{(s-\tau)^{n-1}}{(n-1)!}\left[K_z \sum_{j=0}^{n-1}\left(\sup|u_1^{(j)} - u_2^{(j)}| + \sup|\overline{u_1}^{(j)} - \overline{u_2}^{(j)}|\right)\right.\right. \\
&\left.\left. + MN\int_{s_0}^\tau \sum_{j=0}^{n-1} \sup|u_1^{(j)} - u_2^{(j)}|dr\right]d\tau\right| \\
\leq&\frac{1}{(n-1)!}\left|\int_{s_0}^s (s-\tau)^{n-1}\left(2K_z n\|u_1 - u_2\| + MN\eta n\|u_1 - u_2\|\right)d\tau\right| \\
\leq&\frac{\eta^n}{(n-1)!}(2K_z + MN\eta)\|u_1 - u_2\|,
\end{aligned}$$

where $\overline{u}_i^{(j)} = u_i^{(j)}(\lambda)$, $i = 1, 2$, $j = 0, 1, \ldots, n$.

Since $\frac{\eta^n}{(n-1)!}(2K_z + MN\eta) < 1$, for $u_1(s), u_2(s) \in C(J_1,\mathbb{R})\bigcap C^n(J_2,\mathbb{R})$, the operator γ is a Banach contraction. By Banach contraction principle, the operator γ has a unique fixed point $u^* \in C(J_1,\mathbb{R})\bigcap C^n(J_2,\mathbb{R})$; thus, Equation (3) has a unique solution. □

Next, we obtain the following Ulam stability results.

Theorem 3. *If the assumptions of the Theorem 2 are satisfied, Equation (3) is Hyers–Ulam stable on J_1.*

Proof. Let $u(s) \in C(J_1,\mathbb{R})\bigcap C^n(J_2,\mathbb{R})$ be a unique solution of delay integro-differential equation

$$\begin{cases} u^{(n)}(s) = z\left(s, u^{(0)}, \dots, u^{(0)}(\lambda), \dots, u^{(n-1)}(\lambda), \int_{s_0}^{s} g(\tau, u^{(0)}, \dots, u^{(n-1)})d\tau\right), \ s \in J_2, \\ u(s) = \chi(s), \ s \in J_3, \\ u^{(j)}(s_0) = \chi^{(j)}(s_0), \ j = 1, \dots, n-1. \end{cases} \tag{9}$$

Since $z \in C(J_2 \times \mathbb{R}^{2n+1}, \mathbb{R})$, $\lambda \in C(J_2, J_1)$, from Theorem 1, we have

$$u(s) = \begin{cases} \sum_{j=0}^{n-1} \frac{(s-s_0)^j \chi^{(j)}(s_0)}{j!} + \frac{1}{(n-1)!}\int_{s_0}^{s} (s-\tau)^{n-1} \\ \cdot z\left(\tau, u^{(0)}, \dots, u^{(0)}(\lambda), \dots, u^{(n-1)}(\lambda), \int_{s_0}^{\tau} g(r, u^{(0)}, \dots, u^{(n-1)})dr\right)d\tau, \ s \in J_2, \\ \chi(s), \ s \in J_3. \end{cases} \tag{10}$$

Let $v(s) \in C(J_1,\mathbb{R})\bigcap C^n(J_2,\mathbb{R})$ satisfy the following inequality:

$$\begin{cases} \left|v^{(n)}(s) - z\left(s, v^{(0)}, \dots, v^{(n-1)}(\lambda), \int_{s_0}^{s} g(\tau, v^{(0)}, \dots, v^{(n-1)})d\tau\right)\right| \le \theta, \ s \in J_2, \\ |v(s) - \chi(s)| \le \theta, \ s \in J_3. \end{cases} \tag{11}$$

Let

$$v^{(n)}(s) = z\left(s, v^{(0)}, \dots, v^{(n-1)}(\lambda), \int_{s_0}^{s} g(\tau, v^{(0)}, \dots, v^{(n-1)})d\tau\right) + F(s),$$

from (11), this implies that

$$|F(s)| \le \theta, \ s \in J_2.$$

By Theorem 1, we have

$$\begin{aligned} v(s) = {} & \sum_{j=0}^{n-1} \frac{(s-s_0)^j \chi^{(j)}(s_0)}{j!} + \frac{1}{(n-1)!}\int_{s_0}^{s} (s-\tau)^{n-1} z\left(\tau, v^{(0)}, \dots, v^{(n-1)}(\lambda),\right. \\ & \left.\int_{s_0}^{\tau} g(r, v^{(0)}, \dots, v^{(n-1)})dr\right)d\tau + \frac{1}{(n-1)!}\int_{s_0}^{s} (s-\tau)^{n-1} F(\tau)d\tau, \end{aligned}$$

then

$$\begin{aligned} & \left|v(s) - \sum_{j=0}^{n-1} \frac{(s-s_0)^j \chi^{(j)}(s_0)}{j!} - \frac{1}{(n-1)!}\int_{s_0}^{s} (s-\tau)^{n-1} z\left(\tau, v^{(0)}, \dots, v^{(n-1)}(\lambda),\right.\right. \\ & \left.\left.\int_{s_0}^{\tau} g(r, v^{(0)}, \dots, v^{(n-1)})dr\right)d\tau\right| \\ = & \left|\frac{1}{(n-1)!}\int_{s_0}^{s} (s-\tau)^{n-1} F(\tau)d\tau\right| \end{aligned}$$

$$
\begin{aligned}
&\leq \frac{1}{(n-1)!}\int_{s_0}^{s}(s-\tau)^{n-1}|F(\tau)|d\tau \\
&\leq \frac{1}{(n-1)!}\int_{s_0}^{s}(s-\tau)^{n-1}d\tau\cdot\theta \\
&\leq \eta^n\theta.
\end{aligned}
$$

For all $s \in J_3$,

$$|v(s)-u(s)| = 0.$$

For any $s \in J_2$,

$$
\begin{aligned}
&|v(s)-u(s)| \\
\leq&\left|v(s)-\sum_{j=0}^{n-1}\frac{(s-s_0)^j\chi^{(j)}(s_0)}{j!}-\frac{1}{(n-1)!}\int_{s_0}^{s}(s-\tau)^{n-1}z\Big(\tau,v^{(0)},\ldots,v^{(n-1)},v^{(0)}(\lambda),\right. \\
&\left.\ldots,v^{(n-1)}(\lambda),\int_{s_0}^{\tau}g(r,v^{(0)},\ldots,v^{(n-1)})dr\Big)d\tau\right|+\frac{1}{(n-1)!}\int_{s_0}^{s}(s-\tau)^{n-1}\cdot\Big|z\Big(\tau,v^{(0)}, \\
&\ldots,v^{(n-1)},v^{(0)}(\lambda),\ldots,v^{(n-1)}(\lambda),\int_{s_0}^{\tau}g(r,v^{(0)},\ldots,v^{(n-1)})dr\Big)-z\Big(\tau,u^{(0)}, \\
&\ldots,u^{(n-1)},u^{(0)}(\lambda),\ldots,u^{(n-1)}(\lambda),\int_{s_0}^{\tau}g(r,u^{(0)},\ldots,u^{(n-1)})dr\Big)\Big|d\tau \\
\leq&\eta^n\theta+\frac{1}{(n-1)!}\int_{s_0}^{s}(s-\tau)^{n-1}\Bigg[K_z\sum_{j=0}^{n-1}\Big(|v^{(j)}-u^{(j)}|+|\overline{v}^{(j)}\quad\overline{u}^{(j)}|\Big) \\
&+MN\int_{s_0}^{\tau}\sum_{j=0}^{n-1}|v^{(j)}-u^{(j)}|dr\Bigg]d\tau,
\end{aligned}
$$

where $\overline{u}^{(j)} = u^{(j)}(\lambda)$, $\overline{v}^{(j)} = v^{(j)}(\lambda)$.

From the above inequality, we define the operator A as follows:
for all $s \in J_2$,

$$\Big(Ay^{(j)}\Big)(s) = \eta^n\theta+\frac{1}{(n-1)!}\int_{s_0}^{s}(s-\tau)^{n-1}\left[K_z\sum_{j=0}^{n-1}(y^{(j)}+\overline{y}^{(j)})+MN\int_{s_0}^{\tau}\sum_{j=0}^{n-1}y^{(j)}dr\right]d\tau,$$

for all $s \in J_3$,

$$\Big(Ay^{(j)}\Big)(s) = 0,$$

where $\bar{y}^{(j)} = y^{(j)}(\lambda)$, $j = 0,1,\ldots,n$.

For all $s \in J_2$,

$$
\begin{aligned}
&\Big|\Big(Ay_1{}^{(j)}\Big)(s)-\Big(Ay_2{}^{(j)}\Big)(s)\Big| \\
\leq&\frac{1}{(n-1)!}\int_{s_0}^{s}(s-\tau)^{n-1}\left[K_z\sum_{j=0}^{n-1}\Big(|y_1{}^{(j)}-y_2{}^{(j)}|+|\overline{y_1}^{(j)}-\overline{y_2}^{(j)}|\Big)\right. \\
&\left.+MN\int_{s_0}^{\tau}\sum_{j=0}^{n-1}|y_1{}^{(j)}-y_2{}^{(j)}|dr\right]d\tau \\
\leq&\frac{1}{(n-1)!}\int_{s_0}^{s}(s-\tau)^{n-1}ds(2K_zn+MN\eta n)\|y_1{}^{(j)}-y_2{}^{(j)}\| \\
\leq&\frac{\eta^n}{(n-1)!}(2K_z+MN\eta)\|y_1{}^{(j)}-y_2{}^{(j)}\|,
\end{aligned}
$$

where $\bar{y}_i^{(j)} = y_i^{(j)}(\lambda), i = 1,2, j = 0,1,\ldots,n$.

Since

$$\frac{\eta^n}{(n-1)!}(2K_z + MN\eta) < 1,$$

A is a strict contraction operator.

By the contraction mapping theorem, A has a unique fixed point $\{\omega^{(j)}\}$, so

$$\omega^{(j)}(s) = \eta^n\theta + \frac{1}{(n-1)!}\int_{s_0}^{s}(s-\tau)^{n-1}\left[K_z\sum_{j=0}^{n-1}\left(\omega^{(j)} + \overline{\omega}^{(j)}\right) + MN\int_{s_0}^{\tau}\sum_{j=0}^{n-1}\omega^{(j)}dr\right]d\tau,\ s \in J_2.$$

Since $\left(\omega^{(j)}(s)\right)' \geq 0$, $\omega^{(j)}(s)$ is a nondecreasing function, we have

$$\omega^{(j)}(\lambda(s)) = \overline{\omega}^{(j)}(s) \leq \omega^{(j)}(s),$$

$$\begin{aligned}
\omega^{(j)}(s) &\leq \eta^n\theta + \frac{1}{(n-1)!}\int_{s_0}^{s}(s-\tau)^{n-1}\left(2K_z\sum_{j=0}^{n-1}\omega^{(j)} + MN\int_{s_0}^{\tau}\sum_{j=0}^{n-1}\omega^{(j)}dr\right)d\tau \\
&\leq \eta^n\theta + \frac{1}{(n-1)!}\sum_{j=0}^{n-1}(2K_z + MN\eta)\int_{s_0}^{s}(s-\tau)^{n-1}\omega^{(j)}d\tau \\
&\leq \eta^n\theta + \frac{n}{(n-1)!}(2K_z + MN\eta)\int_{s_0}^{s}(s-\tau)^{n-1}\omega^{(j)}d\tau.
\end{aligned}$$

From Lemma 3, we obtain

$$\omega^{(j)}(s) \leq C\cdot\theta,\ C = \eta^n\exp\left(\frac{(2K_z + MN\eta)\eta^n}{(n-1)!}\right).$$

Since

$$|v(s) - u(s)| \leq \left(Ay^{(j)}\right)(s),$$

then

$$|v(s) - u(s)| \leq \left(Aw^{(j)}\right)(s) = w^{(j)}(s) \leq C\cdot\theta.$$

From Definition 1, Equation (3) is Hyers–Ulam stable. □

Theorem 4. *Assume that* (S_3) *and* (S_4) *hold; then Equation (3) is Hyers–Ulam stable on* J_1.

Proof. Let $u(s) \in C(J_1,\mathbb{R})\bigcap C^n(J_2,\mathbb{R})$ be a solution of delay integro-differential equation

$$\begin{cases}
u^{(n)}(s) = z\left(s, u^{(0)},\ldots,u^{(0)}(\lambda),\ldots,u^{(n-1)}(\lambda),\int_{s_0}^{s}g(\tau,u^{(0)},\ldots,u^{(n-1)})d\tau\right),\ s \in J_2, \\
u(s) = \chi(s),\ s \in J_3, \\
u^{(j)}(s_0) = \chi^{(j)}(s_0),\ j = 1,\ldots,n-1.
\end{cases} \tag{12}$$

Since $z \in C(J_2 \times \mathbb{R}^{2n+1},\mathbb{R})$, $\lambda \in C(J_2,J_1)$, from Theorem 1, we have

$$u(s) = \begin{cases}
\sum_{j=0}^{n-1}\frac{(s-s_0)^j\chi^{(j)}(s_0)}{j!} + \frac{1}{(n-1)!}\int_{s_0}^{s}(s-\tau)^{n-1} \\
\cdot z\left(\tau, u^{(0)},\ldots,u^{(0)}(\lambda),\ldots,u^{(n-1)}(\lambda),\int_{s_0}^{\tau}g(r,u^{(0)},\ldots,u^{(n-1)})dr\right)d\tau,\ s \in J_2, \\
\chi(s),\ s \in J_3.
\end{cases} \tag{13}$$

Let $v(s) \in C(J_1, \mathbb{R}) \bigcap C^n(J_2, \mathbb{R})$ satisfying inequality

$$\begin{cases} \left| v^{(n)}(s) - z\left(s, v^{(0)}, \ldots, v^{(n-1)}(\lambda), \int_{s_0}^{s} g(\tau, v^{(0)}, \ldots, v^{(n-1)}) d\tau \right) \right| \leq \theta, \ s \in J_2, \\ |v(s) - \chi(s)| \leq \theta, \ s \in J_3. \end{cases} \tag{14}$$

Let

$$v^{(n)}(s) = z\left(s, v^{(0)}, \ldots, v^{(n-1)}(\lambda), \int_{s_0}^{s} g(\tau, v^{(0)}, \ldots, v^{(n-1)}) d\tau \right) + F(s),$$

from (14), this implies that

$$|F(s)| \leq \theta, s \in J_2.$$

By Theorem 1, we have

$$\begin{aligned} v(s) = &\sum_{j=0}^{n-1} \frac{(s - s_0)^j \chi^{(j)}(s_0)}{j!} + \frac{1}{(n-1)!} \int_{s_0}^{s} (s - \tau)^{n-1} z\left(\tau, v^{(0)}, \ldots, v^{(n-1)}(\lambda), \right. \\ &\left. \int_{s_0}^{\tau} g(r, v^{(0)}, \ldots, v^{(n-1)}) dr \right) d\tau + \frac{1}{(n-1)!} \int_{s_0}^{s} (s - \tau)^{n-1} F(\tau) d\tau, \end{aligned}$$

then

$$\begin{aligned} &\left| v(s) - \sum_{j=0}^{n-1} \frac{(s - s_0)^j \chi^{(j)}(s_0)}{j!} - \frac{1}{(n-1)!} \int_{s_0}^{s} (s - \tau)^{n-1} z\left(\tau, v^{(0)}, \ldots, v^{(n-1)}(\lambda), \right. \right. \\ &\left. \left. \int_{s_0}^{\tau} g(r, v^{(0)}, \ldots, v^{(n-1)}) dr \right) d\tau \right| \\ =&\left| \frac{1}{(n-1)!} \int_{s_0}^{s} (s - \tau)^{n-1} F(\tau) d\tau \right| \\ \leq&\frac{1}{(n-1)!} \int_{s_0}^{s} (s - \tau)^{n-1} |F(\tau)| d\tau \\ \leq&\frac{1}{(n-1)!} \int_{s_0}^{s} (s - \tau)^{n-1} d\tau \cdot \theta \\ \leq&\eta^n \theta. \end{aligned}$$

For all $s \in J_3$,

$$|v(s) - u(s)| = 0.$$

For any $s \in J_2$,

$$\begin{aligned} &|v(s) - u(s)| \\ =&\left| v(s) - \sum_{j=0}^{n-1} \frac{(s - s_0)^j \chi^{(j)}(s_0)}{j!} - \frac{1}{(n-1)!} \int_{s_0}^{s} (s - \tau)^{n-1} z\left(\tau, u^{(0)}, \ldots, u^{(n-1)}, u^{(0)}(\lambda), \right. \right. \\ &\left. \left. \ldots, u^{(n-1)}(\lambda), \int_{s_0}^{\tau} g(r, u^{(0)}, \ldots, u^{(n-1)}) dr \right) d\tau \right| \\ =&\left| v(s) - \sum_{j=0}^{n-1} \frac{(s - s_0)^j \chi^{(j)}(s_0)}{j!} - \frac{1}{(n-1)!} \int_{s_0}^{s} (s - \tau)^{n-1} z\left(\tau, v^{(0)}, \ldots, v^{(n-1)}, v^{(0)}(\lambda), \right. \right. \\ &\left. \left. \ldots, v^{(n-1)}(\lambda), \int_{s_0}^{\tau} g(r, v^{(0)}, \ldots, v^{(n-1)}) dr \right) d\tau \right| + \left| \frac{1}{(n-1)!} \int_{s_0}^{s} (s - \tau)^{n-1} z\left(\tau, v^{(0)}, \right. \right. \end{aligned}$$

$$\ldots,v^{(n-1)},v^{(0)}(\lambda),\ldots,v^{(n-1)}(\lambda),\int_{s_0}^{\tau}g(r,v^{(0)},\ldots,v^{(n-1)})dr\Big)d\tau$$
$$-\frac{1}{(n-1)!}\int_{s_0}^{s}(s-\tau)^{n-1}z\Big(\tau,u^{(0)},\ldots,u^{(n-1)},u^{(0)}(\lambda),$$
$$\ldots,u^{(n-1)}(\lambda),\int_{s_0}^{\tau}g(r,u^{(0)},\ldots,u^{(n-1)})dr\Big)d\tau\Big|$$
$$\leq\Big|v(s)-\sum_{j=0}^{n-1}\frac{(s-s_0)^j\chi^{(j)}(s_0)}{j!}-\frac{1}{(n-1)!}\int_{s_0}^{s}(s-\tau)^{n-1}z\Big(\tau,v^{(0)},\ldots,v^{(n-1)},$$
$$v^{(0)}(\lambda),\ldots,v^{(n-1)}(\lambda),\int_{s_0}^{\tau}g(r,v^{(0)},\ldots,v^{(n-1)})dr\Big)d\tau\Big|$$
$$+\Big|\frac{1}{(n-1)!}\int_{s_0}^{s}(s-\tau)^{n-1}\Big[e(\tau)|v^{(0)}-u^{(0)}|^l+k(\tau)|v^{(0)}(\lambda)-u^{(0)}(\lambda)|^m$$
$$+\int_{s_0}^{\tau}M(\tau)N(r)|v^{(0)}-u^{(0)}|^n dr\Big]d\tau\Big|,$$

then

$$|v(s)-u(s)|\leq\eta^n\theta+\frac{1}{(n-1)!}\int_{s_0}^{s}(s-\tau)^{n-1}\Big[e(\tau)|v-u|^l+k(\tau)|v(\lambda)-u(\lambda)|^m$$
$$+\int_{s_0}^{\tau}M(\tau)N(r)|v-u|^n dr\Big]d\tau.$$

From Lemma 4, set $h=1$, $a=m$, $b=l$, $c=n$, $w(s)=|v(s)-u(s)|$, $d(s)=\eta^n\theta$, $l(s)=\frac{1}{(n-1)!}$, $m(\tau)=(s-\tau)^{n-1}k(\tau)$, $n(\tau)=(s-\tau)^{n-1}e(\tau)$,$z(r)=(s-\tau)^{n-1}M(\tau)N(r)$; we have

$$|v(s)-u(s)|\leq\eta^n\theta+\frac{1}{(n-1)!}U(s)\exp\Big(\int_{s_0}^{s}V(\tau)d\tau\Big),$$

$$|v(s)-u(s)|\leq\Big[\eta^n+\frac{1}{(n-1)!}\frac{U(s)}{\theta}\exp\Big(\int_{s_0}^{s}V(\tau)d\tau\Big)\Big]\cdot\theta\leq K_{z,\theta}\cdot\theta,$$

where for any $H>0$,

$$K_{z,\theta}=\max_{s\in J_1}\Big\{\eta^n+\frac{1}{(n-1)!}\frac{U(s)}{\theta}\exp\Big(\int_{s_0}^{s}V(\tau)d\tau\Big)\Big\},$$

$$U(s)=\int_{s_0}^{s}\Big[(s-\tau)^{n-1}k(\tau)\Big(mH^{m-1}\eta^n\theta+(1-m)H^m\Big)+g(\tau,s)\Big(lH^{l-1}\eta^n\theta+(1-l)H^l\Big)$$
$$+\int_{s_0}^{\tau}(s-\tau)^{n-1}M(\tau)N(r)\Big(nH^{n-1}\eta^n\theta+(1-n)H^n\Big)dr\Big]d\tau,$$
$$V(s)=\frac{1}{(n-1)!}\int_{s_0}^{s}(s-\tau)^{n-1}M(\tau)N(\tau)nH^{n-1}d\tau.$$

From Definition 1, Equation (3) is Hyers–Ulam stable. □

Theorem 5. *Assume that* (S_3), (S_4) *and* (S_5) *hold; then Equation (3) is Hyers–Ulam–Rassias stable with respect to* $\sigma(s)$ *on* J_1.

Proof. Let $u(s)\in C(J_1,\mathbb{R})\bigcap C^n(J_2,\mathbb{R})$ be a unique solution of delay integro-differential equation

$$\begin{cases} u^{(n)}(s) = z\left(s, u^{(0)}, \ldots, u^{(0)}(\lambda), \ldots, u^{(n-1)}(\lambda), \int_{s_0}^{s} g(\tau, u^{(0)}, \ldots, u^{(n-1)})d\tau\right), \ s \in J_2, \\ u(s) = \chi(s), \ s \in J_3, \\ u^{(j)}(s_0) = \chi^{(j)}(s_0), \ j = 1, \ldots, n-1. \end{cases} \tag{15}$$

Since $z \in C(J_2 \times \mathbb{R}^{2n+1}, \mathbb{R})$, $\lambda \in C(J_2, J_1)$, from Theorem 1, we have

$$u(s) = \begin{cases} \sum\limits_{j=0}^{n-1} \frac{(s-s_0)^j \chi^{(j)}(s_0)}{j!} + \frac{1}{(n-1)!} \int_{s_0}^{s} (s-\tau)^{n-1} \\ \cdot z\left(\tau, u^{(0)}, \ldots, u^{(0)}(\lambda), \ldots, u^{(n-1)}(\lambda), \int_{s_0}^{\tau} g(r, u^{(0)}, \ldots, u^{(n-1)})dr\right)d\tau, \ s \in J_2, \\ \chi(s), \ s \in J_3. \end{cases} \tag{16}$$

Let $v(s) \in C(J_1, \mathbb{R}) \bigcap C^n(J_2, \mathbb{R})$ satisfy the following inequality

$$\begin{cases} \left| v^{(n)}(s) - z\left(s, v^{(0)}, \ldots, v^{(n-1)}(\lambda), \int_{s_0}^{s} g(\tau, v^{(0)}, \ldots, v^{(n-1)})d\tau\right)\right| \leq \sigma(s), \ s \in J_2, \\ |v(s) - \chi(s)| \leq \sigma(s), \ s \in J_3. \end{cases} \tag{17}$$

Let

$$v^{(n)}(s) = z\left(s, v^{(0)}, \ldots, v^{(n-1)}(\lambda), \int_{s_0}^{s} g(\tau, v^{(0)}, \ldots, v^{(n-1)})d\tau\right) + F(s),$$

from (17), this implies that

$$|F(s)| \leq \sigma(s), s \in J_2.$$

By Theorem 1, we have

$$\begin{aligned} v(s) = \sum_{j=0}^{n-1} \frac{(s-s_0)^j \chi^{(j)}(s_0)}{j!} &+ \frac{1}{(n-1)!} \int_{s_0}^{s} (s-\tau)^{n-1} z\left(\tau, v^{(0)}, \ldots, v^{(n-1)}(\lambda),\right. \\ &\left.\int_{s_0}^{\tau} g(r, v^{(0)}, \ldots, v^{(n-1)})dr\right)d\tau + \frac{1}{(n-1)!} \int_{s_0}^{s} (s-\tau)^{n-1} F(\tau)d\tau; \end{aligned}$$

then

$$\begin{aligned} &\left| v(s) - \sum_{j=0}^{n-1} \frac{(s-s_0)^j \chi^{(j)}(s_0)}{j!} - \frac{1}{(n-1)!} \int_{s_0}^{s} (s-\tau)^{n-1} z\left(\tau, v^{(0)}, \ldots, v^{(n-1)}(\lambda),\right.\right. \\ &\left.\left.\int_{s_0}^{\tau} g(r, v^{(0)}, \ldots, v^{(n-1)})dr\right)d\tau \right| \\ =&\left| \frac{1}{(n-1)!} \int_{s_0}^{s} (s-\tau)^{n-1} F(\tau)d\tau \right| \\ \leq& \frac{1}{(n-1)!} \int_{s_0}^{s} (s-\tau)^{n-1} |F(\tau)|d\tau \\ \leq& \frac{1}{(n-1)!} \int_{s_0}^{s} (s-\tau)^{n-1} \sigma(\tau)d\tau. \end{aligned}$$

By Lemma 1 and condition (S_5), we obtain

$$\begin{aligned} &\left| v(s) - \sum_{j=0}^{n-1} \frac{(s-s_0)^j \chi^{(j)}(s_0)}{j!} - \frac{1}{(n-1)!} \int_{s_0}^{s} (s-\tau)^{n-1} z\left(\tau, v^{(0)}, \ldots, v^{(n-1)}(\lambda),\right.\right. \\ &\left.\left.\int_{s_0}^{\tau} g(r, v^{(0)}, \ldots, v^{(n-1)})dr\right)d\tau \right| \end{aligned}$$

$$\leq \int_{s_0}^{s}\int_{s_0}^{s_1}\int_{s_0}^{s_2}\int_{s_0}^{s_3}\cdots\int_{s_0}^{s_{n-1}}\sigma(s_n)ds_n ds_{n-1}\ldots ds_2 ds_1$$
$$\leq L_\sigma{}^n\cdot\sigma(s).$$

For all $s \in J_3$,

$$|v(s) - u(s)| = 0.$$

For any $s \in J_2$,

$$\begin{aligned}
&|v(s) - u(s)|\\
=&\bigg|v(s) - \sum_{j=0}^{n-1}\frac{(s-s_0)^j\chi^{(j)}(s_0)}{j!} - \frac{1}{(n-1)!}\int_{s_0}^{s}(s-\tau)^{n-1}z\bigg(\tau, u^{(0)},\ldots,u^{(n-1)},u^{(0)}(\lambda),\\
&\ldots,u^{(n-1)}(\lambda),\int_{s_0}^{\tau}g(r,u^{(0)},\ldots,u^{(n-1)})dr\bigg)d\tau\bigg|\\
=&\bigg|v(s) - \sum_{j=0}^{n-1}\frac{(s-s_0)^j\chi^{(j)}(s_0)}{j!} - \frac{1}{(n-1)!}\int_{s_0}^{s}(s-\tau)^{n-1}z\bigg(\tau, v^{(0)},\ldots,v^{(n-1)},v^{(0)}(\lambda),\\
&\ldots,v^{(n-1)}(\lambda),\int_{s_0}^{\tau}g(r,v^{(0)},\ldots,v^{(n-1)})dr\bigg)d\tau\bigg| + \bigg|\frac{1}{(n-1)!}\int_{s_0}^{s}(s-\tau)^{n-1}z\bigg(\tau, v^{(0)},\\
&\ldots,v^{(n-1)},v^{(0)}(\lambda),\ldots,v^{(n-1)}(\lambda),\int_{s_0}^{\tau}g(r,v^{(0)},\ldots,v^{(n-1)})dr\bigg)d\tau\\
&-\frac{1}{(n-1)!}\int_{s_0}^{s}(s-\tau)^{n-1}z\bigg(\tau, u^{(0)},\ldots,u^{(n-1)},u^{(0)}(\lambda),\\
&\ldots,u^{(n-1)}(\lambda),\int_{s_0}^{\tau}g(r,u^{(0)},\ldots,u^{(n-1)})dr\bigg)d\tau\bigg|\\
\leq&\bigg|v(s) - \sum_{j=0}^{n-1}\frac{(s-s_0)^j\chi^{(j)}(s_0)}{j!} - \frac{1}{(n-1)!}\int_{s_0}^{s}(s-\tau)^{n-1}z\bigg(\tau, v^{(0)},\ldots,v^{(n-1)},v^{(0)}(\lambda),\\
&\ldots,v^{(n-1)}(\lambda),\int_{s_0}^{\tau}g(r,v^{(0)},\ldots,v^{(n-1)})dr\bigg)d\tau\bigg|\\
&+\bigg|\frac{1}{(n-1)!}\int_{s_0}^{s}(s-\tau)^{n-1}\bigg[e(\tau)|v^{(0)}-u^{(0)}|^l + k(\tau)|v^{(0)}(\lambda)-u^{(0)}(\lambda)|^m\\
&+\int_{s_0}^{\tau}M(\tau)N(r)|v^{(0)}-u^{(0)}|^n dr\bigg]d\tau\bigg|;
\end{aligned}$$

then

$$\begin{aligned}
&|v(s) - u(s)|\\
\leq&L_\sigma{}^n\sigma(s) + \frac{1}{(n-1)!}\int_{s_0}^{s}(s-\tau)^{n-1}\bigg[e(\tau)|v-u|^l + k(\tau)|v(\lambda)-u(\lambda)|^m\\
&+\int_{s_0}^{\tau}M(\tau)N(r)|v-u|^n dr\bigg]d\tau.
\end{aligned}$$

From Lemma 4, set $h = 1$, $a = m$, $b = l$, $c = n$, $w(s) = |v(s) - u(s)|$, $d(s) = L_\sigma{}^n\sigma(s)$, $l(s) = \frac{1}{(n-1)!}$, $m(\tau) = (s-\tau)^{n-1}k(\tau)$, $n(\tau) = (s-\tau)^{n-1}e(\tau)$, $z(r) = (s-\tau)^{n-1}M(\tau)N(r)$; thus, we have

$$|v(s) - u(s)| \leq L_\sigma{}^n\sigma(s) + \frac{1}{(n-1)!}U(s)\exp\bigg(\int_{s_0}^{s}V(\tau)d\tau\bigg),$$

$$|v(s)-u(s)| \le \left[L_\sigma{}^n + \frac{1}{(n-1)!}\frac{U(s)}{\sigma(s)}\exp\left(\int_{s_0}^{s} V(\tau)d\tau\right)\right]\cdot\sigma(s) \le K_\sigma\cdot\sigma(s),$$

where for any $H > 0$,

$$K_\sigma = \max_{s\in J_1}\left\{L_\sigma{}^n + \frac{1}{(n-1)!}\frac{U(s)}{\sigma(s)}\exp\left(\int_{s_0}^{s} V(\tau)d\tau\right)\right\},$$

$$\begin{aligned}U(s) = &\int_{s_0}^{s}\Big[(s-\tau)^{n-1}k(\tau)\Big(mH^{m-1}L_\sigma{}^n\sigma(\tau)+(1-m)H^m\Big)+g(\tau,s)\Big(lH^{l-1}L_\sigma{}^n\sigma(\tau)\\ &+(1-l)H^l\Big)+\int_{s_0}^{\tau}(s-\tau)^{n-1}M(\tau)N(r)\Big(nH^{n-1}L_\sigma{}^n\sigma(r)+(1-n)H^n\Big)dr\Big]d\tau,\\ V(s) = &\frac{1}{(n-1)!}\int_{s_0}^{s}(s-\tau)^{n-1}M(\tau)N(\tau)nH^{n-1}d\tau.\end{aligned}$$

From Definition 2, Equation (3) is Hyers–Ulam–Rassias stable. □

4. Examples

Example 1. *We consider the delay integro-differential equation*

$$\frac{du(s)}{ds} = e^s\left[\frac{1}{|u(s)|+8} + \frac{1}{|u(\lambda(s))|+8} + \frac{1}{64}\int_0^s e^{-\tau}\frac{1}{|u(\tau)|+8}d\tau\right]$$

and the inequality

$$\left|\frac{du(s)}{ds} - e^s\left[\frac{1}{|u(s)|+8} + \frac{1}{|u(\lambda(s))|+8} + \frac{1}{64}\int_0^s e^{-\tau}\frac{1}{|u(\tau)|+8}d\tau\right]\right| \le \sigma(s).$$

Set $z(s,u(s),u(\lambda(s)),v) = e^s\left[\frac{1}{|u(s)|+8}+\frac{1}{|u(\lambda(s))|+8}+\frac{1}{64}v\right]$, $g(s,u(s)) = e^{-s}\frac{1}{|u(s)|+8}$, $s\in[0,2]$.

For any $s\in[0,2]$, *we obtain*

$$\begin{aligned}&|z(s,u_1(s),u_1(\lambda(s)),v_1)-z(s,u_2(s),u_2(\lambda(s)),v_2)|\\ =&\, e^s\left|\frac{(|u_2(s)|-|u_1(s)|)}{(|u_1(s)|+8)(|u_2(s)|+8)}+\frac{(|u_2(\lambda(s))|-|u_1(\lambda(s))|)}{(|u_1(\lambda(s))|+8)(|u_2(\lambda(s))|+8)}+\frac{1}{64}(v_1-v_2)\right|\\ \le&\, \frac{e^s}{64}|u_1(s)-u_2(s)|+\frac{e^s}{64}|u_1(\lambda(s))-u_2(\lambda(s))|+\frac{1}{64}|v_1(s)-v_2(s)|.\end{aligned}$$

Here, $e(s) = \frac{e^s}{64}$, $k(s) = \frac{e^s}{64}$, $M(s) = \frac{e^s}{64}$, $l = m = 1$.

$$|g(s,u_1(s))-g(s,u_2(s))| = e^{-s}\left|\frac{|u_2(s)|-|u_1(s)|}{(|u_1(s)|+8)(|u_2(s)|+8)}\right| \le \frac{e^{-s}}{64}|u_1(s)-u_2(s)|.$$

Here, $N(s) = \frac{e^s}{64}$, $n = 1$.

Thus, (S_1) *and* (S_2) *hold,* $\frac{\eta^n}{(n-1)!}(2K_z+MN\eta) = \frac{23}{50} < 1$. *From Theorem 2, Equation has a unique solution*

$$u(s) = \int_0^s e^\tau\left[\frac{1}{|u(\tau)|+8}+\frac{1}{|u(\lambda(\tau))|+8}+\frac{1}{64}\int_0^\tau e^{-t}\frac{1}{|u(t)|+8}dt\right]d\tau.$$

Let $\sigma(s) = e^s$, $\int_0^s\sigma(\tau) = \int_0^s e^\tau = e^s-1 \le e^s$, *we have* $L_\sigma = 1 > 0$.

As $v(s)$ *satisfies the inequality*

$$\left|\frac{dv(s)}{ds} - e^s\left[\frac{1}{|v(s)|+8}+\frac{1}{|v(\lambda(s))|+8}+\frac{1}{64}\int_0^s e^{-\tau}\frac{1}{|v(\tau)|+8}d\tau\right]\right| \le e^s,$$

we have

$$\left|v(s)-\int_0^s e^{\tau}\left[\frac{1}{|v(\tau)|+8}+\frac{1}{|v(\lambda(\tau))|+8}+\frac{1}{64}\int_0^{\tau}e^{-t}\frac{1}{|v(t)|+8}dt\right]d\tau\right|\leq e^s.$$

Since (S_3), (S_4) *and* (S_5) *hold, from Theorem 5, we have*

$$\begin{aligned}&|v(s)-u(s)|\\&\leq e^s+\int_0^s\left[\frac{e^{\tau}}{64}|v(\tau)-u(\tau)|+\frac{e^{\tau}}{64}|v(\lambda(\tau))-u(\lambda(\tau))|+\int_0^{\tau}\frac{e^{-r}}{64^2}|v(r)-u(r)|dr\right]d\tau\\&\leq\frac{57}{500}e^s.\end{aligned}$$

Hence, the equation is Hyers–Ulam–Rassias stable.

Example 2. *Consider the equation*

$$\frac{du(s)}{ds}=-\frac{1}{8}\frac{1}{|u(s)|+1}-\frac{1}{8}\frac{1}{|u(\lambda(s))|+1}-\frac{1}{64}\int_0^s\frac{1}{|u(\tau)|+1}d\tau.$$

Set $z(s,u(s),u(\lambda(s)),v)=-\frac{1}{8}\frac{1}{|u(s)|+1}-\frac{1}{8}\frac{1}{|u(\lambda(s))|+1}-\frac{1}{64}v$, $g(s,u(s))=\frac{1}{|u(\tau)|+1}$, $s\in[0,2]$.

For any $s\in[0,2]$, *we obtain*

$$\begin{aligned}&|z(s,u_1(s),u_1(\lambda(s)),v_1)-z(s,u_2(s),u_2(\lambda(s)),v_2)|\\&=\frac{1}{8}\left|\frac{(|u_2(s)|-|u_1(s)|)}{(|u_1(s)|+1)(|u_2(s)|+1)}+\frac{1}{8}\frac{(|u_2(\lambda(s))|-|u_1(\lambda(s))|)}{(|u_1(\lambda(s))|+1)(|u_2(\lambda(s))|+1)}+\frac{1}{64}(v_2-v_1)\right|\\&\leq\frac{1}{8}|u_1(s)-u_2(s)|+\frac{1}{8}|u_1(\lambda(s))-u_2(\lambda(s))|+\frac{1}{64}|v_1(s)-v_2(s)|,\end{aligned}$$

$$|g(s,u_1(s))-g(s,u_2(s))|=\left|\frac{|u_2(s)|-|u_1(s)|}{(|u_1(s)|+1)(|u_2(s)|+1)}\right|\leq|u_1(s)-u_2(s)|.$$

Thus, (S_1) *and* (S_2) *hold,* $\frac{\eta^n}{(n-1)!}(2K_z+MN\eta)=\frac{9}{16}<1$. *From Theorem 2, the equation has a unique solution:*

$$u(s)=-\int_0^s\frac{1}{8}\left[\frac{1}{|u(\tau)|+1}+\frac{1}{8}\frac{1}{|u(\lambda(\tau))|+1}+\frac{1}{64}\int_0^{\tau}\frac{1}{|u(t)|+1}dt\right]d\tau.$$

Let $v(s)=e^s$ *and choose* $\theta=\frac{9}{32}$. *We have*

$$\begin{aligned}&\left|\frac{dv(s)}{ds}-\left[-\frac{1}{8}\frac{1}{|v(s)|+1}-\frac{1}{8}\frac{1}{|v(\lambda(s))|+1}-\frac{1}{64}\int_0^s\frac{1}{|v(\tau)|+1}d\tau\right]\right|\\&=\left|\frac{1}{8}\frac{1}{|v(s)|+1}+\frac{1}{8}\frac{1}{|v(\lambda(s))|+1}+\frac{1}{64}\int_0^s\frac{1}{|v(\tau)|+1}d\tau-e^{-s}\right|\leq\frac{9}{32}=\theta.\end{aligned}$$

Since (S_3) *and* (S_4) *hold, from Theorem 4, we have*

$$\begin{aligned}&|v(s)-u(s)|\\&\leq 2\theta+\int_0^s\left[\frac{1}{8}|v(\tau)-u(\tau)|+\frac{1}{8}|v(\lambda(\tau))-u(\lambda(\tau))|+\int_0^{\tau}\frac{1}{64}|v(r)-u(r)|dr\right]d\tau\\&\leq\frac{16}{5}\theta.\end{aligned}$$

Hence, the equation is Hyers–Ulam stable.

5. Conclusions

Based on Gronwall–Bellman inequality, we have proved the Ulam stability of n-th order delay integro-differential equations. By applying Lipschitz conditions and the Banach contraction principle, the existence and uniqueness theorem of a solution was given. In addition, the expression of the solution played a great role in the proof of the main theorems. The Ulam stability of the n-th order delay integro-differential equation is related to many applications, such as the effect of tire dynamics on vehicle shimmy and optimal control of a size-structured population, and the research in this field is still open. In future work, we recommend that interested scholars extend their work to the Ulam stability of a fractional delay integro-differential equation with a Caputo derivative.

Author Contributions: Conceptualization, S.W.; writing—original draft preparation, S.W.; writing—review and editing, S.W. and F.M. All authors have read and agreed to the published version of the manuscript.

Funding: This research received no external funding.

Acknowledgments: The authors thank the reviewers for their helpful suggestions and comments.

Conflicts of Interest: The authors declare that they have no conflict of interest.

References

1. Ulam, S.M. *A Collection of the Mathematical Problems*; Interscience: New York, NY, USA, 1960.
2. Hyers, D.H. On the stability of the linear functional equation. *Proc. Natl. Acad. Sci. USA* **1941**, *27*, 222–224. [CrossRef]
3. Rassias, T.M. On the stability of the linear mapping in banach spaces. *Proc. Am. Math. Soc.* **1978**, *72*, 297–300. [CrossRef]
4. Aoki, T. On the stability of the linear transformation in banach spaces. *J. Math. Soc. Jpn.* **1950**, *2*, 64–66. [CrossRef]
5. Wang J.; Lv, L.; Zhou, Y. Ulam stability and data dependence for fractional differential equations with caputo derivative. *Electron. J. Qual. Theory Differ. Equ.* **2011**, *63*, 1–10. [CrossRef]
6. Liu, K.; Wang, J.; Zhou, Y.; O'Regan D. Hyers-ulam stability and existence of solutions for fractional differential equations with mittag-leffler kernel. *Chaos Solitons Fractals* **2020**, *132*, 1–8. [CrossRef]
7. Liu, K.; Feckan, M.; Wang, J. A fixed-point approach to the hyers-ulam stability of caputo-fabrizio fractional differential equations. *Mathematics* **2020**, *8*, 647. [CrossRef]
8. Jung, S.; Brzdek, J. Hyers-ulam stability of the delay equation $y(t) = y(t-\tau)$. *Abstr. Appl. Anal.* **2010**, *13*, 10. [CrossRef]
9. Zada, A.; Faisal, S.; Li, Y. On the Hyers–Ulam Stability of First-Order Impulsive Delay Differential Equations. *J. Funct. Spaces Appl.* **2016**, *15*, 1–6. [CrossRef]
10. Zada, A.; Shah, S.O. Hyers-Ulam Stability of First-Order Non-Linear Delay Differential Equations with Fractional Integrable Impulses. *Hacet. J. Math. Stat.* **2018**, *47*, 1196–1205. [CrossRef]
11. Luo, D.; Luo, Z. Existence and Hyers-Ulam stability results for a class of fractional order delay differential equations with non-instantaneous impulses. *Math. Slovaca* **2020**, *70*, 1231–1248. [CrossRef]
12. Kendre, S.D.; Unhale, S.I. On existence, uniqueness and Ulam's stability results for boundary value problems of fractional iterative integrodifferential equations. *J. Appl. Math. Comput.* **2020**, *64*, 503–517. [CrossRef]
13. Kucche, K.D.; Shikhare, P. Ulam Stabilities for Nonlinear Volterra Delay Integro-differential Equations. *J. Contemp. Math. Anal.* **2019**, *54*, 276–287. [CrossRef]
14. Huan, D.D.; Gao, H. A note on the existence of stochastic integro-differential equations with memory. *Math. Methods Appl. Sci.* **2015**, *38*, 1–15. [CrossRef]
15. Mokkedem, F.Z.; Fu, X. Approximate controllability of semi-linear neutral integro-differential systems with finite delay. *Appl. Math. Comput.* **2014**, *242*, 202–215. [CrossRef]
16. Desch, W.; Grimmer, R.; Schappacher, W. Wellposedness and wave propagation for a class of integrodifferential equations in Banach space. *J. Differ. Equ.* **1988**, *74*, 391–411. [CrossRef]
17. Gurtin, M.E.; Pipkin, A.C. A general theory of heat conduction with finite wave speed. *Arch. Ration. Mech. Anal.* **1968**, *31*, 113–126. [CrossRef]
18. Fujita, K. Integrodifferential equation which interpolates the heat equation and the wave equation. *Osaka J. Math.* **1997**, *27*, 309–321.
19. Berinde, V. Existence and approximation of solutions of some first order iterative differential equations. *Miskolc Math. Notes* **2010**, *11*, 13–26. [CrossRef]
20. Mi, T.; Stepan, G.; Takacs, D.; Chen, N. Vehicle shimmy modeling with pacejka's magic formula and the delayed tire model. *J. Comput. Nonlinear Dyn.* **2020**, *15*, 031005. [CrossRef]
21. He, Z.; Ni, D.; Zheng, M. Ergodicity and optimal control of a size-structured population model with delay. *J. Syst. Sci. Math. Sci.* **2018**, *38*, 1–15. [CrossRef]

22. Wang, J.; Wei, W. A class of nonlocal impulsive problems for integrodifferential equations in Banach spaces. *Results Math.* **2010**, *58*, 379–397. [CrossRef]
23. Otrocol, D.; Ilea, V. Ulam stability for a delay differential equation. *Cent. Eur. J. Math.* **2013**, *11*, 1296–1303. [CrossRef]
24. Kendre, S.D.; Kharat, V.V.; Narute, R. On existence of solution for mixed iterative integrodifferential equations. *Adv. Differ. Equ. Control Process.* **2015**, *15*, 53–66. [CrossRef]
25. Sevgin, S.; Sevli, H. Stability of a nonlinear Volterra integro-differential equation via a fixed point approach. *J. Nonlinear Sci. Appl.* **2016**, *9*, 200–207. [CrossRef]
26. Kishor, D.K.; Pallavi, U.S. Ulam–Hyers Stability of Integrodifferential Equations in Banach Spaces via Pachpatte's Inequality. *Asian-Eur. J. Math.* **2018**, *11*, 1–19. [CrossRef]
27. Zada, A.; Ali, W.; Park, C. Ulam' type stability of higher order nonlinear delay differential equations via integral inequality of Grönwall-Bellman-Bihari's type. *Appl. Math. Comput.* **2019**, *350*, 60–65. [CrossRef]
28. Folland, G.B. *Advanced Calculus*; Prentice Hall: Indianapolis, IN, USA, 2001.
29. Pachpatte, B.G. *Inequalities for Differential and Integral Equations*; Academic Press: New York, NY, USA, 1998. [CrossRef]
30. Yuan, Z.; Yuan, X.; Meng, F.; Zhang, H. Some new delay integral inequalities and their appplications. *Appl. Math. Comput.* **2009**, *208*, 231–237. [CrossRef]

Σ mathematics

MDPI

Article

Laplace Transform and Semi-Hyers–Ulam–Rassias Stability of Some Delay Differential Equations

Daniela Marian

Department of Mathematics, Technical University of Cluj-Napoca, 28 Memorandumului Street, 400114 Cluj-Napoca, Romania; daniela.marian@math.utcluj.ro

Abstract: In this paper, we study semi-Hyers–Ulam–Rassias stability and generalized semi-Hyers–Ulam–Rassias stability of differential equations $x'(t) + x(t-1) = f(t)$ and $x''(t) + x'(t-1) = f(t)$, $x(t) = 0 \quad \text{if} \quad t \leq 0$, using the Laplace transform. Our results complete those obtained by S. M. Jung and J. Brzdek for the equation $x'(t) + x(t-1) = 0$.

Keywords: semi-Hyers–Ulam–Rassias stability; delay differential equations; Laplace transform

MSC: 44A10; 34K20

Citation: Marian, D. Laplace Transform and Semi-Hyers–Ulam–Rassias Stability of Some Delay Differential Equations. *Mathematics* **2021**, *9*, 3260. https://doi.org/10.3390/math9243260

Academic Editors: Stepan Tersian and Christopher Goodrich

Received: 11 November 2021
Accepted: 14 December 2021
Published: 15 December 2021

1. Introduction

The study of Ulam stability began in 1940, when Ulam posed a problem concerning the stability of homomorphisms (see [1]). In 1941, Hyers [2] gave an answer, in the case of the additive Cauchy equation in Banach spaces, to the problem posed by Ulam [1].

In 1993, Obloza [3] started the study of Hyers–Ulam stability of differential equations. Later, in 1998, Alsina and Ger [4] studied the equation $y'(x) - y(x) = 0$. Many mathematicians have further studied the stability of various equations. For a collection of results regarding this problematic, see [5] or [6].

There are many methods for studying Hyers–Ulam stability of differential equations, such as the direct method, the Gronwall inequality method, the fixed point method, the integral transform method, etc.

We mention that the Laplace transform method was used by H. Rezaei, S. M. Jung and Th. M. Rassias [7] and by Q. H. Alqifiary and S. M. Jung [8] to study the differential equation

$$y^{(n)}(t) + \sum_{k=0}^{n-1} \alpha_k y^{(k)}(t) = f(t).$$

This method was also used in [9], where Laguerre differential equation

$$xy'' + (1-x)y' + ny = 0, \quad n \text{ positive integer}$$

and Bessel differential equation

$$xy'' + y' + xy = 0,$$

was studied. In [10], Mittag-Leffler–Hyers–Ulam stability of the following linear differential equation of first order was studied with this method:

$$u'(t) + lu(t) = r(t),\ t \in I, u, r \in C(I), I = [a, b].$$

In [11], the semi-Hyers–Ulam–Rassias stability of a Volterra integro-differential equation of order I with a convolution type kernel was studied via Laplace transform:

$$y'(t) + \int_0^t y(u)g(t-u)du - f(t) = 0, \quad t \in (0,\infty),$$

$f, g, y : (0,\infty) \to \mathbb{F}$ functions of exponential order and continuous and $\mathbb{F}$ the real field $\mathbb{R}$ or the complex field $\mathbb{C}$.

In [12], the semi-Hyers–Ulam–Rassias stability of the convection partial differential equation was also studied using Laplace transform:

$$\frac{\partial y}{\partial t} + a\frac{\partial y}{\partial x} = 0,\ a > 0,\ x > 0,\ t > 0, y(0,t) = c,\ y(x,0) = 0.$$

In [13], the delay equation

$$y'(t) = \lambda y(t-\tau), \lambda \neq 0, \tau > 0,$$

was studied, using direct method.

In the following, we will study semi-Hyers–Ulam–Rassias stability and generalized semi-Hyers–Ulam–Rassias stability of some equations, with delay of order one and two, with Laplace transform. We complete the results obtained in [13]. Delay differential equations have many applications in various areas of engineering science, biology, physics, etc. The monograph [14] contains some modeling examples from mechanics, chemistry, ecology, biology, psychology, etc. For other applications, see also [15].

We first recall some notions and results regarding the Laplace transform.

Definition 1. *A function $x : \mathbb{R} \to \mathbb{R}$ is called an original function if the following conditions are satisfied:*

1. $x(t) = 0, t < 0;$
2. *x is piecewise continuous;*
3. *$\exists M > 0$ and $\sigma_0 \geq 0$ such that*

$$|x(t)| \leq M \cdot e^{\sigma_0 t}, \quad \forall t \in \mathbb{R}.$$

We denote by $\mathcal{O}$ the set of original functions. We denote by $M(x)$ the set of all numbers that satisfy the condition 3.

The number $\sigma_x = \inf\{\sigma_0 \mid \sigma_0 \in M(x)\}$ is called abscissa of convergence of x.

The functions that appear below are considered original functions. Hence, since in definition of Laplace transform are involved only the values of x on $[0,\infty)$, we may suppose that $x(t) = 0$ for $t < 0$. So by $x(t)$ we understand $x(t)u(t)$, where

$$u(t) = \begin{cases} 0, & \text{if} \quad t \leq 0 \\ 1, & \text{if} \quad t > 0 \end{cases}$$

is the unit step function of Heaviside. We write $x^{(n)}(0)$ instead the lateral limit $x^{(n)}(0^+)$ for $n \geq 0$.

We denote by $\mathcal{L}(x)$ the Laplace transform of the function x, defined by

$$\mathcal{L}(x)(s) = X(s) = \int_0^\infty x(t)e^{-st}dt,$$

on $\{s \in \mathbb{R} \mid s > \sigma_x\}$. It is well known that the Laplace transform is linear and one-to-one if the functions involved are continuous. The inverse Laplace transform will be denoted by $\mathcal{L}^{-1}(X)$ or by $\mathcal{L}^{-1}(\mathcal{L}(x))$.

The following properties are used in the paper:

$$\mathcal{L}(x^{(n)})(s) = s^n \mathcal{L}(x)(s) - s^{n-1}x(0) - s^{n-2}x'(0) - \ldots - x^{(n-1)}(0),$$

$$\mathcal{L}(x(t-a))(s) = e^{-as}X(s),\ a > 0,$$

$$\mathcal{L}^{-1}\left(\frac{1}{s^n}\right)(t) = \frac{t^{n-1}}{(n-1)!}u(t),$$

$$\mathcal{L}(f * g)(s) = \mathcal{L}(f)(s) \cdot \mathcal{L}(g)(s),$$

where $(f * g)(t) = \int_0^t f(t-\tau)g(\tau)d\tau$ is the convolution product of f and g.

In the following, we consider the original functions $x, f : \mathbb{R} \to \mathbb{R}$.

The following Gronwall Lemma is also used in the paper ([16], p. 6):

Lemma 1 ([16]). *Let $x, v, h \in C[\mathbb{R}_+, \mathbb{R}_+]$, h nondecreasing. If*

$$x(t) \le h(t) + \int_{t_0}^{t} v(s)x(s)ds,\ t \ge t_0,$$

then

$$x(t) \le h(t)e^{\int_{t_0}^{t} v(s)ds},\ t \ge t_0.$$

2. Semi-Hyers–Ulam–Rassias Stability of a Delay Differential Equation of Order One

Let $f \in \mathcal{O}$. In what follows, we consider the equation

$$x'(t) + x(t-1) = f(t), \quad x(t) = 0 \quad \text{if} \quad t \le 0, \tag{1}$$

x continuous, piecewise differentiable.

Let $\varepsilon > 0$. We also consider the inequality

$$\left|x'(t) + x(t-1) - f(t)\right| \le \varepsilon, \quad t \in (0, \infty). \tag{2}$$

According to [17], we give the following definition:

Definition 2. *The Equation (1) is called semi-Hyers–Ulam–Rassias stable if there exists a function $k : (0, \infty) \to (0, \infty)$ such that for each solution x of the inequality (2), there exists a solution x_0 of the Equation (1) with*

$$|x(t) - x_0(t)| \le k(t), \forall t \in (0, \infty). \tag{3}$$

Remark 1. *A function $x : (0, \infty) \to \mathbb{R}$ is a solution of (2) if and only if there exists a function $p : (0, \infty) \to \mathbb{R}$ such that*

(1) $|p(t)| \le \varepsilon$, $\forall t \in (0, \infty)$,

(2) $x'(t) + x(t-1) - f(t) = p(t)$, $\forall t \in (0, \infty)$.

Lemma 2. *For $s > 1$ we have*

$$\mathcal{L}^{-1}\left(\frac{1}{s + e^{-s}}\right)(t) = \sum_{n=0}^{[t]} (-1)^n \frac{(t-n)^n}{n!}.$$

Proof. As in [18] (p. 15), for $s > 1$ we have $\frac{e^{-s}}{s} < 1$, hence

$$\begin{aligned}\mathcal{L}^{-1}\left(\frac{1}{s+e^{-s}}\right)(t) &= \mathcal{L}^{-1}\left(\frac{1}{s}\cdot\frac{1}{1+\frac{e^{-s}}{s}}\right)(t) = \mathcal{L}^{-1}\left(\frac{1}{s}\cdot\sum_{n=0}^{\infty}(-1)^n\frac{e^{-ns}}{s^n}\right)(t) \\ &= \sum_{n=0}^{\infty}(-1)^n\mathcal{L}^{-1}\left(\frac{e^{-ns}}{s^{n+1}}\right)(t) = \sum_{n=0}^{\infty}(-1)^n\frac{(t-n)^n}{n!}u(t-n) \\ &= \sum_{n=0}^{[t]}(-1)^n\frac{(t-n)^n}{n!},\end{aligned}$$

where $[t]$ denotes the integer part of the real number t. □

Applying a method used in [19], we prove now that the Laplace transform exist for the functions satisfying (1) and (2).

Theorem 1. *Let $f \in \mathcal{O}$. Let σ_f be abscissa of convergence of f and $M_f > 0$ such that $|f(t)| \leq M_f \cdot e^{\sigma_f t}$, $\forall t > 0$. Then the Laplace transform of x, which is the exact solution of (1) and of x' exist for all $s > \sigma$, where $\sigma = \max\left\{\sigma_f + 1, 2\right\}$.*

Proof. Integrating the relation (1) from 0 to t, we obtain

$$x(t) - x(0) + \int_0^t x(u-1)du = \int_0^t f(u)du,$$

hence

$$x(t) + \int_0^t x(u-1)du = \int_0^t f(u)du.$$

Changing the variable $v = u - 1$ in the first integral, we have

$$x(t) + \int_{-1}^{t-1} x(v)dv = \int_0^t f(u)du,$$

hence

$$x(t) + \int_0^{t-1} x(v)dv = \int_0^t f(u)du.$$

If $\sigma_f > 0$, we obtain

$$\begin{aligned}|x(t)| &\leq \left|\int_0^{t-1} x(v)dv\right| + \left|\int_0^t f(u)du\right| \leq \int_0^t |x(v)|dv + \int_0^t |f(u)|\,du \\ &\leq \int_0^t |x(v)|dv + \int_0^t M_f e^{\sigma_f u}du = \int_0^t |x(v)|dv + \frac{M_f}{\sigma_f}(e^{\sigma_f t} - 1) \leq \int_0^t |x(v)|dv + \frac{M_f}{\sigma_f}e^{\sigma_f t}.\end{aligned}$$

Applying now Gronwall Lemma 1, we obtain

$$|x(t)| \leq \frac{M_f}{\sigma_f}e^{\sigma_f t}e^{\int_0^t dv} = \frac{M_f}{\sigma_f}e^{\sigma_f t}e^t = \frac{M_f}{\sigma_f}e^{(\sigma_f+1)t},$$

that is the function x is of exponential order.

If $\sigma_f = 0$, we obtain

$$|x(t)| \leq \int_0^t |x(v)|dv + \int_0^t M_f du = \int_0^t |x(v)|dv + M_f t.$$

Applying now Gronwall Lemma, we obtain

$$|x(t)| \leq M_f t e^{\int_0^t dv} = M_f t e^t < M_f e^t e^t = M_f e^{2t}, t > 0$$

that is the function x is of exponential order.

From (1), we have

$$|x'(t)| \leq |x(t-1)| + |f(t)| \leq M_x e^{\sigma_x t} + M_f e^{\sigma_f t} \leq 2Me^{\sigma t},$$

where $M = \max\{M_x, M_f\}$ and $\sigma = \max\{\sigma_x, \sigma_f\}$. Hence, x' is of exponential order. □

Theorem 2. *Let $f \in \mathcal{O}$. Let σ_f be abscissa of convergence of f and $M_f > 0$ such that $|f(t)| \leq M_f \cdot e^{\sigma_f t}$, $\forall t > 0$. Then the Laplace transform of x (which is a solution of (2) and of x' exist for all $s > \sigma$, where $\sigma = \max\{2\sigma_f, 2\}$.*

Proof. From (2), we have

$$-\varepsilon \leq x'(t) + x(t-1) - f(t) \leq \varepsilon.$$

Integrating from 0 to t, we obtain

$$-\varepsilon t \leq x(t) + \int_0^t x(u-1)du - \int_0^t f(u)du \leq \varepsilon t,$$

hence

$$-\varepsilon t - \int_0^t x(u-1)du + \int_0^t f(u)du \leq x(t) \leq \varepsilon t - \int_0^t x(u-1)du + \int_0^t f(u)du,$$

Changing the variable $v = u - 1$ in the first integral, we have

$$-\varepsilon t - \int_0^{t-1} x(v)dv + \int_0^t f(u)du \leq x(t) \leq \varepsilon t - \int_0^{t-1} x(v)dv + \int_0^t f(u)du,$$

hence

$$|x(t)| \leq \varepsilon t + \int_0^t |x(v)|dv + \int_0^t |f(u)|du$$

If $\sigma_f > 0$, we obtain

$$|x(t)| \leq \varepsilon t + \int_0^t |x(v)|dv + \int_0^t M_f e^{\sigma_f u}du = \varepsilon t + \int_0^t |x(v)|dv + \frac{M_f}{\sigma_f}\left(e^{\sigma_f t} - 1\right) \leq \int_0^t |x(v)|dv + \varepsilon t + \frac{M_f}{\sigma_f}e^{\sigma_f t}.$$

Applying now Gronwall Lemma, we obtain

$$|x(t)| \leq \left(\varepsilon t + \frac{M_f}{\sigma_f}e^{\sigma_f t}\right)e^{\int_0^t dv} = \left(\varepsilon t + \frac{M_f}{\sigma_f}e^{\sigma_f t}\right)e^t \leq \left(\varepsilon e^{\sigma t} + \frac{M_f}{\sigma_f}e^{\sigma t}\right)e^{\sigma t} = \left(\varepsilon + \frac{M_f}{\sigma_f}\right)e^{2\sigma t},$$

where $\sigma = \max\{1, \sigma_f\}$, that is the function x is of exponential order.

If $\sigma_f = 0$, we obtain

$$|x(t)| \leq \varepsilon t + \int_0^t |x(v)|dv + \int_0^t M_f du = \varepsilon t + \int_0^t |x(v)|dv + M_f t,$$

or

$$|x(t)| \leq \left(\varepsilon + M_f\right)t + \int_0^t |x(v)|dv,$$

Applying now Gronwall Lemma, we obtain

$$|x(t)| \leq \left(\varepsilon + M_f\right)te^{\int_0^t dv} = \left(\varepsilon + M_f\right)te^t < \left(\varepsilon + M_f\right)e^t e^t = \left(\varepsilon + M_f\right)e^{2t}, t > 0$$

that is the function x is of exponential order.

From (2), we have

$$|x'(t)| \leq \varepsilon + |x(t-1)| + |f(t)| \leq \varepsilon + M_x e^{\sigma_x t} + M_f e^{\sigma_f t} \leq (\varepsilon + 2M)e^{\sigma t},$$

where $M = \max\left\{M_x, M_f\right\}$ and $\sigma = \max\left\{\sigma_x, \sigma_f\right\}$. Hence, x' is of exponential order. □

Theorem 3. *If a function $x : (0,\infty) \to \mathbb{R}$ satisfies the inequality (2), where $f \in \mathcal{O}$, then there exists a solution $x_0 : (0,\infty) \to \mathbb{R}$ of (1) such that*

$$|x(t) - x_0(t)| \leq \varepsilon\left(t + \frac{(t-1)^2}{2!} + \cdots + \frac{(t-[t])^{[t]+1}}{([t]+1)!}\right), \quad \forall t \in (0,\infty),$$

that is the Equation (1) is semi-Hyers–Ulam–Rassias stable.

Proof. Let $p : (0,\infty) \to \mathbb{R}$,

$$p(t) = x'(t) + x(t-1) - f(t), \quad t \in (0,\infty). \tag{4}$$

We have

$$\mathcal{L}(p) = s\mathcal{L}(x) - x(0) + e^{-s}\mathcal{L}(x) - \mathcal{L}(f),$$

hence

$$\mathcal{L}(x) = \frac{\mathcal{L}(p)}{s+e^{-s}} + \frac{\mathcal{L}(f)}{s+e^{-s}}.$$

Let

$$x_0(t) = \mathcal{L}^{-1}\left(\frac{\mathcal{L}(f)}{s+e^{-s}}\right)(t), \quad \forall t \in (0,\infty).$$

We remark that $x_0(0) = 0$.
Hence, we obtain

$$\begin{aligned}\mathcal{L}\left[x_0'(t) + x_0(t-1) - f(t)\right] &= s\mathcal{L}(x_0) - x_0(0) + e^{-s}\mathcal{L}(x_0) - \mathcal{L}(f)\\ &= s\frac{\mathcal{L}(f)}{s+e^{-s}} + e^{-s}\frac{\mathcal{L}(f)}{s+e^{-s}} - \mathcal{L}(f) = 0.\end{aligned}$$

Since $\mathcal{L}$ is one-to-one, it follows that

$$x_0'(t) + x_0(t-1) - f(t) = 0,$$

that is x_0 is a solution of (1).
We have

$$\mathcal{L}(x) - \mathcal{L}(x_0) = \frac{\mathcal{L}(p)}{s+e^{-s}},$$

hence

$$\begin{aligned}|x(t) - x_0(t)| &= \left|\mathcal{L}^{-1}\left(\frac{\mathcal{L}(p)}{s+e^{-s}}\right)\right| = \left|\mathcal{L}^{-1}(\mathcal{L}(p)) * \mathcal{L}^{-1}\left(\frac{1}{s+e^{-s}}\right)\right|\\ &= \left|p * \mathcal{L}^{-1}\left(\frac{1}{s+e^{-s}}\right)\right| = \left|\int_0^t p(\tau)\cdot\mathcal{L}^{-1}\left(\frac{1}{s+e^{-s}}\right)(t-\tau)d\tau\right|\\ &\leq \int_0^t |p(\tau)|\cdot\left|\mathcal{L}^{-1}\left(\frac{1}{s+e^{-s}}\right)(t-\tau)\right|d\tau \leq \varepsilon\int_0^t\left|\mathcal{L}^{-1}\left(\frac{1}{s+e^{-s}}\right)(t-\tau)\right|d\tau.\end{aligned}$$

From Lemma 2, we obtain

$$\varepsilon \int_0^t \left| \mathcal{L}^{-1}\left(\frac{1}{s+e^{-s}}\right)(t-\tau) \right| d\tau = \varepsilon \int_0^t \left| \sum_{n=0}^{[t-\tau]} (-1)^n \frac{(t-\tau-n)^n}{n!} \right| d\tau$$
$$\leq \varepsilon \int_0^t \sum_{n=0}^{[t-\tau]} \left| (-1)^n \frac{(t-\tau-n)^n}{n!} \right| d\tau = \varepsilon \int_0^t \sum_{n=0}^{[t-\tau]} \frac{(t-\tau-n)^n}{n!} d\tau.$$

For $t > 1$, we have

$$[t-\tau] = \begin{cases} [t], \tau \in [0, t-[t]] \\ [t]-1, \tau \in (t-[t], t-[t]+1] \\ \dots \\ 0, \tau \in (t-1, t] \end{cases}$$

hence

$$\int_0^t \sum_{n=0}^{[t-\tau]} \frac{(t-\tau-n)^n}{n!} d\tau = \int_0^{t-[t]} \sum_{n=0}^{[t]} \frac{(t-\tau-n)^n}{n!} d\tau + \int_{t-[t]}^{t-[t]+1} \sum_{n=0}^{[t]-1} \frac{(t-\tau-n)^n}{n!} d\tau + \dots + \int_{t-1}^{t} \sum_{n=0}^{0} \frac{(t-\tau-n)^n}{n!} d\tau$$
$$= \int_0^{t-[t]} \left(\frac{(t-\tau-0)^0}{0!} d\tau + \frac{(t-\tau-1)^1}{1!} + \dots + \frac{(t-\tau-[t])^{[t]}}{[t]!} \right) d\tau$$
$$+ \int_{t-[t]}^{t-[t]+1} \left(\frac{(t-\tau-0)^0}{0!} d\tau + \frac{(t-\tau-1)^1}{1!} + \dots + \frac{(t-\tau-[t]-1)^{[t]-1}}{([t]-1)!} \right) d\tau$$
$$\dots$$
$$+ \int_{t-1}^{t} \frac{(t-\tau-0)^0}{0!} d\tau.$$

We obtain

$$\int_0^t \sum_{n=0}^{[t-\tau]} \frac{(t-\tau-n)^n}{n!} d\tau = \int_0^t \frac{(t-\tau-0)^0}{0!} d\tau + \int_0^{t-1} \frac{(t-\tau-1)^1}{1!} d\tau + \dots + \int_0^{t-[t]} \frac{(t-\tau-[t])^{[t]}}{[t]!} d\tau$$
$$= t - \frac{(t-\tau-1)^2}{2!} \Big|_0^{t-1} - \dots - \frac{(t-\tau-[t])^{[t]+1}}{([t]+1)!} \Big|_0^{t-[t]}$$
$$= t + \frac{(t-1)^2}{2!} + \dots + \frac{(t-[t])^{[t]+1}}{([t]+1)!}$$

For $t \in [0,1)$, we have $[t-\tau] = 0$, hence

$$\int_0^t \sum_{n=0}^{[t-\tau]} \frac{(t-\tau-n)^n}{n!} d\tau = \int_0^t d\tau = t.$$

□

3. Semi-Hyers–Ulam–Rassias Stability of a Delay Differential Equation of Order Two

Let $f \in \mathcal{O}$. Next, we consider the equation

$$x''(t) + x'(t-1) = f(t), \quad x(t) = 0 \quad \text{if} \quad t \leq 0, \quad x'(0) = 0, \tag{5}$$

x continuous, piecewise twice differentiable.

Let $\varepsilon > 0$. We also consider the inequality

$$\left| x''(t) + x'(t-1) - f(t) \right| \leq \varepsilon, \quad t \in (0, \infty). \tag{6}$$

Definition 3. *The Equation (5) is called semi-Hyers–Ulam–Rassias stable if there exists a function $k : (0,\infty) \to (0,\infty)$ such that for each solution x of the inequality (6), there exists a solution x_0 of the Equation (5) with*

$$|x(t) - x_0(t)| \le k(t), \forall t \in (0,\infty). \tag{7}$$

Remark 2. *A function $x : (0,\infty) \to \mathbb{R}$ is a solution of (6) if and only if there exists a function $p : (0,\infty) \to \mathbb{R}$ such that*
(1) $|p(t)| \le \varepsilon$, $\forall t \in (0,\infty)$,
(2) $x''(t) + x'(t-1) - f(t) = p(t)$, $\forall t \in (0,\infty)$.

Lemma 3. *For $s > 1$, we have*

$$\mathcal{L}^{-1}\left(\frac{1}{s^2 + se^{-s}}\right)(t) = \sum_{n=0}^{[t]} (-1)^n \frac{(t-n)^{n+1}}{(n+1)!}.$$

Proof. For $s > 1$, we have $\frac{e^{-s}}{s} < 1$, hence

$$\begin{aligned}
\mathcal{L}^{-1}\left(\frac{1}{s^2 + se^{-s}}\right)(t) &= \mathcal{L}^{-1}\left(\frac{1}{s^2} \cdot \frac{1}{1 + \frac{e^{-s}}{s}}\right)(t) = \mathcal{L}^{-1}\left(\frac{1}{s^2} \cdot \sum_{n=0}^{\infty} (-1)^n \frac{e^{-ns}}{s^n}\right)(t) \\
&= \sum_{n=0}^{\infty} (-1)^n \mathcal{L}^{-1}\left(\frac{e^{-ns}}{s^{n+2}}\right)(t) = \sum_{n=0}^{\infty} (-1)^n \frac{(t-n)^{n+1}}{(n+1)!} u(t-n) \\
&= \sum_{n=0}^{[t]} (-1)^n \frac{(t-n)^{n+1}}{(n+1)!}.
\end{aligned}$$

□

Theorem 4. *Let $f \in \mathcal{O}$. Let σ_f be abscissa of convergence of f and $M_f > 0$ such that $|f(t)| \le M_f \cdot e^{\sigma_f t}$, $\forall t > 0$. Then the Laplace transform of x, which is the exact solution of (5) and of x', x'' exist for all $s > \sigma_f$.*

Proof. We can apply Theorem 3.1 from [19]. □

Theorem 5. *Let $f \in \mathcal{O}$. Let σ_f be abscissa of convergence of f and $M_f > 0$ such that $|f(t)| \le M_f \cdot e^{\sigma_f t}$, $\forall t > 0$. Then the Laplace transform of x, which is a solution of (6) and of x', x'' exist for a certain $\sigma > \sigma_f$, for all $s > \sigma$.*

Proof. The proof is similar to that of Theorem 2. □

Theorem 6. *Let $f : \mathbb{R} \to \mathbb{R}$ such that $f \in \mathcal{O}$ and $\left(\mathcal{L}^{-1}\left(\frac{\mathcal{L}(f)}{s^2+se^{-s}}\right)\right)'(0) = 0$. If a function $x : (0,\infty) \to \mathbb{R}$ satisfies the inequality (6), then there exists a solution $x_0 : (0,\infty) \to \mathbb{R}$ of (5) such that*

$$|x(t) - x_0(t)| \le \varepsilon\left(\frac{(t-1)^2}{2!} + \frac{(t-1)^3}{3!} + \cdots + \frac{(t-[t])^{[t]+2}}{([t]+2)!}\right), \quad \forall t \in (0,\infty),$$

that is the Equation (5) is semi-Hyers–Ulam–Rassias stable.

Proof. Let $p : (0,\infty) \to \mathbb{R}$,

$$p(t) = x''(t) + x'(t-1) - f(t), \quad t \in (0,\infty). \tag{8}$$

We have

$$\mathcal{L}(p) = s^2\mathcal{L}(x) - sx(0) - x'(0) + e^{-s}[s\mathcal{L}(x) - x(0)] - \mathcal{L}(f),$$

hence

$$\mathcal{L}(x) = \frac{\mathcal{L}(p)}{s^2 + se^{-s}} + \frac{\mathcal{L}(f)}{s^2 + se^{-s}}.$$

Let

$$x_0(t) = \mathcal{L}^{-1}\left(\frac{\mathcal{L}(f)}{s^2 + se^{-s}}\right)(t), \quad \forall t \in (0, \infty).$$

We remark that $x_0(0) = 0$ and $x_0'(0) = 0$

Hence, we obtain

$$\mathcal{L}\left[x_0''(t) + x_0'(t-1) - f(t)\right] = s^2\mathcal{L}(x_0) - sx_0(0) - x_0'(0) + e^{-s}[s\mathcal{L}(x_0) - x_0(0)] - \mathcal{L}(f)$$
$$= s^2\frac{\mathcal{L}(f)}{s^2 + se^{-s}} + se^{-s}\frac{\mathcal{L}(f)}{s^2 + se^{-s}} - \mathcal{L}(f) = 0.$$

Since $\mathcal{L}$ is one-to-one, it follows that

$$x_0''(t) + x_0'(t-1) - f(t) = 0,$$

that is x_0 is a solution of (5).

We have

$$\mathcal{L}(x) - \mathcal{L}(x_0) = \frac{\mathcal{L}(p)}{s^2 + se^{-s}},$$

hence

$$|x(t) - x_0(t)| = \left|\mathcal{L}^{-1}\left(\frac{\mathcal{L}(p)}{s^2 + se^{-s}}\right)\right| = \left|\mathcal{L}^{-1}(\mathcal{L}(p)) * \mathcal{L}^{-1}\left(\frac{1}{s^2 + se^{-s}}\right)\right|$$
$$= \left|p * \mathcal{L}^{-1}\left(\frac{1}{s^2 + se^{-s}}\right)\right| = \left|\int_0^t p(\tau) \cdot \mathcal{L}^{-1}\left(\frac{1}{s^2 + se^{-s}}\right)(t-\tau)d\tau\right|$$
$$\leq \int_0^t |p(\tau)| \cdot \left|\mathcal{L}^{-1}\left(\frac{1}{s^2 + se^{-s}}\right)(t-\tau)\right|d\tau \leq \varepsilon\int_0^t \left|\mathcal{L}^{-1}\left(\frac{1}{s^2 + se^{-s}}\right)(t-\tau)\right|d\tau.$$

From Lemma 3, we obtain

$$\varepsilon\int_0^t \left|\mathcal{L}^{-1}\left(\frac{1}{s^2 + se^{-s}}\right)(t-\tau)\right|d\tau = \varepsilon\int_0^t \left|\sum_{n=0}^{[t-\tau]}(-1)^n\frac{(t-\tau-n)^{n+1}}{(n+1)!}\right|d\tau$$
$$\leq \varepsilon\int_0^t \sum_{n=0}^{[t-\tau]}\left|(-1)^n\frac{(t-\tau-n)^{n+1}}{(n+1)!}\right|d\tau = \varepsilon\int_0^t \sum_{n=0}^{[t-\tau]}\frac{(t-\tau-n)^{n+1}}{(n+1)!}d\tau.$$

For $t > 1$, we have

$$\int_0^t \sum_{n=0}^{[t-\tau]} \frac{(t-\tau-n)^{n+1}}{(n+1)!} d\tau$$
$$= \int_0^{t-[t]} \sum_{n=0}^{[t]} \frac{(t-\tau-n)^{n+1}}{(n+1)!} d\tau + \int_{t-[t]}^{t-[t]+1} \sum_{n=0}^{[t]-1} \frac{(t-\tau-n)^{n+1}}{(n+1)!} d\tau + \cdots + \int_{t-1}^{t} \sum_{n=0}^{0} \frac{(t-\tau-n)^{n+1}}{(n+1)!} d\tau$$
$$= \int_0^{t-[t]} \left(\frac{(t-\tau-0)^1}{1!} d\tau + \frac{(t-\tau-1)^2}{2!} + \cdots + \frac{(t-\tau-[t])^{[t]+1}}{([t]+1)!} \right) d\tau$$
$$+ \int_{t-[t]}^{t-[t]+1} \left(\frac{(t-\tau-0)^1}{1!} d\tau + \frac{(t-\tau-1)^2}{2!} + \cdots + \frac{(t-\tau-[t]-1)^{[t]}}{[t]!} \right) d\tau$$
$$\ldots$$
$$+ \int_{t-1}^{t} \frac{(t-\tau-0)^1}{1!} d\tau.$$

We obtain

$$\int_0^t \sum_{n=0}^{[t-\tau]} \frac{(t-\tau-n)^{n+1}}{(n+1)!} d\tau = \int_0^t \frac{(t-\tau-0)^1}{1!} d\tau + \int_0^{t-1} \frac{(t-\tau-1)^2}{2!} d\tau + \cdots + \int_0^{t-[t]} \frac{(t-\tau-[t])^{[t]+1}}{([t]+1)!} d\tau$$
$$= -\frac{(t-\tau-0)^2}{2!}\Big|_0^t - \frac{(t-\tau-1)^3}{3!}\Big|_0^{t-1} - \cdots - \frac{(t-\tau-[t])^{[t]+2}}{([t]+2)!}\Big|_0^{t-[t]}$$
$$= \frac{(t-1)^2}{2!} + \frac{(t-1)^3}{3!} + \cdots + \frac{(t-[t])^{[t]+2}}{([t]+2)!}$$

For $t \in [0,1)$, we have $[t-\tau] = 0$, hence

$$\int_0^t \sum_{n=0}^{[t-\tau]} \frac{(t-\tau-n)^{n+1}}{(n+1)!} d\tau = \int_0^t \frac{(t-\tau-0)^1}{1!} d\tau = \frac{(t-1)^2}{2!}.$$

□

4. Generalized Semi-Hyers–Ulam–Rassias Stability of a Delay Differential Equation of Order One

We continue to study generalized semi-Hyers–Ulam–Rassias stability of the Equation (1). Let $\varphi \in \mathcal{O}$. We consider the inequality

$$|x'(t) + x(t-1) - f(t)| \leq \varphi(t), \quad t \in (0, \infty). \tag{9}$$

Definition 4. *The Equation (1) is called generalized semi-Hyers–Ulam–Rassias stable if there exists a function $k : (0,\infty) \to (0,\infty)$ such that for each solution x of the inequality (9), there exists a solution x_0 of the Equation (1) with*

$$|x(t) - x_0(t)| \leq k(t), \forall t \in (0, \infty). \tag{10}$$

Remark 3. *A function $x : (0,\infty) \to \mathbb{R}$ is a solution of (9) if, and only if, there exists a function $p : (0,\infty) \to \mathbb{R}$ such that*

(1) $|p(t)| \leq \varphi(t)$, $\forall t \in (0,\infty)$,
(2) $x'(t) + x(t-1) - f(t) = p(t)$, $\forall t \in (0,\infty)$.

Theorem 7. *If a function $x : (0,\infty) \to \mathbb{R}$ satisfies the inequality (9), where $f, \varphi \in \mathcal{O}$, then there exists a solution $x_0 : (0,\infty) \to \mathbb{R}$ of (1) such that*

$$|x(t) - x_0(t)| \leq \int_0^t \varphi(\tau) \left| \mathcal{L}^{-1}\left(\frac{1}{s+e^{-s}} \right)(t-\tau) \right| d\tau, \tag{11}$$

that is the Equation (1) is generalized semi-Hyers–Ulam–Rassias stable.

Proof. Let $p : (0, \infty) \to \mathbb{R}$,

$$p(t) = x'(t) + x(t-1) - f(t), \quad t \in (0, \infty). \tag{12}$$

As in Theorem 3, for x that is a solution of (9) and Laplace transform of x, x' exists, we have

$$\mathcal{L}(x) = \frac{\mathcal{L}(p)}{s + e^{-s}} + \frac{\mathcal{L}(f)}{s + e^{-s}},$$

and

$$x_0(t) = \mathcal{L}^{-1}\left(\frac{\mathcal{L}(f)}{s + e^{-s}}\right)(t), \quad \forall t \in (0, \infty),$$

is a solution of (1).

We have

$$\mathcal{L}(x) - \mathcal{L}(x_0) = \frac{\mathcal{L}(p)}{s + e^{-s}},$$

hence

$$\begin{aligned}
|x(t) - x_0(t)| &= \left|\mathcal{L}^{-1}\left(\frac{\mathcal{L}(p)}{s + e^{-s}}\right)\right| = \left|\mathcal{L}^{-1}(\mathcal{L}(p)) * \mathcal{L}^{-1}\left(\frac{1}{s + e^{-s}}\right)\right| \\
&= \left|p * \mathcal{L}^{-1}\left(\frac{1}{s + e^{-s}}\right)\right| = \left|\int_0^t p(\tau) \cdot \mathcal{L}^{-1}\left(\frac{1}{s + e^{-s}}\right)(t - \tau) d\tau\right| \\
&\leq \int_0^t |p(\tau)| \cdot \left|\mathcal{L}^{-1}\left(\frac{1}{s + e^{-s}}\right)(t - \tau)\right| d\tau \leq \int_0^t \varphi(\tau) \left|\mathcal{L}^{-1}\left(\frac{1}{s + e^{-s}}\right)(t - \tau)\right| d\tau.
\end{aligned}$$

□

Theorem 8. *Let $\varphi : (0, \infty) \to (0, \infty), \varphi(t) = t^n$. If a function $x : (0, \infty) \to \mathbb{R}$ satisfies the inequality (9), where $f \in \mathcal{O}$, then there exists a solution $x_0 : (0, \infty) \to \mathbb{R}$ of (1) such that*

$$|x(t) - x_0(t)| \leq \frac{t^{n+1}}{n+1} + \frac{(t-1)^{n+2}}{(n+1)(n+2)} + \frac{(t-2)^{n+3}}{(n+1)(n+2)(n+3)} + \cdots + \frac{(t-[t])^{n+[t]+1}}{(n+1)(n+2)\cdots(n+[t]+1)}.$$

Proof. From Theorem 7, we have that if $x : (0, \infty) \to \mathbb{R}$ satisfies the inequality (9), then there exists a solution $x_0 : (0, \infty) \to \mathbb{R}$ of (1) such that

$$|x(t) - x_0(t)| \leq \int_0^t \tau^n \left|\mathcal{L}^{-1}\left(\frac{1}{s + e^{-s}}\right)(t - \tau)\right| d\tau$$

is satisfied. We have

$$\begin{aligned}
&\int_0^t \tau^n \left|\mathcal{L}^{-1}\left(\frac{1}{s + e^{-s}}\right)(t - \tau)\right| d\tau = \int_0^t \tau^n \sum_{n=0}^{[t-\tau]} \frac{(t - \tau - n)^n}{n!} \\
&= \int_0^t \tau^n \frac{(t - \tau - 0)^0}{0!} d\tau + \int_0^{t-1} \tau^n \frac{(t - \tau - 1)^1}{1!} d\tau + \cdots + \int_0^{t-[t]} \tau^n \frac{(t - \tau - [t])^{[t]}}{[t]!} d\tau.
\end{aligned}$$

We have

$$\int_0^t \tau^n \frac{(t - \tau - 0)^0}{0!} d\tau = \frac{\tau^{n+1}}{n+1}\Big|_0^t = \frac{t^{n+1}}{n+1}.$$

Integrating by parts, we have

$$\int_0^{t-1} \tau^n \frac{(t-\tau-1)^1}{1!} d\tau = \int_0^{t-1} \left(\frac{\tau^{n+1}}{n+1}\right)' (t-\tau-1) d\tau = \underbrace{\frac{\tau^{n+1}}{n+1}(t-\tau-1)\Big|_0^{t-1}}_{0} + \int_0^{t-1} \frac{\tau^{n+1}}{n+1} d\tau$$

$$= \frac{\tau^{n+2}}{(n+1)(n+2)}\Big|_0^{t-1} = \frac{(t-1)^{n+2}}{(n+1)(n+2)},$$

$$\int_0^{t-2} \tau^n \frac{(t-\tau-2)^2}{2!} d\tau = \int_0^{t-2} \left(\frac{\tau^{n+1}}{n+1}\right)' \frac{(t-\tau-2)^2}{2!} d\tau = \underbrace{\frac{\tau^{n+1}}{n+1}\frac{(t-\tau-2)^2}{2!}\Big|_0^{t-2}}_{0} + \int_0^{t-2} \frac{\tau^{n+1}}{n+1}\frac{2(t-\tau-2)}{2!} d\tau$$

$$= \int_0^{t-2} \left(\frac{\tau^{n+2}}{(n+1)(n+2)}\right)' \frac{(t-\tau-2)}{1!} d\tau = \frac{\tau^{n+2}}{(n+1)(n+2)}\frac{(t-\tau-2)}{1!}\Big|_0^{t-2} + \int_0^{t-2} \frac{\tau^{n+2}}{(n+1)(n+2)} d\tau$$

$$= \frac{(t-2)^{n+3}}{(n+1)(n+2)(n+3)},$$

...

$$\int_0^{t-[t]} \tau^n \frac{(t-\tau-[t])^{[t]}}{[t]!} d\tau = \int_0^{t-[t]} \left(\frac{\tau^{n+1}}{n+1}\right)' \frac{(t-\tau-[t])^{[t]}}{[t]!} d\tau$$

$$= \underbrace{\frac{\tau^{n+1}}{n+1}\frac{(t-\tau-[t])^{[t]}}{[t]!}\Big|_0^{t-[t]}}_{0} + \int_0^{t-[t]} \frac{\tau^{n+1}}{n+1}\frac{[t](t-\tau-[t])^{[t]-1}}{[t]!} d\tau$$

$$= \int_0^{t-[t]} \left(\frac{\tau^{n+2}}{(n+1)(n+2)}\right)' \frac{(t-\tau-[t])^{[t]-1}}{([t]-1)!} d\tau = \cdots = \frac{(t-[t])^{n+[t]+1}}{(n+1)(n+2)\cdots(n+[t]+1)}.$$

□

5. Generalized Semi-Hyers–Ulam–Rassias Stability of a Delay Differential Equation of Order Two

We are now studying the generalized semi-Hyers–Ulam–Rassias stability of the Equation (5). Let $\varphi \in \mathcal{O}$. We consider the inequality

$$|x''(t) + x'(t-1) - f(t)| \leq \varphi(t), \quad t \in (0,\infty). \tag{13}$$

Definition 5. *The Equation (5) is called generalized semi-Hyers–Ulam–Rassias stable if there exists a function $k : (0,\infty) \to (0,\infty)$ such that for each solution x of the inequality (13), there exists a solution x_0 of the Equation (5) with*

$$|x(t) - x_0(t)| \leq k(t), \forall t \in (0,\infty). \tag{14}$$

Remark 4. *A function $x : (0,\infty) \to \mathbb{R}$ is a solution of (13) if, and only if, there exists a function $p : (0,\infty) \to \mathbb{R}$ such that*

(1) $|p(t)| \leq \varphi(t)$, $\forall t \in (0,\infty)$,

(2) $x''(t) + x'(t-1) - f(t) = p(t)$, $\forall t \in (0,\infty)$.

Theorem 9. *Let $f : \mathbb{R} \to \mathbb{R}$ such that $\left(\mathcal{L}^{-1}\left(\frac{\mathcal{L}(f)}{s^2+se^{-s}}\right)\right)'(0) = 0$. If a function $x : (0,\infty) \to \mathbb{R}$ satisfies the inequality (13), where $f, \varphi \in \mathcal{O}$, then there exists a solution $x_0 : (0,\infty) \to \mathbb{R}$ of (5) such that*

$$|x(t) - x_0(t)| \leq \int_0^t \varphi(\tau) \left|\mathcal{L}^{-1}\left(\frac{1}{s^2+se^{-s}}\right)(t-\tau)\right| d\tau, \tag{15}$$

that is the Equation (5) is generalized semi-Hyers–Ulam–Rassias stable.

Proof. Let $p : (0, \infty) \to \mathbb{R}$,

$$p(t) = x''(t) + x'(t-1) - f(t), \quad t \in (0, \infty). \tag{16}$$

As in Theorem 6, for x that is a solution of (13) and Laplace transform of x, x', x'' exists, we have

$$\mathcal{L}(x) = \frac{\mathcal{L}(p)}{s^2 + se^{-s}} + \frac{\mathcal{L}(f)}{s^2 + se^{-s}},$$

and

$$x_0(t) = \mathcal{L}^{-1}\left(\frac{\mathcal{L}(f)}{s^2 + se^{-s}}\right)(t), \quad \forall t \in (0, \infty),$$

is a solution of (5).

We have

$$\mathcal{L}(x) - \mathcal{L}(x_0) = \frac{\mathcal{L}(p)}{s^2 + se^{-s}},$$

hence

$$\begin{aligned}
|x(t) - x_0(t)| &= \left|\mathcal{L}^{-1}\left(\frac{\mathcal{L}(p)}{s^2 + se^{-s}}\right)\right| = \left|\mathcal{L}^{-1}(\mathcal{L}(p)) * \mathcal{L}^{-1}\left(\frac{1}{s^2 + se^{-s}}\right)\right| \\
&= \left|p * \mathcal{L}^{-1}\left(\frac{1}{s^2 + se^{-s}}\right)\right| = \left|\int_0^t p(\tau) \cdot \mathcal{L}^{-1}\left(\frac{1}{s^2 + se^{-s}}\right)(t-\tau)d\tau\right| \\
&\le \int_0^t |p(\tau)| \cdot \left|\mathcal{L}^{-1}\left(\frac{1}{s^2 + se^{-s}}\right)(t-\tau)\right| d\tau \le \int_0^t \varphi(\tau)\left|\mathcal{L}^{-1}\left(\frac{1}{s^2 + se^{-s}}\right)(t-\tau)\right| d\tau.
\end{aligned}$$

□

Theorem 10. *Let $f : \mathbb{R} \to \mathbb{R}$ such that $f \in \mathcal{O}$ and $\left(\mathcal{L}^{-1}\left(\frac{\mathcal{L}(f)}{s^2+se^{-s}}\right)\right)'(0) = 0$. Let $\varphi : (0, \infty) \to (0, \infty)$, $\varphi(t) = t^n$. If a function $x : (0, \infty) \to \mathbb{R}$ satisfies the inequality (13), then there exists a solution $x_0 : (0, \infty) \to \mathbb{R}$ of (5) such that*

$$|x(t) - x_0(t)| \le \frac{t^{n+2}}{(n+1)(n+2)} + \frac{(t-1)^{n+3}}{(n+1)(n+2)(n+3)} + \cdots + \frac{(t-[t])^{n+[t]+2}}{(n+1)(n+2)\cdots(n+[t]+2)}.$$

Proof. From Theorem 9, we have that if $x : (0, \infty) \to \mathbb{R}$ satisfies the inequality (13), then there exists a solution $x_0 : (0, \infty) \to \mathbb{R}$ of (5) such that

$$|x(t) - x_0(t)| \le \int_0^t \tau^n \left|\mathcal{L}^{-1}\left(\frac{1}{s^2 + se^{-s}}\right)(t-\tau)\right| d\tau$$

is satisfied. We have

$$\begin{aligned}
&\int_0^t \tau^n \left|\mathcal{L}^{-1}\left(\frac{1}{s^2 + se^{-s}}\right)(t-\tau)\right| d\tau = \int_0^t \tau^n \sum_{n=0}^{[t-\tau]} \frac{(t-\tau-n)^{n+1}}{(n+1)!} \\
&= \int_0^t \tau^n \frac{(t-\tau-0)^1}{1!} d\tau + \int_0^{t-1} \tau^n \frac{(t-\tau-1)^2}{2!} d\tau + \cdots + \int_0^{t-[t]} \tau^n \frac{(t-\tau-[t])^{[t]+1}}{([t]+1)!} d\tau.
\end{aligned}$$

Integrating by parts, we have

$$\int_0^t \tau^n \frac{(t-\tau-0)^1}{1!} d\tau = \int_0^t \left(\frac{\tau^{n+1}}{n+1}\right)'(t-\tau)d\tau = \underbrace{\frac{\tau^{n+1}}{n+1}(t-\tau)\Big|_0^t}_{0} + \int_0^t \frac{\tau^{n+1}}{n+1} d\tau$$

$$= \frac{\tau^{n+2}}{(n+1)(n+2)}\Big|_0^t = \frac{t^{n+2}}{(n+1)(n+2)},$$

$$\int_0^{t-1} \tau^n \frac{(t-\tau-1)^2}{2!} d\tau = \int_0^{t-1} \left(\frac{\tau^{n+1}}{n+1}\right)' \frac{(t-\tau-1)^2}{2!} d\tau = \underbrace{\frac{\tau^{n+1}}{n+1}\frac{(t-\tau-1)^2}{2!}\Big|_0^{t-1}}_{0} + \int_0^{t-1} \frac{\tau^{n+1}}{n+1}\frac{2(t-\tau-1)}{2!} d\tau$$

$$= \int_0^{t-1} \left(\frac{\tau^{n+2}}{(n+1)(n+2)}\right)' \frac{(t-\tau-2)}{1!} d\tau = \frac{\tau^{n+2}}{(n+1)(n+2)}\frac{(t-\tau-1)}{1!}\Big|_0^{t-1} + \int_0^{t-1} \frac{\tau^{n+2}}{(n+1)(n+2)} d\tau$$

$$= \frac{(t-1)^{n+3}}{(n+1)(n+2)(n+3)},$$

$$\ldots$$

$$\int_0^{t-[t]} \tau^n \frac{(t-\tau-[t])^{[t]+1}}{([t]+1)!} d\tau = \int_0^{t-[t]} \left(\frac{\tau^{n+1}}{n+1}\right)' \frac{(t-\tau-[t])^{[t]+1}}{([t]+1)!} d\tau$$

$$= \underbrace{\frac{\tau^{n+1}}{n+1}\frac{(t-\tau-[t])^{[t]+1}}{([t]+1)!}\Big|_0^{t-[t]}}_{0} + \int_0^{t-[t]} \frac{\tau^{n+1}}{n+1}\frac{([t]+1)!(t-\tau-[t])^{[t]}}{([t]+1)!} d\tau$$

$$= \int_0^{t-[t]} \left(\frac{\tau^{n+2}}{(n+1)(n+2)}\right)' \frac{(t-\tau-[t])^{[t]-1}}{[t]!} d\tau = \cdots = \frac{(t-[t])^{n+[t]+2}}{(n+1)(n+2)\cdots(n+[t]+2)}.$$

□

6. Conclusions

The use of the Laplace transform in the study of Hyers–Ulam stability of differential equations is relatively recent (2013, see [7]). This method was not used to study the stability of equations with delay. In this paper, we have studied semi-Hyers–Ulam–Rassias stability and generalized semi-Hyers–Ulam–Rassias stability of Equations (1) and (5) using the Laplace transform. Some examples were given. The results obtained complete those of S. M. Jung and J. Brzdek from [13]. This method can be used successfully in the case of other equations with delay, integro-differential equations, partial differential equations or for fractional calculus. In [11], we have already studied a Volterra integro-differential equation of order I with a convolution type kernel and, in [12], the convection partial differential equation. In [20], the Poisson partial differential equation was studied via the double Laplace transform method. We intend to further study other equations.

Funding: This research received no external funding.

Institutional Review Board Statement: Not applicable.

Informed Consent Statement: Not applicable.

Data Availability Statement: Not applicable.

Conflicts of Interest: The author declare no conflict of interest.

References

1. Ulam, S.M. *A Collection of Mathematical Problems*; Interscience: New York, NY, USA, 1960.
2. Hyers, D.H. On the stability of the linear functional equation. *Proc. Natl. Acad. Sci. USA* **1941**, *27*, 222–224. [CrossRef] [PubMed]

3. Obloza, M. Hyers stability of the linear differential equation. *Rocz. Nauk-Dydakt. Pr. Mat.* **1993**, *13*, 259–270.
4. Alsina, C.; Ger, R. On some inequalities and stability results related to exponential function. *J. Inequal. Appl.* **1998**, *2*, 373–380. [CrossRef]
5. Brzdek, J.; Popa, D.; Rasa, I.; Xu, B. *Ulam Stability of Operators*; Elsevier: Amsterdam, The Netherlands, 2018.
6. Tripathy, A.K. *Hyers-Ulam Stability of Ordinary Differential Equations*; Taylor and Francis: Boca Raton, FL, USA, 2021.
7. Rezaei, H.; Jung, S.-M.; Rassias, T. Laplace transform and Hyers-Ulam stability of linear differential equations. *J. Math. Anal. Appl.* **2013**, *403*, 244–251. [CrossRef]
8. Alqifiary, Q.; Jung, S.-M. Laplace transform and generalized Hyers-Ulam stability of linear differential equations. *Electron. J. Differ. Equ.* **2014**, *2014*, 1–11.
9. Biçer, E.; Tunç, C. On the Hyers-Ulam Stability of Laguerre and Bessel Equations by Laplace Transform Method. *Nonlinear Dyn. Syst.* **2017**, *17*, 340–346.
10. Murali, R.; Ponmana Selvan, A. Mittag-Leffler-Hyers-Ulam stability of a linear differential equation of first order using Laplace transforms. *Can. J. Appl. Math.* **2020**, *2*, 47–59.
11. Inoan, D.; Marian, D. Semi-Hyers-Ulam-Rassias stability of a Volterra integro-differential equation of order I with a convolution type kernel via Laplace transform. *Symmetry* **2021**, *13*, 2181. [CrossRef]
12. Marian, D. Semi-Hyers-Ulam-Rassias stability of the convection partial differential equation via Laplace transform. *Mathematics* **2021**, *9*, 2980. [CrossRef]
13. Jung, S.-M.; Brzdek, J. Hyers-Ulam stability of delay equation. *Abstr. Appl. Anal.* **2010**, *13*, 372176.
14. Kolmanovskii, V.; Myshkis, A. *Introduction to the Theory and Applications of Functional Differential Equations*; Kluwer Academic Publishers: Dordrecht, The Netherlands, 1999.
15. Kyrychko, Y.N.; Hogan, S.J. On the use of delay equations in engineering applications. *J. Vib. Control.* **2010**, *16*, 943–960. [CrossRef]
16. Lakshmikantham, V.; Leela, S.; Martynyuk, A.A. *Stability Analysis of Nonlinear Systems*; Marcel Dekker, Inc.: New York, NY, USA, 1989; Volume 125.
17. Castro, L.P.; Simões, A.M. Different Types of Hyers-Ulam-Rassias Stabilities for a Class of Integro-Differential Equations. *Filomat* **2017**, *31*, 5379–5390. [CrossRef]
18. Cohen, A.M. *Numerical Methods for Laplace Transform Inversion (Numerical Methods and Algorithms, 5)*; Springer: Cham, Switzerland, 2007.
19. Cimen, E.; Uncu, S. On the solution of the delay differential equation via Laplace transform. *Comm. Math. App.* **2020**, *11*, 379–387.
20. Abdulah, A.A.; Ahmad, A. The solution of Poisson partial differential equations via double Laplace transform method. *Partial Differ. Equ. Appl. Math.* **2021**, *4*, 100058.

mathematics MDPI

Article

An Epidemic Model with Time Delay Determined by the Disease Duration

Samiran Ghosh [1,†], Vitaly Volpert [2,3,*,†] and Malay Banerjee [1,†]

1 Department of Mathematics and Statistics, IIT Kanpur, Kanpur 208016, India; samiran@iitk.ac.in (S.G.); malayb@iitk.ac.in (M.B.)
2 Institut Camille Jordan, UMR 5208 CNRS, University Lyon 1, 69622 Villeurbanne, France
3 Peoples Friendship University of Russia (RUDN University), 6 Miklukho-Maklaya St, 117198 Moscow, Russia
* Correspondence: volpert@math.univ-lyon1.fr
† These authors contributed equally to this work.

Abstract: Immuno-epidemiological models with distributed recovery and death rates can describe the epidemic progression more precisely than conventional compartmental models. However, the required immunological data to estimate the distributed recovery and death rates are not easily available. An epidemic model with time delay is derived from the previously developed model with distributed recovery and death rates, which does not require precise immunological data. The resulting generic model describes epidemic progression using two parameters, disease transmission rate and disease duration. The disease duration is incorporated as a delay parameter. Various epidemic characteristics of the delay model, namely the basic reproduction number, the maximal number of infected, and the final size of the epidemic are derived. The estimation of disease duration is studied with the help of real data for COVID-19. The delay model gives a good approximation of the COVID-19 data and of the more detailed model with distributed parameters.

Keywords: epidemic model; disease duration; time delay; COVID-19

MSC: 34K60; 92D30

Citation: Ghosh, S.; Volpert, V.; Banerjee, M. An Epidemic Model with Time Delay Determined by the Disease Duration. *Mathematics* **2022**, *10*, 2561. https://doi.org/10.3390/math10152561

Academic Editor: Alexandra Kashchenko

Received: 9 June 2022
Accepted: 15 July 2022
Published: 22 July 2022

1. Introduction

Mathematical modeling of infectious diseases attracts much attention due to successive epidemics, such as HIV, emerging in the 1980s and still continuing [1,2], SARS epidemic in 2002–2003 [3,4], H5N1 influenza in 2005 [5,6] and H1N1 in 2009 [7,8], Ebola in 2014 [9,10]. The ongoing COVID-19 pandemic has stimulated unprecedented efforts of mathematical modeling in epidemiology. A wide variety of mathematical approaches are developed to study epidemiological problems. However, sufficiently simple and validated models still remain in the focus of mathematical modeling in epidemiology.

Modern studies in mathematical epidemiology begin with the SIR model developed in the works by W. O. Kermack and A. G. McKendrick [11–13], stimulated by the Spanish flu epidemic in 1918–1919. Among many developments of such models, we can cite multi-compartment models [14–16], models with a time-varying or nonlinear disease transmission rate [17,18], multi-patch models [19–21], multi-group models incorporating the effect of the heterogeneity of the population [22], and epidemic models with vaccination and other control measures [23,24]. Random movement of individuals in the population is considered in spatiotemporal models in order to describe spatial distributions of susceptible and infected individuals [25,26]. A more detailed literature review can be found in the monographs [27,28] and review articles [29,30].

The conventional SIR model, which includes susceptible (S), infected (I), and recovered (R) compartments, and similar models assume that recovery and death rates at time t are proportional to the number of actively infected individuals $I(t)$ at the same moment of time. This assumption does not take into account disease duration, and it can lead to a large error. In our previous work [31], we showed that this assumption leads to an overestimation of actual recoveries and deaths. Instead, if we use distributed recovery and death rates, properly chosen from real data, the description of the epidemic progression becomes more precise. However, since distributed recovery and death rates are not easily available, we develop a simpler delay model in this work. It gives close results, but it does not require precise immunological data. The model considered in [31] involves distributed recovery and death rates. The model considered in [32] is an extension of the model by incorporating the vaccinated compartment, and the resulting model is an immuno-epidemic model. The delay model, with disease duration delay, considered here is derived from the model proposed in [31] with an appropriate assumption on the recovery and death rate functions. The present model is quite different from the delay model considered in [33] as the delay parameter involved with the earlier model was the measure of the incubation period and the departure of infected individuals from the infected compartment was due to the imposition of quarantine measure. The model proposed and analyzed here is solely dependent on the disease duration period and without imposed quarantine.

Most of the existing delay epidemic models consider time delay either in the disease incidence function or in the susceptible recruitment function (Appendix A). The delay in the recovery and death rates has not been studied yet thoroughly. In this work, we introduce time delay in recovery and death rates with the average disease duration considered as the delay parameter.

In Section 2, we discuss the distributed model and derive the delay model where the discrete time delay estimates average disease duration. We obtain epidemic characterization of the delay model in Section 3. Then, in Section 4, we perform a numerical comparison among the distributed model, delay model, and conventional SIR model with the equivalent parameter values. Next, we discuss a method to estimate the value of disease duration using the real data of disease incidence in Section 5. In Section 6, we validate our delay model with epidemiological data collected during the COVID-19 epidemic. The main outcomes of the proposed model and its epidemiological implications are discussed in the concluding section.

2. Model Formulation

In contrast with the existing compartmental epidemiological models, we start the model derivation by the introduction of the class of newly infected individuals instead of the total number of infected individuals. This approach is appropriate to evaluate daily recovery and death rates. We recall in this section the model with a distributed recovery and death rate [31,33]. We then use this model to derive the delay model and study its properties in the next sections.

2.1. Model with Distributed Parameters

The number of newly infected individuals $J(t)$ is determined by the rate of decrease of the number of susceptible individuals, $J(t) = -S'(t)$. Assuming that

$$N = S(t) + I(t) + R(t) + D(t) \tag{1}$$

is constant, where $I(t)$ is the total number of infected at time t and $R(t)$ and $D(t)$ denote, respectively, recovered and dead, we can write

$$I(t) = \int_0^t J(\eta)d\eta - R(t) - D(t). \tag{2}$$

Following conventional epidemiological models, we set

$$\frac{dS(t)}{dt} = -\beta\frac{S(t)}{N}\,I(t),$$

where β is the disease transmission rate. Let $r(\eta)$ and $d(\eta)$ be the recovery and death rates depending on the time-since-infection η. Then, the number of infected individuals who will recover at time t is given by the expression:

$$\frac{dR(t)}{dt} = \int_0^t r(t-\eta)J(\eta)d\eta,$$

and the number of infected individuals who will die at time t:

$$\frac{dD(t)}{dt} = \int_0^t d(t-\eta)J(\eta)d\eta.$$

Differentiating Equality (1), we obtain

$$\frac{dI(t)}{dt} = \beta\frac{S(t)}{N}\, I(t) - \int_0^t r(t-\eta)J(\eta)d\eta - \int_0^t d(t-\eta)J(\eta)d\eta.$$

Thus, we obtain the following integro-differential equation model:

$$\frac{dS(t)}{dt} = -\beta\frac{S(t)}{N}\, I(t) \quad (= -J(t)), \tag{3a}$$

$$\frac{dI(t)}{dt} = \beta\frac{S(t)}{N}\, I(t) - \int_0^t r(t-\eta)J(\eta)d\eta - \int_0^t d(t-\eta)J(\eta)d\eta, \tag{3b}$$

$$\frac{dR(t)}{dt} = \int_0^t r(t-\eta)J(\eta)d\eta, \tag{3c}$$

$$\frac{dD(t)}{dt} = \int_0^t d(t-\eta)J(\eta)d\eta, \tag{3d}$$

with the initial condition $S(0) = N$, $I(0) = I_0 > 0$ (I_0 is sufficiently small as compared to N), $R(0) = 0$, $D(0) = 0$.

2.2. Reduction to SIR Model

In a particular case, if we assume the uniform distribution of recovery and death rates:

$$r(t-\eta) = \begin{cases} r_0 \ , & t-\tau < \eta \le t \\ 0 \ , & \eta < t-\tau \end{cases}, \quad d(t-\eta) = \begin{cases} d_0 \ , & t-\tau < \eta \le t \\ 0 \ , & \eta < t-\tau \end{cases},$$

where $\tau > 0$ is disease duration, r_0 and d_0 are some constants, and if r_0 and d_0 are small enough, then the model (3) can be reduced to the conventional SIR model (see [31]):

$$\frac{dS(t)}{dt} = -\beta\frac{S(t)}{N}\, I(t), \tag{4a}$$

$$\frac{dI(t)}{dt} = \beta\frac{S(t)}{N}\, I(t) - (r_0 + d_0)I(t), \tag{4b}$$

$$\frac{dR(t)}{dt} = r_0 I(t), \quad \frac{dD(t)}{dt} = d_0 I(t). \tag{4c}$$

However, the approximation of a uniform distribution of recovery and death rates may not be precise since infected individuals are unlikely to recover or die at the beginning of the disease. In the following subsection, we consider another choice of recovery and death rates, which will approximate the real scenario of recovery and death more accurately.

2.3. Delay Model

Let us assume that disease duration is τ, and the individuals $J(t-\tau)$ infected at time $t-\tau$ recover or die at time t with certain probabilities. This assumption corresponds to the following choice of the functions $r(t-\eta)$ and $d(t-\eta)$:

$$r(t-\eta) = r_0\delta(t-\eta-\tau), \quad d(t-\eta) = d_0\delta(t-\eta-\tau),$$

where r_0, d_0 are constants, $r_0 + d_0 = 1$, and δ is the Dirac delta-function. Then,

$$\frac{dR(t)}{dt} = \int_0^t r(t-\eta)J(\eta)d\eta = r_0 J(t-\tau),$$

$$\frac{dD(t)}{dt} = \int_0^t d(t-\eta)J(\eta)d\eta = d_0 J(t-\tau).$$

Note that $J(t)$ is the number of newly infected individuals appearing at time t. If we assume that the first infected case was reported at time $t = 0$, then we can set $J(t) = 0$ for all $t < 0$. Now, integrating the above two equations from 0 to t and assuming that $R(0) = D(0) = 0$, we obtain

$$R(t) = r_0 \int_0^t J(s-\tau)ds = r_0 \int_{-\tau}^{t-\tau} J(y)dy \ = r_0 \int_0^{t-\tau} J(y)dy,$$

$$D(t) = d_0 \int_0^t J(s-\tau)ds = d_0 \int_{-\tau}^{t-\tau} J(y)dy \ = d_0 \int_0^{t-\tau} J(y)dy.$$

Then, instead of (2), we have

$$I(t) = \int_{t-\tau}^t J(s)ds, \tag{5}$$

and from (3b),

$$\frac{dI(t)}{dt} = \beta\frac{S(t)}{N} I(t) - J(t-\tau). \tag{6}$$

From (5) we obtain

$$J(t) = \beta\frac{S(t)}{N} \int_{t-\tau}^t J(s)ds, \quad \frac{dS(t)}{dt} = -J(t). \tag{7}$$

Hence,

$$\frac{dS(t)}{dt} = -\beta\frac{S(t)}{N} \int_{t-\tau}^t J(s)ds = \beta\frac{S(t)}{N} \int_{t-\tau}^t \frac{dS(s)}{ds}ds = -\beta\frac{S(t)}{N} (S(t-\tau) - S(t)). \tag{8}$$

Once we obtain the solution $S(t)$ from (8), then we can find $I(t)$ using the following relation:

$$I(t) = \int_{t-\tau}^t J(s)ds = -\int_{t-\tau}^t \frac{dS(s)}{ds}ds = S(t-\tau) - S(t).$$

Hence, System (3) is reduced to the following delay model:

$$\frac{dS(t)}{dt} = -J(t), \tag{9a}$$

$$\frac{dI(t)}{dt} = J(t) - J(t-\tau), \tag{9b}$$

$$\frac{dR(t)}{dt} = r_0 J(t-\tau), \tag{9c}$$

$$\frac{dD(t)}{dt} = d_0 J(t-\tau), \tag{9d}$$

$$J(t) = \beta\frac{S(t)}{N} I(t), \tag{9e}$$

with $J(t) = 0$ for all $t < 0$. A similar model was proposed in [33] without derivation from the distributed model.

3. Epidemic Characteristics

In this section, we determine the basic reproduction number, the final size of the epidemic, and maximum number of infected individuals for the delay model (9).

3.1. Basic Reproduction Number

To determine the initial exponential growth rate and the basic reproduction number $\mathcal{R}_0$, we use the equations for the infected compartments $I(t)$ considered in the form:

$$\frac{dI(t)}{dt} = \beta\frac{S(t)}{N}\,I(t) - \beta\frac{S(t-\tau)}{N}\,I(t-\tau). \tag{10}$$

Suppose that, at the beginning of the epidemic, $S(t) \approx S_0$ and $S(t-\tau) = S_0$. Then, from (10), we have

$$\frac{dI(t)}{dt} = \beta\frac{S_0}{N}\,(I(t) - I(t-\tau)).$$

Substituting $I(t) = I_0\, e^{\lambda t}$, we have

$$\lambda = \beta\frac{S_0}{N}(1 - e^{-\lambda\tau}). \tag{11}$$

Let $\mathcal{G}(\lambda) = \beta\frac{S_0}{N}(1 - e^{-\lambda\tau})$. Clearly, (11) has a solution $\lambda = 0$ and a non-zero solution with the sign determined by $\mathcal{G}'(0)$. Denote

$$\mathcal{R}_0 = \mathcal{G}'(0) = \beta\tau\frac{S_0}{N}.$$

Let $\mathcal{R}_0 > 1$. This implies, $\mathcal{G}'(0) > 1$. We observe that $\mathcal{G}(\lambda)$ is an increasing function of λ and $\mathcal{G}(\lambda) \to \beta\frac{S_0}{N}$ as $\lambda \to \infty$. This implies that Equation (11) has a positive solution, i.e., there exists $\lambda_* > 0$ such that $\mathcal{G}(\lambda_*) = \lambda_*$. If $\mathcal{R}_0 < 1$, i.e., $\mathcal{G}'(0) < 1$, then

$$\mathcal{G}'(\lambda) = \beta\tau\frac{S_0}{N}e^{-\lambda\tau} < 1$$

for all $\lambda \geq 0$. Therefore, the equation $\mathcal{G}(\lambda) = \lambda$ has no positive solution.

Hence, the basic reproduction number is given by the following expression:

$$\mathcal{R}_0 = \beta\tau\frac{S_0}{N}. \tag{12}$$

Letting $\hat{\lambda} = \lambda/(\beta\frac{S_0}{N})$, we can write Equation (11) in the following form:

$$\hat{\lambda} = 1 - e^{-\mathcal{R}_0\hat{\lambda}}.$$

The solution of this equation determines the initial exponential growth rate, which depends on the single parameter $\mathcal{R}_0$.

3.2. Final Size of the Epidemic

Next, we determine the final size of the susceptible compartment $S_f = \lim_{t\to\infty} S(t)$. From (3a), we obtain:

$$\frac{dS(t)}{dt} = -\beta\frac{S(t)}{N}\int_{t-\tau}^{t} J(\eta)d\eta.$$

Then, integrating from 0 to ∞, we obtain

$$\int_0^\infty \frac{dS}{S} = -\frac{\beta}{N}\int_0^\infty \left(\int_{t-\tau}^{t} J(\eta)d\eta\right)dt.$$

Changing the order of integration, we get

$$\begin{aligned}\ln\frac{S_0}{S_f} &= \frac{\beta}{N}\left[\int_{-\tau}^{0}\left(\int_{0}^{\eta+\tau} J(\eta)dt\right)d\eta + \int_{0}^{\infty}\left(\int_{\eta}^{\eta+\tau} J(\eta)dt\right)d\eta\right] \\ &= \frac{\beta}{N}\left[\int_{-\tau}^{0}(\eta+\tau)J(\eta)d\eta + \int_{0}^{\infty}\tau J(\eta)d\eta\right].\end{aligned}$$

Now, integrating (9a) from 0 to ∞, we have:

$$\int_{0}^{\infty} J(\eta)d\eta = S_0 - S_f. \tag{13}$$

Since $J(t) = 0$ for all $t \in [-\tau, 0]$, then

$$\ln\frac{S_0}{S_f} = \frac{\beta}{N}\left[\int_{0}^{\infty}\tau J(\eta)d\eta\right] = \frac{\beta}{N}\tau(S_0 - S_f). \tag{14}$$

Thus, the final size can be obtained from the equation:

$$\ln\frac{S_0}{S_f} = \frac{\beta}{N}\tau(S_0 - S_f). \tag{15}$$

Integrating (9c) and (9d) from 0 to ∞ and using (13), we obtain:

$$R_f \equiv \lim_{t\to\infty} R(t) = r_0\int_{0}^{\infty} J(s-\tau)ds = r_0\int_{0}^{\infty} J(\eta)d\eta = r_0(S_0 - S_f),$$

$$D_f \equiv \lim_{t\to\infty} D(t) = d_0\int_{0}^{\infty} J(s-\tau)ds = d_0\int_{0}^{\infty} J(\eta)d\eta = d_0(S_0 - S_f).$$

Final size S_f obtained from the numerical simulation and using the Formula (15) is verified for three different values of τ and a range of values of β (Figure 1). Observe that Equation (15) can be written as:

$$\ln\frac{S_0}{S_f} = \mathcal{R}_0\left(1 - \frac{S_f}{S_0}\right). \tag{16}$$

Note that the SIR model (4) gives the same equation for the final size, and also in the SIR model (4), if we assume that $r_0 + d_0 = 1/\tau$, then the expression of $\mathcal{R}_0$ is equivalent for both the SIR model (4) and the delay model (9).

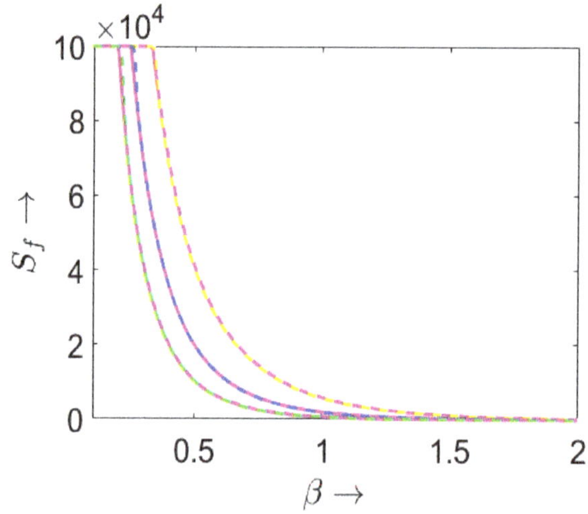

Figure 1. Dependence of S_f on β found analytically by Formula (15) and in numerical simulations of (8) for $\tau = 3$ (upper curves), $\tau = 4$ (middle curves), and $\tau = 5$ (lower curves). The analytical and numerical solutions coincide.

3.3. Maximum Number of Infected Individuals

We now derive an approximate formula for the maximal number of infected individuals for the delay model (9). We have $I(t) = S(t-\tau) - S(t)$. Suppose that $I(t)$ attains its maximum at $t = t_m$. Set $I_m = I(t_m)$, $S_m = S(t_m)$. From the equality $I'(t_m) = 0$, we obtain $S'(t_m - \tau) = S'(t_m)$. This implies

$$\frac{\beta S(t_m-\tau) I(t_m-\tau)}{N} = \frac{\beta S(t_m) I(t_m)}{N}. \tag{17}$$

Substituting the relation $I(t_m) = S(t_m - \tau) - S(t_m)$ in (17), we obtain

$$I(t_m - \tau) = \frac{S_m I_m}{S_m + I_m}. \tag{18}$$

From (8), we have

$$\frac{dS}{dt} = -\frac{\beta S(t)}{N}\Big(S(t-\tau) - S(t)\Big). \tag{19}$$

Integrating (19) from 0 to t_m and changing the variable inside the first integral of the right-hand side, we obtain:

$$\int_0^{t_m} \frac{dS}{S} = -\frac{\beta}{N}\left(\int_{-\tau}^{0} S(t)dt - \int_{t_m-\tau}^{t_m} S(t)dt\right). \tag{20}$$

We assume that $S(t) = S_0$ for all $t \in [-\tau, 0]$ and use the approximation (Figure 2):

$$\int_{t_m-\tau}^{t_m} S(t)dt \approx \frac{\tau}{2} I_m + \tau S_m.$$

Then from (20) we have

$$\ln \frac{S_m}{S_0} = -\frac{\beta}{N}\left(\tau S_0 - \frac{\tau}{2} I_m - \tau S_m\right).$$

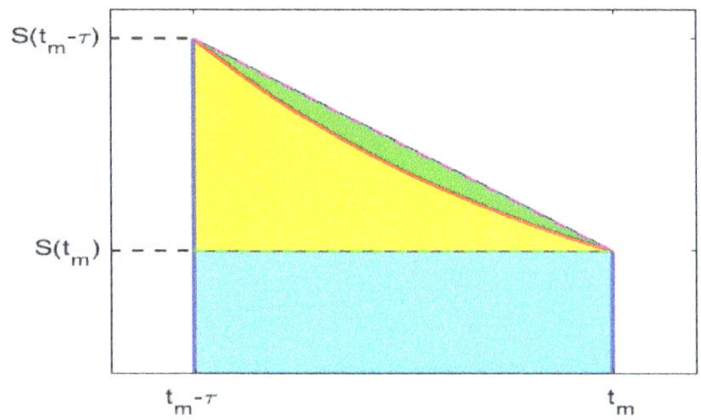

Figure 2. The red curve represents $S(t)$. The integral $\int_{t_m-\tau}^{t_m} S(t)dt$, i.e., the area under the red curve (yellow color region + cyan color region), is approximated by the sum of the areas of the cyan color region, the yellow color region, and the green color region.

Let $x = \frac{I_m}{S_0}$, $y = \frac{S_m}{S_0}$ and $\frac{S_0}{N} \approx 1$. Then we have

$$\ln y = -\beta\tau\left(1 - \frac{1}{2}x - y\right). \tag{21}$$

Again, integrating (19) from $t_m - \tau$ to t_m, we obtain:

$$\int_{t_m-\tau}^{t_m} \frac{dS}{S} = -\frac{\beta}{N}\left(\int_{t_m-\tau}^{t_m} S(t-\tau)dt - \int_{t_m-\tau}^{t_m} S(t)dt\right).$$

Changing the variable inside the first integral of the right-hand side, we get:

$$\ln\frac{S_m}{S(t_m-\tau)} = -\frac{\beta}{N}\left(\int_{t_m-2\tau}^{t_m-\tau} S(t)dt - \int_{t_m-\tau}^{t_m} S(t)dt\right).$$

Now, using the approximation described in Figure 2, we conclude that

$$\ln\frac{S_m}{S(t_m-\tau)} = -\frac{\beta}{N}\left(\tau S(t_m-\tau) + \frac{\tau}{2}I(t_m-\tau) - \tau S_m - \frac{\tau}{2}I_m\right). \tag{22}$$

Using the relation $I(t_m) = S(t_m-\tau) - S(t_m)$, after some transformations, (22) can be written as:

$$\ln\frac{S_m}{S_m + I_m} = -\frac{\beta}{N}\frac{\tau}{2}\Big(I_m + I(t_m-\tau)\Big).$$

Using (18), we obtain:

$$\ln\frac{S_m}{S_m + I_m} = -\frac{\beta}{N}\frac{\tau}{2}\left(I_m + \frac{S_m I_m}{S_m + I_m}\right).$$

Substituting $x = \frac{I_m}{S_0}$, $y = \frac{S_m}{S_0}$ and $\frac{S_0}{N} \approx 1$, we have

$$\ln\frac{y}{x+y} = -\frac{\beta\tau}{2}\left(x + \frac{xy}{x+y}\right). \tag{23}$$

Solving (21) and (23), we can find x, y and, consequently, I_m, S_m.

In Figure 3, we show a comparison between the maximum number of infected obtained by Equations (21) and (23) and the maximum number of infected obtained by direct numerical simulation of the delay model (9). From Figure 3, we can observe that the approximation gives a very close upper bound to the maximum number of infected.

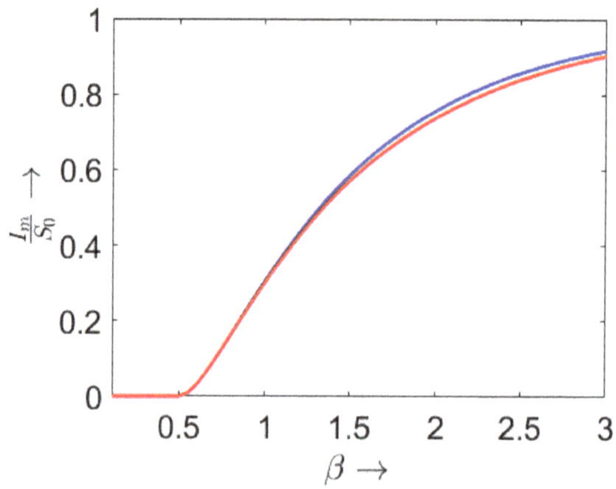

Figure 3. The red curve and the blue curve show the maximum number of infected using the direct numerical simulation of the delay model and using Equations (21) and (23) respectively. Parameter values: $N = 10^5$, $\tau = 4$, $S_0 = N - 1$, $I_0 = 1$.

4. Comparison of Models (3) and (9) and SIR (4)

We compare the results obtained from the distributed model (3), the delay model (9), and the conventional SIR model (4). In [31], we showed that Model (3) can describe the epidemic spread more precisely, and it can exactly capture the recovery and death dynamics by using suitable distributed recovery and death rates. However, the main constraint in using the distributed model (3) is the availability of distributed recovery and death rates. Instead, the average duration of the disease is easier to determine. We show that, in the delay model (9), if we take τ as the mean of the recovery and death distribution functions involved in the distributed model (3), then the delay model (9) gives a close solution to the distributed model (3).

To estimate the recovery and death distributions in the model (3), we use the function *fitdist(:,gamma)* in MATLAB. This function is used to fit a vector of data $X = (x_1, x_2, \cdots, x_n)$ by a gamma distribution of the form $\frac{1}{b^a \Gamma(a)} x^{a-1} e^{-x/b}$, where a and b are the shape and scale parameters. This function gives the maximum likelihood estimators of a and b for the gamma distribution, which are the solutions of the simultaneous equations

$$\log \hat{a} - \Psi(\hat{a}) = \log \left(\bar{X} / \left(\prod_{i=1}^{n} x_i \right)^{1/n} \right),$$

$$\hat{b} = \bar{X} / \hat{a},$$

where $\bar{X}$ is the sample mean of the data X and Ψ is the digamma function given by

$$\Psi(x) = \Gamma'(x) / \Gamma(x).$$

The function *fitdist(:,gamma)* estimates the shape and scale parameters with the 95% confidence interval. Using this statistical technique, we estimated the recovery and death distributions for the model (3) for the data used in [31] and given by the formulas

$$r(t) = \frac{p_0}{b_1^{a_1} \Gamma(a_1)} t^{a_1 - 1} e^{-\frac{t}{b_1}}, \qquad d(t) = \frac{(1 - p_0)}{b_2^{a_2} \Gamma(a_2)} t^{a_2 - 1} e^{-\frac{t}{b_2}},$$

(Figure A1 in Appendix C), where the estimated parameter values are given in Table 1. Here, p_0 is the survival probability, and its estimated value, from the data, is $p_0 = 0.97$ [34].

Table 1. Estimated parameter values (gamma distributions).

Parameters	Estimated Value	95% Confidence Interval
a_1	8.06275	[6.15314, 10.565]
b_1	2.2140	[1.67523, 2.92623]
a_2	6.00014	[3.69566, 9.74161]
b_2	2.19887	[1.32639, 3.64526]

The estimated average time to recovery is 17.85 days and to death is 13.19 days. The value of survival probability p_0 is 0.97 [34], that is, out of 100 infected individuals, 97 infected will recover. This estimate matches with most of the COVID-19 epidemic data from various countries [34,35]. Thus, we can take average disease duration τ as 17.7 days. The corresponding value in the SIR model is $r_0 + d_0 \approx 1/17.7$ days^{-1}.

It is essential to mention here that, instead of a gamma distribution, we can use the Erlang distribution $E_k = \frac{\lambda^k x^{k-1} e^{-\lambda x}}{(k-1)!}, \quad x, \lambda \geq 0$ and $k \in \mathbb{N}$. Since, for lower values of k, e.g., E_1, E_2 distributions, with a reasonable choice of λ, give a significant probability of recovery or death at the beginning of infection, we should look for an Erlang distribution with higher values of k.

We found that the Erlang-8 distribution

$$E_8 = \frac{\lambda^8 x^7 e^{-\lambda x}}{(7)!},$$

with $\lambda = 0.4545$, and the Erlang-6 distribution

$$E_6 = \frac{\lambda^6 x^5 e^{-\lambda x}}{(5)!},$$

with $\lambda = 0.4548$, closely match with the gamma distributions for recovery and death rates respectively, as estimated above. The estimated values of the shape parameters a_1 and a_2 associated with the gamma distributions can be approximated as $a_1 \approx 8$ and $a_2 \approx 6$ for the recovery and death rate distributions, respectively. Thus, one can use the E_8 and E_6 distributions instead of the gamma distributions for recovery and death rates. However, the result will be similar in both cases, and we continue our numerical simulation with the gamma distributions.

Though the parameters of the three models correspond to each other, the distributed model (3) and the delay model (9) both give far different dynamics as compared to the SIR model (4), whereas the distributed model (3) and the delay model (9) give reasonably close dynamics to each other (Figure 4).

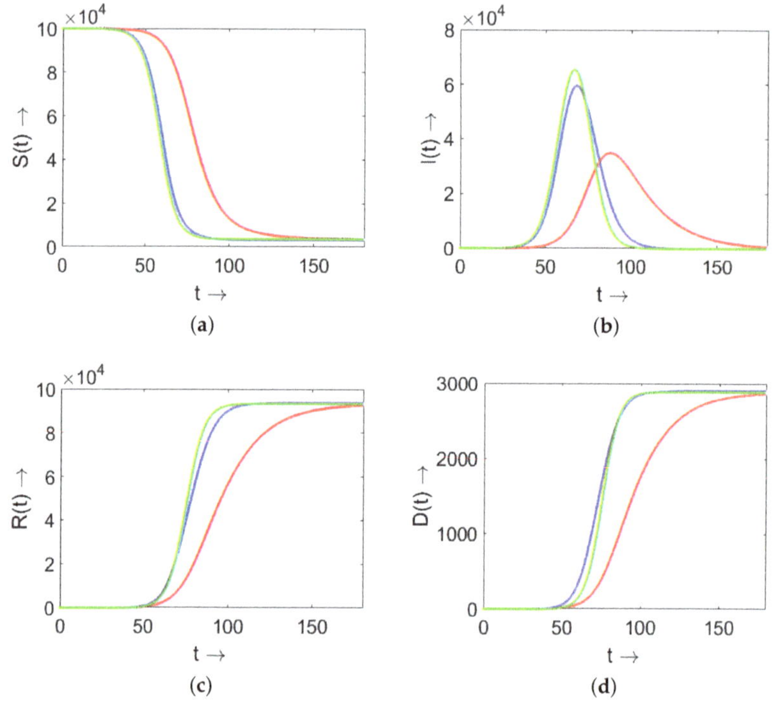

Figure 4. Comparison of the solutions of the distributed model (3) (blue curve), the delay model (9) (green curve), and the conventional SIR model (4) (red curve). (**a**) Susceptible $S(t)$, (**b**) infected $I(t)$, (**c**) recovered $R(t)$, and (**d**) dead $D(t)$. The values of parameters: $N = 10^5$, $I_0 = 1$, $\beta = 0.2$, for the SIR model $r_0 + d_0 = 1/17.7$; for the delay model $\tau = 17.7$; for the distributed model (3): $a_1 = 8.06275$, $b_1 = 2.21407$, $a_2 = 6.00014$, $b_2 = 2.19887$, $p_0 = 0.97$.

The comparison of the final size of epidemic S_f, maximal number of infected I_m, and the time to the maximal number of infected t_m of the distributed model (3) with the gamma distribution, the delay model (9), and the SIR model (4) is shown in Figure 5 for different values of the transmission rate β. As before, the maximal numbers of infected individuals I_m in the models (3) and (9) are sufficiently close, but they are much higher than for the SIR model (4). The times to maximum infected t_m in the models (3) and (9) are reasonably close, but less than for the SIR model (4). The final size of the epidemic S_f is more or less the same for all three models. Similar properties are observed if the gamma distribution is replaced by the Erlang distribution with the corresponding parameters.

This result indicates the relevance of the delay model. If we do not have sufficient individual-level data to estimate the recovery and death distributions, but we have an approximate value of disease duration, then we can describe the epidemic progression in a sufficiently precise way.

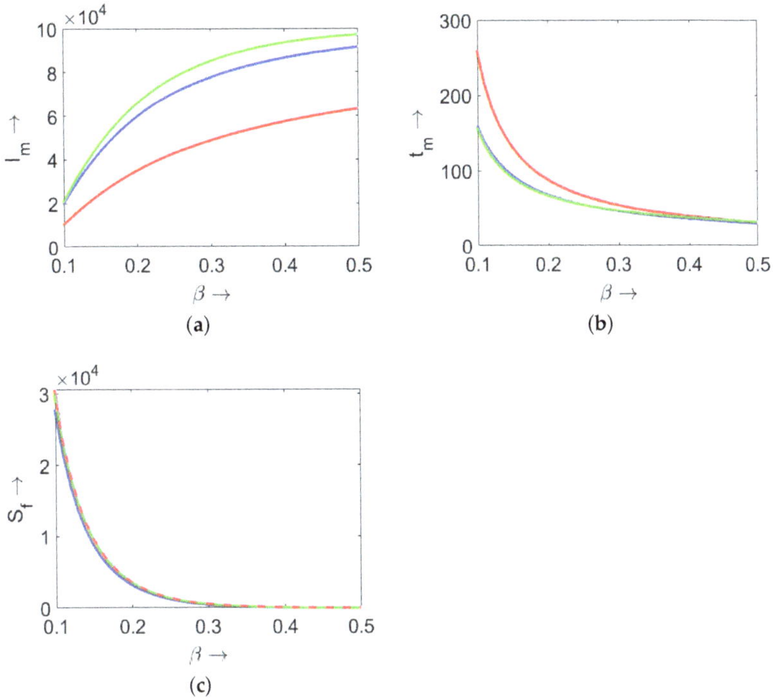

Figure 5. Comparison of the maximal number of infected individuals I_m (**a**), the time to reach the maximal number t_m (**b**), and the final size of the epidemic S_f (**c**) for the distributed model (3) (blue curves), the delay model (9) (green curves), and the SIR model (4) (red curves) for different values of β. The values of parameters: $N = 10^5$, $I_0 = 1$, for the SIR model $r_0 + d_0 = 1/17.7$; for the delay model $\tau = 17.7$; for the distributed model (3): $a_1 = 8.06275$, $b_1 = 2.21407$, $a_2 = 6.00014$, $b_2 = 2.19887$, $p_0 = 0.97$.

5. Determination of Disease Duration from Data

In this section, we determine the disease duration τ from the epidemiological data for the daily number of infected $J(t)$ and the total number of infected individuals $I(t)$, using the equation

$$\frac{dI(t)}{dt} = J(t) - J(t - \tau).$$

Let $I(t)$ have the maximum at $t = t_m$. Set $I(t_m) = I_m$. Then, $J(t_m) = J(t_m - \tau)$, i.e., the daily number of infected is the same at two different time points $t = t_m$ and $t = t_m - \tau$. From the real data of the infected individuals $I(t)$, we can find the day on which the daily number of active cases is maximal, and it determines t_m. From the data of daily reported cases $J(t)$, we can observe that $J(t)$ crosses its maximum at some time before t_m. Now, we have to find the value of $J(t)$ such that $J(t_m)$ will be equal to $J(t_m - \tau)$, which in turn determines the disease duration τ. Hence, considering the delay model, using the real data of daily new cases $J(t)$ and active cases $I(t)$ around a peak, we can find the disease duration τ.

We illustrate this method using the data of $J(t)$ and $I(t)$ taken from [35] for COVID-19 in Italy. We collected the daily new reported data $J(t)$ and active case data $I(t)$ for Italy from 21 February 2020 to 31 May 2021 (which capture the first three peaks in Italy) and from 10 November 2021 to 28 February 2022 (which capture the peak due to Omicron in Italy). To have smoother data, we used the 7-day moving average, the data on the

j-th day replaced by the average data from the $(j-3)$th day to the $(j+3)$th day. As the concerned method is focused on the peaks, the error at the beginning and end of the time interval is not essential. In Italy, during the first peak (in April 2020), the peak of $I(t)$ is attained at $t_m = 51$ (Figure 6a) and the peak of $J(t)$ is attained before on $t = 51$, which is less than t_m (Figure 6b). First, we find that $J(t_m = 51) = 4.17 \times 10^3$ and then find $J(32) = 4.15 \times 10^3 \approx J(t_m = 51)$. This implies $J(t_m - \tau) = J(32)$, and consequently, we can calculate $\tau = 19$ as the disease duration during the first peak. Similarly, during the second peak (in November 2020) and third peak (in March 2021), we estimated the disease duration as $\tau = 20$ days and $\tau = 14$ days, respectively. The peak of epidemic progression due to Omicron in January 2022 is shown in Figure 6c,d, and we estimated the value of τ as 11 days. Similarly, the value of τ is estimated for some other countries (Table 2).

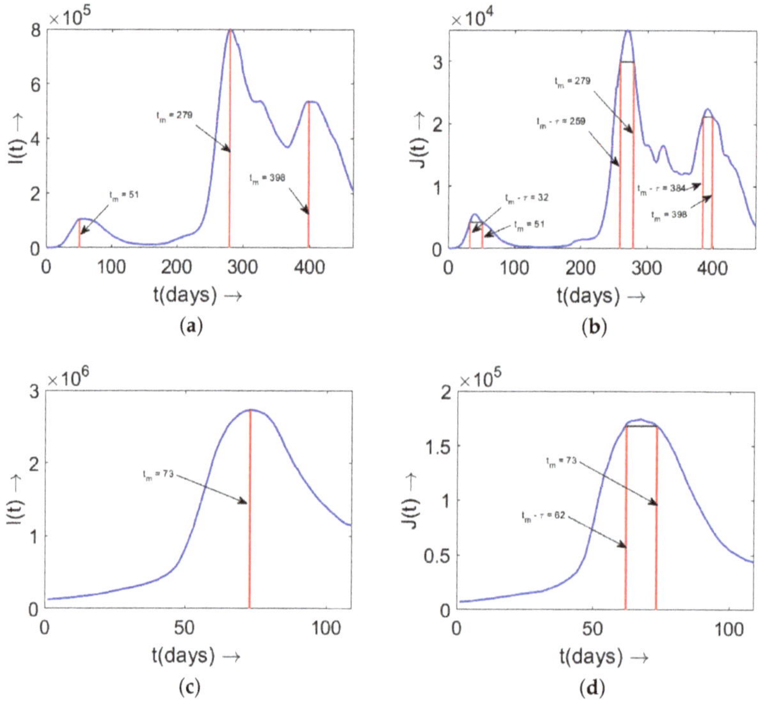

Figure 6. Estimation of the disease duration τ using the data around different peaks of COVID-19 in Italy. (**a**,**b**) Time $t = 0$ corresponds to 21 February 2020. The obtained value of τ is 19 days for the first peak, 20 days for the second peak, and 14 days for the last peak. (**c**,**d**) Time $t = 0$ corresponds to 10 November 2021 (which corresponds to the Omicron outbreak), and the obtained value of τ corresponding to the Omicron outbreak is 11 days.

Table 2. Estimated value of τ for different countries during different outbreaks of the COVID-19 epidemic. The months indicated in the table correspond to the time when the corresponding peak appeared.

Country	Estimated Value of τ (in Days)	Estimated Value of τ (in Days)	Estimated Value of τ (in Days)	Estimated Value of τ (in Days)
	during Peak 1	during Peak 2	during Peak 3	during Peak 4
Italy	19 (April 2020)	20 (November 2020)	14 (March 2021)	11 (January 2022)
Russia	25 (May 2020)	24 (January 2021)	26 (November 2021)	9 (February 2022)
China	16 (February 2020)	-	-	-
Romania	16 (November 2020)	14 (March 2021)	18 (October 2021)	12 (February 2022)
Sweden	20 (July 2020)	20 (December 2020)	19 (April 2021)	14 (February 2022)
Iran	14 (December 2020)	24 (May 2021)	28 (August 2021)	10 (February 2022)

Remark 1. *It is important to note that in the case of the combination of strains, the estimated value of τ corresponds to the weighted average of the strain-specific disease duration. Furthermore, note that this method depends on how the daily cases of infection were reported. However, in many cases, there is a dominant variant during epidemic outbreaks. Thus, the estimated value of τ can be considered as the disease duration corresponding to the dominant variant during a specific epidemic wave.*

Remark 2. *Note that the delay model (9) does not take into account the difference in duration to recovery and the duration to death. If we assume that the death cases are relatively rare (e.g., approximately $\leq 2\%$ in the case of COVID-19), then this difference may not be very essential.*

Remark 3. *Note that this method of the estimation of τ remains the same for time-varying $\beta = \beta(t)$. Thus, the method discussed above does not depend on whether β is a constant or β varies with respect to time. Since the time-varying $\beta(t)$ is capable of incorporating the effect of all possible infected compartments (i.e., exposed $E(t)$, asymptomatic $I_A(t)$, symptomatic $I_S(t)$, hospitalized $H(t)$, etc.) on disease transmission, we can use this method to obtain an estimation of τ for any infectious disease with available data.*

6. Model Validation with Epidemiological Data

In order to validate the delay model (9) and the method of estimation of τ, we compared the results with the epidemiological data. We used the estimated value of τ obtained by the method described above during different peaks of COVID-19.

In Italy, the estimated value of τ is 19 days, 20 days, 14 days, and 11 days during the first peak (April 2020), the second peak (November 2020), the third peak (March 2021), and the fourth peak (January 2022), respectively. We assumed that the disease duration τ remains $\tau = 19$ days from 21 February 2020 to 15 August 2020; $\tau = 20$ days from 16 August 2020 to 19 February 2021; $\tau = 14$ days from 20 February 2021 to 21 May 2021; and 11 days from 10 November 2021 to 28 February 2022 (during Omicron in Italy).

Once these parameter values were determined, we took the number $J(t)$ of daily infected individuals from the epidemiological data [35] and found the sum of daily recoveries and deaths from the expression

$$\Sigma(t) = J(t - \tau). \tag{24}$$

These results were compared with the sum of recoveries and deaths in the data. Figure 7 shows the result of such a comparison for Italy from 21 February 2020 to 21 May 2021 and from 10 November 2021 to 28 February 2022, with the data from [35] (7-day moving average). Recoveries and deaths can also be determined as a proportion of active cases $\sigma(t) = (r_0 + d_0)I(t)$, as is done in the SIR model. Here, $I(t)$ is taken from the data and $r_0 + d_0 = 1/\tau$, and we observed that the SIR model overestimates the sum of recovered and dead. Thus, the delay model (9) gives a good description of the recovery and death compared with the epidemiological data, while the SIR model overestimates them.

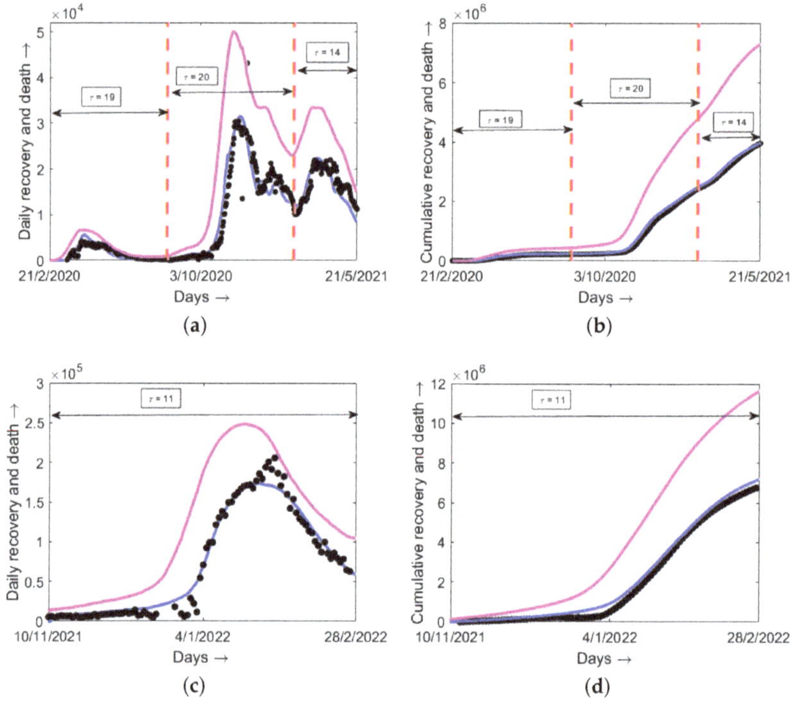

Figure 7. The blue curves show the number $\Sigma(t)$ of recovered and dead in the delay model; the magenta curves correspond to $\sigma(t)$ in the SIR model; the black dots correspond to the 7-day moving average of daily recoveries and death in Italy.

7. Discussion

We proposed a delay model under the assumption that the infected individuals recover or die exactly after an average disease duration τ. Generally, in the case of COVID-19, we observed that the recovery and death distributions follow unimodal or bimodal gamma distributions [34,36]. Estimating these gamma distributions requires individual-level data with the date of onset of disease and the date of recovery or death, which may be very difficult to gather for every country or province. Instead, the only information about the disease duration can help us to obtain sufficiently good results using the delay model. Furthermore, we developed a method to estimate the disease duration from the epidemiological data. It is important to mention here that one can use the Erlang distributions, instead of the gamma distributions, for a compartmental epidemic model with multi-phase disease transition [37].

Let us note that we consider only symptomatic individuals in the model. The influence of asymptomatic individuals is widely discussed in the COVID-19 literature. According to some estimates, they can constitute between 25% and 50% of the total number of cases [38,39]. On the other hand, the infectivity of asymptomatic individuals is much lower than the infectivity of symptomatic individuals because infectivity is proportional to the viral load in the upper respiratory tract [40] and symptoms correlate with viral load. Hence, in the first approximation, we can consider only symptomatic individuals. Further studies are needed to take into account asymptomatic individuals more precisely.

We noticed that during different peaks of COVID-19, the estimated value of τ was different. This difference might be due to different strains or the change of proportion of different infected compartments (such as asymptomatic, hospitalized) that we counted in the same compartment.

The presence of exposed individuals can be taken into account by means of time-dependent infectivity rate $\beta(t-\eta)$. For the individuals infected at time η, their infectivity at time t depends on the difference $t-\eta$. The function $\beta(t-\eta)$ is small if the difference $t-\eta$ is small, which is the case of exposed individuals. This case was studied in [32]. We did not consider the time-dependent infectivity rate in this work since its main objective is to compare the model with distributed recovery and death rates with the delay model.

We compared the final size of the epidemic and maximal number of infected obtained in the Formulas (15), (21), and (23), respectively. Note that these formulae depend on τ and β. Since the outbreak due to Omicron is the only one when the social distancing measures such as lockdowns or isolation were not strictly imposed, we can assume that the transmission rate β is approximately constant. We took the data of the Omicron outbreak in Italy from [35] from 10 November 2021 to 10 December 2021, and we fit the delay model to these 40 days of data and estimated the disease transmission rate β as 0.118. We took the value of disease duration $\tau = 11$ days, which was obtained by using the method discussed in Section 5. Then, using the formula (15), we calculated the final size of the epidemic as 3.387×10^7. Using the formulae (21) and (23), we calculated the maximal number of infected as $I_m = 3.4139 \times 10^6$, whereas the maximal number of infected was $I_m = 2.7317 \times 10^6$ in the data. Thus, the formulae (21) and (23) give a reasonable estimate of the maximal number of infected. Similarly, we obtained an accurate estimate of the maximal number of infected for some other countries (not shown).

Let us finally note that the delay model presented in this work is simple and generic. It describes epidemic progression with two parameters β and τ, which can be easily estimated from the data. Our next goal will be to apply the proposed modeling approach to multi-compartment models consisting of different groups of susceptible and/or infected and to immuno-epidemic models with time-varying recovery and death rates [32]. It is also interesting to check the applicability of the proposed model to other transmissible diseases.

Author Contributions: Model formulation, V.V.; Model analysis, S.G.; Model validation, M.B. All authors contributed equally to the interpretation and discussion of results. All authors have read and agreed to the published version of the manuscript.

Funding. Vitaly Volpert was supported by the Ministry of Science and Higher Education of the Russian Federation (Megagrant agreement no. 075-15-2022-1115).

Institutional Review Board Statement: Not applicable.

Informed Consent Statement: Not applicable.

Data Availability Statement: All data sources are mentioned explicitly.

Conflicts of Interest: The authors declare no conflict of interest.

Appendix A. Review of Delay Models

Time delay in epidemic models accounts for the delay for an individual to become infectious after being infected. Time delay for vector-born diseases characterizes the time needed for the pathogen to reach a certain threshold sufficient for infection transmission. Under the assumption that the infection transmission rate at time t depends on the number of infected at time $t-\tau$ and the number of susceptible at time t, the delay SIR model for vector-born diseases is given by the following system of equations (see [41] and the references therein):

$$\begin{aligned}
\frac{dS(t)}{dt} &= -f(S(t), I(t-\tau)), \\
\frac{dI(t)}{dt} &= f(S(t), I(t-\tau)) - \delta I(t),
\end{aligned}$$

where $S(t)$ represents susceptible and $I(t)$ infectious compartments, the function $f(S(t), I(t-\tau))$ characterizes the disease transmission rate, δ is the clearance rate, and τ is the time delay from the moment of infection to disease transmission. Another type of delay model describes temporary immunity [28]:

$$\begin{aligned}\frac{dS(t)}{dt} &= -f(S(t), I(t)) + \delta I(t-\omega),\\ \frac{dI(t)}{dt} &= f(S(t), I(t)) - \delta I(t),\end{aligned}$$

where ω is the time period after which an infected individual becomes susceptible again.

For long-lasting epidemics such as HIV, new generations of susceptible individuals influence epidemic dynamics. In this case, time delay corresponds to the maturation period after which young adults become susceptible to infection (see [42–44] and the references therein):

$$\begin{aligned}\frac{dS(t)}{dt} &= g(N(t-\tau)) - h((S(t), I(t)),\\ \frac{dI(t)}{dt} &= h(S(t), I(t)) - \delta I(t).\end{aligned}$$

Here, $N(t) = S(t) + I(t)$, $g(N(t-\tau))$ is the susceptible recruitment function, which incorporates the maturation delay τ and $h(S, I)$ is the disease transmission rate.

Appendix B. Positiveness of the Delay Model (9)

We show the positiveness of the solution of the delay model (9). Note that, as per our assumption, $J(t)$ is a positive function. From (9a), we observe that, if $S(t_*) = 0$ at some time point t_*, then $\frac{dS}{dt}|_{t=t_*} = 0$. This implies that $S(t) \geq 0$ for $t > 0$. From (3c) and (3d), we obtain that $R(t)$ and $D(t)$ are both increasing functions, and hence, $R(t)$ and $D(t)$ also remain positive for all t. Next, we prove that $I(t) > 0$. Integrating (9c) from 0 to t, we obtain

$$\begin{aligned}I(t) &= I(0) + \int_0^t J(\eta)d\eta - \int_0^t J(\eta-\tau)d\eta\\ &= I(0) + \int_0^t J(\eta)d\eta - \int_{-\tau}^{t-\tau} J(\eta)d\eta.\end{aligned}$$

Since, $J(t) = 0$ for $t < 0$, we can write:

$$I(t) = I(0) + \int_{t-\tau}^{t} J(\eta)d\eta \geq 0.$$

Therefore, $I(t)$ is positive for all t. This shows the positiveness of the solution of System (9).

Appendix C. Gamma Distributions for Recovery and Death Rates

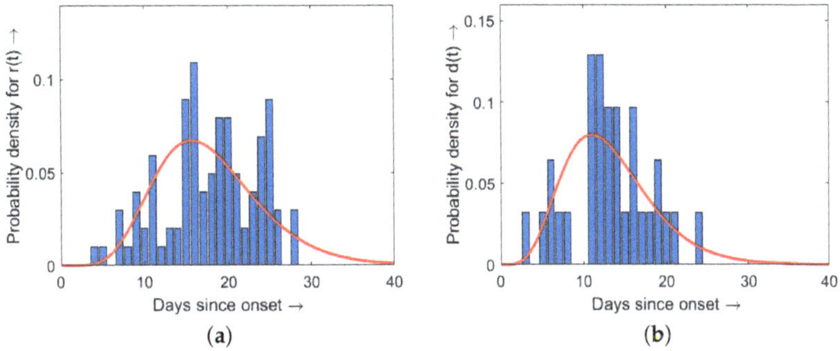

Figure A1. Probability distribution of recovery (**a**) and death (**b**) as a function of time (in days) after the onset of infection. The red curves show the best-fit gamma distributions using the function *"fitdist(:,'gamma')"* in MATLAB.

References

1. Hoch, S.P.F.; Hutwagner, L. Opportunistic candidiasis: An epidemic of the 1980s. *Clin. Infect. Dis.* **1995**, *21*, 897–904. [CrossRef] [PubMed]
2. Chintu, C.; Athale, U.H.; Patil, P.S. Childhood cancers in Zambia before and after the HIV epidemic. *Arch. Dis. Child.* **1995**, *73*, 100–105. [CrossRef] [PubMed]
3. Anderson, R.M.; Fraser, C.; Ghani, A.C.; Donnelly, C.A.; Riley, S.; Ferguson, N.M.; Leung, G.M.; Lam, T.H.; Hedley, A.J. Epidemiology, transmission dynamics and control of SARS: The 2002–2003 epidemic. *Philos. Trans. R. Soc. B: Biol. Sci.* **2004**, *359*, 1091–1105. [CrossRef] [PubMed]
4. Lam, W.K.; Zhong, N.S.; Tan, W.C. Overview on SARS in Asia and the World. *Respirology* **2003**, *8*, S2–S5. [CrossRef] [PubMed]
5. Chen, H.; Smith, G.J.D.; Li, K.S.; Wang, J.; Fan, X.H.; Rayner, J.M.; Vijaykrishna, D.; Zhang, J.X.; Zhang, L.J.; Guo, C.T.; et al. Establishment of multiple sublineages of H5N1 influenza virus in Asia: Implications for pandemic control. *Proc. Natl. Aacd. Sci. USA* **2006**, *103*, 2845–2850. [CrossRef] [PubMed]
6. Kilpatrick, A.M.; Chmura, A.A.; Gibbons, D.W.; Fleischer, R.C.; Marra, P.P.; Daszak, P. Predicting the global spread of H5N1 avian influenza. *Proc. Natl. Aacd. Sci. USA* **2006**, *103*, 19368–19373. [CrossRef]
7. Jain, S.; Kamimoto, L.; Bramley, A.M.; Schmitz, A.M.; Benoit, S.R.; Louie, J.; Sugerman, D.E.; Druckenmiller, J.K.; Ritger, K.A.; Chugh, R. et al. Hospitalized Patients with 2009 H1N1 Influenza in the United States, April–June 2009. *N. Engl. J. Med.* **2009**, *361*, 1935–1944. [CrossRef]
8. Girard, M.P.; Tam, J.S.; Assossou, O.M.; Kieny, M.P. The 2009 A (H1N1) influenza virus pandemic: A review. *Vaccine* **2010**, *28*, 4895–4902. [CrossRef]
9. Frieden, T.R.; Damon, I.; Bell, B.P.; Kenyon, T.; Nichol, S. Ebola 2014—New challenges, new global response and responsibility. *N. Engl. J. Med.* **2014**, *371*, 1177–1180. [CrossRef]
10. WHO Ebola Response Team. Ebola Virus Disease in West Africa — The First 9 Months of the Epidemic and Forward Projections. *N. Engl. J. Med.* **2014**, *371*, 1481–1495. [CrossRef]
11. Kermack, W.O.; McKendrick, A.G. A contribution to the mathematical theory of epidemics. *Proc. R. Soc. A Lond* **1927**, *115*, 700–721.
12. Kermack, W.O.; McKendrick, A.G. Contributions to the mathematical theory of epidemics. II. —The problem of endemicity. *Proc. R. Soc. A Lond* **1932**, *138*, 55–83.
13. Kermack, W.O.; McKendrick, A.G. Contributions to the mathematical theory of epidemics. III.—Further studies of the problem of endemicity. *Proc. R. Soc. A Lond* **1933**, *141*, 94–122.
14. Sharma, S.; Volpert, V.; Banerjee, M. Extended SEIQR type model for COVID-19 epidemic and data analysis. *Math. Biosci. Eng.* **2020**, *17*, 7562–7604. [CrossRef]
15. Khan, M.A.; Atangana, A. Mathematical modeling and analysis of COVID-19: A study of new variant Omicron. *Physica A* **2022**, *599*, 127452. [CrossRef]
16. Brauer, F. Compartmental Models in Epidemiology. In *Mathematical Epidemiology*; Springer: Berlin/Heidelberg, Germany, 2008; pp. 19–79.
17. d'Onofrio, A.; Banerjee, M.; Manfredi, P. Spatial behavioural responses to the spread of an infectious disease can suppress Turing and Turing–Hopf patterning of the disease. *Phys. A Stat. Mech. Appl.* **2020**, *545*, 123773. [CrossRef]
18. Sun, G.-Q.; Jin, Z.; Liu, Q.-X.; Li, L. Chaos induced by breakup of waves in a spatial epidemic model with nonlinear incidence rate. *J. Stat. Mech. Theory Exp.* **2008**, *P08011*, 2008. [CrossRef]

19. Bichara, D.; Iggidr, A. Multi-patch and multi-group epidemic models: A new framework. *J. Math. Biol.* **2018**, *77*, 107–134. [CrossRef]
20. Lahodny, G.E.; Allen, L.J.S. Probability of a disease outbreak in stochastic multipatch epidemic models. *Bull. Math. Biol.* **2013**, *75*, 1157–1180. [CrossRef]
21. McCormack, R.K.; Allen, L.J.S. Multi-patch deterministic and stochastic models for wildlife diseases. *J. Biol. Dyn.* **2007**, *1*, 63–85. [CrossRef]
22. Elbasha, E.H.; Gumel, A.B. Vaccination and herd immunity thresholds in heterogeneous populations. *J. Math. Biol.* **2021**, *83*, 1–23. [CrossRef] [PubMed]
23. Aniţa, S.; Banerjee, M.; Ghosh, S.; Volpert, V. Vaccination in a two-group epidemic model. *Appl. Math. Lett.* **2021**, *119*, 107197. [CrossRef]
24. Faniran, T.S.; Ali, A.; Al-Hazmi, N.E.; Asamoah, J.K.K.; Nofal, T.A.; Adewole, M.O. New Variant of SARS-CoV-2 Dynamics with Imperfect Vaccine. *Complexity* **2022**, *2022*, 1062180. [CrossRef]
25. Ahmed, N.; Wei, Z.; Baleanu, D.; Rafiq, M.; Rehman, M.A. Spatio-temporal numerical modeling of reaction-diffusion measles epidemic system. *Chaos* **2019**, *29*, 103101. [CrossRef]
26. Filipe, J.A.N.; Maule, M.M. Effects of dispersal mechanisms on spatio-temporal development of epidemics. *J. Theor. Biol.* **2004**, *226*, 125–141. [CrossRef]
27. Martcheva, M. *An Introduction to Mathematical Epidemiology*; Springer: Berlin/Heidelberg, Germany, 2015; Volume 61.
28. Brauer, F.; Chavez, C.C.; Feng, Z. *Mathematical Models in Epidemiology*; Springer: Berlin/Heidelberg, Germany, 2019; Volume 32.
29. Hethcote, H.W. The mathematics of infectious diseases. *SIAM Rev.* **2000**, *42*, 599–653. [CrossRef]
30. Hurd, H.S.; Kaneene, J.B. The application of simulation models and systems analysis in epidemiology: A review. *Prev. Vet. Med.* **1993**, *15*, 81–99. [CrossRef]
31. Ghosh, S.; Volpert, V.; Banerjee, M. An epidemic model with time-distributed recovery and death rates. *Bull. Math. Biol.* **2022**, *84*, 78. [CrossRef]
32. Ghosh, S.; Banerjee, M.; Volpert, V. Immuno-epidemiological model-based prediction of further COVID-19 epidemic outbreaks due to immunity waning. *Math. Model. Nat. Phenom.* **2022**, *17*, 9. [CrossRef]
33. Volpert, V.; Banerjee, M.; Petrovskii, S. On a quarantine model of coronavirus infection and data analysis. *Math. Model. Nat. Phenom.* **2020**, *15*, 24. [CrossRef]
34. Paul, S.; Lorin, E. Estimation of COVID-19 recovery and decease periods in Canada using delay model. *Sci. Rep.* **2021**, *11*, 1–15. [CrossRef] [PubMed]
35. Available online: https://www.worldometers.info/coronavirus/ (accessed on 8 May 2022).
36. Verity, R.; Okell, L.C.; Dorigatti, I.; Winskill, P.; Whittaker, C.; Imai, N.; Dannenburg, G.C.; Thompson, H.; Walker, P.G.T.; Fu, H. et al. Estimates of the severity of coronavirus disease 2019: A model-based analysis. *Lancet Infect. Dis.* **2020**, *20*, 669–677. [CrossRef]
37. Arino, J.; Portet, S. A simple model for COVID-19. *Infect. Dis. Model.* **2020**, *5*, 309–315. [CrossRef] [PubMed]
38. Nishiura, H.; Kobayashi, T.; Miyama, T.; Suzuki, A.; Jung, S.; Hayashi, K.; Kinoshita, R.; Yang, Y.; Yuan, B.; Akhmetzhanov, A.R.; others. Estimation of the asymptomatic ratio of novel coronavirus infections (COVID-19). *Int. J. Infect. Dis.* **2020**, *94*, 154–155. [CrossRef] [PubMed]
39. Mizumoto, K.; Kagaya, K.; Zarebski, A.; Chowell, G. Estimating the asymptomatic proportion of coronavirus disease 2019 (COVID-19) cases on board the Diamond Princess cruise ship, Yokohama, Japan, 2020. *Eurosurveillance* **2020**, *25*, 2000180. [CrossRef]
40. Sentis, C.; Billaud, G.; Bal, A.; Frobert, E.; Bouscambert, M.; Destras, G.; Josset, L.; Lina, B.; Morfin, F.; Gaymard, A.; et al. SARS-CoV-2 Omicron Variant, Lineage BA.1, Is Associated with Lower Viral Load in Nasopharyngeal Samples Compared to Delta Variant. *Viruses* **2022**, *14*, 919. [CrossRef]
41. Huang, G.; Takeuchi, Y.; Ma, W.; Wei, D. Global Stability for Delay SIR and SEIR Epidemic Models with Nonlinear Incidence Rate. *Bull. Math. Biol.* **2010**, *72*, 1192–1207. [CrossRef]
42. Mehdaoui, M. A review of commonly used compartmental models in epidemiology. *arXiv* **2021**, arXiv:2110.09642.
43. Cooke, K.; Driessche, P.V.d.; Zou, X. Interaction of maturation delay and nonlinear birth in population and epidemic models. *J. Math. Biol.* **1999**, *39*, 332–352. [CrossRef]
44. Lou, Y.; Zhao, X.-Q. Threshold dynamics in a time-delayed periodic SIS epidemic model. *Discrete Contin. Dyn. Syst. B* **2009**, *12*, 169. [CrossRef]

Σ mathematics

MDPI

Article

Quasinormal Forms for Chains of Coupled Logistic Equations with Delay

Sergey Kashchenko

Regional Scientific and Educational Mathematical Center «Centre of Integrable Systems», P. G. Demidov Yaroslavl State University, 150003 Yaroslavl, Russia; kasch@uniyar.ac.ru

Abstract: In this paper, chains of coupled logistic equations with delay are considered, and the local dynamics of these chains is investigated. A basic assumption is that the number of elements in the chain is large enough. This implies that the study of the original systems can be reduced to the study of a distributed integro–differential boundary value problem that is continuous with respect to the spatial variable. Three types of couplings of greatest interest are considered: diffusion, unidirectional, and fully connected. It is shown that the critical cases in the stability of the equilibrium state have an infinite dimension: infinitely many roots of the characteristic equation tend to the imaginary axis as the small parameter tends to zero, which characterizes the inverse of the number of elements of the chain. In the study of local dynamics in cases close to critical, analogues of normal forms are constructed, namely quasinormal forms, which are boundary value problems of Ginzburg–Landau type or, as in the case of fully connected systems, special nonlinear integro–differential equations. It is shown that the nonlocal solutions of the obtained quasinormal forms determine the principal terms of the asymptotics of solutions to the original problem from a small neighborhood of the equilibrium state.

Keywords: logistic equation; delay; quasinormal form; asymptotic behavior; dynamics

MSC: 34K11

Citation: Kashchenko, S. Quasinormal Forms for Chains of Coupled Logistic Equations with Delay. *Mathematics* **2022**, *10*, 2648. https://doi.org/10.3390/math10152648

Academic Editor: Ferenc Hartung

Received: 3 July 2022
Accepted: 26 July 2022
Published: 28 July 2022

1. Introduction

Currently, special attention is paid to important objects such as chains of interacting oscillators. Such chains arise when modeling many applied problems in radiophysics (see [1–3]), laser optics (see [4–6]), mechanics (see [7,8]), neural network theory (see [9–13]), biophysics (see [14]), mathematical ecology (see [15–18]), etc. This paper investigates the chains of coupled logistic equations with delay that are relevant for biophysics and mathematical ecology.

As a basic example describing certain population size changes, the well-known logistic equation with delay

$$\dot{u} = r[1 - u(t-T)]u \tag{1}$$

is considered. Here, $u(t) > 0$ is the normalized population or the population density, $r > 0$ is the Malthusian parameter, $T > 0$ is the delay associated with the reproductive age of individuals.

Let us recall some well-known facts (see, for example, [19]). In (1), the equilibrium state $u_0 \equiv 1$ is asymptotically stable as $rT \ll \pi/2$, but this equilibrium state is unstable and there is a stable cycle $u_0(t)$ as $rT > \pi/2$. Under the condition

$$0 < rT - \frac{\pi}{2} \ll 1$$

its asymptotic behavior is:

$$u_0(t) = 1+\sqrt{rT - \frac{\pi}{2}}\Big[\xi_0(\tau(1+O(\varepsilon)))\exp\Big(i\frac{2\pi}{T_0}t\Big) + \bar{\xi}_0(\tau(1+O(\varepsilon)))\exp\Big(-i\frac{2\pi}{T_0}t\Big)\Big] + \dots .$$

This cycle is relaxational as $rT \gg 1$. Its asymptotic behavior is presented in [20].

We examine two types of chains of the coupled logistic equations with delay.

Type 1: The chains of the $2N+1$ coupled equations

$$\dot{v}_j(t) = r[1 - v_j(t-T)]v_j(t) + r\sum_{m=-N}^{N} a_{mj}(v_m(t-h) - v_j(t-h)). \tag{2}$$

Here, $j, m = 0, \pm1, \pm2, \dots, \pm N$, $a_{mm} = 0$, and $h \geq 0$. Certain constraints may be imposed on the coupling coefficients a_{mj}. For example, the biologically derived conditions $u_j(t) \geq 0$ must be satisfied for $h = 0$. Therefore, the solutions must keep the quadrant $u_j \geq 0$ $(j = 0, \pm1, \pm2, \dots, \pm N)$ invariant for nonnegative initial conditions $u_j(s) \in C_{[-T,0]}$ $(j = 0, \pm1, \pm2, \dots, \pm N)$. Hence,

$$a_{mj} \geq 0. \tag{3}$$

System (2) has the equilibrium state $u_{j0} = u_0 = 1$ $(j = 0, \pm1, \pm2, \dots, \pm N)$. The substitution

$$v_j = 1 + u_j \tag{4}$$

leads to the system of equations

$$\dot{u}_j(t) = -ru_j(t-T) + r\sum_{m=-N}^{N} a_{mj}(u_m(t-h) - u_j(t-h)) - ru_j(t-T)u_j. \tag{5}$$

Type 2: Here, the site of couplings is the only difference between the chains of coupled equations and (2):

$$\dot{v}_j(t) = r\Big[1 - v_j(t-T) + \sum_{m=-N}^{N} a_{mj}(v_m(t-h) - v_j(t-h))\Big]v_j(t). \tag{6}$$

Substitution (4) converts this system to the system of equations

$$\begin{aligned}\dot{u}_j(t) = &-ru_j(t-T) + r\sum_{m=-N}^{N} a_{mj}(u_m(t-h) - u_j(t-h)) - \\ &ru_j(t-h)u_j + ru_j(t)\sum_{m=-N}^{N}(u_m(t-h) - u_j(t-h)).\end{aligned} \tag{7}$$

The last term of System (7) distinguishes it from System (5).

It is convenient to associate the element $u_j(t)$ with the value of the two-variable function $u(t, x_j)$. Here, x_j is the point of some circle with the angular coordinate $x_j = 2\pi(2N+1)^{-1} \cdot j$. Further, the periodicity condition $u_{j+2N+1}(t) = u(t, x_j + 2\pi) = u_j(t) = u(t, x_j)$ and $a_{m+2N+1,j} = a_{m,j+2N+1} = a_{mj}$ $(m, j = 0, \pm1, \pm2, \dots)$ holds.

We assume the coupling between elements to be homogeneous, i.e.,

$$a_{mj} = a_{m-j}. \tag{8}$$

The basic assumption is that the quantity $(2N+1)$ of elements is large enough:

$$0 < \varepsilon = 2\pi(2N+1)^{-1} \ll 1. \tag{9}$$

The above condition gives ground for moving from the discrete spatial variable x to the continuous variable x.

In this paper, the three most important cases in terms of applications will be considered. In the first case, it is assumed that the system is fully connected and all coupling coefficients are the same: the equalities

$$a_{mj} = \gamma(2N+1)^{-1}(2\pi)^{-1} \tag{10}$$

hold for some coefficient γ. The expression $\gamma\big(2\pi(2N+1)\big)^{-1} \sum\limits_{j=-N}^{N} f(x_j)$ is the partial Darboux sum for the expression $\gamma(2\pi)^{-1} \int_0^{2\pi} f(x)dx$. Thus, under condition (10), the boundary value problem

$$\begin{aligned} \frac{\partial u}{\partial t} = &-ru(t-T,x) + r\gamma\Big[(2\pi)^{-1}\int_0^{2\pi} u(t-h,s)ds - u(t-h,x)\Big] - \\ &ru(t-T,x)u + r\delta\gamma u \cdot \Big[(2\pi)^{-1}\int_0^{2\pi} u(t-h,s)ds - u(t-h,x)\Big] \end{aligned} \tag{11}$$

is the asymptotic approximation for Systems (5) and (7) as $\varepsilon \to 0$. Here, $\delta = 0$ in the case of (5), and $\delta = 1$ in the case of (7).

For Equation (11), the periodic boundary conditions

$$u(t, x+2\pi) \equiv u(t,x) \tag{12}$$

hold. Note that in the case when coefficients a_{i-j} are not identical, the integral term becomes more complicated. We obtain the expression $\frac{1}{2\pi}\int_0^{2\pi} a(s)u(t-h, x+s)ds$ instead of the expression $\frac{1}{2\pi}\int_0^{2\pi} u(t-h,s)ds$, and $\frac{1}{2\pi}\int_0^{2\pi} a(s)ds = 1$.

The local (i.e., in the zero equilibrium state neighborhood) dynamics of the boundary value problem (11) and (12) are studied in Section 2.

Then, we consider the case of so-called diffusional coupling, where

$$a_1 = a_{-1} = \gamma \text{ and } a_k = 0 \text{ for } k \neq \pm 1. \tag{13}$$

Now, from systems (5) and (7), we arrive at the boundary value problem

$$\begin{aligned} \frac{\partial u}{\partial t} = &-ru(t-T,x) + r\gamma\big[u(t-h,x+\varepsilon) - 2u(t-h,x) + u(t-h,x-\varepsilon)\big] - \\ &ru(t-T,x)u(t,x) + r\delta\gamma\big[u(t-h,x+\varepsilon) - \\ &2u(t-h,x) + u(t-h,x-\varepsilon)\big]u(t,x), \quad u(t,x+2\pi) \equiv u(t,x). \end{aligned} \tag{14}$$

If the coefficients a_k $(k \neq \pm 1)$ do not differ much from zero, the dynamic behavior of (14) could change significantly. Thus, we examine a more general (compared to (14)) boundary value problem

$$\begin{aligned} \frac{\partial u}{\partial t} = &-ru(t-T,x) - ru(t-T,x)u(t,x) + \\ &r\gamma\Big(\int_{-\infty}^{+\infty} \big(F_\varepsilon(s) - 2F_0(s) + F_{-\varepsilon}(s)\big)u(t-h,x+s)ds\Big) \times \\ &\big[1 + \delta u(t,x)\big], \quad u(t,x+2\pi) \equiv u(t,x). \end{aligned} \tag{15}$$

Here,

$$\begin{aligned} F_{\pm\varepsilon}(s) &= \frac{1}{\sigma\sqrt{2\pi}} \exp\Big[-(2\sigma^2)^{-1}(s \pm \varepsilon)^2\Big], \\ F_0(s) &= \frac{1}{\sigma\sqrt{2\pi}} \exp\Big[-(2\sigma^2)^{-1}s^2\Big]. \end{aligned}$$

Undoubtedly, the integral expression in (15) can be presented in the form of integrals from 0 to 2π of some function $\tilde{F}(s)$. However, the form of (15) is preferable. Firstly, the asymptotic equality

$$\int_{-\infty}^{+\infty}(F_\varepsilon(s)-2F_0(s)+F_{-\varepsilon}(s))w(x+s)ds = w(x+\varepsilon)-2w(x)+w(x-\varepsilon)+o(1)$$

holds for the fixed function $w(x)$ as $\delta\to 0$. Secondly, it is technically convenient to calculate the importance of further usage of integrals explicitly. For example,

$$\int_{-\infty}^{+\infty}F_\varepsilon(s)\exp(iks)ds = \exp\Big(ik\varepsilon-\frac{1}{2}\delta^2(\varepsilon k)^2\Big). \tag{16}$$

In Section 3, the boundary value problem (15) is examined.

According to the equalities in (13), interactions with one 'neighbor' on the right and one 'neighbor' on the left make a dominating contribution to the couplings between elements as $\varepsilon\to 0$. In the next, fourth, section, the case of coupling coefficient interactions for unidirectional couplings is studied. For $a_1=\gamma, a_j=0$ as $j\neq 1$, the resulting boundary value problem assumes the form

$$\begin{aligned}\frac{\partial u}{\partial t} &= -ru(t-T,x)-ru(t-T,x)u(t,x)+\\ &\quad r\gamma\Big(\int_{-\infty}^{+\infty}(F_\varepsilon(s)-F_0(s))u(t-h,x+s)ds\Big)\cdot\big[1+\delta u(t,x)\big],\\ &\quad u(t,x+2\pi)\equiv u(t,x).\end{aligned} \tag{17}$$

The paper is devoted to the investigation of the behavior of the solutions to the boundary value problems (11), (12); Equations (15) and (17) with initial conditions from some sufficiently small metric $C_{[-T,0]}\times W_{[0,2\pi]}$ ($T_0=\max(T_0,h)$) ε-independent zero equilibrium state neighborhood for small ε. In each of the problems, critical cases are identified in the study of the stability of the zero solution. In critical cases, the characteristic equations of the linearized-at-zero problems have infinitely many roots, with real parts tending to zero as $\varepsilon\to 0$. This is a distinctive feature of the problems under consideration. Thereby, we may speak of the infinite-dimensional critical cases implementation. The standard methods of integral manifolds (see, for example, [21–23]) and normal forms (see, for example, [24]) are not directly applicable for their study. Thus, we employ the methods developed by the author in [25–28]. Their essence lies in the construction of special first-approximation equations called quasinormal forms (QNFs), whose nonlocal dynamics determine the local structure of the initial boundary value problems' solutions. These QNFs are nonlinear boundary value problems of neutral or parabolic types with either one or two spatial variables. The solutions of these QNFs make it possible to determine the principal terms of the asymptotic representations of the considered boundary value problems' solutions.

Section 5 is a natural extension of Section 4. It studies the model of a chain with a unidirectional coupling under the condition that the coupling coefficient between elements takes sufficiently large values. It is about the boundary value problem

$$\dot{N}=r[1-N(t-T,x)]N+\gamma\Big[\int_{-\infty}^{\infty}F(s)N(t,x+s)ds-N\Big], \tag{18}$$

$$N(t,x+2\pi)\equiv N(t,x), \tag{19}$$

where $\gamma\gg 1$. We note that (18) is interpreted as a logistic delay equation with spatially distributed control. The function $F(s)$ describing spatial interactions is given by

$$F(s)=\frac{1}{\sqrt{\mu\pi}}\exp[-\mu^{-1}(s+h)^2],\quad \mu>0.$$

We demonstrate that the dynamic properties of the problem under consideration change significantly depending on the various relations between γ, μ, and h.

We present without proof two analogs of the classical Lyapunov stability theorems in the first approximation statements.

For the linearized-at-zero Equations (11), (15), (17) and (18) with periodic boundary conditions (12), the characteristic equation has the form

$$\lambda + r\exp(-\lambda) = d\Big(\int_{-\infty}^{\infty} F(s,\varepsilon)\exp(iks)ds - 1\Big), \quad k = 0, \pm 1, \pm 2, \dots . \tag{20}$$

Statement 1. *Let the roots of Equation (20) have a negative real part and be separated from the imaginary axis as $\varepsilon \to 0$. Then, an $\varepsilon_0 > 0$ can be found such that, for $\varepsilon \in (0, \varepsilon_0)$, the solutions to the problem under consideration from the sufficiently small ε-independent zero equilibrium state neighborhood tend to zero as $t \to \infty$.*

Statement 2. *Let Equation (20) have a root with a positive real part separated from zero as $\varepsilon \to 0$. Then, the zero equilibrium state of the boundary value problem is unstable for small ε, and there is no attractor of this boundary value problem in some sufficiently small ε-independent zero neighborhood.*

Thus, in the posed problem about local conditions in the zero equilibrium state neighborhood, the dynamics are trivial under the condition of Statement 1, and it cannot be studied by local analysis methods under the condition of Statement 2.

2. Dynamics of Fully Connected Spatially Distributed Chain

In this section, the local dynamics of the boundary value problem (11), (12) are studied. The linearized at zero boundary value problem

$$\begin{gathered}\frac{\partial v}{\partial t} = -rv(t-T,x) + r\gamma\big[M\big(v(t-h,s) - v(t-h,x)\big)\big],\\ v(\tau, x+2\pi) \equiv v(\tau,x)\end{gathered} \tag{21}$$

has the characteristic equation

$$\lambda = -r\exp(-\lambda T) + r\gamma\exp(-\lambda h)[\delta_k - 1], \quad k = 0, \pm 1, \pm 2, \dots, \tag{22}$$

where

$$\delta_k = \begin{cases} 1, & k = 0, \\ 0, & k \neq 0. \end{cases}$$

We obtain this equation from (21) by substituting the elementary Euler solutions $v_k = \exp(ikx + \lambda t)$ $(k = 0, \pm 1, \pm 2, \dots)$.

The case of the small parameter γ is studied in Section 2.1. We fix some γ_1 in such a way that

$$\gamma = \mu\gamma_1 \text{ and } 0 < \mu \ll 1. \tag{23}$$

The general case is studied in Section 2.2.

2.1. Case of Small γ Values

Under the conditions $rT < \pi/2$ and (23), the roots of Equation (22) have separated from zero negative real parts as $\mu \to 0$. For $rT > \pi/2$, Equation (22) has a root with a positive real part separated from zero as $\mu \to 0$. The local dynamics of (11), (12) are not considered in these cases.

We assume that the conditions

$$r_0 T_0 = \frac{\pi}{2}, \quad r = r_0 + \mu r_1, \quad T = T_0 + \mu T_1, \quad \gamma = \mu\gamma_1 \tag{24}$$

hold for some positive r_0 and T_0. In this case, $v_k = \exp(i\pi(2T_0)^{-1}t + ikx)$ is the solution of the linear boundary value problem (21) as well as

$$v(t,x) = \sum_{k=-\infty}^{+\infty} \xi_k \exp\left(i\pi(2T_0)^{-1}t + ikx\right) = \exp\left(i\pi(2T_0)^{-1}t\right) \sum_{k=-\infty}^{+\infty} \xi_k \exp(ikx) = \exp\left(i\pi(2T_0)^{-1}t\right)\xi(x). \tag{25}$$

Then, we seek the solution to the nonlinear boundary value problem (11), (12) in the form

$$u(t,x,\mu) = \mu^{1/2}\Big(\xi(\tau,x)\exp\left(i\pi(2T_0)^{-1}t\right) + \overline{cc}\Big) + \mu u_2(t,\tau,x) + \mu^{3/2}u_3(t,\tau,x) + \ldots, \tag{26}$$

where $\tau = \mu t$ is the 'slow' time, $\xi(\tau,x)$ is the unknown complex amplitude, the functions $u_j(t,\tau,x)$ are $4T_0$-periodic with respect to t and 2π-periodic with respect to x. Here, $\overline{cc}$ means the complex conjugate to the previous term expression.

We insert the formal expression (26) into (11) and collect the coefficients at the same powers of μ. At the first step, we equate the coefficients of $\mu^{1/2}$ and obtain an identity. Then, we collect the coefficients at the first power of μ and obtain the equation for u_2

$$\dot{u}_2 = -ru_2(t-T,x) - r\Big[\xi\exp\Big(-i\frac{\pi}{2} + i\frac{\pi}{2T_0}t\Big) + \bar{\xi}\exp\Big(i\frac{\pi}{2} - i\frac{\pi}{2T_0}t\Big)\Big]\cdot\Big(\xi\exp\Big(i\frac{\pi}{2T_0}t\Big) + \xi\Big).$$

Hence,

$$u_2 = A\xi^2\exp(i\pi(T_0)^{-1}t) + \overline{cc}, \quad A = -\exp(-ir_0)\left(2(i + \exp(-2iT_0))\right)^{-1}.$$

At the third step, we obtain the equation for determining u_3, the solvability condition of which in the indicated class of functions is formulated as

$$\begin{aligned}\frac{\partial\xi}{\partial\tau} &= b\xi + \gamma_0(M(\xi) - \xi) + \beta\xi|\xi|^2,\\ \xi(\tau,x+2\pi) &\equiv \xi(\tau,x).\end{aligned} \tag{27}$$

Here, $M(\xi)$ stands for the mean value with respect to $x \in [0,2\pi]$ of the function $\xi(\tau,x)$:

$$M(\xi) = \frac{1}{2\pi}\int_0^{2\pi}\xi(\tau,x)dx.$$

The following equalities hold for the coefficients in (27):

$$\begin{aligned} b &= \Big(1 + \frac{\pi^2}{4}\Big)^{-1}\Big[\Big(\frac{\pi}{2} + i\Big)r_1 + \lambda_0^2 T_1\Big(1 - i\frac{\pi}{2}\Big)\Big],\\ \gamma_0 &= \gamma_1 r_0\exp\left(-i\pi h(2T_0)^{-1}\right)\cdot\left[i\pi(2T_0)^{-1} - r_0\exp\left(-i\pi(2T_0)^{-1}\right)\right]^{-1},\\ \beta &= -\lambda_0[3\pi - 2 + i(\pi+6)]\Big(10\Big(1 + \frac{4}{\pi^2}\Big)\Big)^{-1}, \quad \Re\beta < 0. \end{aligned}$$

In the considered case, the next statement indicates the boundary value problem (27) to be the QNF for the boundary value problem (11), (12).

Theorem 1. *Let the conditions (23) and (24) be satisfied, and let the boundary value problem (27) have the solution $\xi(\tau,x)$ for $\tau \geq \tau_0$. Then, the function*

$$u(t,x,\mu) = \mu^{1/2}\Big(\xi(\tau,x)\exp\left(i\pi(2T_0)^{-1}t\right) + \overline{cc}\Big) + \mu\left(A\xi^2(\tau,x)\exp(i\pi(T_0)^{-1}t) + \overline{cc}\right)$$

satisfies the boundary value problem (11), (12) up to $O(\mu^{3/2})$.

We note that the conditions of zero solution in (27) asymptotic stability consist in the fulfillment of the inequalities

$$\Re b < 0, \quad \Re(b - \gamma_0) < 0. \tag{28}$$

For $\Re b > 0$, the QNF (27) has the homogeneous cycle $\rho_0 \exp(i\omega_0 t)$, and

$$\rho_0 = \left(- \Re b \cdot (\Re\beta)^{-1}\right)^{1/2}, \quad \omega_0 = \Im b + \rho_0^2 \Im\beta.$$

The same cycle under the same condition exists in the logistic Equation (1). The cycle in Equation (1) is orbitally stable, while the orbital stability in (27) requires the following inequalities to be valid:

$$(1) \qquad \rho_0 \Re\beta - \Re\gamma_0 < 0, \tag{29}$$

$$(2) \qquad |\gamma_0|^2 - 2\rho_0^2 (\Re\beta \cdot \Re\gamma_0 + \Im\beta \cdot \Im\gamma_0) > 0. \tag{30}$$

A value of γ_0 can be selected such that either (29) or (30) does not hold. We note that stability (instability) condition fulfillment can be achieved by delay coefficient h variation.

In addition to one cycle, the QNF (27) can have the cycles

$$\rho_k \exp(i\omega_k t + ikx) \quad (k = 0, \pm 1, \pm 2, \dots).$$

These cycles exist under the condition $\Re(b - \gamma_0) > 0$ and

$$\rho_k = \rho^0 = \left(- \Re(b - \gamma_0) \cdot (\Re\beta)^{-1}\right)^{1/2}, \quad \omega_k = \omega^0 = \Im(b - \gamma_0) + \rho_k^2 \Im\beta. \tag{31}$$

The above cycles are orbitally stable if the inequalities

(1) $(\rho^0)^2 \Re\beta + \Re\gamma_0 < 0,$

(2) $|\gamma_0|^2 + 2(\rho^0)^2 (\Re\beta \cdot \Re\gamma_0 + \Im\beta \cdot \Im\gamma_0) > 0$

hold. Strict unfulfillment of at least one of these inequalities implies instability of all cycles.

The problem of the spatially inhomogeneous step-like cycle's existence is more intriguing.

At the first instance, we note that Equation (27) is periodic with respect to t and 2π-periodic piecewise continuous with respect to x solution

$$\rho(x)\exp(i\omega^0 t), \quad \rho(x) = \begin{cases} \rho^0, & x \in (0, \pi), \\ -\rho^0, & x \in (\pi, 2\pi). \end{cases}$$

One can construct families of $2\pi\omega_0^{-1}$-periodic with respect to t and 2π-periodic piecewise continuous with respect to x solutions $\rho(x, k_1, k_2, \alpha)\exp(i\omega_0 t)$, where

$$\rho(x, k_1, k_2, \alpha) = \begin{cases} \rho^0 \exp(i2\pi\alpha^{-1} k_1 x), & x \in (0, \alpha), \quad k_1 = \pm 1, \pm 2, \dots, \\ \rho^0 \exp(i2\pi(2\pi - \alpha)^{-1} k_2 x), & x \in (\alpha, 2\pi - \alpha), \quad k_2 = \pm 1, \pm 2, \dots. \end{cases}$$

Obviously, constructions of this kind extend to solutions with an arbitrary number of 'steps'.

What is more intriguing, these are the cycles consisting of two different steps with respect to 'amplitude' on the interval $[0, 2\pi]$. To construct them, we arbitrarily fix the parameters $\alpha \in (0, 2\pi)$ and $\varphi_{1,2} \in (0, 2\pi)$. We assume

$$u_0(t, x) = \rho(x)\exp(i\omega t), \quad \rho(x) = \begin{cases} \rho_1 \exp(i\varphi_1), & x \in (0, \alpha), \\ \rho_2 \exp(i\varphi_2), & x \in (\alpha, 2\pi). \end{cases} \tag{32}$$

Let $\varphi = \varphi_2 - \varphi_1$. We insert (32) into (26). Then, we obtain the system of polynomial equations

$$i\omega\rho_j = (b - \gamma_0)\rho_j + \gamma_0 P + \beta\rho_j^3, \quad (j = 1, 2). \tag{33}$$

Here, $P = (2\pi)^{-1}\gamma_0\big(\alpha\rho_1 + (1-\alpha)\rho_2\exp(i\varphi)\big)$.

The system (33) represents two complex or four real equations of five real variables $\rho_1, \rho_2, \alpha, \varphi$ and ω. We proceed with the real-valued notation of this system:

$$\rho_1 = \Re(b-\gamma_0)\rho_1 + \rho_1^3\Re\beta + \Re\gamma_0 P, \tag{34}$$

$$\omega\rho_1 = \Im(b-\gamma_0)\rho_1 + \rho_1^3\Im\beta + \Im\gamma_0 P, \tag{35}$$

$$\rho_2 = \Re(b-\gamma_0)\rho_2 + \rho_2^3\Re\beta + \Re\big(\gamma_0\exp(-i\varphi)P\big), \tag{36}$$

$$\omega\rho_2 = \Im(b-\gamma_0)\rho_2 + \rho_2^3\Im\beta + \Im\big(\gamma_0\exp(-i\varphi)P\big), \tag{37}$$

First, we provide the expressions for $\rho_{1,2}^3$ from (34) and (36):

$$\begin{aligned}\rho_1^3 &= \big[\big(1-\Re(b-\gamma_0)\big)\rho_1 - \Re(\gamma_0 P)\big](\Re\beta)^{-1},\\ \rho_2^3 &= \big[\big(1-\Re(b-\gamma_0)\big)\rho_2 - \Re(\gamma_0\exp(-i\varphi)P)\big](\Re\beta)^{-1}.\end{aligned}$$

Then, we substitute them into (35) and (37) instead of $\rho_{1,2}^3$, respectively. As a result, we obtain the linear system with the 2×2 matrix B of the form

$$B\begin{pmatrix}\rho_1\\ \rho_2\end{pmatrix} = \omega\begin{pmatrix}\rho_1\\ \rho_2\end{pmatrix}.$$

If the real positive eigenvalue $\omega = \omega(\alpha,\varphi)$ of this matrix can be determined, we obtain the eigenvector $\rho_2 = c(\alpha,\varphi)\rho_1$. Taking this equality into consideration in (34) and (36), we obtain the expressions for $\rho_j = \rho_j(\alpha,\varphi)$ $(j = 1, 2)$. Finally, another variable is eliminated via the equality

$$c(\alpha,\varphi) = \rho_2(\alpha,\varphi)\big(\rho_1(\alpha,\varphi)\big)^{-1}.$$

Numerical investigations are carried out in this way.

2.2. Case of Parameter γ 'Middle' Values

We restrict ourselves to considering the boundary value problem (11), (12) in the case when the parameters h and T coincide, namely $h = T$, which is interesting for mathematical ecology problems. Then, the characteristic Equation (22) splits into two:

(1) $\lambda = -r\exp(-\lambda T)$,
(2) $\lambda = -r(1+\gamma)\exp(-\lambda T)$.

Moreover, each root of the last equation is repeated infinitely many times. Let the inequality $rT < \pi/2$ hold. Thus, the size of each isolated population does not oscillate in the positive equilibrium state neighborhood. We assume that the problem of the stationery stability in (11), (12) has a critical case: the relations

$$r_0(1+\gamma_0)T_0 = \frac{\pi}{2} \tag{38}$$

hold for some $r = r_0, \gamma = \gamma_0$ and $T = T_0$. From here, the linear boundary value problem (21) has infinitely many periodical solutions $u_k(t,x) = \exp(ikx + i\omega_0 t)$, $k = 1, 2, \ldots$, $\omega_0 = \pi(2T_0)^{-1} = r_0(1+\gamma_0)$. This implies that under the condition $M(\xi(x)) = 0$, the function $u_0(t,x) = \xi(x)\exp(i\omega_0 t)$ is also a solution of (21). We introduce a small parameter $\mu : 0 < \mu \ll 1$. Let

$$r = r_0 + \mu r, \quad \gamma = \gamma_0 + \mu\gamma, \quad T = T_0 + \mu T_1$$

in (11), (12). We seek solutions to this boundary value problem in the form of formal asymptotic series

$$u(t,x,\mu) = \mu^{1/2}\Big(\xi(\tau,x)\exp\left(i\omega_0 t\right) + \overline{cc}\Big) + \mu u_2(t,\tau,x) + \mu^{3/2}u_2(t,\tau,x) + \ldots, \quad (39)$$

where $\tau = \mu t$, $\xi(\tau,x)$ is the unknown amplitude, and the functions $u_j(t,\tau,x)$ are $2\pi/\omega_0$-periodic with respect to t and 2π-periodic with respect to x. The key condition is that the function $\xi(\tau,x)$ has a zero mean with respect to the spatial variable:

$$M(\xi(\tau,s)) = 0. \quad (40)$$

We insert (39) into (11). First, we perform standard actions to obtain the equation for u_2:

$$\begin{aligned}\frac{\partial u_2}{\partial t} &= -r_0 u_2(t-T,x) + r_0\gamma_0\Big[M\big(u_2(t-T,s)\big) - u_2(t-T,x)\Big] - \\ &\quad r_0(1+\delta\gamma_0)\xi^2(\tau,x)\exp(-i\omega_0 T_0 + 2i\omega_0 t) + \overline{cc}.\end{aligned} \quad (41)$$

We seek the solution of (41) in the form

$$u_2(t,\tau,x) = u_{20}(t,\tau)\exp(2i\omega_0 t) + \overline{cc} + u_{21}(t,\tau,x)\exp(2i\omega_0 t) + \overline{cc}$$

and $M(u_{21}(t,\tau,s)) = 0$. Then,

$$\begin{aligned}u_{20}(t,\tau) &= C_1 M(\xi^2(\tau,s)),\\ u_{21}(t,\tau,x) &= C_2\big(\xi^2(\tau,x) - M(\xi^2(\tau,s))\big),\\ C_1 &= -\big(2i\omega_0 + r_0\exp(-i\omega_0 T_0)\big)^{-1} r_0(1+\delta\gamma_0)\exp(-i\omega_0 T_0),\\ C_2 &= -\big(2i\omega_0 + r_0(1+\gamma_0)\exp(-i\omega_0 T_0)\big)^{-1} r_0(1+\delta\gamma_0)\exp(-i\omega_0 T_0).\end{aligned}$$

At the next step, we collect the coefficients at $\mu^{3/2}$ in the formal identity and obtain the equation for u_3 in the form

$$\begin{aligned}\frac{\partial u_3}{\partial t} &= -r_0 u_3(t-T,x) + r_0\gamma_0\Big[M\big(u_3(t-T,s)\big) - u_3(t-T,x)\Big] + \\ &\quad D_1(\tau,x)\exp(i\omega_0 t) + \overline{cc} + D_3(\tau,x)\exp(3i\omega_0 t) + \overline{cc}.\end{aligned}$$

The $D_3(\tau,x)$-independent in the indicated class of functions solvability condition of this equation is the validity of the equality

$$D_1(\tau,x) - M(D_1(\tau,x)) = 0.$$

We take into account the explicit form of $D_1(\tau,x)$ and obtain from this equality the boundary value problem as the QNF to find $\xi(\tau,x)$:

$$\frac{\partial\xi}{\partial\tau} = b_1\xi + \beta_1\xi|\xi^2| + \beta_2\bar{\xi}M(\xi^2), \quad (42)$$

$$\xi(\tau,x+2\pi) \equiv \xi(\tau,x), \quad M(\xi(\tau,s)) = 0. \quad (43)$$

The formulas

$$\begin{aligned} b_1 &= \left(1+\frac{\pi^2}{4}\right)^{-1}\left[\left(\frac{\pi}{2}+i\right)(r_1(1+\gamma_0)+\gamma_1 r_0)+r_0^2(1+\gamma_0^2)T_1\left(1-i\frac{\pi}{2}\right)\right],\\ \beta_1 &= -r(1+\delta\gamma_0)\big(\exp(-2i\omega_0 T_0)+\exp(i\omega_0 T_0)\big)C_2\left(1+i\frac{\pi}{2}\right)^{-1},\\ \beta_2 &= -r\Big[(1+\delta\gamma_0)\big(\exp(-2i\omega_0 T_0)+\exp(i\omega_0 T_0)\big)(C_1-C_2)+\\ &\quad \delta\gamma_0\exp(-2i\omega_0 T_0)C_1\Big]\left(1+i\frac{\pi}{2}\right)^{-1} \end{aligned}$$

hold for the coefficients in (42).

Let us sum things up.

Theorem 2. *Let condition (38) be satisfied, and the boundary value problem (42), (43) has the bounded solution $\xi(\tau,x)$ as $\tau\to\infty$. Then, the function*

$$u(t,x,\mu)=\mu^{1/2}\Big(\xi(\tau,x)\exp\left(i\omega_0 t\right)+\overline{cc}\Big)+\mu u_2(t,\tau,x)$$

satisfies the boundary value problem (11), (12) up to $O(\mu^{3/2})$.

Periodic with respect to t and 2π-periodic piecewise continuous with respect to x solutions to the boundary value problem (11), (12) could also be determined in explicit form. However, it is not considered in this paper. We only refer to the paper [29]. In a similar situation, families of step-like solutions to the QNF are constructed, its stability is studied, and a comparison with experimental data is performed.

3. Chain Dynamics in Case of Diffusional Couplings

The boundary value problem (15) is examined. Let $\delta=0$ for definiteness. Then, the linearized on the zero equilibrium state boundary value problem has the form

$$\frac{\partial u}{\partial t}=-ru(t-T,x)+r\gamma\int_{-\infty}^{+\infty}F(s,\varepsilon)u(t-h,x+s)ds, \tag{44}$$

$$u(t,x+2\pi)\equiv u(t,x). \tag{45}$$

Here, we assume that function $F(s,\varepsilon)$ is given by

$$F(s,\varepsilon)=F_\varepsilon(s)-2F_0(s)+F_{-\varepsilon}(s). \tag{46}$$

Depending on the parameter σ, three fundamentally different events can be distinguished. The first and the simplest of them assumes the parameter $\sigma>0$ to be somehow fixed and, naturally, independent of the small parameter ε. This case is studied in Section 3.1. In Section 3.2, we assume that there is a value of $\sigma_0>0$ such that

$$\sigma=\varepsilon\sigma_0. \tag{47}$$

The critical case of infinite dimension mentioned above is realized under this condition. Finally, in Section 3.3, we assume the parameter σ to be even smaller: $\sigma=o(\varepsilon)$. More precisely, for some fixed $\sigma_0>0$, we consider the relation

$$\sigma=\varepsilon^2\sigma_0. \tag{48}$$

This case is the most complicated and intriguing. It naturally generalizes the case of 'purely diffusional' couplings for which $\sigma\sim 0$.

3.1. Chain Dynamics for Fixed σ Value

In Formula (46), we arbitrarily fix the value $\sigma_0 > 0$. The inequality

$$0 < r < \frac{\pi}{2} \tag{49}$$

is the necessary and sufficient condition for the real parts of all eigenvalues of the characteristic Equation (20) to be negative.

For $r = \pi/2$, Equation (20) has exactly two pure imaginary roots $\lambda_\pm = \pm i\pi/2$, and the real parts of the remaining roots are negative and separated from zero as $\varepsilon \to 0$. Thus, the conditions of the well-studied Andronov–Hopf bifurcation are satisfied. Let

$$r = \frac{\pi}{2} + \varepsilon^2 r_1 \tag{50}$$

for the arbitrarily fixed value r_1.

Then, for $\varepsilon \ll 1$, the roots $\lambda_\pm(\varepsilon)$ of Equation (20) close to $\lambda_\pm$ are as follows:

$$\begin{aligned} \lambda_+(\varepsilon) =& \overline{\lambda}_-(\varepsilon), \\ \lambda_+(\varepsilon) =& i\frac{\pi}{2} + \varepsilon^2\lambda_{10} + O(\varepsilon^4), \\ \text{where } \lambda_{10} =& (1 + \frac{\pi^2}{4})^{-1}(\frac{\pi}{2} + i)r_1. \end{aligned} \tag{51}$$

Under these conditions and for sufficiently small ε, the boundary value problem (15) has a two-dimensional stable local integral invariant manifold $\mathcal{M}(\varepsilon)$ in the zero equilibrium state neighborhood, on which this boundary value problem can be written as a special scalar complex ordinary differential equation

$$\frac{d\xi}{d\tau} = \lambda_{10}\xi + g\xi|\xi|^2, \tag{52}$$

where $\tau = \varepsilon^2 t$ is a slow time, and $\xi(\tau)$ is a slowly varying amplitude in the asymptotic presentations of solutions on the manifold $\mathcal{M}(\varepsilon)$

$$u = \varepsilon\Big[\xi(\tau)\exp\Big(i\frac{\pi}{2}t\Big) + \bar{\xi}(\tau)\exp\Big(-i\frac{\pi}{2}t\Big)\Big] + \varepsilon^2 u_2(t,\tau) + \varepsilon^3 u_3(t,\tau) + \dots . \tag{53}$$

Here, the functions $u_j(t,\tau)$ are 4-periodic with respect to t. We insert the formal expression (53) into (15) and collect the coefficients at the same powers of ε. First, we equate the coefficients at ε^2 to obtain

$$u_2 = \frac{2-i}{5}\xi^2\exp(i\pi t) + \frac{2+i}{5}\bar{\xi}^2\exp(-i\pi t). \tag{54}$$

At the next step, from the solvability condition of the resulting equation with respect to u_3, we obtain the necessity of satisfying the relation (52), where

$$g = -\frac{\pi}{2}\Big[3\pi - 2 + i(\pi + 6)\Big] \cdot \Big(10\Big(1 + \frac{4}{\pi^2}\Big)\Big)^{-1}. \tag{55}$$

Let us formulate the resulting statements. Their proofs are well-known (see, for example, [19]).

Theorem 3. *Let $r_1 < 0$. Then, for all sufficiently small ε, the solution of the boundary value problem (15) from some sufficiently small ε-independent equilibrium state $u_0 = 0$ neighborhood tends to zero as $t \to \infty$.*

Theorem 4. *Let $r_1 > 0$. Then, all the solutions of Equation (52) except the zero solution tend to an orbitally stable cycle*

$$\begin{aligned}\xi_0(\tau) =& \Big[10\frac{\pi}{2}r_1(3\pi-2)^{-1}\Big]^{\frac{1}{2}}\xi_0\exp(i\phi_0\tau),\\ \phi_0 =& \Im\lambda_{10}+\xi_0^2\Im g,\end{aligned} \tag{56}$$

and the solutions ($\not\equiv 1$) from $\mathcal{M}(\varepsilon)$ tend to cycle

$$u_0(t,\varepsilon) = \varepsilon\Big[\xi_0(\varepsilon^2 t)\exp\Big(i\frac{\pi}{2}t\Big) + \bar{\xi}_0(\varepsilon^2 t)\exp\Big(-i\frac{\pi}{2}t\Big)\Big] + O(\varepsilon^2) \tag{57}$$

as $t \to \infty$.

Thus, in the considered case, the boundary value problem (15) can have only a homogeneous cycle $1 + u_0(t,\varepsilon)$ in a zero neighborhood, which is a logistic Equation (1) under the condition (50). Apparently, the case considered here is of no interest.

3.2. Chain Dynamics for σ Values of ε Order

Here, we assume that the condition (47) holds. Then, the characteristic Equation (20) has the set of roots $\lambda_m(\varepsilon)$ and $\overline{\lambda}_m(\varepsilon)$ $(m = 0, \pm 1, \pm 2, \ldots)$, the real parts of which tend to zero as $\varepsilon \to \infty$. The representation

$$\begin{aligned}\lambda_m(\varepsilon) + \Big(\frac{\pi}{2} + \varepsilon^2 r_1\Big)\exp(-\lambda_m(\varepsilon)) =& d\Bigg(\int_{-\infty}^{\infty} F(s,\varepsilon)\exp(ims)ds - 1\Bigg) = \\ & d(\cos(\varepsilon m)\exp(-\varepsilon^2 m^2\sigma_0^2) - 1).\end{aligned} \tag{58}$$

holds for these roots.

From here, we obtain that the asymptotic equality

$$\lambda_m(\varepsilon) = i\frac{\pi}{2} + \varepsilon^2\lambda_1 + \ldots, \quad \lambda_1 = \lambda_{10} - \Big(1 + i\frac{\pi}{2}\Big)^{-1} d\Big(\frac{1}{2} + \sigma_0^2\Big)m^2$$

holds for each integer m.

Each of the above roots corresponds to the solution $v_m(t,x)$ of the boundary value problem (44), (45) for which

$$v_m(t,x) = \exp(i\frac{\pi}{2}t + imx)\nu_m(\tau),$$

where $\nu_m(\tau) = \nu_m\exp((-\varepsilon^2\lambda_1 + O(\varepsilon^4))t)$.

Let us introduce the formal series

$$\begin{aligned}u(t,x,\varepsilon) =& \varepsilon\Big[\exp\Big(i\frac{\pi}{2}t\Big)\sum_{m=-\infty}^{\infty}\xi_m(\tau)\exp(imx) + \\ & \exp\Big(-i\frac{\pi}{2}t\Big)\sum_{m=-\infty}^{\infty}\bar{\xi}_m(\tau)\exp(-imx)\Big] + \\ & \varepsilon^2 u_2(t,\tau,x) + \varepsilon^3 u_3(t,\tau,x) + \ldots.\end{aligned} \tag{59}$$

Here, $\tau = \varepsilon^2 t$ is a slow time, $\xi_m(\tau)$ are the unknown slowly varying amplitudes, and the functions $u_j(t,\tau,x)$ are periodic with respect to t and x. We note that Formula (59) defines a solution set of the linear boundary value problem (44), (45) in the linear approximation, i.e., for $u_j \equiv 0$.

Expression (59) can be significantly simplified. For this purpose, we assume

$$\xi(\tau, x) = \sum_{m=-\infty}^{\infty} \xi_m(\tau) \exp(imx).$$

Then, it follows from (59) that

$$u(t,x,\varepsilon) = \varepsilon\Big[\xi(\tau,x)\exp\Big(i\frac{\pi}{2}t\Big) + \bar{\xi}(\tau,x)\exp\Big(-i\frac{\pi}{2}t\Big)\Big] + \varepsilon^2 u_2(t,\tau,x) + \varepsilon^3 u_3(t,\tau,x) + \dots . \tag{60}$$

We insert (60) into (15) and equate the coefficients of the same powers of ε in the resulting formal identity. At the first step, the identity holds for ε^1. At the second step, we collect the coefficients at ε^2 and obtain the equality (54), where $\xi = \xi(\tau, x)$. At the next step, we obtain the boundary value problem for determining $\xi(\tau, x)$ from the solvability condition of the resulting equation with respect to u_3:

$$\frac{\partial \xi}{\partial \tau} = d_0 \frac{\partial^2 \xi}{\partial x^2} + \lambda_{10}\xi + g\xi|\xi|^2, \qquad \xi(t, x + 2\pi) \equiv \xi(\tau, x). \tag{61}$$

Here, $d_0 = (1 + i\pi/2)^{-1}(1/2 + \sigma_0^2)$ and the coefficients λ_{10} and g are the same as in (51) and (55), respectively.

We formulate the basic results.

Theorem 5. *Let the boundary value problem (61) have the bounded solution $\xi_0(\tau, x)$ as $\tau \to \infty$. Then, the function*

$$u_0(t,x,\varepsilon) = \varepsilon\Big[\xi_0(\tau,x)\exp\Big(i\frac{\pi}{2}t\Big) + \bar{\xi}_0(\tau,x)\exp\Big(-i\frac{\pi}{2}t\Big)\Big] + \varepsilon^2\frac{2-i}{5}\xi^2\exp(i\pi t) + \frac{2+i}{5}\bar{\xi}^2\exp(-i\pi t)$$

satisfies the boundary value problem (15) up to $O(\varepsilon^4)$.

The problem of the existence and stability of an exact solution to (15), which is close to the corresponding solution of the boundary value problem (61) as $\varepsilon \to 0$, arises. It can be solved, for example, if $\xi_0(\tau, x)$ is a periodic solution with the property of coarseness. By coarseness, we mean the following: If $\xi_0(\tau, x) \equiv const \cdot \exp(i\omega\tau + imx)$, then only one multiplier of the linearized on $\xi_0(\tau, x)$ boundary value problem is equal to Modulo 1. In other cases, the coarseness condition is that only two multipliers of the linearized on $\xi_0(\tau, x)$ boundary value problem are equal to Modulo 1.

Theorem 6. *Let $\xi_0(\tau, x)$ be the coarse periodic solution of the boundary value problem (61) with period ω_0. Then, for all sufficiently small ε, the boundary value problem (15) has the periodic with respect to t solution $u_0(t, x, \varepsilon)$ with period $\omega_0 + O(\varepsilon)$ with the same stability as $\xi_0(\tau, x)$. The asymptotic equality*

$$u_0(t,x,\varepsilon) = \varepsilon(\xi_0((1+O(\varepsilon))\varepsilon^2 t, x)\exp\Big(i\frac{\pi}{2}t\Big) + \bar{\xi}_0((1+O(\varepsilon))\varepsilon^2 t, x)\exp\Big(-i\frac{\pi}{2}t\Big) + \ldots + O(\varepsilon^4). \tag{62}$$

holds for this solution.

The proof of Theorem 5 follows directly from the above construction of the boundary value problem (15) solution asymptotics. The justification of Theorem 6 is standard but cumbersome, so we omit it.

3.3. Chain Dynamics for $\sigma = O(\varepsilon^2)$

Here, we assume that the condition (48) holds. We distinguish the roots of the characteristic Equation (20) with real parts tending to zero as $\varepsilon \to 0$. This equation's roots $\lambda = \lambda(k)$ are calculated from the formula

$$\lambda + (r_0 + \varepsilon^2 r_1)\exp(-\lambda) = d\Big(\int_{-\infty}^{\infty} F(s,\varepsilon)\exp(iks)ds - 1\Big) = d(\cos(z)\exp(-\varepsilon^4\sigma_0^2 z^2) - 1), \tag{63}$$

where $z = \varepsilon k$. The vanishing of the right-hand side in (63) up to $O(1)$ (as $\varepsilon \to 0$) is responsible for the real parts of the roots tending to zero. Those numbers $k = k(\varepsilon)$ satisfy this condition for which $\cos(z) \sim 1$. We introduce the notation to describe such numbers. We fix an arbitrary integer n and let $\theta_n = \theta_n(\varepsilon) \in [0,1)$ be the expression that complements the value $2\pi n\varepsilon^{-1}$ to an integer. It appears that the function $\theta_n(\varepsilon)$ can be considered identically zero. The point is that the parameter ε introduced above is determined as $\varepsilon = 2\pi(1+2N)^{-1}$. Therefore, $2\pi n\varepsilon^{-1} = n(1+2N)$, which is an integer.

Then, the set of numbers $k(\varepsilon)$ of the roots $\lambda(k(\varepsilon))$ consists of the values

$$k(\varepsilon) = 2\pi n\varepsilon^{-1} + m, \quad m, n = 0, \pm 1, \pm 2, \ldots \tag{64}$$

in the considered case.

It is convenient to denote these roots by $\lambda_{m,n}(\varepsilon)$. We obtain the asymptotic expression

$$\lambda_{m,n}(\varepsilon) = i\frac{\pi}{2} - \varepsilon^2\Big(1 + i\frac{\pi}{2}\Big)^{-1}(m^2 + 4\pi^2\sigma_0^2 n^2) + O(\varepsilon^4)$$

for them.

We follow the algorithm investigated above and introduce the formal series

$$u = \varepsilon\Big[\exp\Big(i\frac{\pi}{2}t\Big)\sum_{m=-\infty}^{\infty}\sum_{n=-\infty}^{\infty}\xi_{m,n}(\tau)\exp(i(2\pi n\varepsilon^{-1} + m)x) + \varepsilon\Big(-i\frac{\pi}{2}t\Big)\sum_{m=-\infty}^{\infty}\sum_{n=-\infty}^{\infty}\bar{\xi}_{m,n}(\tau)\exp(-i(2\pi n\varepsilon^{-1} + m)x)\Big] + \varepsilon^2 u_2(t,\tau,x) + \varepsilon^3 u_3(t,\tau,x) + \ldots, \tag{65}$$

where $\tau = \varepsilon^2 t$, and the functions $u_j(t,\tau,x)$ are periodic with respect to t and x.

Let $y = 2\pi\varepsilon^{-1}x$ and

$$\xi(\tau,x,y) = \sum_{m=-\infty}^{\infty}\sum_{n=-\infty}^{\infty}\xi_{m,n}(\tau)\exp(iny + imx).$$

Then, we can simplify expression (65)

$$u = \varepsilon\Big[\exp\Big(i\frac{\pi}{2}t\Big)\xi(\tau,x,y) + \exp\Big(-i\frac{\pi}{2}t\Big)\bar{\xi}(\tau,x,y)\Big] + \varepsilon^2 u_2 + \varepsilon^3 u_3 + \ldots. \tag{66}$$

We insert (66) into (15) and equate the coefficients at the same powers of ε. First, we determine $u_2(\tau,t,x)$. Then, from the solvability condition of the equation with respect to u_3, we obtain the expression for $\xi(\tau,x,y)$, determining:

$$\frac{\partial\xi}{\partial\tau} = \Big(1 + i\frac{\pi}{2}\Big)^{-1}\cdot\Big(\frac{\partial^2\xi}{\partial x^2} + 4\pi^2\sigma_0^2\frac{\partial^2\xi}{\partial y^2}\Big) + \lambda_{10}\xi + g\xi|\xi|^2, \tag{67}$$

$$\xi(\tau, x + 2\pi, y) \equiv \xi(\tau, x, y + 2\pi) \equiv \xi(\tau, x, y), \tag{68}$$

where the coefficients λ_{10} and g are the same as in (52).

Ideologically, the basic results of this subsection repeat Theorems 5 and 6. We cite an analogue of Theorem 5 as an example.

Theorem 7. *Let $\xi_0(\tau, x, y)$ be the bounded solution of the boundary value problem (67), (68) as $\tau \to \infty$. Then, the function*

$$\begin{aligned} u_0(t, x, \varepsilon) = 1 + \varepsilon\Big[&\exp\Big(i\frac{\pi}{2}t\Big)\xi_0(\varepsilon^2 t, x, 2\pi^{-1}x) + \\ &\exp\Big(-i\frac{\pi}{2}t\Big)\bar{\xi}_0(\varepsilon^2 t, x, 2\pi\varepsilon^{-1}x)\Big] + \varepsilon^2 u_2 \end{aligned} \tag{69}$$

satisfies the boundary value problem (15) up to $O(\varepsilon^3)$.

The boundary value problems (61) and (67), (68) have been numerically investigated by many authors (see, for example, [30]). It has been shown that complicated and irregular oscillations are typical for such boundary value problems, especially for (67), (68). The formulas (60) and (66), which couple these boundary value problem solutions with the boundary value problem (15) solutions, allow us to formulate the same conclusion about the solutions of (15).

4. Cooperative Dynamics in Chains with Unidirectional Coupling

We consider the boundary value problem (17) in which the equality

$$F(s, \varepsilon) = F_\varepsilon(s) - F_0(s)$$

holds for the function $F(s, \varepsilon)$. Further, relation (47) holds for the parameter σ.

We assume that the equilibrium state $u_0 = 1$ of logistic Equation (1) is asymptotically stable in the absence of couplings. Thus, the values of parameter r satisfy the inequality

$$0 < r < \frac{\pi}{2}. \tag{70}$$

Section 4.1 analyses the linearized at zero boundary value problem, and the nonlinear boundary value problem, which is the QNF, is constructed in Section 4.2.

4.1. Linear Analysis

In the considered case, the characteristic equation for the linearized on u_0 boundary value problem takes the form

$$\lambda + r\exp(-\lambda) = d(\exp(iz - \sigma_0^2 z^2) - 1), \tag{71}$$

where $d > 0$, $z = \varepsilon k$, $k = 0, \pm 1, \pm 2, \ldots$. We study the location of the roots of Equation (71) in order to make a conclusion about the stability of the equilibrium state in the boundary value problem (17).

We present several simple statements about the roots of (71) without proofs.

Lemma 1. *For $z \in [\pi(2n+1), \pi(2n+2)]$ $(n = 0, \pm 1, \pm 2, \ldots)$ Equation (71) has no roots with a zero real part as $d > 0$.*

Lemma 2. *For every $z \in (2\pi n, \pi(2n+1))$, there exists $d > 0$ such that Equation (71) has a root with a zero real part as $d = d_z$.*

We introduce the notation: $d(r) = \min\limits_{-\infty < z < \infty} d_z = d_{z(r)}$.

Then, the equilibrium state of the boundary value problem (17) is asymptotically stable as $d \in (0, d(r))$. For $d = d(r)$ and $z = z(r)$, Equation (71) has roots $\lambda_{\pm}(r)$ with zero real part: $\lambda_{\pm}(r) = \pm i\omega(r)$ $(\omega(r) > 0)$.

Lemma 3. *The inequalities*

$$0 < z(r) < \pi, \quad \frac{\pi}{2} < \omega(r) < \frac{3\pi}{2}$$

hold for the values of $\omega(r)$ and $z(r)$.

We consider the questions about the asymptotic behavior of the expressions $d(r)$, $\omega(r)$ and $z(r)$ for $r \to 0$ and for $r \to \pi/2$ separately.

First, let $r \to 0$. We denote by ω_0 the root from the interval $(\pi/2, \pi)$ of the equation $\tan\omega = -\omega^{-1}$. Let

$$c_0 = (1 + \sigma_0^2)\omega_0^2(\omega_0^2 + 4), \quad z_0 = \omega_0 c_0^{-1}.$$

Lemma 4. *The asymptotic equalities*

$$d(r) = c_0 r^{-1}(1 + o(1)), \quad \omega(r) = \omega_0 + o(1), \quad z(r) = z_0 r(1 + o(1))$$

hold as $r \to 0$.

Then, let $r = \pi/2 - \mu$ and $0 < \mu \ll 1$. Now, by $z_{00} \in (0, \pi/2)$, we denote the least root of equation $\cos z = (\pi/4 + 1)^{-1/2}$. Then, $\min z_{00} = \pi/2(\pi^2/4 + 1)^{-1/2}$. We assume

$$c_{00} = \frac{\pi}{2}\Big[\Big(\frac{\pi^2}{4} + 1\Big)^{\frac{1}{2}} \exp(-\sigma_0^2 z_{00}^2) - 1\Big], \quad (c_0 < 0),$$

$$\omega_{00} = c_{00}\frac{\pi}{2}\Big(\frac{\pi^2}{4} + 1\Big)^{-\frac{1}{2}\exp(-\sigma_0^2 z_{00}^2)} - 1.$$

Lemma 5. *For all sufficiently small μ, the asymptotic equalities*

$$\begin{aligned} d(r) &= c_{00}\mu(1 + o(1)), \\ \omega(r) &= \frac{\pi}{2} + \omega_{00}\mu(1 + o(1)), \\ z(r) &= z_{00} + o(1) \end{aligned}$$

hold.

The justifications of Lemmas (4) and (5) are quite simple but cumbersome. Therefore, we omit them.

Further, we fix the value $r_0 \in (0, \pi/2)$ and arbitrary values r_1 and d_1. Let

$$r = r_0 + \varepsilon^2 r_1, \quad d = d(r_0) + \varepsilon^2 d_1 \tag{72}$$

in (17).

Below, let $\theta = \theta(\varepsilon) \in [0, 1)$ be the expression that complements the quantity $z(r_0)\varepsilon^{-1}$ to an integer. We study the asymptotic behavior of the close to imaginary axis roots of Equation (71). We denote them by $\lambda_m(\varepsilon)$ and $\overline{\lambda}_m(\varepsilon)$ $(m = 0, \pm 1, \pm 2, \ldots)$. The equalities

$$\lambda_m(\varepsilon) = i\omega(r) + \varepsilon i R_1(\theta + m) + \varepsilon^2(R_{20} + (\theta + m)^2 R_2) + \ldots \tag{73}$$

hold, where

$$\begin{aligned} R_1 &= (1 - r_0 \exp(-i\omega(r_0)))^{-1} d(r_0) z(r_0) \times \\ &\quad (1 + 2i\sigma_0^2) \exp(-\sigma_0^2 z^2(r_0) + iz_0(r_0)), \\ R_{20} &= (1 - r_0 \exp(-i\omega(r_0)))^{-1} \times \\ &\quad [d_1(1 - \exp(-\sigma_0^2 z^2(r_0) + iz_0(r_0)) - 1) - r_1 \exp(-i\omega(r_0))], \\ R_2 &= (1 - r_0 \exp(-i\omega(r_0)))^{-1} \Big[\frac{1}{2} r_0 \exp(-i\omega(r_0)) R_1^2 + \\ &\quad d(r_0)\Big(2\sigma_0^2 z^2(r_0) - \Big(\sigma_0^2 + \frac{1}{2}\Big)\Big) \exp(-\sigma_0^2 z^2(r_0) + iz(r_0))\Big]. \end{aligned}$$

It is significant that

$$\Im R_1 = 0 \text{ and } \Re R_2 < 0. \tag{74}$$

4.2. Construction of Quasinormal Form

We introduce the formal series

$$\begin{aligned} u = &\varepsilon\Big(\exp(i\omega(r_0)t) \sum_{m=-\infty}^{\infty} \xi_m(\tau) \exp(i(z(r_0)\varepsilon^{-1} + \theta + m)x + \varepsilon i R_1(\theta + m)t) + \\ &\exp(-i\omega(r_0)t) \sum_{m=-\infty}^{\infty} \bar{\xi}_m(\tau) \exp(-i(z(r_0)\varepsilon^{-1} + \theta + m)x - \\ &\varepsilon i R_1(\theta + m)t)\Big) + \varepsilon^2 u_2(t, \tau, x, \varepsilon) + \varepsilon^3 u_3(t, \tau, x, \varepsilon) + \dots, \quad \tau = \varepsilon^2 t. \end{aligned} \tag{75}$$

The above expression can be simplified significantly. Let

$$\xi(\tau, y) = \sum_{m=-\infty}^{\infty} \xi_m(\tau) \exp(imy), \quad y = x + \varepsilon R_1 t.$$

Then, it is possible to proceed from (75) to the presentation

$$\begin{aligned} u = &\varepsilon(\exp(i(\omega(r_0) + \varepsilon R_1\theta)t + i(z(r_0)\varepsilon^{-1} + \theta)x)\xi(\tau, y) + \\ &\exp(-i(\omega(r_0) + \varepsilon R_1\theta)t - i(z(r_0)\varepsilon^{-1} + \theta)x)\bar{\xi}(\tau, y)) + \\ &\varepsilon^2 u_2(t, \tau, x, y) + \varepsilon^3 u_3(t, \tau, x, y) + \dots. \end{aligned} \tag{76}$$

The functions appearing here, $u_j(t, \tau, x, y)$, are periodic with respect to t, x, and y.

We insert (76) into (17). Then, performing standard techniques, we determine $u_2(t, \tau, x, y)$:

$$\begin{aligned} u_2(t, \tau, x, y) = &u_{20}|\xi(\tau, y)|^2 + u_{21}\xi^2(\tau, y) \exp((2i(\omega(r_0) + \varepsilon R_1\theta)t + 2i(z(r_0)\varepsilon^{-1} + \theta)x) + \\ &\bar{u}_{21}\bar{\xi}^2(\tau, y) \exp((-2i\omega(r_0) + \varepsilon R_1\theta)t - 2i(z(r_0)\varepsilon^{-1} + \theta)x), \end{aligned}$$

where

$$\begin{aligned} u_{20} &= -2\cos\omega(r_0), \\ u_{21} &= -2r\cos(2\omega(r_0))[2i\omega(r_0) + r_0 \exp(-2i\omega(r_0)) - \\ &\quad d(r_0)(exp(-2i\omega(r_0) - 4\sigma_0^2 z^2(r_0)) - 1)]^{-1}. \end{aligned}$$

At the next step, we obtain the equation for $u_3(t, \tau, x, y)$. From its solvability condition in the indicated class of functions, we arrive at the boundary value problem for $\xi(\tau, y)$, determining:

$$\frac{\partial \xi}{\partial \tau} = R_2 \frac{\partial^2 \xi}{\partial y^2} - i\theta R_2 \frac{\partial \xi}{\partial y} + (R_{20} + \theta^2 R^2)\xi + q\xi|\xi|^2, \tag{77}$$

$$\xi(\tau, y + 2\pi) \equiv \xi(\tau, y). \tag{78}$$

The equality

$$q = r_0(1 - r_0\exp(-i\omega(r_0)))^{-1}[2\cos(\omega(r_0))(1 + \exp(-i\omega(r_0)) - u_{21}(\exp(i\omega(r_0)) + \exp(-2i\omega(r_0)))].$$

holds for the coefficient q.

We introduce the notation to formulate the basic result. We arbitrarily fix the value $\theta_0 \in [0,1)$, and let $\varepsilon_n(\theta_0)$ be a sequence such that $\varepsilon_n(\theta_0) \to 0$ as $n \to \infty$, and the equality $\theta(\varepsilon_n(\theta_0)) = \theta_0$ holds for each n.

From above, we obtain the following statement.

Theorem 8. *Let, for some $\theta = \theta_0$, the boundary value problem (77), (78) have the bounded solution $\xi_0(\tau, y)$ as $\tau \to \infty$, $y \in [0, 2\pi]$. Then, under condition (47) and for $\varepsilon = \varepsilon_n(\theta_0)$, the function*

$$u_0(t,x,\varepsilon) = \varepsilon(\exp(i(\omega(r_0) + \varepsilon R_1\theta_0)t + i(z(r_0)\varepsilon^{-1} + \theta_0)x)\xi_0(\tau,y) + \exp(-i(\omega(r_0) + \varepsilon R_1\theta_0)t - i(z(r_0)\varepsilon^{-1} + \theta_0)x)\bar{\xi}_0(\tau,y)),$$

$$\tau = \varepsilon^2 t, \quad y = x + \varepsilon R_1 t$$

satisfies the boundary value problem (17) up to $O(\varepsilon^2)$.

Therefore, the boundary value problem (77), (78) is the QNF for (17).

5. Dynamics of Logistic Delay Equation with Large Coefficient of Spatially Distributed Control

In this section, we study the logistic delay equation with large coefficient of spatially distributed control of the form

$$\dot{N} = r[1 - N(t - T, x)]N + \gamma\Big[\int_{-\infty}^{\infty} F(s)N(t, x+s)ds - N\Big]. \tag{79}$$

The dependence of the functions $N(t,x)$ on the spatial variable x is assumed to be periodic:

$$N(t, x + 2\pi) \equiv N(t,x). \tag{80}$$

Thus, we fix the space $C_{[-T,0]\times[0,2\pi]}$ as a phase space of the boundary value problem (79), (80).

Function $F(s)$ describing spatial interactions is defined by

$$F(s) = \frac{1}{\sqrt{\mu\pi}}\exp[-\mu^{-1}(s+h)^2], \quad \mu > 0. \tag{81}$$

We note that $\int_{-\infty}^{\infty} F(s)ds = 1$. Apparently, study of the problem (79) and (80) is of great interest, provided that parameter μ appearing in (81) is sufficiently small:

$$0 < \mu \ll 1. \tag{82}$$

This condition arises naturally in many applied problems (see, for example, [31]). The assumption that the coefficient γ is large enough, i.e.,

$$\gamma \gg 1 \tag{83}$$

allows us to apply special asymptotic methods. In the next section, we study the local dynamics of solutions to the boundary value problem (79) and (80) under the conditions (82) and (83). The corresponding constructions are based on the results from [28]. Section 5.2 considers the local dynamics (i.e., in a small equilibrium state neighborhood) of the problem (79), (80). Critical cases are distinguished in the stability problem. The distinctive feature of these critical cases is that they have infinite dimension. As a basic result, nonlinear boundary value problems of parabolic type are constructed that do not contain small and large parameters. Their nonlocal dynamics determine the behavior of the solutions of problem (79), (80) from small equilibrium state neighborhood $N_0 = 1$. The corresponding investigation is based on the papers [26,28]. We immediately pay attention to one of the conclusions obtained in Sections 5.1 and 5.2. As it turns out, complicated bifurcation phenomena in the problem (79), (80) can appear even for sufficiently small values of the delay time T. Here, we use the results obtained in the paper [32].

5.1. Boundary Value Problem Reduction to Parabolic-Type Equation

This section is divided into three parts. The first two sections assume that the deviation h is asymptotically small, i.e., function $F(s)$ is close to symmetric. In Part 1, the parameters γ^{-1}, μ and h^2 are assumed to be of the same order. It is shown that the nonlocal dynamics of specially constructed boundary value problems of parabolic type determine, in general, the dynamic properties of problem (79), (80). The corresponding structures are called slowly oscillating since they are formed mainly on low modes. The diffusive properties of the initial equation are assumed to be small in Part 2. In terms of problem coefficients, this means the qualified smallness of parameters μ and h^2 compared to γ^{-1}. The appropriate range of their change is indicated below. In this case, we demonstrate that the rapidly oscillating (i.e., formed on asymptotically large modes) regimes are distinctive for the boundary value problem (79), (80). In order to find them, special families of nonlinear parabolic boundary value problems are constructed. In Part 3, we study the dynamics of problem (79), (80) under the condition of $F(s)$ essential dissymmetry when parameter h is not small.

Thus, we demonstrate that the boundary value problem (79), (80) dynamics essentially depend on the relations between parameters γ^{-1}, μ, and h.

5.1.1. Slowly Oscillating Structures

Let

$$\varepsilon = \gamma^{-1}, \quad 0 < \varepsilon \ll 1.$$

Here, we assume that the parameters ε, μ, and h^2 are of the same order: for some fixed, positive k and h_1, we obtain

$$\mu = k\varepsilon, \quad h = \varepsilon^{1/2} h_1. \tag{84}$$

After dividing (79) by γ, we consider the resulting 'main' part, which is the linear boundary value problem

$$\varepsilon \frac{\partial u}{\partial t} = \int_{-\infty}^{\infty} F(s) u(t, x+s) ds - u, \quad u(t, x+2\pi) \equiv u(t,x). \tag{85}$$

The characteristic equation of (85) is of the form

$$\varepsilon \lambda_m = \exp[i\varepsilon^{1/2} h_1 m - \varepsilon k m^2] - 1, \quad m = 0, \pm 1, \pm 2, \dots . \tag{86}$$

Hence, we obtain the asymptotic formulas

$$\lambda_m = i\varepsilon^{-1/2} h_1 m - \Big(k + \frac{1}{2} h_1^2\Big) m^2 + O(\varepsilon^{1/2}) \tag{87}$$

for the roots $\lambda_m = \lambda_m(\varepsilon)$. Thus, infinitely many roots of Equation (86) tend to the imaginary axis as $\varepsilon \to 0$. This gives us reason to regard the considered critical case in the stability problem to be infinite-dimensional. The methodology of studying such systems is developed in [26,28]. We use the appropriate results here. For this purpose, we introduce the formal series

$$u = \sum_{m=-\infty}^{\infty} \xi_m(t) \exp(imy) + \varepsilon u_1(t, y) + \dots , \tag{88}$$

where $y = x + \varepsilon^{1/2}h_1 t$. We insert (88) into (79) and equate the coefficients at the same power of ε. We obtain the infinite system of ordinary differential equations to determine the function $\xi_m(t)$. As it turns out, this system can be written as one complex parabolic equation of the Ginzburg–Landau type for the function

$$\xi(t,y) = \sum_{m=-\infty}^{\infty} \xi_m(t)\exp(imy)$$

$$\frac{\partial \xi}{\partial t} = \left(k + \frac{1}{2}h_1^2\right)\frac{\partial^2 \xi}{\partial y^2} + r[1 - \xi(t-T, y-\Delta)]\xi, \tag{89}$$

$$\xi(t, y+2\pi) \equiv \xi(t,y), \tag{90}$$

where $\Delta = \Delta(\varepsilon) = (\varepsilon^{-1/2}h_1 T)_{\text{ mod } 2\pi}$.

Theorem 9. *Let, for some fixed $\Delta = \Delta_0 \in [0, 2\pi]$, the boundary value problem (89), (90) be bounded together with the time derivative solution $\xi_0(t,y)$ as $t \to \infty$. Then, as determined from the equality $\Delta(\varepsilon) = \Delta_0$, for the sufficiently small ε_n, the function*

$$N(t, x, \varepsilon_n) = \xi_0(t, x + \varepsilon_n^{-1/2}h_1 t)$$

satisfies the boundary value problem (79), (80) up to $O(\varepsilon_n^{1/2})$.

Theorem 10. *On conditions of Theorem 9, let $\xi_0(t,y)$ be a periodic solution of the problem (89), (90), and let only two of its multipliers be equal to Modulo 1. Then, for all sufficiently small ε_n, the boundary value problem (79), (80) has a periodic solution $N_0(t,x,\varepsilon)$ of the same stability as $\xi_0(t,y)$, and*

$$N_0(t,x,\varepsilon) = \xi_0((1 + o(\varepsilon_n^{1/2}))t, x + \varepsilon_n^{-1/2}h_1 t) + O(\varepsilon^{1/2}).$$

5.1.2. Rapidly Oscillating Structures

Here, we demonstrate that the decrease of diffusion coefficients (k and h_1) can lead to the appearance of rapid oscillation with respect to spatial and time variable families of structures. Conditionally, we can divide them into two types. Proportional decrease of coefficients k and h_1, which play the role of diffusion, leads to the appearance of the first type. The structures are formed in the neighborhood of asymptotic large modes. However, the product of diffusion coefficients and the (asymptotically large) value of the corresponding modes is of an asymptotically small quantity. In other words, the squares of the corresponding modes coincide in order with the reciprocal of deviation of spatial variables. The second type of structures arises only when one diffusion coefficient, k, decreases. Here also, rapidly oscillating structures are formed due to the interaction of a large number of modes far apart from each other. However, the principal difference from structures of the first type is that the values of modes themselves coincide in order with the reciprocal of the deviation of the spatial variable but not the values of the squares of the modes. Let us consider these cases separately.

Case 1. *Structures of the 'first' type.*

Let

$$\mu = \varepsilon^2 k_1, \quad h = \varepsilon h_2 \tag{91}$$

for some fixed positive k_1 and h_2.

We arbitrarily fix z as real, and let $\theta = \theta(\varepsilon, z)$ be the value from the semi-open interval $[0,1)$ that complements the expression $z\varepsilon^{-1/2}$ to an integer. We consider the integer set

$$(z\varepsilon^{-1/2} + \theta)m + n, \quad m, n = 0, \pm 1, \pm 2, \ldots .$$

For these numbers, the characteristic Equation (86) has the set of roots similar to (87)

$$\lambda_{m,n} = i\varepsilon^{-1/2}h_2zm + i(\theta m + n)h_2 - \Big(k_1 + \frac{1}{2}h_2^2\Big)z^2m^2 + O(\varepsilon^{1/2}).$$

Then, the family of the boundary value problems depending on the parameter z

$$\frac{\partial\xi}{\partial t} = z^2\Big(k_1 + \frac{1}{2}h_2^2\Big)\frac{\partial^2\xi}{\partial y^2} + h_2\Big(\theta\frac{\partial\xi}{\partial y} + \frac{\partial\xi}{\partial v}\Big) + r\xi[1 - \xi(t - T, y - \delta, v)], \qquad (92)$$

$$\xi(t, y + 2\pi, v) \equiv \xi(t, y, v) \equiv \xi(t, y, v + 2\pi) \qquad (93)$$

plays a role in the boundary value problem (89), (90) in the considered case. Here, $\delta = (\varepsilon^{-1/2}h_2z + h_2\theta) \mod 2\pi$.

Theorem 11. *Let, for some fixed* $\delta = \delta_0$ *and* $z = z_0$, *the boundary value problem (92), (93) be bounded together with a derivative with respect to t solution* $\xi_0(t, y, v)$ *as* $t \to \infty$. *Then, as determined from the equality* $\delta(\varepsilon) = \delta_0$, *for the sufficiently small* ε_n, *the function*

$$N(t, x, \varepsilon) = \xi_0\big(t, (z_0\varepsilon^{-1/2} + \theta)x + (\varepsilon^{-1/2}h_2z_0 + h_2\theta)t, x\big)$$

satisfies the boundary value problem (79), (80) up to $O(\varepsilon^{1/2})$.

The 'first' type of structure can also be formed by the interaction of a larger number of modes. We use constructions from [32] to demonstrate this.

We fix an arbitrarily natural number m_0 and real numbers $z_1, \ldots, z_{m_0}$. We consider the set of integer numbers

$$\sum_{j=1}^{m_0}(z_j\varepsilon^{-1/2} + \theta_j)m_j + n_j, \quad m_j, n_j = 0, \pm1, \pm2, \ldots.$$

For modes with these numbers, the equation

$$\frac{\partial\xi}{\partial t} = \Big[z_1\frac{\partial}{\partial y_1} + \ldots + z_{m_0}\frac{\partial}{\partial y_{m_0}}\Big]^2\Big(k_1 + \frac{1}{2}h_2^2\Big)\xi + h_2\Big(\theta_1\frac{\partial\xi}{\partial y_1} + \ldots + \theta_{m_0}\frac{\partial\xi}{\partial y_{m_0}} + \frac{\partial\xi}{\partial v_1} + \ldots + \frac{\partial\xi}{\partial v_{m_0}}\Big) + r[1 - \xi(t - T, y_1 - \delta_1, \ldots, y_{m_0} - \delta_{m_0}, v_1, \ldots, v_{m_0})]\xi$$

plays the role of the boundary value problem (92), (93) with 2π-periodic boundary conditions with respect to each spatial variable, and

$$\delta_j = (\varepsilon^{-1/2}h_2z_j + h_2\theta_j) \mod 2\pi.$$

Similarly to Theorem 11, the corresponding statement about coupling with the solutions of the boundary value problem (79), (80) is formulated for the solutions of this boundary value problem.

Remark 1. *The structures considered here that rapidly oscillate with respect to spatial variables arise when the coefficients k and* h_1 *in (89) are also asymptotically small.*

In this part, the case of $k = \varepsilon k_1$ and $h_1 = \varepsilon^{1/2}h_2$ is considered. Of course, one can investigate a more general case, when for some positive α, k_1 and h_2, the equalities

$$k = \varepsilon^{1+\alpha}k_1, \quad h_1 = \varepsilon^{\frac{1+\alpha}{2}}h_2$$

hold. For such k and h, the changes in the corresponding constructions are not fundamental, so we do not dwell on them.

Case 2. *Structures of the 'second' type.*

Here, the coefficient h is assumed to be the same as in (84). Further,

$$\mu = \varepsilon^2 k_1.$$

We consider the integer set $(2\pi h_1^{-1}\varepsilon^{-1/2} + \theta)m + n$, *where* $\theta \in [0,1)$ *is such that the expression in brackets is an integer,* $m, n = 0, \pm 1, \pm 2, \ldots$. *The characteristic Equation (86) has the set of roots* $\lambda_{m,n}$ *for which*

$$\lambda_{m,n} = ih_1(\theta m + n)\varepsilon^{-1/2} - \left(\frac{4\pi^2}{h_1^2}k_1 m^2 + \frac{1}{2}h_1^2(\theta m + n)^2\right) + O(\varepsilon^{1/2}).$$

We apply the above construction and obtain the resulting boundary value problem

$$\frac{\partial \xi}{\partial t} = 4\pi^2 h_1^{-2} k_1 \frac{\partial^2 \xi}{\partial y^2} + \frac{h_1^2}{2}\left(\theta\frac{\partial}{\partial y} + \frac{\partial}{\partial v}\right)^2 \xi + r[1 - \xi(t - T, y - \delta, v - \kappa)]\xi, \quad (94)$$

$$\xi(t, y + 2\pi, v) \equiv \xi(t, y, v) \equiv \xi(t, y, v + 2\pi), \quad (95)$$

where

$$\delta = (h_1 T\theta\varepsilon^{-1/2})_{\mod 2\pi}, \quad \kappa = (h_1 T\varepsilon^{-1/2})_{\mod 2\pi}.$$

We introduce some notation in order to formulate an analogue of Theorem 9 in the considered situation. We fix an arbitrary $\kappa = \kappa_0 \in [0,1)$ *and the sequence* $\varepsilon_p \to 0$ *of the roots of equation* $\kappa(\varepsilon_p) = \kappa_0$. *Let* θ_0 *be the arbitrary limit point of the sequence* $\theta(\varepsilon_p)$. *Let* $\theta(\varepsilon_{p_q}) \to \theta_0$ *for the sequence* ε_{p_q}. *Finally,* $\sigma_0 \in [0,1)$ *denotes the arbitrary limit point of the sequence* $\sigma(\varepsilon_{p_q})$, *and let* $\varepsilon_R \subset \varepsilon_{p_q}$ *and* $\sigma(\varepsilon_R) \to \sigma_0$.

Theorem 12. *Let, for some* θ_0, σ_0, *and* κ_0, *the boundary value problem (94), (95) be bounded together with a derivative with respect to t solution* $\xi_0(t, y, v)$. *Then, for* $\sigma = \sigma_0$, $\kappa = \kappa_0$, $\theta = \theta_0$, *and* $\varepsilon = \varepsilon_R \to 0$, *the function*

$$N(t, x, \varepsilon) = \xi_0\big(t, (2\pi h_1^{-1}\varepsilon_R^{-1/2} + \theta_0)x + h_1\theta_0\varepsilon_R^{-1/2}t, x + h_1\varepsilon^{-1/2}t\big)$$

satisfies the boundary value problem (79), (80) up to $O(\varepsilon^{1/2})$.

5.1.3. Case of Essentially Asymmetric Function

Here, we assume parameter h to not be small but to be close to some number rationally commensurate with π. This means, that for some relatively prime integers m_1 and m_2,

$$h = \frac{\pi m_1}{m_2} - \varepsilon^{1/2}h_1. \quad (96)$$

We assume that $m = Mn$, where $n = 0, \pm 1, \pm 2, \ldots$, $M = 2m_2$ if m_1 is even, or $M = 2m_2$ if m_1 is odd. Here, we repeat the constructions from Section 5.1.1 and obtain, similar to (89), (90), the boundary value problem

$$\frac{\partial \xi}{\partial t} = M^2\left(k + \frac{1}{2}h_1^2\right)\frac{\partial^2 \xi}{\partial y^2} + r[1 - \xi(t - T, y - \Delta)]\xi,$$

$$\xi(t, y + 2\pi) \equiv \xi(t, y).$$

The formula

$$N(t, x, \varepsilon) = \xi\big(t, M(x - \varepsilon^{-1/2}h_1 t)\big) + O(\varepsilon^{1/2})$$

establishes a relation between its solutions and the solutions of problem (79), (80). Accordingly, for (91), we arrive at the boundary value problem

$$\begin{gathered}\frac{\partial\xi}{\partial t} = z^2M^2\left(k_1 + \frac{1}{2}h_2^2\right)\frac{\partial^2\xi}{\partial y^2} + h_2M\frac{\partial\xi}{\partial v} + r[1-\xi(t-T,y-\delta,v)]\xi,\\ \xi(t,y+2\pi,v) \equiv \xi(t,y,v) \equiv \xi(t,y,v+2\pi).\end{gathered} \tag{97}$$

The solutions of this boundary value problem and of the boundary value problem (79), (80) are coupled by the equality

$$N(t,x,\varepsilon) = \xi\big(t, M(z\varepsilon^{-1/2}+\theta)x + M(\varepsilon^{-1/2}h_2z + h_2\theta), Mx\big) + O(\varepsilon^{1/2}).$$

Satisfaction of only one condition $\mu = \varepsilon^2k_1 \quad (h = \varepsilon^{1/2}h_1)$ is a more interesting situation. Let $\theta = \theta(\varepsilon) \in [0, M)$ be a value which complements the expression $\pi m_1(m_2h_1\varepsilon^{1/2})^{-1}$ to an integer multiple of M. We examine the set of integers $K = \{(\pi m_1(m_2h_2\varepsilon^{1/2})^{-1} + \theta)p\}$, $p = 0, \pm1, \pm2, \ldots$. Then, for the roots of Equation (86) with numbers m from K and $n = 0, \pm1, \pm2, \ldots$, we obtain

$$\lambda_{m,n} = ih_1(\theta p + n)\varepsilon^{-1/2} - \left[\frac{\pi^2m_1^2}{m_2^2}k_1p^2 - \frac{1}{2}h_1^2(\theta p + n)^2\right] + O(\varepsilon^{1/2}).$$

Here, the boundary value problem

$$\begin{gathered}\frac{\partial\xi}{\partial t} = \frac{\pi^2m_1^2}{m_2^2}k_1\frac{\partial^2\xi}{\partial y^2} + \frac{1}{2}h_1^2\left(\theta\frac{\partial}{\partial y} + \frac{\partial}{\partial v}\right)\xi + r[1-\xi(t-T,y-\delta,v-\kappa)]\xi,\\ \xi(t,y+2\pi,v) \equiv \xi(t,y,v) \equiv \xi(t,y,v+2\pi)\end{gathered}$$

is the analogue of problem (97). Definitely in the situations under consideration, there is also a connection between the solutions of the constructed boundary value problems and the asymptotic (with respect to residual) solutions of the boundary value problem (79), (80). As in Section 5.1.1, boundary value problems similar to those given but with a large number of spatial variables appear when taking into account the larger number of modes. We do not dwell on this in more detail.

5.2. Large Coefficient γ-Induced Bifurcations

Upon condition (83), we study the behavior of solutions of the boundary value problem (79), (80) in a sufficiently small equilibrium state $N_0 \equiv 1$ neighborhood. The characteristic quasipolynomial of a boundary value problem linearized on N_0 has the form

$$\varepsilon\lambda = -\varepsilon r\exp(-\lambda T) + \exp(ihm - \mu m^2) - 1, \quad 0 < \varepsilon \ll 1, \quad m = 0, \pm1, \pm2, \ldots. \tag{98}$$

As in Section 5.1, we restrict ourselves to the most interesting and important situations depending on the relationship between the parameters ε, h, and μ. In Section 5.2.1, we assume that condition (84) holds: $h = \sqrt{\varepsilon}h_1$, $\mu = k\varepsilon$. Below, we demonstrate that Andronov–Hopf bifurcation occurs in (79), (80) even for small values of the delay parameter $T \sim \varepsilon^{1/2}$. The periodic solution bifurcating from the equilibrium state N_0 turns out to be rapidly oscillating in time. In Section 5.2.2, the relations $h = \varepsilon h_2$, $\mu = k_1\varepsilon^2$ are assumed to be valid. In this case, the corresponding bifurcation process has an infinite dimension: infinitely many roots of the characteristic Equation (98) tend to the imaginary axis as $\varepsilon \to 0$. We construct quasinormal forms, i.e., the families of complex parabolic (and degenerate parabolic) boundary value problems whose nonlocal dynamics determine the behavior of the initial boundary value problem (79), (80) solutions in the small neighborhood of N_0 for small ε. In Section 5.2.3, even more complicated families of quasinormal forms are constructed to determine the dynamic properties of problem (79), (80) under the constraint $\mu = k_1\varepsilon^2$. The conclusions are given in Section 5.2.4.

It is natural to choose the delay time T as the main bifurcation parameter. We recall that the bifurcation value for T is determined from the equality $2rT = \pi$ in Equation (79). In the cases considered here, we demonstrate that the bifurcation parameter can be asymptotically small.

5.2.1. Bifurcation Analysis upon Condition $h = \varepsilon^{1/2}h_1$, $\mu = k\varepsilon$

In (98), we assume

$$\lambda = i\omega \quad (\omega > 0), \quad \omega = \varepsilon^{-1/2}h_1 + \omega_2, \quad T = \varepsilon^{1/2}T_1.$$

Then, we obtain

$$\begin{aligned} r\cos(h_1 T_{1m}) &= -(k + \frac{1}{2}h_1^2)m^2, \\ r\sin(h_1 T_{1m}) &= \omega_2. \end{aligned} \tag{99}$$

up to $O(\varepsilon^{1/2})$. If it exists, let T_{1m}, $m = 1, 2, \ldots$ be the least positive root of Equation (99). Obviously, there is a finite number of such roots. Let T_1^0 be the least of them. Let $T_1^0 = T_{1m_0}$. We formulate two statements about the roots of Equation (98) that are simple but cumbersome proofs that are omitted.

Lemma 6. *Let $T_1 < T_1^0$. Then, for all sufficiently small ε, the Equation (98) roots separate from zero negative real parts as $\varepsilon \to 0$.*

Lemma 7. *Let $T_1 > T_1^0$. Then, for all sufficiently small ε, Equation (98) has a root separate from the zero positive real part as $\varepsilon \to 0$.*

Thus, in the context of the above lemmas, the issue of the boundary value problem (79), (80) local dynamics is solved trivially.

Let us study the behavior of the solutions of the problem (79), (80) in the N_0 neighborhood close to the critical case condition

$$T_1 = T_1^0 + \varepsilon^{1/2}T_{01}.$$

Then, the characteristic Equation (98) has the coupling of the roots $\lambda_{1,2}(\varepsilon)$ of the form

$$\lambda_{1,2}(\varepsilon) = \pm i(\varepsilon^{-1/2}h_1 + \omega_2) + O(\varepsilon^{1/2}).$$

The real parts of the remaining roots of Equation (98) are negative and zero-separated as $\varepsilon \to 0$. In this case, for small ε, the boundary value problem (79), (80) has a two-dimensional stable local invariant integral manifold in the (small) N_0 neighborhood, on which this boundary value problem can be represented in the form of the scalar complex equation up to the summands of the $O(\varepsilon^{1/2})$ order:

$$\frac{\partial \xi}{\partial \tau} = \alpha\xi + d|\xi|^2\xi, \tag{100}$$

where $\tau = \varepsilon^{1/2}t$ is a 'slow' time. The solution $N(t, x, \varepsilon)$ on this manifold is coupled to solutions of Equation (100) by the relation

$$\begin{aligned} N(t, x, \varepsilon) = \varepsilon^{1/4}\big[\xi(\tau)\exp(im_0 x + i(\varepsilon^{-1/2}h_1 m_0 + \omega_2)t) + \bar{\xi}(\tau)\exp(-im_0 x - \\ i(\varepsilon^{-1/2}h_1 m_0 + \omega_2)t)\big] + \varepsilon^{1/2}u_2(t, \tau, x) + \varepsilon^{3/4}u_3(t, \tau, x) + \ldots . \end{aligned} \tag{101}$$

Here, the functions $u_j(t, \tau, x)$ are periodic with respect to first and third arguments, with periods $2\pi(\varepsilon^{-1/2}h_1 m_0 + \omega_2)^{-1}$ and 2π, respectively.

Regarding the dynamics of Equation (100) (and hence the boundary value problem (79), (80) in the N_0 neighborhood), one needs to find the coefficients α and d. To accomplish this, we insert the formal series (101) into (79) and equate the coefficients at the same powers of ε. At the second step, we obtain

$$u_2(t,\tau,x) = u_{20}|\xi|^2 + u_{21}\xi^2\exp(2im_0x + 2i(\varepsilon^{-1/2}h_1m_0 + \omega_2)t) + \\ \bar{u}_{21}\bar{\xi}^2\exp(-2im_0x - 2i(\varepsilon^{-1/2}h_1m_0 + \omega_2)t)$$

and

$$\begin{aligned} u_{20} &= 2\cos(T_1^0h_1m_0), \\ u_{21} &= -r\big(\exp(-2iT_1^0h_1m_0)(2i\omega_2 + 4m_0^2k + r\exp(-2iT_1^0h_1m_0))\big)^{-1}. \end{aligned}$$

From the solvability condition obtained at the third-step equation with respect to $u_3(t,\tau)$, we obtain

$$\begin{aligned} d &= -\ r\big[1 + \exp(-2iT_1^0h_1m_0) - r\exp(-iT_1^0h_1m_0)(2i\omega_2 + 4m_0^2k + \\ &\quad r\exp(-2iT_1^0h_1m_0))^{-1}\big], \\ \alpha &= irh_1T_1^0m_0\exp(-iT_1^0h_1m_0) - \Big(k + \frac{1}{2}h_1^2\Big)m_0^2. \end{aligned}$$

We note that each of the quantities $\Re\alpha$ and $\Re d$ can be either positive or negative, depending on the values of the parameters T_1^0, m_0, r, k, and h_1. As an example, we make one statement about the dynamics of problem (79), (80).

Theorem 13. *Let $\Re\alpha > 0$ and $\Re d < 0$. Then, for all sufficiently small ε, the boundary value problem (79), (80) has a stable periodic solution $N_0(t,x,\varepsilon)$ in the N_0 neighborhood, for which*

$$N_0(t,x,\varepsilon) = 1 + 2\varepsilon^{1/4}\rho_0\cos(m_0x + \varepsilon^{-1/2}h_1m_0 + \omega_2 + \varepsilon^{1/2}\varphi_0 + O(\varepsilon^{3/4}))t + O(\varepsilon^{1/2}),$$

where

$$\rho_0 = \big(\Re\alpha(-\Re d)^{-1}\big)^{1/2}, \quad \varphi_0 = \Im\alpha + \rho_0^2\Im d.$$

Remark 2. *The results presented here could be obtained by studying the bifurcations from the equilibrium state $\xi_0 \equiv 1$ in the boundary value problem (89), (90).*

5.2.2. High-Mode Bifurcations upon Condition $\mu = \varepsilon^2k_1$, $h = \varepsilon h_2$

It is assumed here that the conditions $h = \varepsilon h_2$, $\mu = k_1\varepsilon^2$ are satisfied. Under these conditions, we study the behavior of the solutions of the problem (79), (80) from a small N_0 neighborhood. First, we consider the characteristic Equation (98). For $T = 0$, its roots have negative real parts (separated from zero as $\varepsilon \to 0$). Let us demonstrate that there are roots with a close to zero real part as $T \sim \varepsilon^{1/2}$, and the numbers (modes) $m \sim \varepsilon^{-1/2}$ correspond to them. In (98), we assume

$$T = \varepsilon^{1/2}T_1, \quad m = c\varepsilon^{-1/2} + \theta_c, \quad \lambda = i\varepsilon^{-1/2}h_2c + i\omega(c),$$

where $\theta_c = \theta_c(\varepsilon) \in [0,1)$ is the value that complements the previous summand $c\varepsilon^{-1/2}$ to an integer. Then, we obtain the equality

$$i\omega(c) = -r\exp(-ih_2T_1c) - \Big(k_1 + \frac{1}{2}h_2^2\Big)c^2 \quad (102)$$

(up to $O(\varepsilon^{1/2})$). Let us determine the least value of $T_1 = T_1^0$ for which this equation is solvable with respect to c, i.e., for some $c = c_0$, the relation

$$r\cos(h_2T_1^0c_0) = -\Big(k_1 + \frac{1}{2}h_2^2\Big)c_0^2 \quad (103)$$

holds. We denote by x_0 the least positive root of the equation

$$2x = -x.$$

Then, the following simple statements hold.

Lemma 8. *For T_1^0 and c_0, the equalities*

$$\begin{aligned} T_1^0 &= \frac{1}{2}x_0\Big(k_1 + \frac{1}{2}h_2^2\Big)^{1/2}(2 - r\cos x_0)^{-1/2}, \\ c_0 &= (-r\cos x_0)^{-1/2}\Big(k_1 + \frac{1}{2}h_2^2\Big)^{-1/2} \end{aligned}$$

hold.

Lemma 9. *Let $T_1 < T_1^0$. Then, for all sufficiently small ε, the roots of Equation (98) have negative real parts (separated from zero as $\varepsilon \to 0$).*

Lemma 10. *Let $T_1 > T_1^0$. Then, for all sufficiently small ε, Equation (98) has a root with a positive real part (separated from zero as $\varepsilon \to 0$).*

In the context of Lemmas 9 and 10, the behavior of the solutions of the problem (79), (80) in small (ε-independent) neighborhood of N_0 is determined in the standard way.

Below, we assume that a case close to critical in the stability problem of N_0 is realized. Let, for some arbitrary constant T_{11}, the equality

$$T_1 = T_1^0 + \varepsilon^{1/2}T_{11}$$

hold. In this case, infinitely many roots of Equation (98) tend to the imaginary axis as $\varepsilon \to 0$, and there are no roots with a positive zero-separated as $\varepsilon \to 0$ real part. Thus, the critical case of an infinite dimension is realized in the N_0 stability problem. Let us apply the technique of [26,28] to study the local dynamics of problem (79), (80) for small ε.

First, we note that all modes that correspond to roots of Equation (98) close to the imaginary axis are asymptotically large and have the leading asymptotic term $c_0\varepsilon^{-1/2}$. In this regard, we consider all modes with numbers $m = m(\varepsilon)$ for which

$$m(\varepsilon) = c_0\varepsilon^{-1/2} + \theta_0 + b\varepsilon^{-1/4} + \theta_1, \tag{104}$$

where $\theta_0 = \theta_{c_0}$, b is arbitrarily fixed, and $\theta_1 = \theta(b,\varepsilon) \in [0,1)$ complements the value of $b\varepsilon^{-1/4}$ to an integer. The roots $\lambda = \lambda_{m(\varepsilon)}$ of Equation (98) with numbers $m(\varepsilon)$ satisfy the asymptotic equalities

$$\lambda = ih_2c_0\varepsilon^{-1/2} + ih_2b\varepsilon^{-1/4} + i\omega(c_0) + i\varepsilon^{1/4}\Delta b + \varepsilon^{1/2}\lambda_2 + O(\varepsilon^{3/4}).$$

Here, the following designations are accepted:

$$\Delta = rh_2T_1^0\exp(-ih_2T_1^0c_0) + i2c_0\Big(k_1 + \frac{1}{2}h_2^2\Big), \quad \Im\Delta = 0,$$

$$\lambda_2 = -\sigma b^2 - 2c_0\theta_0\Big(k_1 + \frac{1}{2}h_2^2\Big) + r\exp(-ih_2T_1^0c_0)\big(i\omega(c_0)T_1^0 + ih_2c_0T_{11}\big),$$

where

$$\sigma = \Big(k_1 + \frac{1}{2}h_2^2\Big)\left(1 + \frac{1}{2}c_0^2h_2^2(T_1^0)^2\right) + i\omega(c_0)\frac{1}{2}h_2^2(T_1^0)^2.$$

Another notation is used below. Let $\Omega = \Omega(\varepsilon)$ be the set of all such values of b for which the values of $b\varepsilon^{-1/4}$ are integers from $-\infty$ to ∞.

Let us introduce the formal series

$$N = 1 + \varepsilon^{1/4}\Big[\exp((ih_2\varepsilon^{-1/2}c_0 + i\omega(c_0))t + (i\varepsilon^{-1/2}c_0 + \theta_0)x)\sum_{b\in\Omega}\xi_b(\tau)\exp iby + \exp(-(ih_2\varepsilon^{-1/2}c_0 + i\omega(c_0))t - i(\varepsilon^{-1/2}c_0 + \theta_0)xby)\sum_{b\in\Omega}\bar{\xi}_b(\tau)\exp(-iby) + \theta_0 x\Big] + \varepsilon^{1/2}u_2(t,\tau,x,y) + \varepsilon^{3/4}u_3(t,\tau,x,y) + \dots, \tag{105}$$

where

$$\tau = \varepsilon^{1/2}t, \quad y = \varepsilon^{-1/4}x + (\varepsilon^{-1/4}h_2 + \varepsilon^{1/4}\Delta)t.$$

The dependence on the first, third, and fourth arguments of function $u_j(t,\tau,x,y)$ is periodic, with periods $2\pi(h_2\varepsilon^{-1/2}c_0 + \omega(c_0))^{-1}, 2\pi(\varepsilon^{-1/2}c_0 + \theta_0$, and 2π, respectively. We insert (105) into (79) and perform standard operations. At the second step, we obtain

$$u_2(t,\tau,x,y) = u_{20}(\tau,y)|\xi|^2 + u_{21}(t,\tau,x,y)\xi^2 + \bar{u}_{21}(t,\tau,x,y)\bar{\xi}^2$$

and

$$\begin{aligned} u_{20}(\tau,x) &= 2(\cos x_0)|\xi|^2, \\ u_{21} &= -r\exp(-2ix_0)\Big[2i\omega(c_0) + r\exp(2ix_0) + \Big(k_1 + \frac{1}{2}h_2^2\Big)4c_0^2\Big]^{-1} \times \\ &\quad \exp\big(2i[(h_2\varepsilon^{-1/2}c_0 + \omega(c_0))t + (\varepsilon^{-1/2}c_0 + \theta_0)x]\big). \end{aligned}$$

At the third step, from the solvability condition of the resulting equation with respect to u_3, we obtain the equation for determining the unknown amplitude

$$\begin{gathered} \xi(\tau,y) = \Big(\sum_{b\in\Omega}\xi_b\exp iby\Big)\exp\Big(i\Big[r\omega(c_0)T_1^0 + h_2c_0T_{11}\cos x_0 - 2c_0\theta_0\Big(k_1 + \frac{1}{2}h_2^2\Big)\Big]\Big), \\ \frac{\partial\xi}{\partial\tau} = \sigma\frac{\partial^2\xi}{\partial y^2} + \beta\xi + d|\xi|^2\xi, \end{gathered} \tag{106}$$

where

$$\begin{aligned} \beta &= rh_2c_0T_{11}\sin x_0 \\ d &= -r\Big\{2(\cos x_0)(1 + \exp(-ix_0)) - \\ &\quad (\exp(ix_0) + \exp(-2ix_0))r\exp(-2ix_0)\Big[2i\omega(c_0) + \\ &\quad r\exp(-2ix_0) + \Big(k_1 + \frac{1}{2}h_2^2\Big)4c_0^2\Big]^{-1}\Big\}. \end{aligned}$$

We note that there are no boundary conditions for Equation (106). The point is that the function with respect to argument y contains an arbitrary set of harmonics. We present one of the variants of strict statements about relations between the solutions of (106) and the solutions of the boundary value problem (79), (80).

Theorem 14. *Let Equation (106) have an R-periodic with respect to argument y solution $\xi(\tau, y)$. Then, for $\varepsilon \to 0$, the function*

$$\begin{aligned} N(t,x,\varepsilon) &= 1+\varepsilon^{1/4}\Big[\xi(\varepsilon^{1/2}t,(\varepsilon^{-1/4}+\theta_R)x+(\varepsilon^{-1/4}h_2+\varepsilon^{1/4}\Delta)t)\times \\ &\exp(i[h_2\varepsilon^{-1/4}c_0+\omega(c_0)]t+i[\varepsilon^{-1/2}c_0+\theta_0]x)+\bar{\xi}(\varepsilon^{1/2}t,(\varepsilon^{-1/4}+\theta_R)x+ \\ &(\varepsilon^{-1/4}h_2+\varepsilon^{1/4}\Delta)t)\exp(-i[h_2\varepsilon^{-1/4}c_0+\omega(c_0)]t-i[\varepsilon^{-1/2}c_0+\theta_0]x)\Big]+ \\ &\varepsilon^{1/2}u_2(t,\tau,y,x) \end{aligned}$$

satisfies the boundary value problem (79), (80) up to $O(\varepsilon^{3/4})$, where the expression $\theta_R = \theta_R(\varepsilon) \in [0, 2\pi/R)$ complements the summand $\varepsilon^{-1/4}$ to an integer multiple of $2\pi/R$.

5.2.3. Reduction to Spatially Two-Dimensional Parabolic Equations

As noted above, the local dynamics of the problem (79), (80) essentially depend on the relations between the parameters ε, h, and μ. Two of the most important cases are analyzed in Sections 5.2.1 and 5.2.2 with some model 'relations' between small parameters. Here, we dwell on another important scenario that is fundamentally different from the previous ones. We construct nonlinear parabolic equations with two spatial variables called the quasinormal forms to study local dynamics of the problem (79), (80) in N_0 neighborhood.

We consider a model situation where

$$h = \varepsilon h_2, \quad \mu = k_0\varepsilon^{7/2}, \quad T = \varepsilon^{1/2}T_1. \tag{107}$$

Let $m = m(\varepsilon)$ be such asymptotically large modes for which

$$m(\varepsilon) = \frac{2\pi h}{h_2}\varepsilon^{-1} + c\varepsilon^{-1/2} + \theta_1 + b\varepsilon^{-1/4} + \theta_2, \tag{108}$$

where $n = 0, \pm 1, \pm 2, \ldots$, the parameter c is determined below, the values of b are arbitrary, the value $\theta_1 = \theta_1(\varepsilon) \in [0, 1)$ complements the sum of two previous terms to an integer, and $\theta_2 = \theta_2(\varepsilon) \in [0, 1)$ complements the expression $b\varepsilon^{-1/4}$ to an integer. For the roots of the characteristic Equation (98) with numbers (108), the asymptotic formulas

$$\lambda = -r\exp(-\lambda\varepsilon^{-1/2}T_1) + ih_2c\varepsilon^{-1/2} + ih_2b\varepsilon^{-1/4} + i(\theta_1+\theta_2)h_2 - \frac{1}{2}h_2^2c^2 + \ldots$$

hold. In order to determine the stability boundary of N_0 for the problem (79), (80) in the range of parameter T_1, we assume

$$\lambda = ih_2c\varepsilon^{-1/2} + ih_2b\varepsilon^{-1/4} + i\omega + \varepsilon^{1/4}\lambda_1 + \varepsilon^{1/2}\lambda_2 + \ldots. \tag{109}$$

At the first step of the asymptotic analysis, from (109), we arrive at the equality

$$i\omega = -r\exp(-ih_2cT_1) - \frac{1}{2}h_2^2c^2. \tag{110}$$

The least value of $T_1 = T_1^0$ for which Equation (110) is solvable for some $c = c_0$ is determined from the relations (103) as $k_1 = 0$, i.e.,

$$\begin{aligned} c_0 &= (-r\cos x_0)^{1/2}2^{-1/2}h_2, \\ T_1^0 &= 2^{-3/2}x_0h_2(-r\cos x_0)^{1/2}. \end{aligned}$$

Here, the statements of Lemmas 9 and 10 also hold. Thus, we assume below that a case close to critical in the stability problem of N_0 is realized. Let, for some constant T_{11}, the equality

$$T_1 = T_1^0 + \varepsilon^{1/2}T_{11}$$

hold. Similar to the previous part, infinitely many roots of Equation (98) tend to the imaginary axis as $\varepsilon \to 0$, and there are no roots with a positive zero-separated as $\varepsilon \to 0$ real part. However, there are 'essentially' more such roots in this case. Let us explain the above. For this purpose, we obtain expressions for λ_1 and λ_2:

$$\begin{aligned}
\lambda_1 &= i\Delta_0 b, \quad \Delta_0 = rh_2T_1^0\exp(-x_0) + ic_0h_2^2, \quad \Im\Delta = 0,\\
\lambda_2 &= -\sigma b^2 - k_0h_2^{-2}4\pi^2n^2 + \beta_0,\\
\beta_0 &= -c_0\theta_1(c_0)h_2^2 + r\exp(-x_0)\big(i\omega_0T_1^0 + ih_2c_0T_{11}\big),\\
i\omega_0 &= -r\exp(-x_0) - \frac{1}{2}h_2^2c_0^2,\\
\sigma_0 &= \frac{1}{2}h_2^2\left(1 + \frac{1}{2}c_0^2h_2^2(T_1^0)^2\right) + i\omega_0\frac{1}{2}h_2^2(T_1^0)^2.
\end{aligned} \tag{111}$$

The expression (111) differs from the similar formula for λ_2 in the previous part by the presence of parameter n, which takes all integer values $n = 0, \pm1, \pm2, \ldots$. Hence, we obtain that the quantity ξ_b is also an h_2-periodic function with respect to x in the basic formula of the form (105) in the considered case: $\xi_b = \xi_b(\tau, x)$. Thus, we repeat the Equation (106) construction technique and obtain the more complicated equation

$$\frac{\partial\xi}{\partial\tau} = \sigma_0\frac{\partial^2\xi}{\partial y^2} + k_0\frac{\partial^2\xi}{\partial x^2} + \beta_0\xi + d_0|\xi|^2\xi \tag{112}$$

with h_2-periodic boundary conditions with respect to x, and d_0 differs from the value d appearing in (106) only by the presence of $k_1 = 0$ in the appropriate formula.

For the dynamics of (79), (80), Equation (112) plays the same role as Equation (106) with the conditions from Section 5.1. We do not dwell on this in more detail.

5.2.4. Case of 'Intelligently' Small Parameters h and μ

To complete the picture, we briefly consider the simplest situation when both parameters h and μ are 'intelligently' small:

$$h = \varepsilon^2 h_0, \quad \mu = \varepsilon^2 k_0. \tag{113}$$

The bifurcation value of the delay coefficient $T = T_0$ satisfies the equality $T = \pi(2r)^{-1}$. Let $T = T_0 + \varepsilon T_{01}$ in (79), (80). Then, infinitely many roots $\lambda_m = \lambda_m(\varepsilon)$ of Equation (98) tend to the imaginary axis as $\varepsilon \to 0$, and there are no roots with a positive zero-separated as $\varepsilon \to 0$ real part. Therefore, the critical case of an infinite dimension is realized here, too.

Let us introduce the formal series

$$\begin{aligned}
N = {} & 1 + \varepsilon^{1/2}\Big[\exp\Big(i\frac{\pi}{2T_0}t\Big)\xi(\tau,x) + \exp\Big(-i\frac{\pi}{2T_0}t\Big)\bar\xi(\tau,x)\Big] + \\
& + \varepsilon u_2(t,\tau,x) + \varepsilon^{3/3}u_2(t,\tau,x) + \ldots,
\end{aligned} \tag{114}$$

where $\tau = \varepsilon t$, and $u_j(t,\tau,x)$ are periodic with respect to first and third arguments with $4T_0$ and 2π periods, respectively. We insert (114) into (79) and perform standard operations. At the third step, we arrive at the boundary value problem for determining the unknown, slowly varying amplitude $\xi(\tau, x)$:

$$\frac{\partial\xi}{\partial\tau} = \Big(1 + i\frac{\pi}{2}\Big)^{-1}\Big[k_0\frac{\partial^2\xi}{\partial x^2} + h_0\frac{\partial\xi}{\partial x} + r_0^2T_{11}\Big] + g|\xi|^2\xi, \tag{115}$$

$$\xi(\tau, x + 2\pi) \equiv \xi(\tau, x), \tag{116}$$

where

$$g = -r[3\pi - 2 + i(\pi + 6)]\Big(10\Big(1 + \frac{\pi^2}{4}\Big)\Big)^{-1}.$$

The coupling between solutions of the problem (115), (116) and asymptotic with respect to residual solutions of the problem (79), (80) is determined by Formula (114). We note that for a periodic solution of (115), (116) of the form $\xi_0(\tau, x) = Const \cdot \exp(i\omega\tau + ikx)$, one can formulate a stronger result about the existence (and inheritance of the stability properties) of a periodic solution of the problem (79), (80), which is close to

$$\varepsilon^{1/2}\Big[\xi_0(\tau, x)\exp\Big(i\Big(\frac{\pi}{2T_0} + O(\varepsilon)\Big)t\Big) + \bar{\xi}_0(\tau, x)\exp\Big(-i\Big(\frac{\pi}{2T_0} + O(\varepsilon)\Big)t\Big)\Big]$$

as $\varepsilon \to 0$.

6. Conclusions

It has been shown that the considered critical cases in the stability problem of the distributed chain of logistic equations with delay have an infinite dimension. This leads to the fact that description of their local dynamics is reduced to the study of the nonlocal behavior of boundary value problems of Ginzburg–Landau type solutions. It is known (see, for example, [30]) that the dynamics of such objects can be complicated, and they are characterized by irregular oscillations, multistability phenomena, etc. The dynamic effects essentially depend on the choice of couplings. It has been shown that in a number of cases the solutions are rapidly and slowly oscillating with respect to spatial variable components. The basic results define the structure of problems that are asymptotic with respect to residual solutions to the initial boundary value. The problem of existence, stability, and more complicated asymptotic expansions of exact solutions close to those constructed can be solved, for example, for the case of periodic solutions of normalized equations.

We considered separately the role of the above parameter $\theta = \theta(\varepsilon) \in [0, 1)$. We recalled that the dynamic properties of the initial system are determined by the QNF (49), (50), which includes the parameter θ. The dynamics of (49), (50) and hence of the boundary value problem (9), (10) may change for different values of this parameter. This is shown in detail in [31]. This implies that an infinite process of forward and reverse bifurcations can occur as $\varepsilon \to 0$.

Below, we formulate one more conclusion of the general plan. It was shown above that the quasinormal forms that determine the dynamics of the initial boundary value problem are equations of Ginzburg–Landau type. We note that parabolic boundary value problems with one and two spatial variables can act as quasinormal forms depending on the coefficient σ of the function $F(s, \varepsilon)$ ((12), (13)). The stability of the simplest solutions of these equations is studied in [33]. In particular, it has been established that their stability properties are determined to a large extent by the imaginary components of the diffusion coefficients and of the Lyapunov quantity (coefficients g and q in (49) and (50)). Numerical analysis of the corresponding criterion makes it possible to formulate the conclusion about the instability of all the simplest solutions of the form $\cdot \exp(i\omega t + ikx)$. Thus, solution synchronization is a rather rare phenomenon in the considered chains.

It has been demonstrated that the study of the dynamics of logistic equations with delay is reduced to nonlinear dynamics analysis of special families of the parabolic and degenerately parabolic boundary value problems for large values of the coefficient of spatially distributed control. In particular, the phenomenon of hypermultistability is described.

In the study of local dynamics, bifurcation phenomena can be realized in the equilibrium state neighborhood even for asymptotically small delays. Here, the critical case has an infinite dimension in the stability problem. Analogues of the normal form, so-called quasinormal forms, are constructed in this situation, which are universal nonlinear boundary value problems of the parabolic type. Their nonlocal dynamics determine the local behavior of the solutions of the initial boundary value problem.

Funding: This work was supported by the Russian Science Foundation (project no. 21-71-30011).

Institutional Review Board Statement: Not applicable.

Informed Consent Statement: Not applicable.

Data Availability Statement: Not applicable.

Conflicts of Interest: The author declares no conflict of interest. The funder had no role in the design of the study; in the collection, analyses, or interpretation of data; in the writing of the manuscript, or in the decision to publish the results.

References

1. Maurer, J.; Libchaber, A. Effect of the Prandtl number on the onset of turbulence in liquid 4He. *J. Phys. Lett.* **1982**, *41*, 515. [CrossRef]
2. Kuznetsov, S.P.; Ponomarenko, V.I.; Seleznev, E.P. Autonomous system generating hyperbolic chaos: Circuit simulation and experiment. *Izv. Vyssh. Uchebn. Zaved. Prikl. Nelin. Dinam.* **2013**, *21*, 17–30.
3. Pikovsky, A.S.; Rosenblum, M.G.; Kurths, J. *Synchronization: A Universal Concept in Nonlinear Sciences*; Cambridge University Press: Cambridge, UK, 2001.
4. Brun, E.; Derighette, B.; Meier, D.; Holzner, R.; Raveni, M. Observation of order and chaos in a nuclear spin-flip laser. *J. Opt. Soc. Am. B* **1985**, *2*, 156. [CrossRef]
5. Dangoisse, D.; Glorieux, P.; Hennequin, D. Chaos in a CO_2 laser with modulated parameters: Experiments and numerical simulations. *Phys. Rev. A* **1987**, *36*, 4775. [CrossRef] [PubMed]
6. Chembo, Y.K.; Jacquot, M.; Dudley, J.M.; Larger, L. Ikeda-like chaos on a dynamically filtered supercontinuum light source. *Phys. Rev. A* **2016**, *94*, 023847. [CrossRef]
7. Thompson, J.M.T.; Stewart, H.B. *Nonlinear Dynamics and Chaos*; Wiley: Chichester, UK, 1986.
8. Foss, J.; Longtin, A.; Mensour, B.; Milton, J. Multistability and delayed recurrent loops. *Phys. Rev. Lett.* **1996**, *76*, 708. [CrossRef]
9. Sysoev, I.V.; Ponomarenko, V.I.; Kulminskiy, D.D.; Prokhorov, M.D. Recovery of couplings and parameters of elements in networks of time-delay systems from time series. *Phys. Rev. E* **2016**, *94*, 052207. [CrossRef]
10. Ponomarenko, V.I.; Kulminskiy, D.D.; Prokhorov, M.D. Chimeralike states in networks of bistable time-delayed feedback oscillators coupled via the mean field. *Phys. Rev. E* **2017**, *96*, 022209. [CrossRef]
11. Haken, H. *Brain Dynamics: Synchronization and Activity Patterns in Pulse-Coupled Neural Nets with Delays and Noise*; Springer: Berlin/Heidelberg, Germany, 2002.
12. Osipov, G.V.; Kurths, J.; Zhou, C. *Synchronization in Oscillatory Networks*; Springer: Berlin, Germany, 2007.
13. Afraimovich, V.S.; Nekorkin, V.I.; Osipov, G.V.; Shalfeev, V.D. *Stability, Structures and Chaos in Nonlinear Synchronization Networks*; World Scientific: Singapore, 1994.
14. Karavaev, A.S.; Ishbulatov, Y.M.; Ponomarenko, V.I.; Bezruchko, B.P.; Kiselev, A.R.; Prokhorov, M.D. Autonomic control is a source of dynamical chaos in the cardiovascular system. *Chaos* **2019**, *29*, 121101. [CrossRef]
15. Kuang, Y. *Delay Differential Equations: With Applications in Population Dynamics*; Mathematics in Science and Engineering; Academic Press: Boston, MA, USA, 1993; Volume 410, p. 191.
16. Wu, J. *Theory and Applications of Partial Functional Differential Equations*; Applied Mathematical Sciences; Springer: New York, NY, USA, 1996; Volume 119, 439p.
17. Gourley, S.A.; Sou, J.W.-H.; Wu, J.H. Nonlocality of reaction-diffusion equations induced by delay: Biological modeling and nonlinear dynamics. *J. Math. Sci.* **2004**, *124*, 5119–5153. [CrossRef]
18. Kashchenko, S.A. Corporate Dynamics in Chains of Coupled Logistic Equations with Delay. *Comput. Math. Math. Phys.* **2021**, *61*, 1063–1074. [CrossRef]
19. Kashchenko, S.A. Local Dynamics of Logistic Equation with Delay and Diffusion. *Mathematics* **2021**, *9*, 1566. [CrossRef]
20. Kashchenko, S.A. Asymptotics of the solutions of the generalized hutchinson equation. *Automat. Control Comp. Sci.* **2013**, *47*, 470–494. [CrossRef]
21. Hale, J.K. *Theory of Functional Differential Equations*, 2nd ed.; Springer: New York, NY, USA, 1977; 626p.
22. Hartman, P. *Ordinary Differential Equations*, 2nd ed.; Classics in Applied Mathematics; Society for Industrial and Applied Mathematics (SIAM): Philadelphia, PA, USA, 2002; Volume 38, 642p.
23. Marsden, J.E.; McCracken, M.F. *The Hopf Bifurcation and Its Applications*; Applied Mathematical Sciences; Springer: New York, NY, USA, 1976; Volume 19, 421p.
24. Oster, G.; Guckenheimer, J. *Bifurcation Phenomena in Population Models*; Applied Mathematical Sciences; Springer: New York, NY, USA, 1976; Volume 19, pp. 327–353.
25. Kashchenko, S.A. On quasinormal forms for parabolic equations with small diffusion. *Sov. Math. Dokl.* **1988**, *37*, 510–513.
26. Kaschenko, S.A. Normalization in the systems with small diffusion. *Int. J. Bifurc. Chaos Appl. Sci. Eng.* **1996**, *6*, 1093–1109. [CrossRef]
27. Kashchenko, I.S.; Kashchenko, S.A. Dynamics of the Kuramoto equation with spatially distributed control. *Comm. Nonlin. Sci. Numer. Simulat.* **2016**, *34*, 123–129. [CrossRef]
28. Kashchenko, S.A. The Ginzburg–Landau equation as a normal form for a second-order difference-differential equation with a large delay. *Comput. Math. Math. Phys.* **1998**, *38*, 443–451.

29. Grigorieva, E.V.; Kashchenko, S.A. Rectangular structures in the model of an optoelectronic oscillator with delay. *Phys. D Nonlinear Phenom.* **2021**, *417*, 132818. [CrossRef]
30. Akhromeeva, T.S.; Kurdyumov, S.P.; Malinetskii, G.G.; Samarskii, A.A. *Nonstationary Structures and Diffusion Chaos*; Nauka: Moscow, Russia, 1992; 544p.
31. Kashchenko, I.S.; Kashchenko, S.A. Infinite Process of Forward and Backward Bifurcations in the Logistic Equation with Two Delays. *Nonlinear Phenom. Complex Syst.* **2019**, *22*, 407–412. [CrossRef]
32. Kashchenko, I.S.; Kashchenko, S.A. Dynamics of Strongly Coupled Spatially Distributed Logistic Equations with Delay. *Comput. Math. Math. Phys.* **2015**, *55*, 607–617. [CrossRef]
33. Kashchenko, A.A. Analysis of running waves stability in the Ginzburg–Landau equation with small diffusion. *Automat. Control Comp. Sci.* **2015**, *49*, 514–517. [CrossRef]

mathematics

MDPI

Article

Mathematical Modeling and Stability Analysis of a Delayed Carbon Absorption-Emission Model Associated with China's Adjustment of Industrial Structure

Leilei Han, Haokun Sui and Yuting Ding *

Department of Mathematics, Northeast Forestry University, Harbin 150040, China
* Correspondence:dingyt@nefu.edu.cn

Abstract: Global warming has brought about enormous damage, therefore, some scholars have begun to conduct in-depth research on peak carbon dioxide emissions and carbon neutrality. In this paper, based on the background of China's upgrading industrial structure and energy structure, we establish a delayed two-dimensional differential equation model associated with China's adjustment of industrial structure. Firstly, we analyze the existence of the equilibrium for the model. We also analyze the characteristic roots of the characteristic equation at each equilibrium point for the model, then, we analyze the stability of the equilibrium point for the model according to the characteristic root, and discuss the existence of Hopf bifurcation of the system by using bifurcation theory. Secondly, we derive the normal form of Hopf bifurcation by using the multiple time scales method. Then, through the official real data, we present the range of some parameters in the model, and determine a set of parameters by reasonable analysis. The validity of the theoretical results is verified by numerical simulations. Finally, we use the real data to forecast the time of peak carbon dioxide emissions and carbon neutralization. Eventually, we put forward some suggestions based on the current situation of carbon emission and absorption in China, such as planting trees to increase the growth rate of carbon absorption, deepening industrial reform and optimizing energy structure to reduce carbon emissions.

Keywords: carbon absorption-emission model; time delay; multiple time scales method; normal form; Hopf bifurcation

MSC: 34K18; 37L10

Citation: Han, L.; Sui, H.; Ding, Y. Mathematical Modeling and Stability Analysis of a Delayed Carbon Absorption-Emission Model Associated with China's Adjustment of Industrial Structure. *Mathematics* **2022**, *10*, 3089. https://doi.org/10.3390/math10173089

Academic Editors: Mariano Torrisi and Mustafa R.S. Kulenovic

Received: 6 July 2022
Accepted: 23 August 2022
Published: 27 August 2022

1. Introduction

Unreasonable development has caused environmental destruction, therefore, it is the general trend to protect the environment and save energy. Global collaboration promotes the rapid development of the world; immoderate use of natural resources, however, has given rise to land degradation, deforestation and biodiversity loss, and so on. Three wastes in industrial production cause soil pollution, water pollution and air pollution, the rapid development of the global secondary industry promotes the burning of fossil fuels in large quantities, and the greenhouse gas released intensifies the greenhouse effect, causing global warming. The melting of the polar ice cap causes the sea level to rise, and some river deltas with low altitude and fertile land are submerged. At the same time, it also causes seawater to pour into the harbor, which pollutes underground water sources and aggravates the salinization of land. We can know from the notice issued by "The State of Global Climate 2020" that the global average temperature in 2020 was about 1.2 degrees Celsius higher than the pre-industrial level. In the face of natural disasters, human beings are extremely helpless. In order to slow down the trend of climate warming, the United Nations adopted the United Nations Framework Convention on Climate Change in New York on 9 May 1992. In 1997, the Kyoto Protocol of the United Nations Framework Convention on Climate Change was successfully formulated, and it provided legally binding quantitative emission reduction and emission limitation targets for developed countries. In December 2017, twenty-nine countries around the world had signed the Joint Statement on Carbon Neutrality. By September 2019, 66 countries had agreed at the United Nations Climate Action Summit that lucid waters and lush mountains are invaluable assets, and had formed the Climate Ambition Alliance. All these measures have accelerated global carbon neutrality. Britain, Sweden, France, Denmark, New Zealand, Hungary and other countries have written the goal of carbon neutrality into their laws. The EU announced that it will become the first "carbon neutral" land in the world in 2050.

China is a big carbon emitter, so it is imperative to promote peak carbon dioxide emissions and achieve carbon neutrality. According to the data of the seventh national census, China's population has exceeded 1.4 billion, accounting for 21.5% of the world's total population. Abundant human resources have promoted the rapid development of the secondary industry, which is dominated by manufacturing. China's economy is developing steadily, among which the traditional manufacturing industry with high energy consumption and high carbon emission is still the main industry in China. In 2019, China's total carbon emissions reached 10.17 billion tons, accounting for 28% of the global carbon emissions, and China's industrial carbon emissions accounted for more than 50% of China's total carbon emissions. Therefore, Zhang et al. [1] suggested that adjusting the industrial structure and the energy structure have become two obstacles on the road of carbon neutrality in China. Cai et al. [2] used standard methods to calculate urban carbon dioxide emissions, and established a data set of urban carbon dioxide emissions in China. As the largest developing country in the world and a responsible big country, China passed the Energy Conservation Law of the People's Republic of China on 1 November 1997 in order to slow down the global warming trend and play a leading role among developing countries. China released the white paper "China's Policies and Actions to Address Climate Change" in October 2008. In the meantime, China also actively participates in global climate change negotiations, strengthens communication, coordination and cooperation with other countries in the world, and makes contributions to jointly addressing the challenges of climate change and promoting global sustainable development. In September 2020, China proposed at the United Nations General Assembly that carbon dioxide emissions would peak before 2030, and that it strives to achieve carbon neutrality before 2060; In 2021, at the National People's Congress, peak carbon dioxide emissions and carbon neutrality were written into the government work report for the first time. In the same year, the basic ideas and important measures to realize peak carbon dioxide emissions and carbon neutrality were put forward at the ninth meeting of the Central Committee of Finance and Economics. At the National People's Congress in 2021, peak carbon dioxide emissions and carbon neutrality were written into the government work report for the first time, and China put forward the basic ideas and important measures to realize peak carbon dioxide emissions and carbon neutrality at the ninth meeting of the Central Committee of Finance and Economics in the same year.

China is a big carbon emitting country and a big energy consumption country. In 2010, the proportion of carbon emissions from coal in primary energy accounted for about 70%. For this reason, Zou et al. [3] found that the research and development of new energy will greatly promote the realization of carbon neutralization in China. New energy has become the protagonist of the third energy transformation, and will lead the future of carbon neutrality. In [4–7], the authors suggest that developing low-carbon cities, optimizing industrial structure, reducing carbon emissions from steel industry, improving carbon emission reduction technology and reducing carbon sequestration cost are important measures for China to realize peak carbon dioxide emissions and carbon neutrality ahead of schedule.

In the field of applied mathematics, there are a few researches on China's carbon neutrality. Wang et al. [8] innovatively constructed traditional Markov probability transfer matrix and spatial Markov probability transfer matrix to explore the temporal and spatial evolution of China's urban carbon emission performance and predict the long-term trend of carbon emission performance. Chen [9] put forward the energy supply and demand model under two related carbon emission scenarios, namely, China's planned peak and advanced peak scenarios, and suggested that low carbon would be a basic feature of the change of energy supply and demand structure, and non-fossil energy would replace oil as the second largest energy source. Industrial structure and energy consumption structure all have significant influence on carbon dioxide emissions, especially industrial energy intensity. In [10], Guo used economic accounting methods to estimate the potential of China's industrial carbon emission reduction from the perspective of structural emission reduction and intensity emission reduction, and further discussed the influence of industrial internal structure adjustment and energy structure optimization on industrial carbon emission peak and emission reduction potential. According to the data, during the 20 years from 2000 to 2019, the proportion of coal decreased from the original peak of 72.5% to 57.7%, and the natural gas resources increased from 2.2% to 8.4%. Li et al. [11] used the generalized Weng model to predict the regional natural gas production in China, and the prediction results show that the peak natural gas production will reach 323 billion cubic meters per year in 2036. In [12], the scholars investigate the relationship between energy consumption, economic growth and carbon dioxide emissions in Pakistan by using the annual time series data from 1965 to 2015. The estimation results of ARDL show that energy consumption and economic growth have both increased CO_2 emissions in Pakistan in the short and long term. In [13], based on China's provincial panel data from 2004 to 2016, Liu et al. empirically analyzed the impact of ecological civilization construction on carbon emission intensity by using spatial Durbin model based on STIRPAT model. The above-mentioned scholars only consider one of carbon emission and carbon absorption, but not both. We know that only by considering both of them can we accurately and reasonably forecast the time when China will achieve peak carbon dioxide emissions and carbon neutrality. In this paper, we selected industrial structure and energy consumption structure as the influencing factors of carbon emissions.

As the processes of carbon emission and carbon absorption are time-varying processes, we can describe them by continuous differential equations. Furthermore, considering that carbon emission and carbon absorption are not only related to the current time, but also to the past time, we can use the delayed differential equation model to describe the phenomenon of the dynamic system of carbon emission and carbon absorption more truly and accurately. There is a lot of research work on delayed differential equations in many fields, such as biology, medicine, physics, and so on [14–18]. At present, there are few research achievements in describing carbon emission and carbon absorption model by using delayed differential equations, so the purpose of this paper is to use delayed differential equations to describe carbon emission and carbon absorption model.

The motivation of this paper is as follows. Firstly, according to the Chinese government's goal of achieving peak carbon dioxide emissions by 2030 and carbon neutrality by 2060, we want to make some predictions and analyze whether China can achieve it under the current policy based on the carbon absorption and emission model. If there is some gap between the simulated results of the model and the ideal goal, we can put forward some policy suggestions to achieve China's peak carbon dioxide emissions carbon neutrality goal by combining the model with the actual situation. Secondly, considering that many scholars have studied the peak carbon dioxide emissions and carbon neutrality in China from different fields, but there are few related studies on the use of delayed differential equations to describe this problem, and we try to establish a carbon absorption and emission model from the perspective of delayed differential equations to analyze the problem, and analyze this problem from different angles to see if we can get new results. Thirdly, this paper establishes a two-dimensional delayed differential equation model of carbon emission and carbon absorption, which is different from models models cited in the literature [3–13]. We focus on analyzing the existence and stability of equilibrium point, and the existence of system bifurcation, and studying the long-term change process of carbon emission and carbon absorption. The models cited in the literature [3–13] include traditional Markov probability transfer matrix and spatial Markov probability transfer matrix, energy supply and demand model, generalized Weng's model, spatial Durbin model based on STIRPAT model, etc. The above models do not analyze the amount of carbon absorption, but the two-dimensional delayed differential equation proposed by us is not only related to carbon emission, but also to carbon absorption. We also use the knowledge of differential equations to analyze the stability of the model, focusing on the long-term stability of carbon emission and absorption, and so on.

The rest of the content is arranged as follows. In Section 2, we establish a delayed carbon absorption-emission model based on the carbon emission and carbon absorption. In Section 3, we analyze the existence and stability of equilibria and the existence of Hopf bifurcation for the model with time delay. In Section 4, we derive the normal form of the Hopf bifurcation of the above model and analyze the stability of the bifurcating periodic solutions. In Section 5, we present numerical simulations to verify the correctness of our analysis. Finally, the conclusion is drawn in Section 6.

2. Mathematical Modeling

In this paper, we consider carbon emission and carbon absorption together, and analyze the problem of carbon neutrality under China's industrial adjustment. With the rapid development of economy and technology, we assume that carbon emissions and absorption are in a competitive relationship as a whole; this is because in the early stage of China's economic development, the proportion of traditional industries has increased year by year. In 2007, the added value of China's secondary industry accounted for 47.6% of the total proportion. At the same time, China's clean energy development technology is not mature enough, the coal consumption is large and the utilization rate is low. In order to achieve economic growth, traditional high-carbon emission industries are developed, and natural resources are over-exploited, resulting in a significant increase in carbon emissions, immature carbon storage technology, and a corresponding reduction in carbon absorption. As the global climate is gradually warming, the greenhouse effect is obvious year on year, and mankind is facing serious natural disasters. China has gradually realized this great development idea of lucid waters and lush mountains are invaluable assets. In order to implement this correct development idea, our government is actively committed to reducing the coal proportion, improving the energy utilization rate, developing clean energy, shifting from the traditional high-carbon secondary industry to the green and sustainable tertiary industry, reducing carbon emissions, increasing the vegetation coverage, and striving to build a green city. When we only consider the competitive relationship between carbon emission and absorption, we can obtain the following model,

$$\begin{cases} \dfrac{dx(t)}{dt} = x(t)(a_1 - \dfrac{a_1 S_1}{N_2} y(t)), \\ \dfrac{dy(t)}{dt} = y(t)(a_2 - \dfrac{a_2 S_2}{N_1} x(t)), \end{cases} \tag{1}$$

where a_1 represents the annual growth rate of carbon emission, a_2 represents the annual growth rate of carbon absorption, $x(t)$ represents China's carbon emission amount at time t, $y(t)$ represents China's carbon absorption amount at time t, N_1 means the maximum capacity of carbon emissions and N_2 means the maximum capacity of carbon absorption. S_1 means the competition coefficient coefficient of carbon emissions relative to carbon absorption and S_2 represents the competition coefficient of carbon absorption relative to carbon emission.

We think that adding carbon adsorption saturation term to the model will make the model more realistic. This is because China has a vast territory, diverse climates, wide latitudes, and a large distance from the sea. In addition, the terrain is different, and the terrain types and mountain ranges are diverse, which leads to various combinations of temperature and precipitation and different combinations of water temperatures form different types of forest vegetation. This is because the net carbon absorbed by each vegetation is the same under certain conditions every year. Furthermore, from the technical point of view, we know that the progress of carbon storage technology promotes the increase of carbon absorption, but with the relative backwardness of technology, the carbon storage technology will improve relatively slowly, resulting in the decrease of the change rate of carbon storage.

Considering that the dual wheels of optimizing industrial structure and energy structure proposed by Guo [10] could make great contributions to national emission reduction, we can use the quadratic function simulated by previous articles to express the relationship between time and carbon emissions. We can assume that the distance between annual carbon emissions and peak carbon emissions represents the speed of carbon emissions, which is reasonable, because the smaller the distance between them, the larger the carbon emissions, and the smaller the slope of the curve. In practice, it shows that as the industrial structure is gradually transferred from the secondary industry to the tertiary industry, the energy structure is also changed from coal-based primary energy to natural gas-based clean energy, and the carbon emission changes slowly.

We know that there will be a series of processes from the transformation of industrial structure and technology research and development to the application of technology in time production, which will take a certain amount of time. If the relationship between carbon emission and carbon absorption in 2022 is simulated, the carbon emission reduction technology in 2022 will increase compared with the carbon emission when the technology is mature, because the carbon emission reduction technology is just successful but immature. Therefore, we should choose the distance from the peak to the carbon emissions before 2022 as the factor that will affect the carbon emissions in 2022. Increased investment from the government in carbon emission reduction technologies and the rapid development of carbon emission reduction technologies will accelerate the transformation of industrial structure and energy structure, as well as increasing the efficiency during the period of putting into use. For this reason, we establish the following model, the descriptions of these parameters are given in Table 1, and we note that these parameters are all positive,

$$\begin{cases} \dfrac{dx}{dt} = x(a_1 - \dfrac{a_1 S_1}{N_2} y) + k(m - x(t-\tau)), \\ \dfrac{dy}{dt} = y(a_2 - \dfrac{a_2 S_2}{N_1} x - \dfrac{a_2}{N_2} y). \end{cases} \tag{2}$$

For convenience, we denote that

$$c_1 = \frac{a_1 S_1}{N_2},\ b_2 = \frac{a_2 S_2}{N_1},\ c_2 = \frac{a_2}{N_2},$$

then, model (2) becomes

$$\begin{cases} \dfrac{dx}{dt} = x(a_1 - c_1 y) + k(m - x(t-\tau)), \\ \dfrac{dy}{dt} = y(a_2 - b_2 x - c_2 y). \end{cases} \tag{3}$$

According to the initial condition of the system (3), we present a theorem about the nonnegtivity of solution of the system (3).

Theorem 1. *If $x(0) > 0$, $y(0) > 0$, the solution $x(t)$, $y(t)$ of the system (3) with $\tau = 0$ is positive.*

Table 1. Descriptions of variables and parameters in the model (2).

Symbol	Description	Unit
x	Carbon emissions amount	10^2 Mt
y	Carbon absorption amount	10^2 Mt
a_1	Annual growth rate of carbon emissions	-
a_2	Annual growth rate of carbon absorption	-
k	The influence coefficient of energy structure reform on x	-
m	The peak of carbon emissions	10^2 Mt
N_1	The maximum capacity of carbon emissions	10^2 Mt
N_2	The maximum capacity of carbon absorptions	10^2 Mt
S_1	The copetitive coefficient of carbon emissions relative to carbon absorptions	-
S_2	The copetitive coefficient of carbon absorption relative to carbon emissions	-
τ	Time-delay for carbon emission reduction technology to be applied to actual production	year

Proof. First, we prove $y(t) > 0$ when $t > 0$ under the positive initial condition of the system (3) with $\tau = 0$.

We assume that $y(t)$ is not always positive for $t > 0$ and make t_1 be the first time that $y(t_1) = 0,\ y'(t_1) < 0$. According to the second equation of the system (3), we can obtain $y'(t_1) = 0$. The two conclusions we obtain are contradictory. Therefore, under the positive initial condition, the solution $y(t)$ of the system (3) is positive for $t > 0$. Then, we prove $x(t) > 0$ when $t > 0$ under the positive initial condition of the system (3) with $\tau = 0$. We assume that $x(t)$ is not always positive for $t > 0$ and make t_2 be the first time that $x(t_2) = 0,\ x'(t_2) < 0$. According to the first equation of the system (3), we can obtain $x'(t_2) = km > 0$. The two conclusions we reach are contradictory. Therefore, under the positive initial condition, the solution $x(t)$ of the system (3) with $\tau = 0$ is also positive for $t > 0$. □

Remark 1. *We prove if $x(0) > 0,\ y(0) > 0$, the solution $x(t),\ y(t)$ of the system (3) with $\tau = 0$ is positive. It is also not easy for us to prove the solution of the system (3) is positive when $\tau > 0$. However, according to the numerical simulation of a group of real parameters, we find that the solution of the system (3) is always positive, which is not contradictory to the positivity of the solution of the system (3).*

Next, we will consider the dynamics phenomena of the system (3).

3. Stability Analysis of Equilibrium and Existence of Hopf Bifurcation

In this section, we will discuss the stability of equilibria and the existence of Hopf bifurcation for system (3).

3.1. Existence Of Equilibrium Point

When the parameters of system (3) meet the following assumptions

$$(H_1)\ k - a_1 > 0, \tag{4}$$

system (3) has a boundary equilibrium $E_1 = (x^{(1)}, 0)$, where

$$x^{(1)} = \frac{km}{k - a_1}.$$

When the parameters of system (3) meet the following assumptions

$$(H_2)\begin{cases}\sqrt{(c_1a_2+(k-a_1)c_2)^2-4c_1c_2b_2km}>0,\\ c_1a_2+(k-a_1)c_2+\sqrt{(c_1a_2+(k-a_1)c_2)^2-4c_1c_2b_2km}>0,\\ c_1a_2-(k-a_1)c_2-\sqrt{(c_1a_2+(k-a_1)c_2)^2-4c_1c_2b_2km}>0,\end{cases} \tag{5}$$

system (3) has a positive equilibrium $E_2=(x^{(2)},y^{(2)})$, where

$$x^{(2)}=\frac{c_1a_2+(k-a_1)c_2+\sqrt{(c_1a_2+(k-a_1)c_2)^2-4c_1c_2b_2km}}{2c_1b_2},$$

$$y^{(2)}=\frac{c_1a_2-(k-a_1)c_2-\sqrt{(c_1a_2+(k-a_1)c_2)^2-4c_1c_2b_2km}}{2c_1c_2}.$$

When the parameters of system (3) meet the following assumptions

$$(H_3)\begin{cases}\sqrt{(c_1a_2+(k-a_1)c_2)^2-4c_1c_2b_2km}>0,\\ c_1a_2+(k-a_1)c_2-\sqrt{(c_1a_2+(k-a_1)c_2)^2-4c_1c_2b_2km}>0,\\ c_1a_2-(k-a_1)c_2+\sqrt{(c_1a_2+(k-a_1)c_2)^2-4c_1c_2b_2km}>0,\end{cases} \tag{6}$$

system (3) has a positive equilibrium $E_3=(x^{(3)},y^{(3)})$, where

$$x^{(3)}=\frac{c_1a_2+(k-a_1)c_2-\sqrt{(c_1a_2+(k-a_1)c_2)^2-4c_1c_2b_2km}}{2c_1b_2},$$

$$y^{(3)}=\frac{c_1a_2-(k-a_1)c_2+\sqrt{(c_1a_2+(k-a_1)c_2)^2-4c_1c_2b_2km}}{2c_1c_2}.$$

3.2. Stability and Existence of Hopf Bifurcation for $E_1=(x^{(1)},0)$

When (H_1) holds, system (3) has equilibrium E_1, similar to the calculation method in [19–22], we calculate the stability of the equilibrium E_1 and the existence of Hopf bifurcation. The characteristic equation of system (3), evaluated at E_1, is given as follows:

$$\lambda(\lambda-a_1+e^{-\lambda\tau}k)=0. \tag{7}$$

Note that $\lambda=0$ is always the root of the Equation (7). Next, we only need to consider the following equation,

$$\lambda-a_1+e^{-\lambda\tau}k=0. \tag{8}$$

When $\tau=0$, Equation (8) becomes

$$\lambda+k-a_1=0, \tag{9}$$

it leads to $\lambda_1=-(k-a_1)<0$, due to (H_1) holds.

When $\tau>0$, we try to discuss the existence of Hopf bifurcation. We assume that $\lambda=i\omega(\omega>0)$ is a pure imaginary root of Equation (8). Substituting it into Equation (8) and separating the real and imaginary parts, we obtain:

$$\begin{cases}k\sin(\omega\tau)=\omega,\\ k\cos(\omega\tau)=a_1.\end{cases} \tag{10}$$

Equation (10) derives the following results,

$$Q_1 \triangleq \sin(\omega_1 \tau_1) = \frac{\omega_1}{k}, \ R_1 \triangleq \cos(\omega_1 \tau_1) = \frac{a_1}{k}. \tag{11}$$

Adding the square of the two equations, we obtain

$$\omega_1^2 - a_1^2 + k^2 = 0, \tag{12}$$

then it gives $\omega_1 = \sqrt{k^2 - a_1^2}$, which makes sense due to the assumptions (H_1). We obtain the expression of $\tau_1^{(j)}$ as follows:

$$\tau_1^{(j)} = \begin{cases} \dfrac{\arccos(R_1) + 2j\pi}{\omega_1}, Q_1 > 0, \\ \dfrac{-\arccos(R_1) + 2(j+1)\pi}{\omega_1}, Q_1 < 0, \ j = 0, \ 1, \ 2, \ 3, \ 4, \cdots. \end{cases} \tag{13}$$

Let $\lambda = \lambda(\tau)$ be the root of Equation (8), satisfying $\lambda(\tau_1^{(j)}) = \mathrm{i}\omega_1$. Differentiating both sides of (8) with respective to τ gives that

$$\mathrm{Re}(\frac{d\lambda}{d\tau})^{-1}|_{\tau=\tau_1^{(j)}} = \frac{k^2 - a_1^2}{k\omega_1^2} > 0. \tag{14}$$

Theorem 2. *When the parameters of system (3) meet the assumptions* (H_1)*, for any of* $\tau \geqslant 0$*, characteristic Equation (7) has a zero root. When* $\tau = \tau_1^{(j)}$*, characteristic Equation (7) has a zero root and a pair of pure imaginary roots, and when* $\tau \in [0, \tau_1^{(0)})$*, Equation (7) has a zero root, and other roots have negative real parts, when* $\tau > \tau_1^{(0)}$*, the equilibrium* E_1 *of system (3) is unstable.*

3.3. Stability and Existence of Hopf Bifurcation for $E_{2,3}$

Next, we analyze the stability of system (3) for $E_i = (x^{(i)}, y^{(i)})$ $(i = 2, 3)$, and the characteristic equation of system (3), evaluated at E_i, is given by

$$\lambda^2 + (-a_1 + c_1 y^{(i)} + c_2 y^{(i)})\lambda + c_2 y^{(i)}(-a_1 + c_1 y^{(i)}) - c_1 b_2 x^{(i)} y^{(i)} + (k\lambda + kc_2 y^{(i)})e^{-\lambda\tau} = 0. \tag{15}$$

When $\tau = 0$, Equation (15) becomes

$$\lambda^2 + T_2^{(i)}\lambda + D_2^{(i)} = 0, \tag{16}$$

where

$$T_2^{(i)} = (k - a_1 + c_1 y^{(i)} + c_2 y^{(i)}), \ D_2^{(i)} = c_2 y^{(i)}(k - a_1 + c_1 y^{(i)}) - c_1 b_2 x^{(i)} y^{(i)}.$$

where $(x^{(i)}, y^{(i)}) = (x^{(2)}, y^{(2)})$, the parameters of system (3) meet the assumptions (H_2), we can prove that

$$T_2^{(2)} > 0, \ D_2^{(2)} = -y^{(2)}\sqrt{(c_1 a_2 + (k - a_1)c_2)^2 - 4c_1 c_2 b_2 km} < 0, \tag{17}$$

thus, E_2 is unstable when $\tau = 0$.

When $(x^{(i)}, y^{(i)}) = (x^{(3)}, y^{(3)})$ and the parameters of system (3) satisfy the assumptions (H_3), we can prove that

$$T_2^{(3)} > 0, \ D_2^{(3)} = y^{(3)}\sqrt{(c_1 a_2 + (k - a_1)c_2)^2 - 4c_1 c_2 b_2 km} > 0, \tag{18}$$

thus, E_3 is locally asymptotically stable when $\tau = 0$. When $\tau > 0$, we try to discuss the existence of Hopf bifurcation. We assume that $\lambda = i\omega(\omega > 0)$ is a pure imaginary root of Equation (15). Substituting it into Equation (15) and separating the real and imaginary parts, we obtain:

$$\begin{cases} \omega^2 + c_2y^{(i)}(a_1 - c_1y^{(i)}) + c_1b_2x^{(i)}y^{(i)} = k\omega\sin(\omega\tau) + kc_2y^{(i)}\cos(\omega\tau), \\ \omega(a_1 - c_1y^{(i)} - c_2y^{(i)}) = k\omega\cos(\omega\tau) - kc_2y^{(i)}\sin(\omega\tau), \end{cases} \tag{19}$$

Equation (19) derives the following results,

$$\begin{aligned} Q_2^{(i)} &\triangleq \sin(\omega\tau) = \frac{k\omega(\omega^2 + c_2y^{(i)}(a_1 - c_1y^{(i)}) + c_1b_2x^{(i)}y^{(i)}) - kc_2y^{(i)}\omega(a_1 - c_1y^{(i)} - c_2y^{(i)})}{k^2\omega^2 + k^2c_2^2y^{(i)2}}, \\ R_2^{(i)} &\triangleq \cos(\omega\tau) = \\ &\frac{k\omega^2(a_1 - c_1y^{(i)}) + c_1b_2x^{(i)}y^{(i)}) + kc_2y^{(i)}(\omega^2 + c_2y^{(i)}(a_1 - c_1y^{(i)}) + c_1b_2x^{(i)}y^{(i)})}{k^2\omega^2 + k^2c_2^2y^{(i)2}}. \end{aligned} \tag{20}$$

Adding the square of the two equations, we obtain

$$\omega^4 + T_3^{(i)}\omega^2 + D_3^{(i)} = 0, \tag{21}$$

where

$$\begin{aligned} T_3^{(i)} &= 2c_2y^{(i)}(a_1 - c_1y^{(i)}) + 2c_1b_2x^{(i)}y^{(i)} + (a_1 - c_1y^{(i)} - c_2y^{(i)})^2 - k^2, \\ D_3^{(i)} &= 2c_1c_2b_2x^{(i)}y^{(i)2}(a_1 - c_1y^{(i)}) + (c_2y^{(i)}(a_1 - c_1y^{(i)}))^2 + (c_1b_2x^{(i)}y^{(i)})^2 - (kc_2y^{(i)})^2. \end{aligned}$$

For convenience, we let $\omega^2 = z$, Equation (21) becomes

$$h(z) = z^2 + T_3^{(i)}z + D_3^{(i)} = 0. \tag{22}$$

When the parameters of system (3) meet the following assumptions—$D_3^{(i)} < 0$, Equation (22) has one positive root z_2; If $T_3^{(i)} > 0, D_3^{(i)} > 0$ hold, Equation (22) has no positive root; If $T_3^{(i)} < 0, D_3^{(i)} > 0$ hold, Equation (22) has two positive roots z_3, z_4. We hypothesize that Equation (22) has positive roots z_n $(n = 2, 3, 4)$, then $\omega_n = \sqrt{z_n}$ $(n = 2, 3, 4)$. From (20), we can solve the critical value of time delay,

$$\tau_n^{(j)} = \begin{cases} \dfrac{\arcsin(Q_2^{(i)}) + 2j\pi}{\omega_n}, R_2 > 0, \\ \dfrac{-\arcsin(Q_2^{(i)}) + 2(j+1)\pi}{\omega_n}, R_2 < 0, \ n = 2,\ 3,\ 4,\ j = 0,\ 1,\ 2, \cdots. \end{cases} \tag{23}$$

Let $\lambda = \lambda(\tau)$ be the root of (15), satisfying $\lambda(\tau_n^{(j)}) = i\omega_n$ $(n = 2, 3, 4)$. Differentiating both sides of Equation (15) with respective to τ gives that:

$$\begin{aligned} \mathrm{Re}(\frac{d\lambda}{d\tau})^{-1}|_{\tau=\tau_n^{(j)}} &= \frac{2\omega_n^2 + 2c_2y^{(i)}(a_1 - c_1y^{(i)}) + 2c_1b_2x^{(i)}y^{(i)} + (a_1 - c_1y^{(i)} - c_2y^{(i)})^2 - k^2}{k^2\omega_n^2 + k^2c_2^2y^{(i)2}} \\ &= h'(z_n) \neq 0. \end{aligned} \tag{24}$$

Theorem 3. *Considering the stability of E_2 and E_3 for system (3), we come to the following conclusions:*
(1) When (H_2) holds, the equilibrium E_2 is unstable for any $\tau \geqslant 0$;
(2) When (H_3) holds, we discuss the stability of equilibrium E_3 of system (3) below.
(a) When $T_3^{(3)} > 0, D_3^{(3)} > 0$ hold, Equation (22) has no positive root, the equilibrium E_3 is locally asymptotically stable for any $\tau \geqslant 0$;

(b) If $D_3^{(3)} < 0$ holds, Equation (22) has one positive roots z_2, then when $\tau \in [0, \tau_2^{(0)})$, the equilibrium E_3 is locally asymptotically stable, and unstable when $\tau > \tau_2^{(0)}$;

(c) If $T_3^{(3)} < 0, D_3^{(3)} > 0$ hold, system (3) undergoes a Hopf bifurcation at the trivial equilibrium E_3 when $\tau = \tau_n^{(j)}$ $(n = 3, 4;\ j = 0,\ 1,\ 2, \cdots)$. Then, $\exists m \in N$ makes $0 < \tau_4^{(0)} < \tau_3^{(0)} < \tau_4^{(1)} < \tau_4^{(1)} < \cdots < \tau_3^{(m-1)} < \tau_4^{(m)} < \tau_4^{(m+1)}$. When $\tau \in [0, \tau_4^{(0)}) \cup \bigcup_{l=1}^{m} (\tau_3^{(l-1)}, \tau_4^{(l)})$, the equilibrium E_3 of the system (3) is locally asymptotically stable, and when $\tau \in \bigcup_{l=0}^{m-1} (\tau_4^{(l)}, \tau_3^{(l)}) \cup (\tau_4^{(m)}, +\infty)$, the equilibrium E_3 is unstable.

Proof.

(1) When (H_2) and $\tau = 0$ hold, we can prove $T_2^{(2)} > 0,\ D_2^{(2)} < 0$, that is Equation (16) has a positive root, so equilibrium E_2 of system (3) with $\tau = 0$ is unstable;

(2) When $T_3^{(3)} > 0, D_3^{(3)} > 0$ hold, we can prove $T_2^{(3)} > 0,\ D_2^{(3)} > 0$, that is, Equation (16) has two negative roots, so equilibrium E_3 of system (3) with $\tau = 0$ is locally asymptotically stable:

- (a) When $T_3^{(3)} > 0, D_3^{(3)} > 0$ hold, Equation (22) has no positive root, the equilibrium E_3 is locally asymptotically stable for any $\tau \geqslant 0$;
- (b) When $D_3^{(3)} < 0$ holds, Equation (22) has one positive root z_2, and $Sign(\mathrm{Re}(\frac{d\lambda}{d\tau})^{-1}_{\tau=\tau_2^{(j)}}) = Sign(h'(z_2)) > 0$, and thus, all the roots of Equation (22) have negative real parts for $\tau \in [0, \tau_2^{(0)})$, and Equation (22) has at least one pair of roots with positive real part when $\tau > \tau_2^{(0)}$;
- (c) If $T_3^{(3)} < 0, D_3^{(3)} > 0$ hold, $h(z) = 0$ has two positive roots z_3 and z_4, and $Sign(\mathrm{Re}(\frac{d\lambda}{d\tau})^{-1}_{\tau=\tau_3^{(j)}}) = Sign(h'(z_3)) < 0$ and $Sign(\mathrm{Re}(\frac{d\lambda}{d\tau})^{-1}_{\tau=\tau_4^{(j)}}) = Sign(h'(z_4)) > 0$, thus, there exists $m \in N$, such that all the roots of Equation (15) have negative real parts when$\tau \in [0, \tau_4^{(0)}) \cup \bigcup_{l=1}^{m} (\tau_3^{(l-1)}, \tau_4^{(l)})$, and Equation (15) has at least one root with a positive real part when $\tau \in \bigcup_{l=0}^{m-1} (\tau_4^{(l)}, \tau_3^{(l)}) \cup (\tau_4^{(m)}, +\infty)$, and the conclusion is immediate.

□

4. Normal Form of Hopf Bifurcation

In Section 3, we have shown that the equilibrium $E_2 = (x^{(2)}, y^{(2)})$ is unstable when $\tau = 0$, and the equilibrium $E_3 = (x^{(3)}, y^{(3)})$ is locally asymptotically stable when $\tau = 0$. To reflect the actual situation, we focus on the delay from technological innovation to practical production. Therefore, we consider the time-delay τ as a bifurcation parameter and denote the critical value $\tau = \tau_c = \tau_n^{(j)}$, where $\tau_n^{(j)}$ is given in (23). When $\tau = \tau_n^{(j)}$, characteristic Equation (21) has a pair of pure imaginary roots $\lambda = \pm i\omega$. Therefore, system (3) undergoes a Hopf bifurcation at equilibrium E_3. In this section, we derive the normal form of Hopf bifurcation for the system (3) by using the multiple time scales method given in [23,24].

In order to normalize the delay, we first re-scale the time t by using $t \mapsto t/\tau$, then translate the equilibrium $E_3 = (x^{(3)}, y^{(3)})$ to the origin, that is,

$$\begin{cases} \widetilde{x} = x - x^{(3)}, \\ \widetilde{y} = y - y^{(3)}, \end{cases}$$

For convenience, we still use x and y to represent $\tilde{x}$ and $\tilde{y}$ respectively, so Equation (3) is transformed into:

$$\begin{cases} \dfrac{dx}{dt} = \tau(a_1 x - c_1 x^{(3)} y - c_1 xy - c_1 y^{(3)} x - kx(t-1)), \\ \dfrac{dy}{dt} = -\tau(y + y^{(3)})(b_2 x + c_2 y). \end{cases} \tag{25}$$

Equation (25) can also be written as:

$$\dot{Z}(t) = \tau N_1 Z(t) + \tau N_2 Z(t-1) + \tau F(Z(t), Z(t-1)), \tag{26}$$

where

$$Z(t) = (x(t), y(t))^T,\ Z(t-1) = (x(t-1), y(t-1))^T, F(Z(t), Z(t-1)) = (x(t-1), y(t-1))^T,$$

and

$$N_1 = \begin{pmatrix} a_1 - c_1 y^{(3)} & -c_1 x^{(3)} \\ -b_2 y^{(3)} & -c_2 y^{(3)} \end{pmatrix},\ N_2 = \begin{pmatrix} -k & 0 \\ 0 & 0 \end{pmatrix}.$$

We let h be eigenvector corresponding to eigenvalue $\lambda = i\omega\tau$ of Equation (26), and h^* be the eigenvector corresponding to eigenvalue $\lambda = -i\omega\tau$ of adjoint matrix of Equation (26), satisfying

$$< h^*, h >= \overline{h^*}^T h = 1. \tag{27}$$

By calculating, we have

$$h = (1, -\frac{b_2 y^{(3)}}{i\omega + c_2 y^{(3)}})^T,\ h^* = d(\frac{i\omega - c_2 y^{(3)}}{c_1 x^{(3)}}, 1)^T,\ d = \frac{c_1 x^{(3)}}{c_1 x^{(3)} + b_2 y^{(3)}}. \tag{28}$$

We treat the delay τ as the bifurcation parameter, let $\tau = \tau_c + \varepsilon\mu$, where $\tau_c = \tau_n^{(j)}$ $(j = 0, 1, 2, \cdots)$ is the Hopf bifurcation critical value, μ is perturbation parameter, ε is dimensionless scale parameter. Suppose system (26) undergoes a Hopf bifurcation from the trivial equilibrium at the critical point $\tau = \tau_c$, and then, by the MTS method, the solution of (26) is assumed as follows:

$$Z(t) = Z(T_0, T_1, T_2, \cdots) = \sum_{k=1}^{+\infty} \varepsilon^k Z_k(T_0, T_1, T_2, \cdots), \tag{29}$$

where

$$Z(T_0, T_1, T_2, \cdots) = (x(T_0, T_1, T_2, \cdots), y(T_0, T_1, T_2, \cdots))^T,$$
$$Z_k(T_0, T_1, T_2, \cdots) = (x_k(T_0, T_1, T_2, \cdots), y_k(T_0, T_1, T_2, \cdots))^T,$$

and the derivative with regard to t is transformed into

$$\frac{d}{dt} = \frac{\partial}{\partial T_0} + \varepsilon\frac{\partial}{\partial T_1} + \varepsilon^2\frac{\partial}{\partial T_2} + \cdots = D_0 + \varepsilon D_1 + \varepsilon^2 D_2 + \cdots, \tag{30}$$

where D_i is differential operator, and

$$D_i = \frac{\partial}{\partial T_i}\ (i = 0, 1, 2, 3, \cdots).$$

From (26), we have

$$\dot{Z}(t) = \varepsilon D_0 Z_1 + \varepsilon^2 D_1 Z_1 + \varepsilon^3 D_2 Z_1 + \varepsilon^2 D_0 Z_2 + \varepsilon^3 D_1 Z_2 + \varepsilon^3 D_0 Z_3 + \cdots. \tag{31}$$

We expand $x(T_0-1,\varepsilon(T_0-1),\varepsilon^2(T_0-1),\cdots)$ at $x(T_0-1,T_1,T_2,\cdots)$ by the Taylor expansion, that is,

$$x(t-1)=\varepsilon x_{1,\tau_c}+\varepsilon^2 x_{2,\tau_c}+\varepsilon^3 x_{3,\tau_c}-\varepsilon^2 D_1 x_{1,\tau_c}-\varepsilon^3 D_2 x_{1,\tau_c}-\varepsilon^3 D_1 x_{2,\tau_c}+\cdots, \tag{32}$$

where $x_{j,\tau_c}=x_j(T_0-1,T_1,T_2,\cdots)$, $j=1,2,3\cdots$.

We substitute Formulas (29)–(32) into Equation (26), then comparing the coefficients of $\varepsilon,\varepsilon^2$ and ε^3 on both sides of the equation, respectively. Then, we obtain the following expressions, respectively,

$$\begin{aligned}&D_0x_1-\tau_c(a_1x_1-c_1x^{(3)}y_1-c_1x_1y^{(3)}-kx_{1,\tau_c})=0,\\&D_0y_1+\tau_c y^{(3)}(b_2x_1+c_2y_1)=0.\end{aligned} \tag{33}$$

$$\begin{aligned}&D_0x_2-\tau_c(a_1x_2-c_1x^{(3)}y_2-c_1x_2y^{(3)}-kx_{2,\tau_c})\\&=\mu(a_1x_1-c_1x^{(3)}y_1-c_1x_1y^{(3)}-kx_{1,\tau_c})-\tau_c(c_1x_1y_1-kD_1x_{1,\tau_c})-D_1x_1,\\&D_0y_2+\tau_c y^{(3)}(b_2x_2+c_2y_2)\\&=-(\mu y^{(3)}+\tau_c y_1)(b_2x_1+c_2y_1)-D_1y_1.\end{aligned} \tag{34}$$

$$\begin{aligned}&D_0x_3-\tau_c(a_1x_3-c_1x^{(3)}y_3-c_1x_3y^{(3)}-kx_{3,\tau_c})\\&=\mu(a_1x_2-c_1x_2y_1-c_1x^{(3)}y_2-c_1x_2y^{(3)}+kx_{2,\tau_c}+kD_1x_{1,\tau_c})-\tau_c(c_1x_2y_1+c_1x_1y_2-\\&kD_2x_{1,\tau_c}-kD_1x_{2,\tau_c})-D_1x_2-D_2x_1,\\&D_0y_3+\tau_c y^{(3)}(b_2x_3+c_2y_3)\\&=-\tau_c(y_2(b_2x-1+c_2y_1)+y_1(b_2x_2+c_2y_2))-\mu(y_1(b_2x_1+c_2y_1)+y^{(3)}(b_2x_2+c_2y_2))\\&-D_1y_2-D_2y_1.\end{aligned} \tag{35}$$

Equation (33) has the solution with following form,

$$Z_1=Ghe^{i\omega\tau_cT_0}+\overline{Gh}e^{-i\omega\tau_cT_0}, \tag{36}$$

where h is given by (28). Equation (34) is a linear non-homogeneous equation, and the non-homogeneous equation has a solution if and only if a solvability condition is satisfied. That is, the right-hand side of (34) should be orthogonal to every solution of the adjoint homogeneous problem. Thus, we solve (36) into the right part of equation (34), and the coefficient vector of $e^{i\omega\tau_cT_0}$ is noted as m_1, by $<h^*,m_1>=0$, so we can solve $\frac{\partial G}{\partial T_1}$, namely,

$$\frac{\partial G}{\partial T_1}=M\mu G, \tag{37}$$

where

$$M=\frac{c_1x^{(3)}(y^{(3)}b_2+y^{(3)}c_2h_2)-(c_2y^{(3)}+i\omega)(-a_1+c_1x^{(3)}h_2+c_1y^{(3)}+ke^{-i\omega\tau_c})}{(c_2y^{(3)}+i\omega)(-\tau_cke^{-i\omega\tau_c}+1)-c_1x^{(3)}h_2},$$

$$h_2=-\frac{b_2y^{(3)}}{i\omega+c_2y^{(3)}},$$

with

$$x^{(3)}=\frac{c_1a_2+(k-a_1)c_2-\sqrt{(c_1a_2+(k-a_1)c_2)^2-4c_1c_2b_2km}}{2c_1b_2},$$

$$y^{(3)}=\frac{c_1a_2-(k-a_1)c_2+\sqrt{(c_1a_2+(k-a_1)c_2)^2-4c_1c_2b_2km}}{2c_1c_2}.$$

We solve Equation (34), as μ is a small disturbance coefficient, and we only consider the influence of μ on low-order terms, thus, we obtain its solutions with following form:

$$\begin{aligned} x_2 &= g_1 e^{2i\omega\tau_c T_0} + c.c. + l_1, \\ y_2 &= g_2 e^{2i\omega\tau_c T_0} + c.c. + l_2, \end{aligned} \tag{38}$$

where $c.c.$ stands for the complex conjugate of the preceding terms, then, we substitute solutions (38) into (34), and we obtain

$$\begin{aligned} g_1 &= K_1 S G^2,\ l_1 = P_1 R G\overline{G}, \\ g_2 &= K_2 S G^2,\ l_2 = P_2 R G\overline{G}, \end{aligned} \tag{39}$$

with

$$\begin{aligned} K_1 &= (2i\omega + c_2 y^{(3)})(-c_1 h_2) + c_1 x^{(3)}(c_2 h_2^2 + b_2 h_2), \\ K_2 &= (2i\omega + c_1 y^{(3)} - a_1 + ke^{-2i\omega\tau_c})(-c_2 h_2^2 - b_2 h_2) + c_1 b_2 y^{(3)} h_2, \\ S &= ((2i\omega + c_2 y^{(3)})(2i\omega + c_1 y^{(3)} - a_1 + ke^{-2i\omega\tau_c}) - c_1 b_2 y^{(3)} x^{(3)})^{-1}, \\ P_1 &= -c_1 x^{(3)}(b_2(\overline{h_2} + h_2) + 2c_2 h_2 \overline{h_2}) + c_2 c_1 y^{(3)}(\overline{h_2} + h_2), \\ P_2 &= -c_1 b_2 y^{(3)}(\overline{h_2} + h_2) + (c_1 y^{(3)} + k - a_1)(b_2(\overline{h_2} + h_2) + 2c_2 h_2 \overline{h_2}), \\ R &= (-c_2 y^{(3)}(k - a_1 + c_1 y^{(3)}) + c_1 b_2 x^{(3)} y^{(3)})^{-1},\ h_2 = -\frac{b_2 y^{(3)}}{i\omega + c_2 y^{(3)}}. \end{aligned} \tag{40}$$

Next, substituting solution (36) and (38) into (35), and with the coefficient vector of $e^{i\omega\tau_c T_0}$ noted as m_2, by solvability condition, we have $< h^*, m_2 >= 0$. Note that μ is a disturbance parameter, and μ^2 has little influence for small unfolding parameter, thus, we can ignore the $\mu^2 G$ term, then $\frac{\partial G}{\partial T_2}$, can be solved to yield

$$\frac{\partial G}{\partial T_2} = HG^2\overline{G}, \tag{41}$$

where

$$\begin{aligned} H =& \frac{(i\omega + c_2 y^{(3)})(-\tau_c c_1)(K_1 S\overline{h_2} + K_2 S + P_1 R h_2 + P_2 R)}{(i\omega + c_2 y^{(3)})(k\tau_c e^{-i\omega\tau_c} - 1) + c_1 x^{(3)} h_2} \\ &+ \frac{\tau_c b_2 c_1 x^{(3)}(K_1 S\overline{h_2} + K_2 S + P_1 R h_2 + P_2 R) + 2\tau_c c_2 c_1 x^{(3)}(K_2 S\overline{h_2} + P_2 R h_2)}{(i\omega + c_2 y^{(3)})(k\tau_c e^{-i\omega\tau_c} - 1) + c_1 x^{(3)} h_2}, \\ h_2 =& -\frac{b_2 y^{(3)}}{i\omega + c_2 y^{(3)}}, \end{aligned}$$

with

$$\begin{aligned} x^{(3)} &= \frac{c_1 a_2 + (k - a_1)c_2 - \sqrt{(c_1 a_2 + (k - a_1)c_2)^2 - 4c_1 c_2 b_2 km}}{2c_1 b_2}, \\ y^{(3)} &= \frac{c_1 a_2 - (k - a_1)c_2 + \sqrt{(c_1 a_2 + (k - a_1)c_2)^2 - 4c_1 c_2 b_2 km}}{2c_1 c_2}. \end{aligned}$$

Let $G \to G/\varepsilon$, we obtain the normal form of Hopf bifurcation of system (26) truncated at the cubic order terms:

$$\dot{G} = M\mu G + HG^2\overline{G}, \tag{42}$$

where M is given in (37), and H given in (41).

With the polar coordinate $G = re^{i\theta}$, substituting that expression into Equation (42), we obtain the amplitude equation of Equation (42) on the center manifold as

$$\begin{cases} \dot{r} = \mathrm{Re}(M)\mu r + \mathrm{Re}(H)r^3, \\ \dot{\theta} = \mathrm{Im}(M)\mu + \mathrm{Im}(H)r^2. \end{cases} \tag{43}$$

Theorem 4. *When* $\frac{\mathrm{Re}(M)\mu}{\mathrm{Re}(H)} < 0$, *system* (26) *has periodic solutions.*

(1) *If* $\mathrm{Re}(M)\mu < 0$, *then the periodic solution reduced on the center manifold is unstable;*
(2) *If* $\mathrm{Re}(M)\mu > 0$, *then the periodic solution reduced on the center manifold is stable.*

5. Numerical Simulations

First of all, in this section, we will analyze and reasonably select some parameters in system (3) based on the official actual data. Then, based on the selected parameters, we use Matlab software to simulate the stable equilibrium and periodic solution of the system (3). Finally, we put forward some reasonable carbon emission reduction measures for China according to the simulation results.

5.1. Determination of Parameter Values

Firstly, we present the carbon emissions from 2000 to 2018 (see Table 2).

Table 2. Annual carbon emission data (the unit of carbon emission is 10^2 million ton).

Year	Carbon Emissions	Year	Carbon Emissions	Year	Carbon Emissions
2000	31.52	2007	65.62	2014	113.34
2001	32.84	2008	74.85	2015	111.07
2002	36.38	2009	81.53	2016	112.24
2003	43.08	2010	91.35	2017	115.53
2004	49.47	2011	102.76	2018	118.83
2005	58.08	2012	105.65		
2006	62.49	2013	112.44		

Based on the data in Table 2, we analyze the peak value and peak time of China's carbon emissions and also predict the amount of carbon emissions in 2022. We use carbon emissions data from 2000 to 2018 (Table 2) to simulate a quadratic function of carbon emissions over time, as shown in Figure 1. Figure 1 shows that the maximum value will appear around 2029, with a value of 13.8135 billion tons. Each hollow red circle in Figure 1 represents the real data of annual carbon emissions, the black curve represents the quadratic function simulation of these data, and the red hollow five pointed star represents the simulated maximum value. Then, we assume that the predicted maximum value is the peak value of carbon emissions, namely, maximum = m. We have also reasonably predicted the carbon emissions in 2022, which will be 13.2087 billion tons. In this way, the peak of carbon emissions can be achieved before 2030, which is consistent with the national policy requirements.

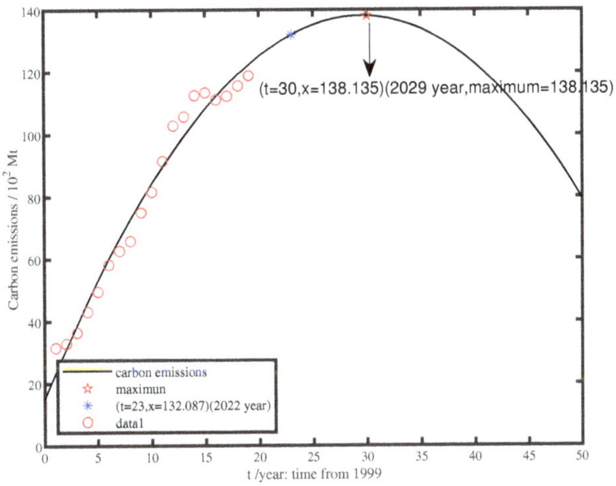

Figure 1. Carbon emission data from 2000 to 2018 and fitting curve.

Therefore, because the meaning of parameter m in model (3) is the maximum peak value of carbon emissions, combined with Figure 1, we take $m = 138.135$.

Next, we assume that this year's natural growth rate is the difference between this year's carbon emissions and last year's carbon emissions divided by last year's carbon emissions, that is, $a_{1,j} = \frac{x_j - x_{j-1}}{x_j}$ $(j = 2001, 2002, \cdots)$, and we calculated the annual natural growth rate of carbon emissions and simulated it with a first-order function curve. Each blue asterisk in Figure 2 represents the natural growth rate of carbon emissions each year, and the blue line represents the simulation image of a function of these data, as shown in Figure 2.

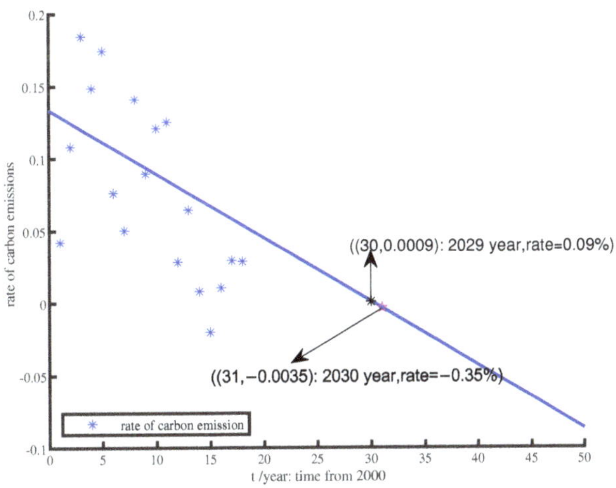

Figure 2. Analysis of the natural growth rate of carbon emissions and fitting curve.

Figure 2 shows that 2029 is the last year when the natural growth rate of carbon emissions is positive with 0.09%, and it turns negative by 2030 with −0.35%.

It is common sense that the maximum capacity of carbon emissions should be greater than the peak of carbon emissions, carbon absorption is the same, so we choose $N_1 = 2m = 276.27$, $N_2 = 1.1m = 151.9485$, whose units are both 10^2 million ton. Since we chose a competitive model, we chose competition factors of $S_1 = 2$ and $S_2 = 0.5$ to make carbon emissions and carbon sequestration competitive. We assume natural growth rate of carbon emissions of between 0.14 and 0.05, thus, we choose $a_1 = 0.14,\ a_2 = 0.2,\ k = 0.5$.

Based on the above analysis, we take one group of parameters as follows,

$$a_1 = 0.14,\ a_2 = 0.2,\ k = 0.5\ S_1 = 2\ S_2 = 0.5\ N_1 = 276.27,\ N_2 = 151.9485,\ m = 138.135.$$

5.2. Simulation Results

We select the above group of parameters given in Section 5.1, that is,

$$a_1 = 0.14,\ a_2 = 0.2,\ k = 0.5\ S_1 = 2\ S_2 = 0.5\ N_1 = 276.27,\ N_2 = 151.9485,\ m = 138.135.$$

After calculation, we find that the group of parameters satisfies hypothesis conditions (H_1) and (H_3), the hypothesis condition (H_2) is not satisfied, that is, E_1 and E_3 exist, but E_2 does not exist. Since E_1 is a boundary equilibrium, we should actually discuss the stability of the non-trivial equilibrium, so we will discuss the stability of the equilibrium E_3 in the following part, and $E_3 = (119.81, 119.82)$; from Equation (17), we calculate that $T_2 = 0.7365 > 0,\ D_2 = 0.0815 > 0$. Thus, equilibrium E_3 is locally asymptotically stable when $\tau = 0$. We select initial value (132, 50), and the simulation result of the stable equilibrium E_3 is shown in Figure 3.

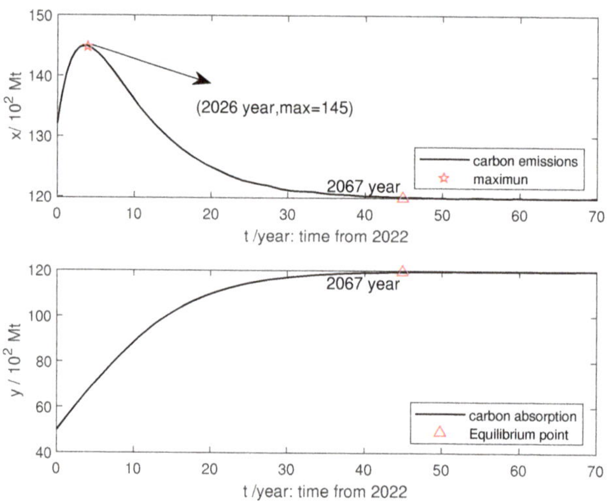

Figure 3. Equilibrium E_3 of system (3) is locally asymptotically stable when $\tau = 0$.

Remark 2. *From Figure 3, we take $\tau = 0$, which indicates that the impact of technological innovation on carbon emissions is instantaneous. We conclude that China will reach the carbon peak in 2026, and the peak value is about 14.5 billion tons. With time going by, the carbon emissions will become smaller and smaller, and gradually reach stability in 2067. The stable value is at about 11.981 billion tons, carbon absorption will increase with time and stabilize at 11.982 billion tons around 2067. For this reason, if China implements the current policy, it will achieve peak carbon dioxide emissions by 2030, but not carbon neutrality by 2060. Therefore, China should adopt stronger policies to lay the foundation for carbon neutrality. In Figure 1, we can see that China's peak carbon dioxide emissions time is 2029, with a peak value of 13.81 billion tons, while in Figure 3, the simulation results show that China has completed peak carbon dioxide emissions in an earlier time and the peak value will increase. As the coefficients in our model are constant, but in real life, the coefficients of the model may change with time. Another reason is that our model does not consider too many factors, such as the influence of construction industry and carbon sink, which leads to a slight deviation in our simulation results. However, our simulation results are at least consistent with the realization of peak carbon dioxide emissions before 2030.*

After that, we consider the time of carbon peak at the difference of the influence factors of industrial structure and energy structure on carbon emissions (see Figure 4).

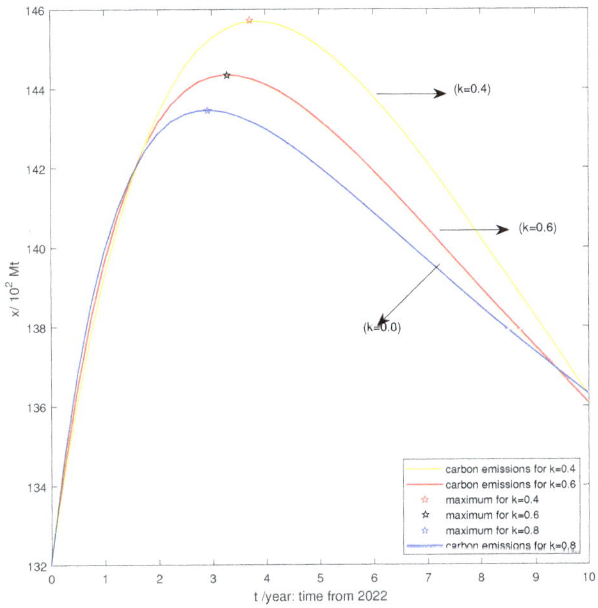

Figure 4. Change of carbon emission under different values for the influence coefficient of energy structure reform on carbon emissions amount k.

Remark 3. *From Figure 4, when the influence coefficient of energy structure reform on carbon emissions amount k increases, that is, with the optimization of industrial structure and the improvement of energy structure, the time for China to reach the carbon peak will become shorter and shorter. When* $k = 0.4$*, we predict that the peak value of carbon will reach 14.573 billion tons in April 2026. When* $k = 0.6$*, China will reach the peak of carbon in April 2025, with a peak of 14.43 billion tons. When* $k = 0.8$*, we predict that China will reach peak carbon dioxide emissions in 2025, with a peak of 14.34 billion tons. This is reasonable because when China's emission reduction policy is effectively implemented, corresponding policies are introduced, new development of new energy exploration and application technologies is achieved, and industrial reform is conducted in depth. China's secondary industry with high carbon emissions will be transformed into a green and sustainable tertiary industry in an all-round way. The proportion of clean energy, mainly natural gas, will be greatly increased, and the peak value of carbon emissions will be reduced while reaching the maximum value ahead of time.*

Later, we select the previous data, and when the natural growth rate of carbon absorption increases, we arrive at the following conclusions: (see Figure 5).

Remark 4. *With the increase of natural growth rate of carbon absorption, the peak value of carbon emissions becomes smaller and smaller, and the time for carbon to reach the peak value becomes shorter and shorter, and the time for carbon neutrality becomes shorter. The red line in Figure 5 shows the apparent trend of carbon emissions and carbon absorption at* $a_2 = 0.1$*. China will reach peak carbon dioxide emissions around 2028, but it will take nearly one hundred years to achieve carbon neutrality. The blue curve shows the change trend of carbon emissions and carbon absorption at* $a_2 = 0.2$*, and it is predicted that China will reach peak carbon dioxide emissions around 2026 and be carbon neutral in 2072. The black curve shows the change trend of carbon emissions and carbon absorption at* $a_2 = 0.3$*. It can be seen that China will reach peak carbon dioxide emissions* *around 2026 and become carbon neutral in 2057. Although China can achieve peak carbon dioxide emissions by 2030 at different natural growth rates of carbon absorption, China cannot achieve carbon neutrality by 2060 at a lower natural growth rate of carbon absorption. It also shows that with the country's emphasis on ecological protection and green development, people have a clearer understanding of green development, saving energy, planting trees, increasing forest vegetation coverage and increasing urban green space, which leads to an increase in the natural growth rate of carbon absorption. The smaller the carbon peak, the shorter the time to achieve carbon neutrality. In Figure 5, we can see that when the natural growth rate of carbon absorption reaches 0.3, it is possible for China to achieve carbon neutrality by 2060. As the natural growth rate of carbon absorption is relatively high, in order to achieve China's goal of carbon neutrality by 2060, we should not only consider increasing the natural growth rate of carbon absorption to achieve carbon neutrality, but also consider optimizing the industrial structure and energy structure to reduce the natural growth rate of carbon emissions. Therefore, we also need to deepen the industrial reform and optimize the energy structure to reduce the natural growth rate of China's carbon emissions.*

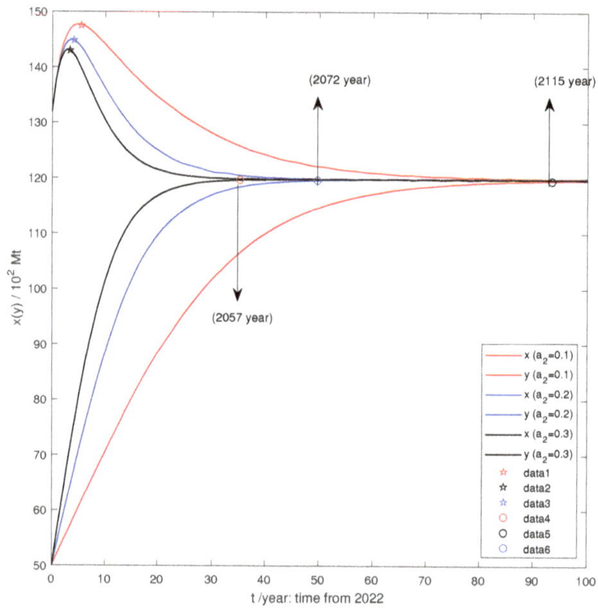

Figure 5. Analysis of the influence of natural growth rate of carbon absorption on carbon absorption and emission.

Further on, we find that Formula (22) has only one positive root, so we calculate that $\tau_1^{(0)} = 3.606$. From Theorem 3, we know that when $\tau \in [0, \tau_1^{(0)})$, the equilibrium E_3 is locally asymptotically stable and unstable when $\tau > \tau_1^{(0)}$. From Equations (37) and (41), we have

$$\mathrm{Re}(M) = 0.1955 > 0;\ \mathrm{Re}(H) = -3.51 * 10^{-7} < 0;\ r = \sqrt{-\frac{\mathrm{Re}(M)\mu}{\mathrm{Re}(H)}} > 0. \quad (44)$$

When $\tau = 0.5 < \tau_1^{(0)} = 3.606$, the simulation result of the stable equilibrium E_3 is as shown in Figure 6.

Remark 5. *From Figure 6, carbon emissions x reached their peak around 2060, with a peak of about 14.6 billion tons, and then decreased year by year and gradually stabilized, and they became stable* *around 2063. Carbon absorption y tends to be stable around 2067. Once carbon emissions and carbon absorption are stable, the value of carbon emissions is about 11.9 billion tons, and the value of carbon absorption is about 12 billion tons. If this continues, it will be difficult for China to achieve carbon neutrality before 2060. Therefore, China needs to take some measures, such as improving the level of carbon emission reduction technology to reduce the carbon emissions of the steel industry.*

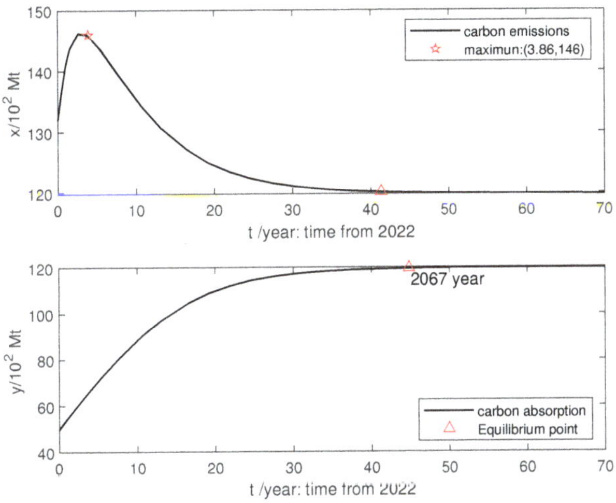

Figure 6. When $\tau = 0.5$, the system (3) is locally asymptotically stable at the equilibrium point E_3.

When $\tau = 3.61 > \tau_1^{(0)} = 3.606$, from Theorem 4, we learn that the system (3) has a stable periodic solution at the at the equilibrium E_3, as shown in Figure 7.

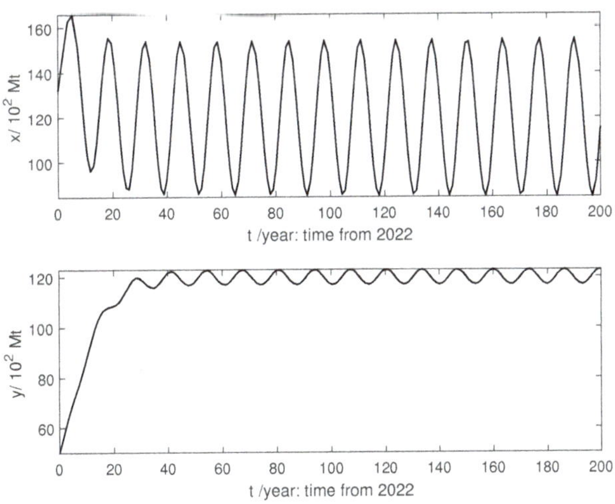

Figure 7. When $\tau = 3.61$, the system (3) has a stable periodic solution near the equilibrium E_3.

Remark 6. *From Figure 7, when $\tau = 3.61$, the system (3) is locally asymptotically stable at the equilibrium E_3, which is consistent with (4). $\tau = 3.61$, that is, when the technical level is applied to the actual production of carbon emission reduction, the time required becomes longer, we can see that carbon emissions and carbon absorption fluctuate periodically, and the period is about 13 years. As a result of the long delay time, it is inconsistent with the actual production level at present, so we do not consider the practical application of this situation.*

6. Conclusions

In this paper, considering the competitive relationship between carbon emission and carbon absorption, we set up a new two-dimensional differential equation model with time delay to make some predictions and analyze whether China can achieve it under the current policy, which depends on China's technology research and development level and government policy investment. In practice, the parameters of the model are variable. In order to simplify the problem, the parameters of the model (3) are constant coefficients. At the same time, the model in this paper does not consider too many factors. The simulation process of the model may be different from the real process. For example, the peak value of the simulation will be higher than the future peak value because we have not fully considered the carbon emission reduction measures, but on the whole, the stability of our model is consistent with the actual one. In addition, we theoretically analyzed the existence and stability of the equilibrium and the existence of Hopf bifurcation, and we also derive the normal form of Hopf bifurcation for the system (3) by using the multiple time scales method. After that, we selected a set of data for numerical analysis to verify our theoretical analysis results, we find that equilibrium E_3 of system (3) is locally asymptotically stable when $\tau = 0$. When $\tau = 3.61$, the system (3) has a stable periodic solution near the equilibrium E_3 and we find from Figure 4 that the optimization and adjustment of industrial structure and energy structure has an important impetus to China's realization of peak carbon dioxide emissions and carbon neutrality. When the industrial structure is optimized and the energy structure is improved, the time for China to reach peak carbon dioxide emissions will be shortened (see Figure 4).

Next, our numerical analysis also shows that when the natural growth rate of carbon absorption increases, the time for China to achieve carbon peak carbon dioxide emissions will be shortened and the peak value will also decrease (see from Figure 5). From Figure 5, we predict that when the natural growth rate of carbon absorption is 0.3, China will achieve carbon neutrality before 2060. As the natural growth rate of carbon absorption is actually too high, we also need to deepen the industrial reform and optimize the energy structure to reduce the natural growth rate of China's carbon emissions. Therefore, based on the above research, this paper emphasizes planting trees and improving the level of carbon storage technology to improve the natural growth rate of carbon absorption and carbon emission reduction technology, and improving the development and application technology of new energy to achieve in-depth industrial structure adjustment and energy structure optimization. The above measures are of great significance to China's realization of peak carbon dioxide emissions by 2030 and carbon neutrality by 2060.

Author Contributions: Writing—original draft preparation: L.H. and H.S.; funding acquisition: L.H., H.S. and Y.D.; methodology and supervision: Y.D. All authors have read and agreed to the published version of the manuscript.

Funding: This study was funded by Fundamental Research Funds for the Central Universities of China (No. 2572022DJ06) and College Students Innovations Special Project funded by Northeast Forestry University of China (No. 202210225155).

Institutional Review Board Statement: Not applicable.

Informed Consent Statement: Not applicable.

Data Availability Statement: The authors confirm that the date supporting the findings of this study are available within the article.

Conflicts of Interest: All authors declare no conflict of interest in this paper.

References

1. Zhang, G.X.; Zhang, P.D.; Xiu, J.; Chai, J. Are energy conservation and emission reduction policy measures effective for industrial structure restructuring and upgrading? *Chin. J. Popul. Resour.* **2018**, *1*, 12–27. [CrossRef]
2. Cai, B.F.; Wang, J.N.; Yang, S.Y.; Mao, Y.Q.; Cao, L.B. Carbon dioxide emissions from cities in China based on high resolution emission gridded data. *Chin. J. Popul. Resour.* **2017**, *15*, 58–70. [CrossRef]

3. Zou, C.N.; Xiong, B.; Xue, H.Q.; Zheng, D.W.; Ge, Z.X.; Wang, Y.; Jiang, L.Y.; Pan, S.Q.; Wu, S.D. The role of new energy in carbon neutral. *Petrol. Explor. Dev.* **2021**, *48*, 480–491. [CrossRef]
4. Zhang, Y.X.; Yin, J.P.; Fu, Y.; Wang, J.X.; Wang, G.S. The research of carbon emission and carbon sequestration potential of forest vegetation in China. *Meteorol. Environ. Res.* **2021**, *12*, 24–31.
5. Du, X.W. China's low-carbon transition for addressing climate change. *Adv. Clim. Chang. Res.* **2016**, *1*, 105–108. [CrossRef]
6. Feng, X.P. Carbon dioxide emissions reduction technology and its application prospects in the steel industry. *Baosteel Tech. Res.* **2010**, *s1*, 131.
7. Feng, R.; Dai, B.Z.; Su, H. Effect of China's industrial structure adjustment on carbon emissions. *Ecol. Econ.* **2017**, *2*, 117–124.
8. Wang, S.J.; Gao, S.; Huang, Y.Y.; Shi, C.Y. Spatiotemporal evolution of urban carbon emission performance in China and prediction of future trends. *Acta Geogr. Sin.* **2020**, *30*, 757–774. [CrossRef]
9. Chen, J.H. An empirical study on China's energy supply-and-demand model considering carbon emission peak constraints in 2030. *Engineering* **2017**, *3*, 512–517. [CrossRef]
10. Guo, C.X. Estimation of emission reduction potential in China's industrial sector. *Chin. J. Popul. Resour.* **2015**, *3*, 223–230. [CrossRef]
11. Li, S.Q.; Zhang, B.S.; Tang, X. Forecasting of China's natural gas production and its policy implications. *Petrol. Sci.* **2016**, *13*, 592–603. [CrossRef]
12. Muhammad, K.K.; Muhammad, I.K.; Muhammad, R. The relationship between energy consumption, economic growth and carbon dioxide emissions in Pakistan. *Financ. Innov.* **2020**, *6*, 56–68.
13. Liu, K.; Tao, Y.M.; Wu, Y.; Wang, C.X. How does ecological civilization construction affect carbon emission intensity? Evidence from Chinese provinces'panel data. *Chin. J. Popul. Resour.* **2020**, *18*, 97–102.
14. Sahoo, D.; Samanta, G.P. Comparison between two tritrophic food chain models with multiple delays and anti-predation effect. *Int. J. Biomath.* **2021**, *14*, 53–100. [CrossRef]
15. Khajanchi, S. Chaotic dynamics of a delayed tumor immune interaction model. *Int. J. Biomath.* **2020**, *13*, 1–33. [CrossRef]
16. Tessema, M.K.; Chirove, F.; Sibanda, P. Modeling control of foot and mouth disease with two time delays. *Int. J. Biomath.* **2019**, *12*, 1–37. [CrossRef]
17. Ren, H.P.; Li, W.C.; Liu, D. Hopf bifurcation analysis of Chen circuit with direct time delay feedback. *Chin. Phys. B* **2010**, *3*, 164–175.
18. Zhang, M.M.; Wang, C.J.; Mei, D.C. Effect of time delay on the upper bound of the time derivative of information entropy in a stochastic dynamical. *Chin. Phys. B* **2011**, *20*, 122–126. [CrossRef]
19. Orosz, G. Hopf bifurcation calculations in delayed systems. *Mech. Eng.* **2004**, *48*, 189–200.
20. Awang, N.A.; Maan, N.; Sulain, M.D. Tumour-natural killer and cD8+ t cells interaction model with delay. *Mathematics* **2022**, *10*, 2193. [CrossRef]
21. Liu, X.; Ding, Y. Stability and numerical simulations of a new SVIR model with two delays on COVID-19 booster vaccination. *Mathematics* **2022**, *10*, 1772. [CrossRef]
22. Wang, J.; Wang, Y. Study on the stability and entropy complexity of an energy-saving and emission-reduction model with two delays. *Entropy* **2016**, *18*, 371. [CrossRef]
23. Nayfeh, A.H. Order reduction of retarded nonlinear systems—The method of multiple scales versus center-manifold reduction. *Nonlin. Dyn.* **2008**, *51*, 483–500. [CrossRef]
24. Das, S.L.; Chatterjee, A. Multiple scales without center manifold reductions for delay differential equations near Hopf bifurcations. *Nonlin. Dyn.* **2002**, *30*, 323–335. [CrossRef]

mathematics MDPI

Article

Asymptotics of Solutions to a Differential Equation with Delay and Nonlinearity Having Simple Behaviour at Infinity

Alexandra Kashchenko

Centre of Integrable Systems, P. G. Demidov Yaroslavl State University, 150003 Yaroslavl, Russia; a.kashchenko@uniyar.ac.ru

Abstract: In this paper, we study nonlocal dynamics of a nonlinear delay differential equation. This equation with different types of nonlinearities appears in medical, physical, biological, and ecological applications. The type of nonlinearity in this paper is a generalization of two important for applications types of nonlinearities: piecewise constant and compactly supported functions. We study asymptotics of solutions under the condition that nonlinearity is multiplied by a large parameter. We construct all solutions of the equation with initial conditions from a wide subset of the phase space and find conditions on the parameters of equations for having periodic solutions.

Keywords: delay; asymptotics; large parameter; relaxation oscillations; periodic solutions

MSC: 34K25; 34K13

Citation: Kashchenko, A. Asymptotics of Solutions to a Differential Equation with Delay and Nonlinearity Having Simple Behaviour at Infinity. *Mathematics* **2022**, *10*, 3360. https://doi.org/10.3390/math10183360

Academic Editor: Andrei D. Polyanin

Received: 29 July 2022
Accepted: 13 September 2022
Published: 16 September 2022

1. Introduction

Differential equations with delay

$$\dot{x} = G(x, x(t-\tau)), \tag{1}$$

where x is from $\mathbb{R}^n$, G is some continuous function, and $\tau > 0$ is a delay time, arise as mathematical models in different areas of science (see [1,2] and references therein). Many studies are devoted to the construction of solutions or the analysis of the stability of solutions to differential equations with delay [3–11].

Consider differential equation with delay

$$\dot{u} + \nu u = \lambda F(u(t-T)). \tag{2}$$

Here, u is a scalar real function, and parameters ν and λ and delay time T are positive. This equation plays an important role in mathematical modelling and is of great interest for fundamental research.

This equation simulates a process of production and destruction where the single state variable u decays with a rate ν proportional to u at the present and is produced with a rate dependent on the value of u some time in the past. Such processes arise in many biological applications, for example, in normal and pathological behaviour of control systems in the physiology of blood cell production and respiration and periodic or irregular activity in neural networks (see Table 1 in [12], paper [13] and references therein).

Equation (2) with compactly supported nonlinearity simulates an oscillator with nonlinear delayed feedback with an RC low-pass filter of the first order [14,15]. Additionally, Equation (2) with another nonlinear functions F occurs in laser optics [1,16] and in mathematical ecology [2,17].

There are many studies on the dynamics of this equation: its dynamics were studied in the case of piecewise constant [13], monotone [18,19], or compactly supported nonlinearity [20] in the case of positive and negative feedback [21]. Asymptotics of solutions [22] and the existence of periodic solutions [23] were studied in the case of a singularly perturbed equation:

$$\varepsilon \dot{u} + u = F(u(t-T)), \quad (0 < \varepsilon \ll 1).$$

In [24], the authors determined how dynamics of this differential equation when ε is small related with dynamics of this equation in the case of $\varepsilon = 0$. In [25,26], the authors proposed methods to reconstruct Equation (2) from time series.

For systems of two [27], three [28] and $N > 3$ [29]-coupled oscillators (2) with compactly supported nonlinearity F and $\lambda \gg 1$, asymptotics of relaxation solutions were constructed.

Using simple renormalizations, we can obtain that the coefficient ν in (2) is equal to one. Therefore, without limiting generality, below, we consider case $\nu = 1$.

In the present work, we analytically study behaviour at $t \to +\infty$ of solutions to Equation (2) with initial conditions from a wide subset of the phase space $C[-T, 0]$ under conditions

$$\lambda \gg 1$$

and

$$F(x) = \begin{cases} b, & x \le p_L, \\ f(x), & p_L < x < p_R, \\ d, & x \ge p_R, \end{cases} \tag{3}$$

where $p_L < 0 < p_R$.

We assume that nonlinear function $f(x)$ is bounded and piecewise-smooth. We consider positive, negative, and zero values of parameters b and d (but we assume that at least one of the parameters b or d is nonzero, because if $b = d = 0$, then F is a compactly supported function, and this case has been studied in [20]).

This type of function, $F(u)$, is a generalization of two important applications [12,15] regarding types of nonlinearity: compactly supported and piecewise constant nonlinearities. The class of nonlinearity $F(u)$ is broad because constants $p_L < 0$, $p_R > 0$, b, and d are arbitrary, and conditions on function f are quite general. Therefore, this type of nonlinearity may occur in many applied problems, and the results obtained in this paper can be directly applied to study dynamics of the mathematical models with certain nonlinear functions F (if function F satisfies conditions (3)).

We analytically draw a conclusion about qualitative and quantitative properties of solutions to Equation (2) with arbitrary function F (satisfying conditions (3)) with initial conditions from a wide subset of the phase space and give numerical illustrations of the obtained results. It is important to mention that it is impossible to obtain such a result using only numerical methods because it is impossible to iterate through all functions F from the considered class and through all the considered initial conditions.

The method of investigation in this paper is the following.

1. We select two sets of initial conditions: S_- and S_+. The set S_- consists of continuous functions $u(s)$, ($s \in [-T, 0]$), such that $u(s) \le p_L$ on $s \in [-T, 0)$, and $u(0) = p_L$. The set S_+ consists of continuous functions $u(s)$, ($s \in [-T, 0]$), such that $u(s) \ge p_R$ on $s \in [-T, 0)$, and $u(0) = p_R$.

2. We take initial conditions from sets S_- and S_+ and construct asymptotics at $\lambda \to +\infty$ of all solutions to Equation (2) using the method of steps [30].

3. By the asymptotics of solutions, we draw conclusions about the behaviour of solutions at $t \to +\infty$.

In this paper we conclude that two types of behaviour at $t \to +\infty$ of solutions to Equation (2) with initial conditions from the set S_+ or S_- are possible: (1) the solution tends to a constant at $t \to +\infty$, or (2) after the pre-period, the solution becomes a cycle.

The idea of the proof that after the pre-period, the solution becomes a cycle is the following: 1. it follows from the form of sets S_- and S_+ and properties of function $F(u)$, that on the first step ($t \in [0, T]$) all solutions from the set S_- (S_+) coincide with each other. Thus, all solutions with initial conditions from S_- (S_+) coincide with each other for all $t \ge 0$; 2. if we take initial conditions from one of these sets (S_- or S_+) and if there exists a time moment t_* such that $u(t_* + s)$ (where $s \in [-T, 0]$) belongs to the chosen set, then there exists a periodic solution to Equation (2).

4. We generalize obtained results to the wide sets of initial conditions $u(s) \geq p_R$ (or $u(s) \leq p_L$) at $s \in [-T, 0]$.

The paper has the following structure: in Sections 2–5, we construct asymptotics of solutions to Equation (2) considering cases of different signs of b and d under condition $bd \neq 0$; in Sections 6 and 7 we consider cases $b \neq 0$ and $d = 0$; and in Sections 8 and 9, we consider cases $b = 0$ and $d \neq 0$. In Section 10, we generalize results of Sections 2–9 to wide sets of initial conditions $u(s) \geq p_R$ (or $u(s) \leq p_L$) at $s \in [-T, 0]$.

2. Asymptotics of Solutions in the Case $b > 0$ and $d > 0$

Firstly, we consider asymptotics of the solution to Equation (2) with initial conditions from S_+. We solve our equation using the method of steps.

On the first step (on the segment $t \in [0, T]$), the function $u(t - T)$ is greater than or equal to p_R, which is why on this segment, Equation (2) has the form

$$\dot{u} + u = \lambda d. \tag{4}$$

Hence, on this time segment, the solution to Equation (2) has the form

$$u(t) = p_R e^{-t} + \lambda d(1 - e^{-t}). \tag{5}$$

Because $d > 0$ and λ is sufficiently large, we obtain $u(t) > p_R$ on $t \in [0, T]$. Therefore, Equation (2) has the form of (4) on the next step $t \in [T, 2T]$ and so on (Equation (2) has the form of (4); until then $u(t) < p_R$). However, at $\lambda \gg 1$, the condition $u(t) = p_R e^{-t} + \lambda d(1 - e^{-t}) < p_R$ is not true for all $t \geq 0$, so Equation (2) has the form of (4) for all $t \geq 0$, and the solution has the form of (5) for all $t \geq 0$ (see Figure 1).

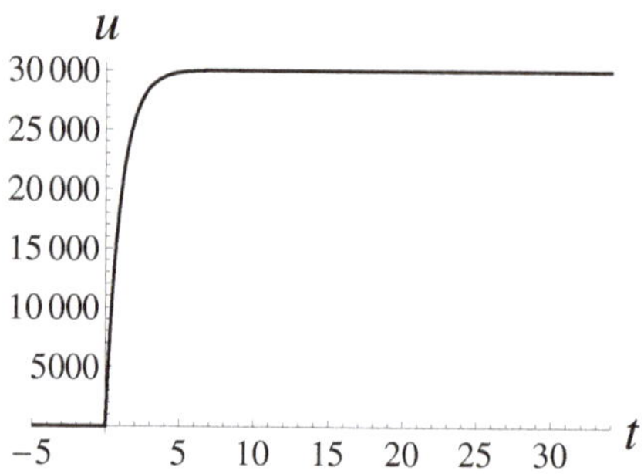

Figure 1. Solution to Equation (2) with initial conditions from S_+ in the case $b > 0$ and $d > 0$. Values of parameters: $\lambda = 10^4$, $T = 5$, $p_L = -1$, $p_R = 2$, $b = 2$, $d = 3$.

Secondly, we take initial conditions from S_- and construct asymptotics for these initial conditions.

Then, on the first step (on the segment $t \in [0, T]$), the function $u(t - T)$ is less than or equal to p_L, which is why on this segment, Equation (2) has the form

$$\dot{u} + u = \lambda b. \tag{6}$$

It follows from (6) that the solution has the form

$$u(t) = p_L e^{-t} + \lambda b(1 - e^{-t}). \tag{7}$$

Therefore,

$$u(T) = p_L e^{-T} + \lambda b(1 - e^{-T}). \tag{8}$$

Lemma 1. *The leading part of the asymptotics of the solution to Equation (2) on the segment $t \in [T, 2T]$ coincides with the leading part of the asymptotics of the solution to the Cauchy problem (4) and (8). The solution to Equation (2) in this interval has the form*

$$u(t) = \lambda b(1 - e^{-T})e^{-(t-T)} + \lambda d(1 - e^{-(t-T)}) + o(\lambda). \tag{9}$$

Proof. On the segment $t \in [0, T]$, the solution to Equation (2) has the form of (7). This expression is an increasing function of t because $\lambda b > 0$ and $p_L < 0$. Therefore, (7) is greater than p_L for all $t \in [0, T]$. It is easy to see that expression (7) is less than p_R for all $t \in [0, \delta)$, where

$$\delta = \ln\left(1 + \frac{p_R - p_L}{\lambda b - p_R}\right), \tag{10}$$

and is greater than p_R for all $t \in (\delta, T]$. Note that δ is asymptotically small by λ at $\lambda \to +\infty$ (it has order $O(\lambda^{-1})$).

It follows from the estimation of the expression (7) that on the segment $t \in [T, T + \delta]$, Equation (2) has the form

$$\dot{u} + u = \lambda f(u(t - T)), \tag{11}$$

and on the interval $t \in (T + \delta, 2T]$, it has the form of (4).

At the segment $t \in [T, T + \delta]$, the exact solution to Equation (2) (which is Equation (11) in this interval) has the form

$$u(t) = (p_L e^{-T} + \lambda b(1 - e^{-T}))e^{-(t-T)} + \lambda \int_{T}^{t} e^{s-t} f(u(s - T))ds. \tag{12}$$

Function f is bounded; therefore there exists a constant M such that $|f(u(s - T))| < M$ for all $s \in [T, T + \delta]$. Thus,

$$\left|\lambda \int_{T}^{t} e^{s-t} f(u(s - T))ds\right| \leq \lambda \int_{T}^{t} |e^{s-t} f(u(s - T))|ds \leq \lambda \int_{T}^{t} M ds \leq \lambda \int_{T}^{T+\delta} M ds = \lambda \delta M \leq M_1, \tag{13}$$

where M_1 is some constant. The last inequality is true because δ has order $O(\lambda^{-1})$ at $\lambda \to +\infty$.

Note that on the interval $t \in [T, T + \delta]$

$$0 \leq \lambda d(1 - e^{-(t-T)}) \leq \lambda d(1 - e^{-(T+\delta-T)}) \leq M_2, \tag{14}$$

(where M_2 is some constant), δ has order $O(\lambda^{-1})$ at $\lambda \to +\infty$. It follows from inequalities (13) and (14) that on the segment $t \in [T, T + \delta]$, the leading terms of asymptotics at $\lambda \to +\infty$ of expressions (12) and (9) coincide.

On the segment $t \in [T + \delta, 2T]$, the exact solution to Equation (2) (which is Equation (4) in this interval) has the form

$$\begin{aligned} u(t) = {} & \lambda b(1 - e^{-T})e^{-(t-T)} + \lambda d(1 - e^{-(t-T)}e^{\delta}) + \\ & (p_L e^{-(T+\delta)} + \lambda \int_{T}^{T+\delta} e^{s-(T+\delta)} f(u(s - T))ds)e^{-(t-(T+\delta))}. \end{aligned} \tag{15}$$

Since $\delta = O(\lambda^{-1})$ at $\lambda \to +\infty$, then on the segment $t \in [T + \delta, 2T]$, the leading terms of asymptotics at $\lambda \to +\infty$ of expressions (15) and (9) coincide. Thus, the solution to Equation (2) has the form of (9) on the whole segment $t \in [T, 2T]$.

The exact solution to the Cauchy problem (4), (8) has the form

$$u(t) = \lambda b(1 - e^{-T})e^{-(t-T)} + \lambda d(1 - e^{-(t-T)}) + p_L e^{-t}. \tag{16}$$

It is easy to see that the leading terms of asymptotics at $\lambda \to +\infty$ of expressions (16) and (9) coincide on the whole segment $t \in [T, 2T]$.

Thus, on this segment, the leading part of asymptotics of solution to Equation (2) coincides with the leading part of asymptotics of the solution to the Cauchy problem (4) and (8). □

Expression (9) is greater than p_R for all $t \in [T, +\infty)$. Therefore, Equation (2) has the form of (4) for all $t \geq T + \delta$, and the solution of Equation (2) has the form of (9) for all $t \geq T$ (see Figure 2).

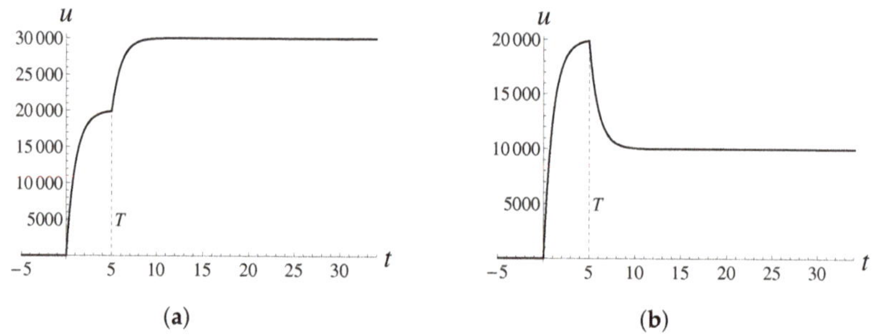

Figure 2. Typical graphs of solutions to Equation (2) with initial conditions from S_- in the case $b > 0$ and $d > 0$ if (**a**) $d > b > 0$ and (**b**) $b > d > 0$. Values of parameters: $\lambda = 10^4$, $T = 5$, $p_L = -1$, $p_R = 2$, $b = 2$, (**a**) $d = 3$, and (**b**) $d = 1$.

Therefore, in the case $b > 0$ and $d > 0$, all solutions with initial conditions from sets S_+ and S_- tend to the constant λd at $t \to +\infty$.

3. Asymptotics of Solutions in the Case $b < 0$ and $d < 0$

Initially, we consider asymptotics of solution to Equation (2) with initial conditions from S_+. In the first step (on the segment $t \in [0, T]$), function $u(t-T)$ is greater or equal than p_R, which is why in this segment Equation (2) has the form of (4). Therefore, for $t \in [0, T]$, the solution of Equation (2) has the form of (5).

In this case, $d < 0$, so we obtain $u(t) < p_L$ for $t \in [\delta, T + \delta]$, where $\delta = O(\lambda^{-1})$ at $\lambda \to +\infty$; therefore, Equation (2) has the form of (6) in the segment $t \in [T + \delta, 2T + \delta]$. As in the previous case, in the time segment $t \in [T, T + \delta]$, the solution $u(t)$ depends on the values of the function f, but this dependence is smaller than the leading term of the asymptotics of the solution, and this leading term of the asymptotics of the solution coincides with the leading term of the asymptotics of the solution to the Cauchy problem (6),

$$u(T) = p_R e^{-T} + \lambda d(1 - e^{-T}).$$

Hence, it follows that the solution of Equation (2) with initial conditions from set S_+ has the form

$$u(t) = \lambda d(1 - e^{-T})e^{-(t-T)} + \lambda b(1 - e^{-(t-T)}) + o(\lambda). \quad (17)$$

Since $b < 0$ and $d < 0$, expression (17) is less then p_L for all $t \in [T, +\infty)$. This is why Equation (2) has the form of (6) for all $t \in [T + \delta, +\infty)$, and Formula (17) holds for all $t \geq T$.

Now, we study asymptotics of the solution to Equation (2) with the initial conditions from S_-.

On the segment $t \in [0, T]$, the function $u(t-T)$ is less than or equal to p_L, which is why on this segment Equation (2) has the form of (6), and its solution has the form of (7).

As $b < 0$, we obtain $u(t) < p_L$, and Equation (2) has the form of (6); until then, $u(t) > p_L$. However, expression (7) is less than p_L for all $t > 0$. This is why solution has the form of (7) for all $t \in [0, +\infty)$.

Therefore, in the case that $b < 0$ and $d < 0$, all solutions with initial conditions from sets S_+ and S_- tend to the constant λb at $t \to +\infty$.

4. Asymptotics of Solutions in the Case $b < 0$ and $d > 0$

Firstly, we consider the asymptotics of the solution to Equation (2) with initial conditions from S_+.

In the first step (in the segment $t \in [0, T]$), the function $u(t-T)$ is greater than or equal to p_R, which is why on this segment, Equation (2) has the form of (4), and the solution to Equation (2) has the form of (5). As in Section 2, we identify that Expression (5) is greater than p_R for all $t > 0$; therefore, Equation (2) has the form of (4) for all $t > 0$. This is why the solution of (2) with initial conditions from S_+ does not depend on the values of f and b and has the form of (5) for all $t > 0$.

Similarly, the solution of Equation (2) with initial conditions from S_- does not depend on the values of f and d and for all $t > 0$ has the form of (7).

Therefore, in the case that $b < 0$ and $d > 0$, the solutions with initial conditions from S_+ tend to the constant λd, and solutions with initial conditions from S_- tend to the constant λb at $t \to +\infty$.

5. Asymptotics of Solutions in the Case $b > 0$ and $d < 0$

In this section, we study behaviour of solutions with initial conditions from sets S_+ and S_- under the assumption that $b > 0$ and $d < 0$.

Firstly, we take initial conditions from S_+ and begin to construct asymptotics of solutions. Then, on the first step $t \in [0, T]$, Equation (2) has the form of (4) and solution has the form of (5) and

$$u(T) = \lambda d(1 - e^{-T} + o(1)). \tag{18}$$

Since $d < 0$, there exists an asymptotically small λ value $\delta_1 > 0$ such that $p_L < u(t) < p_R$ for $t \in (0, \delta_1)$ and $u(t) < p_L$ for all $t \in (\delta_1, T]$. Therefore, on the segment $t \in [T + \delta_1, 2T]$, Equation (2) has the form of (6). In the segment $t \in [T, T + \delta_1]$, the solution to Equation (2) depends on the values of the function f, but the leading term of the asymptotics of the solution to Equation (2) coincides with the leading term of the asymptotics of the solution to Equation (6) with initial conditions from (18). This is why in the whole segment $t \in [T, 2T]$, the solution has the form of (17). Note that in the case that $b > 0$ and $d < 0$, Expression (17) is an increasing function.

Since $u(T) < 0$ and (17) increases to the positive value, there exists an asymptotically small by λ value $\delta_2 < 0$ and value $t_1 > T + \delta_1$, such that $u(t_1) = 0$ and $u(t_1 + \delta_2) = p_L$. It follows from the definition of t_1 and δ_2 that Equation (2) has the form of (6) on the segment $t \in [T + \delta_1, t_1 + \delta_2 + T]$. It easily follows from (17) that

$$e^{-(t_1 - T)} = b/(b - d(1 - e^{-T})), \tag{19}$$

and, consequently,

$$u(t_1 + T) = \lambda b(1 - e^{-T} + o(1)). \tag{20}$$

Note that expression (20) is greater than p_R when $\lambda \gg 1$. Thus, for $t > t_1 + T + \delta_3$ (where $\delta_3 > 0$ denotes an asymptotically small by λ value such that $u(t_1 + \delta_3) = p_R$), until then, the $u(t) < p_R$ solution Equation (2) has the form of (4). Therefore, for $t > t_1 + T + \delta_3$, until then, the $u(t) < p_R$ solution to Equation (2) has the form of

$$u(t) = (\lambda b(1 - e^{-T}) - \lambda d)e^{-(t-(t_1+T))} + \lambda d + o(\lambda). \tag{21}$$

Expression (21) is a decreasing function, and there exists $t = t_2$ such that (21) is equal to zero. Additionally, for $t_* = t_2 + o(1)$, it is true that $u(t_*) = p_R$ and $u(t_* + s) > p_R$ for all $s \in [-T, 0)$. Thus, at the point $t = t_*$, we return to the initial situation (the function $u(t_* + s)$ belongs to the set S_+). This is why if we take this function as the initial conditions for Equation (2), we obtain a periodic solution to this equation with an amplitude of the order $O(\lambda)$ (see Formulas (18) and (20)) and period

$$t_* = 2T + \ln\left(\frac{(b(1-e^{-T}) - d)(b - d(1-e^{-T}))}{-bd}\right) + o(1). \tag{22}$$

We mention that the logarithm in Formula (22) is positive because its argument is greater than 1 for all $b > 0$, $d < 0$, and $T > 0$.

Note that there exists a point $t_L = t_1 + \delta_2$ such that $u(t_L) = p_L$ and $u(s + t_L) < p_L$ on the segment $s \in [-T, 0)$. Additionally, we stress that if we take an initial function such that it is less than or equal to p_L in some segment of the length T: $s \in [\tilde{t} - T, \tilde{t})$ and is equal to p_L at the point $\tilde{t}$, then the solution to Equation (2) on the next interval $t \in [\tilde{t}, \tilde{t} + T]$ does not depend on the "history" values of $u(s + \tilde{t})$ on $s \in [-T, 0)$. This is why if we consider the initial conditions from the set S_- and construct the asymptotics of the solution to Equation (2), we obtain the periodic solution obtained earlier in this section, but this solution will be shifted.

From the results of Sections 2–5, we derive the following theorem.

Theorem 1. *Let $bd \neq 0$. Then, Equation (2) with sufficiently large $\lambda > 0$ has a cycle with initial conditions from S_+ or S_- if and only if $b > 0$ and $d < 0$. This sign-changing cycle $u_*(t)$ has asymptotics*

$$\begin{aligned}
&u_*(t) = p_R e^{-(t-nt_*)} + \lambda d(1 - e^{-(t-nt_*)}), && t \in [nt_*, nt_* + T],\\
&u_*(t) = \lambda d(1 - e^{-T})e^{-(t-(T+nt_*))} + \lambda b(1 - e^{-(t-(T+nt_*))}) + o(\lambda), && \\
& && t \in [nt_* + T, nt_* + t_1 + T],\\
&u_*(t) = (\lambda b(1 - e^{-T}) - \lambda d)e^{-(t-(t_1+T+nt_*))} + \lambda d + o(\lambda), && \\
& && t \in [nt_* + t_1 + T, (n+1)t_*].
\end{aligned} \tag{23}$$

at $\lambda \to +\infty$ (where $n = 0, 1, 2, \ldots$ represents the number of periods of the cycle), and the period of this cycle t_* is given in (22).

Note that Formula (23) was obtained from Formulas (5), (17), and (21) using a shift in the time variable t by n periods t_* of solution $u_*(t)$.

It should also be noted that all shifts of cycle $u_*(t + C)$ where $C \in \mathbb{R}$ are solutions to Equation (2), but we consider them as a single object.

A cycle of Equation (2) in the case that $b > 0$ and $d < 0$ is shown in Figure 3.

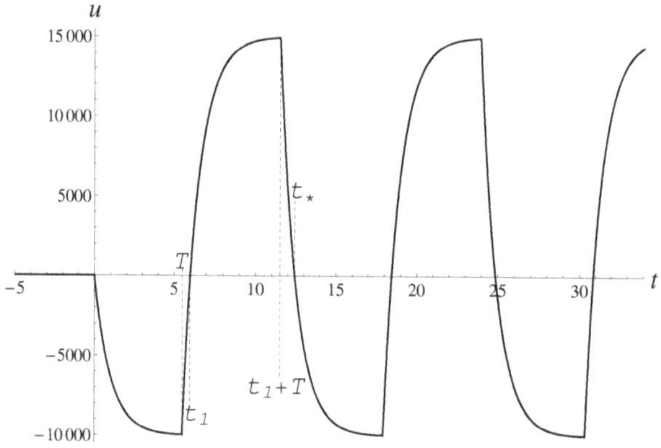

Figure 3. Cycle of Equation (2) in the case that $b > 0$ and $d < 0$. Values of parameters: $\lambda = 10^4$, $T = 5.5$, $p_L = -2$, $p_R = 3$, $b = 1.5$, and $d = -1$.

6. Asymptotics of Solutions in the Case $b > 0$ and $d = 0$

Firstly, we consider initial conditions from S_+. Then, on the first step $t \in [0, T]$, Equation (2) has the form

$$\dot{u} + u = 0. \quad (24)$$

Therefore, the solution has the form

$$u(t) = p_R e^{-t}. \quad (25)$$

Since the solution to (25) belongs to the interval $u \in (0, p_R)$ in the interval $t \in (0, T]$, then in the segment $t \in [T, 2T]$, it depends on the values of function f. It has the form

$$u(t) = p_R e^{-t} + \lambda \int_T^t e^{s-t} f(p_R e^{T-s}) ds. \quad (26)$$

In this segment, the asymptotics of the solution to (2) crucially depend on the values of the integral in Formula (26). Below, we assume that this integral preserves its sign on the segment $t \in (T, 2T]$ (if the integral changes its sign, then we cannot construct the asymptotics of the solution at the segment $t \in [2T, 3T]$ for an arbitrary unknown function f). Consider the first case:

$$\int_T^t e^{s-t} f(p_R e^{T-s}) ds > 0 \text{ for all } t \in (T, 2T]. \quad (27)$$

Then, expression (26) is greater than p_R on the segment $t \in [T + \delta_1, 2T]$ (here, $\delta_1 \geq 0$ is some asymptotically small by λ value; it has order $O(\lambda^{-1})$ at $\lambda \to +\infty$). In the segment $t \in [2T, 2T + \delta_1]$, the leading term of the asymptotics of the solution to Equation (2) coincides with the leading term of the asymptotics of the solution to Equation (24) with the initial conditions

$$u(2T) = p_R e^{-2T} + \lambda \int_T^{2T} e^{s-2T} f(p_R e^{T-s}) ds,$$

and in the segment $t \in [2T + \delta_1, 3T]$, Equation (2) has the form of (24). This is why in the whole segment $t \in [2T, 3T]$, the solution to (2) has the form of

$$u(t) = \lambda \Big(\int_T^{2T} e^{s-2T} f(p_R e^{T-s}) ds + o(1) \Big) e^{-(t-2T)}. \quad (28)$$

Note that Expression (28) is greater than p_R in the segment with length $O(\ln \lambda)$ at $\lambda \to +\infty$ (and this is why Equation (2) has the form of (24) in this segment), and this expression decreases and tends to zero at $t \to +\infty$. Therefore, there exists a time moment $t_* = 2T + (1 + o(1)) \ln \lambda > 3T$ such that $u(t_*) = p_R$ and $u(t_* + s) > p_R$ on the interval $s \in [-T, 0)$. Thus, we come to the initial situation (the function $u(t_* + s)$ belongs to the set S_+), and if we take this function as the initial conditions to our equation, then we obtain a positive relaxation cycle of Equation (2) with the amplitude $O(\lambda)$ and period $t_* = 2T + (1 + o(1)) \ln \lambda$.

We obtain the following result.

Theorem 2. *Let $b > 0$ and $d = 0$, and (27) holds. Then, for all sufficiently large $\lambda > 0$, Equation (2) has a positive relaxation cycle with the asymptotics*

$$
\begin{aligned}
&u(t) = p_R e^{-(t-nt_*)}, \qquad t \in [nt_*, nt_* + T],\\
&u(t) = p_R e^{-(t-nt_*)} + \lambda \int\limits_{T+nt_*}^{t} e^{s-t} f(p_R e^{nt_*+T-s}) ds, \quad t \in [nt_* + T, nt_* + 2T],\\
&u(t) = \lambda \Big(\int\limits_{nt_*+T}^{nt_*+2T} e^{s-nt_*-2T} f(p_R e^{nt_*+T-s}) ds + o(1) \Big) e^{-(t-nt_*-2T)},\\
&\qquad t \in [nt_* + 2T, (n+1)t_*],
\end{aligned} \tag{29}
$$

(where $n = 0, 1, 2, \ldots$ represents number of periods of cycle) and the period $t_* = 2T + (1 + o(1)) \ln \lambda$ at $\lambda \to +\infty$.

Consider the second case:

$$
\int\limits_{T}^{t} e^{s-t} f(p_R e^{T-s}) ds < 0 \text{ for all } t \in (T, 2T]. \tag{30}
$$

Then, expression (26) is less than p_L in the segment $t \in [T + \delta_2, 2T]$ (here, $\delta_2 > 0$ denotes an asymptotically small by λ value such that $u(T + \delta_2) = p_L$), and this is why Equation (2) in the segment $t \in [2T + \delta_2, 3T]$ has the form of (6). Thus, in the segment $t \in [2T, 3T]$, the solution has the form

$$
u(t) = \lambda \Big(\int\limits_{T}^{2T} e^{s-2T} f(p_R e^{T-s}) ds - b + o(1) \Big) e^{-(t-2T)} + \lambda b. \tag{31}
$$

Note that expression (31) is an increasing function and that there exists a time moment $t_1 > 2T + \delta_2$ such that $u(t_1) = 0$. It is easy to see that

$$
e^{-(t_1-2T)} = \frac{b}{b - \int\limits_{T}^{2T} e^{s-2T} f(p_R e^{T-s}) ds}. \tag{32}
$$

On the segment $t \in [2T + \delta_2, t_1 + T + \delta_3]$ equation has the form of (6), and therefore, Formula (31) holds for the solution in this segment (here, $\delta_3 < 0$ is an asymptotically small by λ value that denotes a time moment such that $u(t_1 + \delta_3) = p_L$).

It follows from (32) that

$$
u(t_1 + T + \delta_3) = \lambda b (1 - e^{-T} + o(1)). \tag{33}
$$

Since the value (33) is positive and has order $O(\lambda)$ at $\lambda \to +\infty$, then Equation (2) has the form of (24) in the time interval $t \in [t_1 + \delta_4 + T, t_*)$ (here, $\delta_4 > 0$ denotes an asymptotically small by λ value such that $u(t_1 + \delta_4) = p_R$, and t_* denotes a first time moment such that $t_* > t_1 + T + \delta_4$ and $u(t_*) = p_R$). Therefore, the solution has the form

$$
u(t) = \lambda b (1 - e^{-T} + o(1)) e^{-(t-(t_1+T))}. \tag{34}
$$

Note that $t_* = t_1 + T + (1 + o(1)) \ln \lambda$. This is why $u(t_* + s) > p_R$ for all $s \in [-T, 0)$. Thus, $u(t_* + s)$ belongs to the set S_+, and therefore, if we take this function as the initial condition, we get a sign-changing relaxation cycle with the amplitude of the order $O(\lambda)$ and period $O(\ln \lambda)$ at $\lambda \to +\infty$.

If we consider initial conditions from the set S_-, then on the first step $t \in [0, T]$, the equation has the form of (6) and the solution has the form of (7). Since $b > 0$, there exists an asymptotically small by λ value $\delta > 0$ such that $u(\delta) = p_R$ and $u(t) > p_R$ for all $t \in [\delta, T]$.

Then, for all $t > T + \delta$, until then, the $u(t) = p_R$ equation has the form of (24) and the solution has the form

$$u(t) = \lambda b(1 - e^{-T} + o(1))e^{-(t-T))}. \tag{35}$$

We denote as t_R a time moment such that $t_R > T$ and $u(t_R) = p_R$. This value exists because Expression (35) decreases and tends to zero at $t \to +\infty$. Note that $t_R = O(\ln \lambda)$ at $\lambda \to +\infty$. Therefore, function $u(t_R + s)$ ($s \in [-T, 0]$) belongs to the set S_+, and we return to a problem considered earlier in this section.

From the results of this section we obtain the following statement.

Theorem 3. *Let $b > 0$, $d = 0$, and condition (30) holds. Then, for all sufficiently large $\lambda > 0$, Equation (2) has a sign-changing relaxation cycle with the asymptotics*

$$\begin{aligned}
&u(t) = p_R e^{-(t-nt_*)}, && t \in [nt_*, nt_* + T],\\
&u(t) = p_R e^{-(t-nt_*)} + \lambda \int\limits_{T+nt_*}^{t} e^{s-t} f(p_R e^{nt_*+T-s})ds, && t \in [nt_* + T, nt_* + 2T],\\
&u(t) = \lambda\Big(\int\limits_{nt_*+T}^{nt_*+2T} e^{s-nt_*-2T} f(p_R e^{nt_*+T-s})ds - b + o(1)\Big)e^{-(t-nt_*-2T)} + \lambda b, && \\
& && t \in [nt_* + 2T, nt_* + t_1 + T],\\
&u(t) = \lambda b(1 - e^{-T} + o(1))e^{-(t-(nt_*+t_1+T))}, && t \in [nt_* + t_1 + T, (n+1)t_*],
\end{aligned}$$

(where $n = 0, 1, 2, \ldots$ represents the number of periods of a cycle) and period $t_* = t_1 + T + (1 + o(1)) \ln \lambda$ at $\lambda \to +\infty$.

The cycles of Equation (2) in the case that $b > 0$ and $d = 0$ are shown in Figure 4.

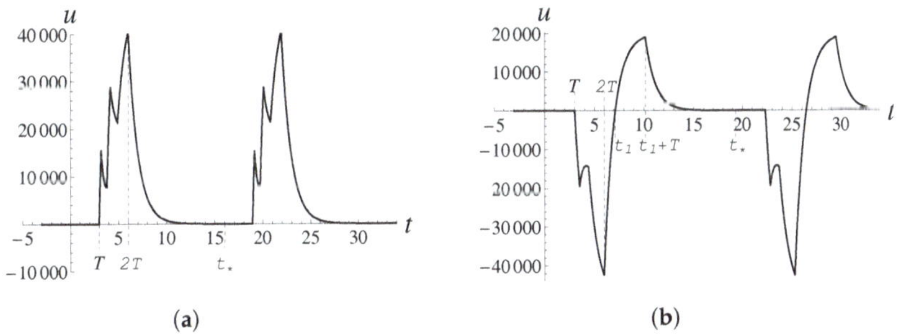

Figure 4. Relaxation cycles of Equation (2) in the case that $b > 0$ and $d = 0$; function $f(u)$ satisfies the condition (**a**) (27) (**b**) (30). Values of parameters: $\lambda = 10^4$, $T = 3$, $p_L = -1$, $p_R = 2$, $b = 2$, and $d = 0$.

7. Asymptotics of Solutions in the Case $b < 0$ and $d = 0$

Firstly, consider initial conditions from S_+. As in the previous section, in the interval $t \in [0, T]$, the solution has the form of (25), and in the interval $t \in [T, 2T]$, it has the form of (26).

If condition (27) holds, then this case is absolutely similar to the case in Section 6, and we obtain the following result.

Theorem 4. *Let $b < 0$, $d = 0$, and (27) holds. Then for all sufficiently large $\lambda > 0$, Equation (2) has a positive relaxation cycle with the asymptotics (29) and period $t_* = 2T + (1 + o(1)) \ln \lambda$ at $\lambda \to +\infty$.*

If condition (30) is true, then there exists an asymptotically small by λ value $\delta > 0$ such that $u(T + \delta) = p_L$ and $u(t) < p_L$ in the interval $t \in (T + \delta, 2T]$. That is why in the segment $t \in [2T + \delta, 3T]$, the equation has the form of (6), and the solution has the form of (31) in the segment $t \in [2T, 3T]$. One can easily see that under conditions $b < 0$ and (30), Expression (31) is less than p_L for all $t > 2T$. This is why Equation (2) has the form of (6), and the solution has the asymptotics of (31) for all $t > 3T$.

Therefore, in the case that $b < 0$ and $d = 0$, if Condition (30) is true, then all solutions with initial conditions from S_+ tend to a constant λb at $t \to +\infty$.

Now, consider initial conditions from S_-. Then, absolutely similarly as in Section 3, the solution has the asymptotics of (7) for all $t > 0$.

Thus, in the case that $b < 0$ and $d = 0$, all solutions with initial conditions from S_- tend to a constant λb at $t \to +\infty$.

8. Asymptotics of Solutions in the Case $b = 0$ and $d < 0$

Firstly, consider initial conditions from S_-. Then, on the first step, $t \in [0, T]$, Equation (2) has the form of (24) and solution has the form

$$u(t) = p_L e^{-t}. \tag{36}$$

It follows from (36) that in the segment $t \in [0, T]$, function $u(t)$ satisfies the inequality $p_L < u(t) < 0$, which is why in the second step, $t \in [T, 2T]$, the solution has the form

$$u(t) = p_L e^{-t} + \lambda \int_T^t e^{s-t} f(p_L e^{T-s}) ds. \tag{37}$$

If function $f(u)$ satisfies the condition

$$\int_T^t e^{s-t} f(p_L e^{T-s}) ds < 0 \text{ for all } t \in (T, 2T], \tag{38}$$

then there exists an asymptotically small by λ value $\delta > 0$ such that Expression (37) is less than p_L on the interval $t \in (T + \delta, 2T]$. It is easy to see that on the segment $t \in [2T, 3T]$, the leading term of the asymptotics of the solution to Equation (2) coincides with the leading term of the asymptotics of the solution to Equation (24) with the initial condition

$$u(2T) = p_L e^{-2T} + \lambda \int_T^{2T} e^{s-2T} f(p_L e^{T-s}) ds. \tag{39}$$

This is why, in the segment $t \in [2T, 3T]$, the solution to Equation (2) has the form

$$u(t) = \lambda \Big(\int_T^{2T} e^{s-2T} f(p_L e^{T-s}) ds + o(1) \Big) e^{-(t-2T)}. \tag{40}$$

Note that Expression (40) is less than p_L in the segment $t \in [2T, 3T]$, which is why Equation (2) has the form of (24) until the Function (40) becomes greater than p_L. There exists a value $t_* > 3T$ such that $u(t_*) = p_L$ and $u(t) < p_L$ for all $t \in (2T, t_*)$. This is why at the point $t = t_*$, we return to the initial situation: the function $u(t_* + s)$ ($s \in [-T, 0)$) belongs to the set S_-. Therefore, if we consider the function $u(t_* + s)$ as the initial conditions of Equation (2), then we get a negative relaxation cycle. Note that it follows from (40) that $t_* - 2T = (1 + o(1)) \ln \lambda$ at $\lambda \to +\infty$.

We obtain the following statement.

Theorem 5. *Let $b = 0$, $d < 0$, and let condition (38) be true. Then, for all sufficiently large $\lambda > 0$, Equation (2) has a negative relaxation cycle with the asymptotics*

$$
\begin{aligned}
&u(t) = p_L e^{-(t-nt_*)}, && t \in [nt_*, nt_* + T],\\
&u(t) = p_L e^{-(t-nt_*)} + \lambda \int\limits_{T+nt_*}^{t} e^{s-t} f(p_L e^{nt_*+T-s}) ds, && t \in [nt_* + T, nt_* + 2T],\\
&u(t) = \lambda \Big(\int\limits_{nt_*+T}^{nt_*+2T} e^{s-nt_*-2T} f(p_L e^{nt_*+T-s}) ds + o(1) \Big) e^{-(t-nt_*-2T)}, &&\\
& && t \in [nt_* + 2T, (n+1)t_*],
\end{aligned}
\tag{41}
$$

(where $n = 0, 1, 2, \ldots$ represents the number of periods of a cycle) and period $t_* = 2T + (1 + o(1)) \ln \lambda$ at $\lambda \to +\infty$.

If the function $f(u)$ satisfies the condition

$$
\int\limits_{T}^{t} e^{s-t} f(p_L e^{T-s}) ds > 0 \text{ for all } t \in (T, 2T],
\tag{42}
$$

then there exists an asymptotically small by λ value $\delta_1 > 0$ such that $u(T + \delta_1) = p_R$, $u(t) > p_R$ in the interval $(T + \delta_1, 2T]$. Thus, in the segment $t \in [2T, 3T]$, the leading term of the asymptotics of the solution to Equation (2) coincides with the leading term of the asymptotics of the solution to Equation (4) with the initial conditions of (39). This is why this time segment solution has the asymptotics

$$
u(t) = \lambda \Big(\int\limits_{T}^{2T} e^{s-2T} f(p_L e^{T-s}) ds - d + o(1) \Big) e^{-(t-2T)} + \lambda d.
\tag{43}
$$

Since $d < 0$, Expression (43) is decreasing, and there exists a time value t_1 such that $t_1 > 2T$ and Expression (43) is equal to zero at the point t_1 and greater than zero in the interval $t \in (2T, t_1)$. Note that until $u(t) < p_R$, Equation (2) has the form of (4), and the solution has the form of (43). Since λ is sufficiently large, there exists an asymptotically small by λ values $\delta_2 < 0$ and $\delta_3 > 0$ such that $u(t_1 + \delta_2) = p_R$ and $u(t_1 + \delta_3) = p_L$. The length of the interval $(T + \delta_1, t_1 + \delta_2)$ is greater than T, and the solution in this interval is greater than p_R, which is why Equation (2) has the form of (4) in the segment $t \in [t_1 + \delta_2, t_1 + \delta_2 + T]$ and the solution has the form of (43) in this interval.

It is easy to see that

$$
u(t_1 + \delta_3 + T) = \lambda d(1 - e^{-T} + o(1)).
\tag{44}
$$

Since the solution is less than p_L in the interval of the length of delay ($t \in (t_1 + \delta_3, t_1 + \delta_3 + T]$), and $u(t_1 + \delta_3 + T)$ is negative and has the order $O(\lambda)$, Equation (2) has the form of (24) in the segment of the length $(1 + o(1)) \ln \lambda$ (until the solution becomes greater than p_L), and the solution has the form

$$
u(t) = \lambda d(1 - e^{-T} + o(1)) e^{-(t-(t_1+T))}.
\tag{45}
$$

Expression (45) is negative and increases. There exists a time moment $t_* > t_1 + T + \delta_3$ such that Expression (45) is less than p_L for all $t \in [t_1 + T + \delta_3, t_*)$ and is equal to p_L at the point $t = t_*$. Thus, function $u(t_* + s)$ belongs to the set S_-: $u(t_*) = p_L$ and $u(t_* + s) < p_L$ for all $s \in [-T, 0)$. Therefore, if we take this function as the initial conditions of Equation (2), then we get a sign-changing relaxation cycle of this equation with the period $t_* = t_1 + T + (1 + o(1)) \ln \lambda$.

If we take initial functions from S_+, then at the first step, $t \in [0, T]$, the equation has the form of (4) and solution has the form of (5). Then, there exists an asymptotically small by λ value $\delta_4 > 0$ such that $u(t) < p_L$ for all $t \in (\delta_4, T]$. Since, for $t \in [\delta_4, T + \delta_4]$, the solution is less than p_L, Equation (2) has the form of (24), and the solution has the form

$$u(t) = \lambda d(1 - e^{-T} + o(1))e^{-(t-T)} \tag{46}$$

for $t > T + \delta_4$; until then $u(t) > p_L$.

It follows from (46) that there exists a value t_L such that $u(t_L) = p_L$ and $u(s + t_L) < p_L$ in the interval $s \in [-T, 0)$. Therefore, oin the segment $t \in [t_L - T, t_L]$, the solution belongs to the set S_-, which is why we have reduced the problem to the previously studied one.

From the above reasoning, we obtain the following statement.

Theorem 6. *Let $b = 0$, $d < 0$, and let condition (42) hold. Then, for all sufficiently large $\lambda > 0$, Equation (2) has a sign-changing relaxation cycle with the asymptotics*

$$\begin{aligned}
&u(t) = p_L e^{-(t-nt_*)}, && t \in [nt_*, nt_* + T],\\
&u(t) = p_L e^{-(t-nt_*)} + \lambda \int\limits_{T+nt_*}^{t} e^{s-t} f(p_L e^{nt_*+T-s})ds, && t \in [nt_* + T, nt_* + 2T],\\
&u(t) = \lambda\Big(\int\limits_{nt_*+T}^{nt_*+2T} e^{s-nt_*-2T} f(p_L e^{nt_*+T-s})ds - d + o(1)\Big)e^{-(t-nt_*-2T)} + \lambda d, && t \in [nt_* + 2T, nt_* + t_1 + T],\\
&u(t) = \lambda d(1 - e^{-T} + o(1))e^{-(t-(nt_*+t_1+T))}, && t \in [nt_* + t_1 + T, (n+1)t_*],
\end{aligned}$$

(where $n = 0, 1, 2, \dots$ represents the number of periods of cycle) and period $t_* = t_1 + T + (1 + o(1)) \ln \lambda$ at $\lambda \to +\infty$.

The cycles of Equation (2) in the case that $b = 0$ and $d < 0$ are shown in Figure 5.

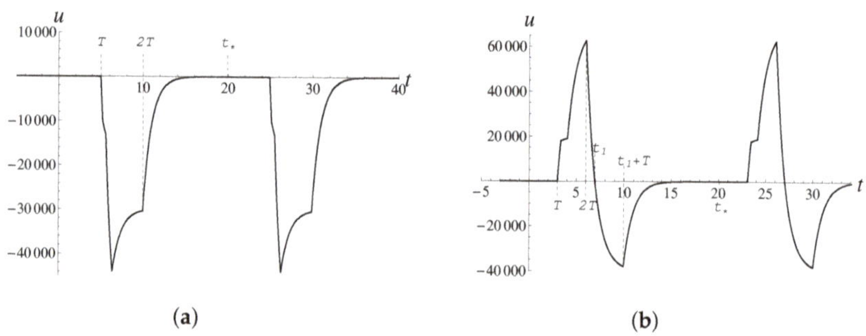

Figure 5. Relaxation cycles of Equation (2) in the case that $b = 0$ and $d < 0$ and function $f(u)$ satisfies the conditions of (**a**) (38) and (**b**) (42). Values of parameters: $\lambda = 10^4$, $p_L = -1.5$, $p_R = 2.5$, $b = 0$, (**a**) $T = 5$, $d = -2$, (**b**) $T = 3$, and $d = -4$.

9. Asymptotics of Solutions in the Case $b = 0$ and $d > 0$

Firstly, consider the initial conditions from S_+. Similar to the case in Section 2, we obtain that for all $t \geq 0$, the solution has the form of (5).

Therefore, in the case that $b = 0$ and $d > 0$, all solutions with initial conditions from the set S_+ tend to a constant λd at $t \to +\infty$.

Now consider the initial conditions from S_-. If function f satisfies Inequality (38), then we obtain that Equation (2) has a negative relaxation cycle (all the reasoning is the same as in Section 8).

The following statement is true.

Theorem 7. *Let $b = 0$, $d > 0$, and let condition (38) be true. Then, for all sufficiently large $\lambda > 0$, Equation (2) has a negative relaxation cycle with the asymptotics of (41) and period $t_* = 2T + (1 + o(1)) \ln \lambda$ at $\lambda \to +\infty$.*

Let us construct the asymptotics of the solution to Equation (2) in the case that function f satisfies the inequality (42). Similarly to Section 8, in the segment $t \in [0, T]$, the solution has the form of (36), in the segment $t \in [T, 2T]$, it has the form of (37), and in the segment $t \in [2T, 3T]$, it has the form of (43). Since Expression (43) is greater than p_R for all $t > 2T$, Equation (2) has the form of (4) for all $t > 3T$, and the solution has the form of (43) for all $t > 2T$.

Thus, in the case that $b = 0$ and $d > 0$, under the condition that function f satisfies Inequality (42), all solutions with initial conditions from the set S_- tend to a constant λd at $t \to +\infty$.

10. Discussion and Conclusions

If we fix the values of b and d, function f, and the set of initial conditions (S_+ or S_-), then for all initial conditions from the chosen set, we obtain an identical behaviour at $t \to +\infty$ (because all solutions with initial conditions from the set S_+ (or S_-) coincide with each other in the segment $t \in [0, T]$, and, therefore, for all $t \geq 0$).

In Sections 2–9 we derived that the behaviour at $t \to +\infty$ of the solutions to Equation (2) with the initial conditions from sets S_+ and S_- may be only of two types: (1) solutions tend to a constant at $t \to +\infty$ or (2) we obtain a cycle.

The following generalization of this result takes place.

Theorem 8. *If we replace the equality $u(0) = p_R$ ($u(0) = p_L$) with the inequality $u(0) \geq p_R$ ($u(0) \leq p_L$, respectively) in the definition of the set S_+ (or S_-, respectively), then the behaviour of the solutions at $t \to +\infty$ does not change.*

Theorem 8 means that if a solution with initial conditions from S_+ tends to a constant at $t \to +\infty$, then a solution with initial conditions satisfying inequality $u(s) \geq p_R$ for all $s \in [-T, 0]$ tends to the same constant at $t \to +\infty$; if we take initial conditions from S_+ and obtain a cycle, then taking initial conditions satisfying inequality $u(s) \geq p_R$, we get the same cycle (but it may be shifted).

The same result is valid for the set S_-.

Proof. Let us prove that if in the definition of S_+, we replace equality $u(0) = p_R$ with inequality $u(0) > p_R$, then the behaviour of the solution does not change.

Denote $u(0)$ as u_0. Since for all $s \in [-T, 0]$, Inequality $u(s) \geq p_R$ holds, then Equation (2) has the form of (4) on the segment $t \in [0, T]$, and the solution has form

$$u_+(t) = u_0 e^{-t} + \lambda d(1 - e^{-t}). \tag{47}$$

Two situations are possible:

(1) There exists a time moment $t_0 > 0$ such that expression (47) is greater than p_R for all $t \in [0, t_0)$ and is equal to p_R at $t = t_0$;

(2) For all $t > 0$, Expression (47) is greater than p_R.

If the first situation occurs, then the function $u_+(t_0 + s)$ ($s \in [-T, 0]$) belongs to the set S_+. All solutions with initial conditions from S_+ for fixed values b and d and function f have the same behaviour, which is why, in this case, for the considered initial conditions, we have the same behaviour of solutions as for the initial conditions from S_+.

The second situation is possible only in the case that $d > 0$ (for all $d \leq 0$ and $u_0 > p_R$, there exists $t_0 > 0$ such that $u_+(t_0) = p_R$). In this situation, for all $t \geq 0$, Equation (2) has the form of (4), and the solution has the form of (47) for all $t \geq 0$. Expression (47) tends to λd at $t \to +\infty$. Since in all cases where $d > 0$, the solutions with initial conditions from S_+

tend to λd at $t \to +\infty$ (see Sections 2, 4 and 9), then in this situation, for the considered initial conditions, we have the same behaviour of solutions as for initial conditions from S_+.

The proof of the Theorem for set S_- is absolutely similar as the proof for the set S_+. □

We have studied the nonlocal dynamics of an equation with delay and nonlinearity having simple behaviour at infinity. This type of nonlinearity is interesting because, on one hand, it is a quite general class of functions, and on the other hand, it is a generalization of two important for application types of nonlinearity: compactly supported and piecewise constant nonlinearities. The key assumption that the nonlinear function F is multiplied by a large parameter λ allows us to construct the asymptotics of all the solutions from the wide sets of initial conditions.

We have studied behaviour at $t \to +\infty$ of the solutions to (2) for wide sets of initial conditions and conclude that two types of behaviour are possible: (1) the solution tends to a constant or (2) after the pre-period, the solution becomes a cycle.

It is important to mention that it is impossible to obtain such general results using numerical simulation because it is impossible to iterate through all the considered functions F and initial conditions. Additionally, even if we take a certain function F and initial conditions, the simulation of this equation is a difficult problem, because the parameter λ is large.

We have found conditions on signs b and d under the condition that $bd \neq 0$ for having a cycle of Equation (2). This cycle has an amplitude of the order $O(\lambda)$ and period of the order $O(1)$ at $\lambda \to +\infty$. We have found conditions on sign b (d) under condition $d = 0$ ($b = 0$, respectively) for having relaxation cycles of Equation (2). Depending on the properties of the function f, this cycle may be sign-changing or sign-preserving.

It is important to mention that most found cycles (see Theorems 1, 3, 6) do not exist in the case of compactly supported nonlinearity [20].

In the future, it will be interesting to study the dynamics of several coupled Equation (2) and to analyse the dependence of the dynamics of the system on the type of coupling.

Funding: This research was funded by The Council on Grants of the President of the Russian Federation grant number MK-2510.2022.1.1.

Data Availability Statement: Not applicable.

Conflicts of Interest: The author declares no conflict of interest. The funder had no role in the design of the study; in the collection, analyses, or interpretation of data; in the writing of the manuscript; or in the decision to publish the results.

References

1. Erneux, T. *Applied Delay Differential Equations*; Springer Science & Business Media: Berlin/Heidelberg, Germany, 2009. [CrossRef]
2. Lakshmanan, M.; Senthilkumar, D.V. *Dynamics of Nonlinear Time-Delay Systems*; Springer Science & Business Media: Berlin/Heidelberg, Germany, 2011. [CrossRef]
3. Zenir, K. Stabilization for Solutions of Plate Equation with Time-Varying Delay and Weak-Viscoelasticity in $\mathbb{R}^n$. *Russ. Math.* **2020**, *64*, 21–33. [CrossRef]
4. Rao, R.; Lin, Z.; Ai, X.; Wu, J. Synchronization of Epidemic Systems with Neumann Boundary Value under Delayed Impulse. *Mathematics* **2022**, *10*, 2064. [CrossRef]
5. Jajarmi, A.; Baleanu, D.; Vahid, K.Z.; Pirouz, H.M.; Asad, J.H. A new and general fractional Lagrangian approach: A capacitor microphone case study. *Results Phys.* **2021**, *31*, 104950. [CrossRef]
6. Yang, X.; Wang, H.; Zhu, Q. Event-triggered predictive control of nonlinear stochastic systems with output delay. *Automatica* **2022**, *140*, 110230. [CrossRef]
7. Kashchenko, A.A. Multistability in a system of two coupled oscillators with delayed feedback. *J. Differ. Equ.* **2019**, *266*, 562–579. [CrossRef]
8. Kashchenko, A.A. Non-rough Relaxation Solutions of a System with Delay and Sign-Changing Nonlinearity. *Nonlinear Phenom. Complex Syst.* **2019**, *22*, 190–195.
9. Glyzin, S.D.; Kolesov, A.Y.; Marushkina, E.A. Relaxation oscillations in a system of two pulsed synaptically coupled neurons. *Autom. Control Comput. Sci.* **2017**, *51*, 658–665. [CrossRef]
10. Hammad, H.A.; Zayed, M. Solving a System of Differential Equations with Infinite Delay by Using Tripled Fixed Point Techniques on Graphs. *Symmetry* **2022**, *14*, 1388. [CrossRef]

11. Preobrazhenskaya, M.M. A relay Mackey—Glass model with two delays. *Theor. Math. Phys.* **2020**, *203*, 524–534. [CrossRef]
12. an der Heiden, U.; Mackey, M.C. The dynamics of production and destruction: Analytic insight into complex behavior. *J. Math. Biol.* **1982**, *16*, 75–101. [CrossRef]
13. an der Heiden, U.; Walther, H.O. Existence of chaos in control systems with delayed feedback. *J. Differ. Equ.* **1983**, *47*, 273–295. [CrossRef]
14. Kislov, V.Y.; Dmitriev, A.S. Nonlinear Stochastization of Oscillations in Radio Engineering and Electronic Systems. In *Problems of Modern Radio Engineering and Electronics*; Nauka: Moscow, Russia, 1987; pp. 154–169.
15. Kilias, T.; Kelber, K.; Mogel, A.; Schwarz, W. Electronic chaos generators—Design and applications. *Int. J. Electron.* **1995**, *79*, 737–753. [CrossRef]
16. Larger, L.; Lee, M.W.; Goedgebuer, J.P.; Elflein, W.; Erneux, T. Chaos in coherence modulation: Bifurcations of an oscillator generating optical delay fluctuations. *JOSA B* **2001**, *18*, 1063–1068. [CrossRef]
17. Arino, J.; Van Den Driessche, P. Time delays in epidemic models. In *Delay Differential Equations and Applications*; Springer: Berlin/Heidelberg, Germany, 2006; pp. 539–578.
18. Krisztin, T.; Walther, H.O. Unique periodic orbits for delayed positive feedback and the global attractor. *J. Dyn. Differ. Equ.* **2001**, *13*, 1–57. [CrossRef]
19. Krisztin, T.; Vas, G. Large-amplitude periodic solutions for differential equations with delayed monotone positive feedback. *J. Dyn. Differ. Equ.* **2011**, *23*, 727–790. [CrossRef]
20. Kaschenko, S.A. Asymptotic Behavior of Relaxation Oscillations in Systems of Difference-Differential Equations with a Compactly Supported Nonlinearity. I. *Differ. Equ.* **1995**, *31*, 1275–1285.
21. Stoffer, D. Delay equations with rapidly oscillating stable periodic solutions. *J. Dyn. Differ. Equ.* **2008**, *20*, 201–238. [CrossRef]
22. Ivanov, A.F.; Sharkovsky, A.N. Oscillations in singularly perturbed delay equations. In *Dynamics Reported*; Springer: Berlin/Heidelberg, Germany, 1992; pp. 164–224. [CrossRef]
23. Mallet-Paret, J.; Nussbaum, R.D. Global continuation and asymptotic behaviour for periodic solutions of a differential-delay equation. *Ann. Mat. Pura Appl.* **1986**, *145*, 33–128. [CrossRef]
24. Kashchenko, I.; Kaschenko, S. Normal and quasinormal forms for systems of difference and differential-difference equations. *Commun. Nonlinear Sci. Numer. Simul.* **2016**, *38*, 243–256. [CrossRef]
25. Bezruchko, B.; Karavaev, A.; Ponomarenko, V.; Prokhorov, M. Reconstruction of time-delay systems from chaotic time series. *Phys. Rev. E* **2001**, *64*, 056216. [CrossRef]
26. Prokhorov, M.; Ponomarenko, V.; Karavaev, A.; Bezruchko, B. Reconstruction of time-delayed feedback systems from time series. *Phys. D Nonlinear Phenom.* **2005**, *203*, 209–223. [CrossRef]
27. Kashchenko, A.A. Relaxation modes of a system of diffusion coupled oscillators with delay. *Commun. Nonlinear Sci. Numer. Simulat.* **2021**, *93*, 105488. [CrossRef]
28. Kashchenko, A.A. Influence of coupling on the dynamics of three delayed oscillators. *Izv. Vuz. Appl. Nonlinear Dyn.* **2021**, *29*, 869–891. [CrossRef]
29. Kashchenko, A.A. Dependence of the dynamics of a model of coupled oscillators on the number of oscillators. *Dokl. Math.* **2021**, *104*, 355–359. [CrossRef]
30. Hale, J.; Lunel, S.M.V. *Introduction to Functional Differential Equations*; Springer: Berlin/Heidelberg, Germany, 1993.

mathematics MDPI

Article

Forecasting the Effect of Pre-Exposure Prophylaxis (PrEP) on HIV Propagation with a System of Differential– Difference Equations with Delay

Mostafa Adimy [1,†], Julien Molina [1,†], Laurent Pujo-Menjouet [1,*,†], Grégoire Ranson [1,2,†] and Jianhong Wu [2,†]

1 Univ Lyon, Université Claude Bernard Lyon 1, CNRS UMR5208, Inria, Institut Camille Jordan, F-69603 Villeurbanne, France
2 Laboratory for Industrial and Applied Mathematics (LIAM), Department of Mathematics and Statistics, York University, Toronto, ON M3J 1P3, Canada
* Corresponding: pujo@math.univ-lyon1.fr
† These authors contributed equally to this work.

Abstract: The HIV/AIDS epidemic is still active worldwide with no existing definitive cure. Based on the WHO recommendations stated in 2014, a treatment, called Pre-Exposure Prophylaxis (PrEP), has been used in the world, and more particularly in France since 2016, to prevent HIV infections. In this paper, we propose a new compartmental epidemiological model with a limited protection time offered by this new treatment. We describe the PrEP compartment with an age-structure hyperbolic equation and introduce a differential equation on the parameter that governs the PrEP starting process. This leads us to a nonlinear differential–difference system with discrete delay. After a local stability analysis, we prove the global behavior of the system. Finally, we illustrate the solutions with numerical simulations based on the data of the French Men who have Sex with Men (MSM) population. We show that the choice of a logistic time dynamics combined with our Hill-function-like model leads to a perfect data fit. These results enable us to forecast the evolution of the HIV epidemics in France if the populations keep using PrEP.

Keywords: HIV; AIDS; PrEP; differential–difference system; discrete delay; France

MSC: 92D30

Citation: Adimy, M.; Molina, J.; Pujo-Menjouet, L.; Ranson, G.; Wu, J. Forecasting the Effect of Pre-Exposure Prophylaxis (PrEP)on HIV Propagation with a System of Differential–Difference Equations with Delay. *Mathematics* **2022**, *10*, 4093. https://doi.org/10.3390/math10214093

Academic Editor: Alexandra Kashchenko

Received: 15 September 2022
Accepted: 26 October 2022
Published: 2 November 2022

1. Introduction

Since its onset in the early 1980s and its clear identification in 1983, Human Immunodeficiency Virus (HIV) and then Acquired Immune Deficiency Syndrome (AIDS) have still comprised one of the most deadly active worldwide epidemics. In the 2019 UNAIDS study, about 38 million persons lived with HIV, 1.7 million became infected, and 690,000 died of AIDS-related diseases (UNAIDS, Global HIV & AIDS statistics—2020 fact sheet: https://www.unaids.org/en/resources/fact-sheet) (accessed on 13 September 2022), becoming one of the most serious public health challenges.

It is well known now that this infection evolves in three stages: first a short acute phase where flu-like symptoms appear, followed by a symptom-free chronic phase that lasts between 10 and 15 years. It eventually ends up with AIDS when the virus has killed enough TCD4, leading to the failure of the immune system (https://www.hiv.gov/hiv-basics/overview/about-hiv-and-aids/symptoms-of-hiv) (accessed on 13 September 2022).

Note here that the latency stage appears as one of the crucial problems. Indeed, the dormant period of the virus drastically delays HIV/AIDS diagnosis if not detected and plays a major role in the epidemic's spread (see Figure 1 in [1]).

Despite extensive investigations, there is still no existing therapy that helps the organism to fully get rid of the virus.

However, since 1996, AntiRetroviral Therapy (ART), consisting of a combination of three (or more) antiretroviral agents taken daily, has appeared to reduce significantly the presence of the virus under a detectable threshold. Currently, not only efficient at avoiding the fatality of the disease, ART allows also HIV-infected individuals stop spreading the disease. In 2019, 25.4 million of them successfully accessed antiretroviral therapy, (UNAIDS, Global HIV & AIDS statistics—2020 fact sheet: https://www.unaids.org/en/resources/fact-sheet (accessed on 13 September 2022); World Health Organization (WHO)—HIV/AIDS: https://www.who.int/news-room/fact-sheets/detail/hiv-aids (accessed on 13 September 2022).

In the late 2010s, Pre-Exposure Prophylaxis (PrEP) was introduced as a new way of preventing HIV transmission. This successful treatment addresses HIV-free individuals showing a high risk of becoming infected. PrEP consists of taking a combination of two antiretrovirals in two different protocols: either on a daily basis (continuous treatment) or on demand (discrete treatment), which is just at least 2 h before and 2 days after sexual intercourse. Every 3 months, continuous PrEP users need to have a global Sexually Transmitted Infections (STIs) screening in order to obtain a prescription for another 3 months (World Health Organization (WHO)—HIV/AIDS: https://www.who.int/news-room/fact-sheets/detail/hiv-aids; https://www.who.int/teams/global-hiv-hepatitis-and-stis-programmes/hiv/prevention/pre-exposure-prophylaxis) (accessed on 13 September 2022). Theoretically, they can stop anytime, but they are practically more likely to choose at the end of each quarter. We remind here that PrEP is preventive and does not cure HIV. However, it effectively reduces HIV transmission (World Health Organization (WHO)—HIV/AIDS: https://www.who.int/news-room/fact-sheets/detail/hiv-aids) (accessed on 13 September 2022).

Our objective here was to design a new model to mathematically forecast the influence of PrEP users among high-risk profiles on the epidemic. The application of our study focused only on the French population, where PrEP has been used since 2016, and is currently followed by an average of 20,000 individuals [2].

In the past few decades, many epidemiological models have been used to describe HIV's dynamics. Some of them used the standard Susceptible (S)–Infected (I)–Infected under ART (C) with low viral charge–Infected with AIDS symptoms (A) ($SICA$) model (see [3] for instance), and for a good review, we suggest [4,5].

It has only been in the past few years that new models including a PrEP user compartment appeared and started to receive our attention. A good example is the preliminary work [6], where the authors suggested a vaccination approach, which could be seen as a precursor to PrEP. Their numerical simulations showed that the epidemic spread could be controlled thanks to vaccination, even if the basic reproduction number remains above 1. In [7,8], an explicit PrEP compartment was included in the $SICA$ model. The parameters in [8] were adjusted with clinical data and PrEP's effectiveness mathematically proven. In [9], the authors divided the PrEP compartment according to the adherence of users to the treatment. They showed that, with at least 70% of PrEP users in the male homosexual population, the HIV epidemic could be effectively controlled. Finally, in [10], PrEP was combined with screening and the result was compared to Portuguese data showing that these two processes appeared necessary to control the HIV epidemic.

In our paper, we introduce a new approach with a Susceptible–Infected–Protected (SIP) model. Inspired by [8,11], it includes an age structure on the PrEP (protected) compartment, corresponding to the time spent after the onset of the new 3-month treatment period. Once the term is reached, the user chooses either to keep taking PrEP or to stop it, becoming susceptible again. On the other hand, individuals of the S compartment may decide to start or resume this preventative process and, hence, reach the P population.

Our goal was to propose a more accurate model than that of [8] that still possible to handle analytically by considering a more complex susceptible interaction $F(t,S)$ depending both on time t (through a function ψ) and the total S population (through a function f), which can be seen as a political or economic decision made depending on the size of the HIV-exposed population(see Section 2 for details). After standard modifications, we prove in Section 2 that our new model can be written as a nonlinear differential–difference system with discrete delay. As presented below in Sections 3 and 4, the stability analysis is then possible when the ψ term is constant. However, since it may take a while to convince a population set to start PrEP, it appears natural to us that ψ may follow a logistic equation. The model becomes then too challenging to be investigated in an analytical way, and thus, numerical simulations take over this work in Section 5. Thanks to this new assumption, we show eventually that it is possible to fit the data with realistic values. Before this, we proceed to its well-posedness and stability study and investigate the constant and non-constant joining PrEP rate subcases in Section 3 and 4. Then, we compare our theoretical work to official clinical French data in order to understand the role of PrEP's dynamics on the HIV/AIDS epidemic in Section 5. With some numerical simulations, we observe that, by choosing a logistic equation for the nonlinear joining PrEP rate and a Hill function for the dynamics of $f(S)$, we perfectly fit our data.

2. Introducing Our Model

In order to keep the model as simple as possible, we considered only three compartments: Susceptible (S), individuals that may be infected by HIV; Infected (I) and Protected (P), individuals on PrEP treatment (see Figure 1). The total population is

$$N(t) = S(t) + I(t) + P(t).$$

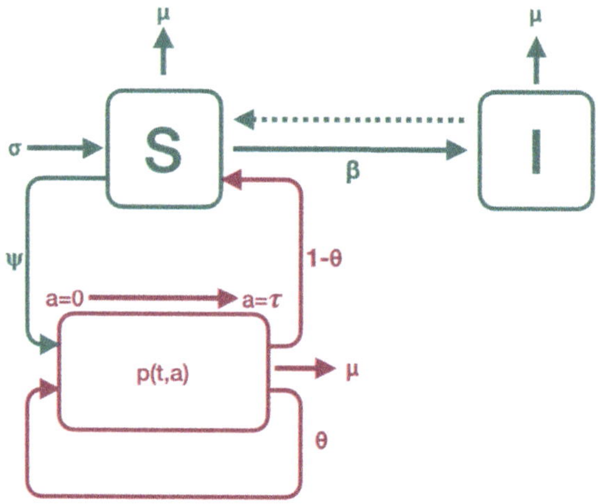

Figure 1. Schematic representation of the compartmental model (1). Continuous arrows represent movements between compartments. Dashed ones represents the transmission of the infection.

To take into account the limited protection duration offered by PrEP, we structured the compartment of protected individuals by age. Here, age a corresponds to the time since the last test and the renewal of PrEP treatment. The maximum duration of the protection period is generally three months, $\tau = 3$ months. Therefore, $a \in [0, \tau]$. If an individual decides to renew the treatment, the age a is reset to zero. We denote by $p(t, a)$ the population on PrEP at time t who started their new treatment period a days ago. Thus, the total population of PrEP users at time t is

$$P(t) = \int_0^\tau p(t, a)da.$$

The model was designed taking into account the input and output rates of each compartment with appropriate parameters (see Figure 1). At each time t, there is a constant number of individuals (source term σ) who become susceptible by reaching the age of sexual consent, becoming single again, or deciding to start new intercourse experiences.

At the same time, some susceptible individuals become infected with HIV at a rate β. A part,

$$F(t, S(t)) = \psi(t) f(S(t)),$$

of the susceptible individuals decide to start PrEP. The choice of functions f and ψ allows us to consider many scenarios. The function f is an increasing function of the total population of susceptible individuals with $f(0) = 0$. Examples could be

$$f(S) = S^n \quad \text{or} \quad f(S) = \frac{S^n}{1 + S^n}, \quad n \geq 1.$$

The first choice is well adapted to rich countries or countries with a low number of susceptible individuals (the proposed treatment, for example the case $f(S) = S, n = 1$, is proportional to the total population of susceptible individuals). The second choice is better adapted to poor countries or countries with a large number of susceptible individuals, which, for budgetary reasons, cannot increase the treatment indefinitely. The fact that the function ψ is time-dependent is dictated by the data we wish to use on PrEP, which began in 2016 in France and continues to increase. For cost reasons, this PrEP prescription rate will eventually reach a maximum threshold. A well-fitting example of function ψ is

$$\psi(t) = \psi_0 + \frac{\kappa_1 t^m}{t^m + \kappa_2}, \quad m \geq 1, \ \kappa_1, \ \kappa_2 > 0.$$

For the analytical study of the model, we assumed that this threshold has already been reached and, therefore, considered

$$\psi \equiv K := \psi_0 + \kappa_1$$

to be a constant. We can also choose $t \mapsto \psi(t)$ as a solution of the logistic equation with K as the carrying capacity. Finally, we supposed that the disease and treatment do not affect mortality (death rate μ is consequently the same for all). The system satisfied by S and I is then given, for all $t > 0$, by

$$\begin{cases} S'(t) &= \sigma - \beta I(t)S(t) - \mu S(t) - Kf(S(t)) + (1-\theta)p(t,\tau), \\ I'(t) &= \beta I(t)S(t) - \mu I(t) \end{cases} \tag{1}$$

The density p satisfies, for $t > 0$, the following age-structured partial differential equation:

$$\begin{cases} \dfrac{\partial p}{\partial t}(t,a) + \dfrac{\partial p}{\partial a}(t,a) = -\mu p(t,a), \quad 0 < a < \tau, \\ p(t,0) = Kf(S(t)) + \theta p(t,\tau). \end{cases} \tag{2}$$

We remind here that $a \in [0, \tau]$ is the time elapsed from the new period of time under treatment. If an individual decides to renew the treatment, the age a is reset to zero. We denote by $p(t,a)$ the population under PrEP at time t who started their new treatment period a days ago. The initial condition is given by

$$S(0) = S_0, \quad I(0) = I_0 \quad \text{and} \quad p(0,a) = p_0(a), \quad 0 < a < \tau.$$

The boundary condition

$$p(t,0) = Kf(S(t)) + \theta p(t,\tau),$$

represents individuals who renewed their PrEP, $\theta p(t,\tau)$, or those who started it, $Kf(S(t))$.

Using the characteristics method and the boundary condition from (2) (see [12]), we obtain, for $t > 0$ and $a \in [0, \tau]$,

$$p(t,a) = \begin{cases} e^{-\mu a} p(t-a, 0), & t > a, \\ e^{-\mu t} p(0, a-t) = e^{-\mu t} p_0(a-t), & 0 \leq t \leq a. \end{cases} \tag{3}$$

To write Equation (3) in a convenient form, we supposed that the initial condition p_0 is continuous on $[0, \tau]$ and satisfies the compatibility condition

$$p_0(0) = Kf(S_0) + \theta p_0(\tau).$$

We put

$$\varphi(t) := e^{-\mu t} p_0(-t), \quad -\tau \leq t \leq 0,$$

and we define the function

$$u(t) := p(t, 0), \quad t \geq 0.$$

We then obtain from (3) the expression

$$p(t, \tau) = e^{-\mu\tau} \begin{cases} u(t-\tau), & t > \tau, \\ \varphi(t-\tau), & 0 \leq t \leq \tau. \end{cases}$$

This means that we can extend the function u to the interval $[-\tau, 0]$, by putting $u(t) = \varphi(t)$ for $t \in [-\tau, 0]$. Then, we have directly $p(t, \tau) = e^{-\mu\tau} u(t-\tau)$, for all $t \geq 0$. Consequently, using the boundary condition of the system (2), u satisfies the difference equation:

$$u(t) = \begin{cases} Kf(S(t)) + \theta e^{-\mu\tau} u(t-\tau), & t > 0, \\ \varphi(t), & -\tau \leq t \leq 0. \end{cases}$$

Furthermore, the total population $P(t)$ can be explicitly expressed, for $t \geq 0$, in terms of the function u:

$$P(t) = \int_0^\tau e^{-\mu a} u(t-a) da = e^{-\mu t} \int_{t-\tau}^t e^{\mu a} u(a) da.$$

Thus, we obtain the complete model, for $t > 0$,

$$\begin{cases} S'(t) &= \sigma - \beta I(t)S(t) - \mu S(t) - Kf(S(t)) + (1-\theta)e^{-\mu\tau} u(t-\tau), \\ I'(t) &= \beta I(t)S(t) - \mu I(t), \\ u(t) &= Kf(S(t)) + \theta e^{-\mu\tau} u(t-\tau), \end{cases} \tag{4}$$

with the initial condition:

$$S(0) = S_0, \quad I(0) = I_0 \quad \text{and} \quad u(t) = \varphi(t), \quad t \in [-\tau, 0]. \tag{5}$$

Knowing that $P(t) = e^{-\mu t} \int_{t-\tau}^t e^{\mu a} u(a) da$, we obtain

$$P'(t) = -\mu P(t) + Kf(S(t)) - (1-\theta)e^{-\mu\tau} u(t-\tau).$$

We then have

$$N'(t) = S'(t) + I'(t) + P'(t) = \sigma - \mu N(t).$$

We easily obtain

$$N(t) = \left(N_0 - \frac{\sigma}{\mu}\right) e^{-\mu t} + \frac{\sigma}{\mu} \to \frac{\sigma}{\mu}, \quad \text{as } t \to +\infty. \tag{6}$$

3. Mathematical Analysis

In this section, we discuss the well-posedness of the model, the steady-states, the basic reproduction number, and the local asymptotic stability.

3.1. Well-Posedness of the Model

The problem (4) and (5) is a coupled system of nonlinear differential and difference equations with discrete delay. We directly derive the following proposition about the well-posedness of the model.

Proposition 1. *For any nonnegative initial condition (S_0, I_0, φ), where φ is a nonnegative continuous function on $[-\tau, 0]$, there exists a unique nonnegative solution to Problem (4) and (5) defined on $[0, +\infty)$. Moreover, this solution is uniformly bounded on $[0, +\infty)$.*

Proof. We first solve the system (4) and (5) on the interval $[0, \tau]$. In this case, since u is completely defined, the Cauchy–Lipschitz theorem gives the existence and uniqueness of the solution on $[0, \tau]$, and this solution is nonnegative. Then, we repeat this method on each interval of type $[k\tau, (k+1)\tau]$ with $k \in \mathbb{N}$. Thus, we obtain a unique nonnegative solution on the interval $[0, +\infty)$. Furthermore, using (6) and the fact that $S(t) + I(t) + u(t) \leq S(t) + I(t) + P(t) = N(t)$, we deduce that (S, I, u) is uniformly bounded on $[0, +\infty)$. □

3.2. Steady-States and Basic Reproduction Number

In this subsection, we compute the steady-states of the system and study their local asymptotic stability. Let us consider a steady-state (S^*, I^*, u^*) of (4). We then have

$$\begin{cases} 0 &= \sigma - \beta I^* S^* - \mu S^* - K f(S^*) + (1-\theta) e^{-\mu\tau} u^*, \\ 0 &= (\beta S^* - \mu) I^*, \\ u^* &= K f(S^*) + \theta e^{-\mu\tau} u^*. \end{cases} \tag{7}$$

The third equation of the system (7) leads to

$$u^* = \frac{K f(S^*)}{1 - \theta e^{-\mu\tau}}.$$

We remark that, as $\theta \in (0,1)$, we always have $1 - \theta e^{-\mu\tau} > 0$.

Assume that $I^* = 0$. Then, the first equation of (7) implies that S^* satisfies the equation:

$$\Phi(S^*) := S^* + \frac{K(1 - e^{-\mu\tau})}{\mu(1 - \theta e^{-\mu\tau})} f(S^*) = \frac{\sigma}{\mu}. \tag{8}$$

Since Φ is increasing, tends to infinity, and satisfies $\Phi(0) = 0$, we obtain the existence of a unique S^* such that $\Phi(S^*) = \sigma/\mu$. We can therefore write $S^* = \Phi^{-1}(\sigma/\mu)$. Thus, we obtain the disease-free steady-state:

$$(S^*, I^*, u^*) = \left(\Phi^{-1}(\sigma/\mu) \,,\, 0 \,,\, \frac{K f(\Phi^{-1}(\sigma/\mu))}{1 - \theta e^{-\tau\mu}} \right). \tag{9}$$

Now, suppose that $S^* = \mu/\beta$. We immediately obtain that

$$u^* = \frac{K f(\mu/\beta)}{1 - \theta e^{-\mu\tau}}.$$

We inject these two last expressions into the first equation of (7) to obtain

$$I^* = \frac{\sigma}{\mu} - \Phi\left(\frac{\mu}{\beta}\right),$$

where the function Φ is given by the expression (8). Then, $I^* > 0$ exists if and only if

$$\Phi^{-1}\left(\frac{\sigma}{\mu}\right) > \frac{\mu}{\beta}.$$

Let us define the basic reproduction number $\mathcal{R}_0$ as a threshold for the existence of the endemic steady-state:

$$\mathcal{R}_0 := \frac{\beta}{\mu} \Phi^{-1}\left(\frac{\sigma}{\mu}\right).$$

Hence, we obtain the existence of a unique endemic steady-state:

$$(S^*, I^*, u^*) = \left(\frac{\mu}{\beta}, \frac{\sigma}{\mu} - \Phi\left(\frac{\mu}{\beta}\right), \frac{Kf(\mu/\beta)}{1-\theta e^{-\mu\tau}}\right) \tag{10}$$

if and only if

$$\mathcal{R}_0 > 1.$$

We will need to know the variation of $\mathcal{R}_0$ as a function of $\tau \in [0, +\infty)$. We have the following lemma.

Lemma 1. *The basic reproduction number $\tau \in [0, +\infty) \mapsto \mathcal{R}_0(\tau)$ is a decreasing function such that*

$$\mathcal{R}_0(0) = \frac{\beta\sigma}{\mu^2} \quad \textit{and} \quad \mathcal{R}_0(\infty) = \frac{\beta}{\mu}\Phi_\infty^{-1}\left(\frac{\sigma}{\mu}\right),$$

with

$$\Phi_\infty(S) := S + \frac{K}{\mu}f(S).$$

Proof. Consider the dependence of the function Φ on τ by putting

$$\Phi(S,\tau) := S + \frac{K(1-e^{-\mu\tau})}{\mu(1-\theta e^{-\mu\tau})}f(S).$$

We want to study the variation of $\tau \mapsto \mathcal{R}_0(\tau) = \frac{\beta}{\mu}\Phi^{-1}\left(\frac{\sigma}{\mu}, \tau\right)$. Then, we set $S(\tau) := \Phi^{-1}(\sigma/\mu, \tau)$. In fact, we have $\Phi(S(\tau), \tau) = \sigma/\mu$. By differentiating, we deduce that

$$\frac{\partial\Phi}{\partial S}(S(\tau),\tau)\frac{d}{d\tau}S(\tau) + \frac{\partial\Phi}{\partial\tau}(S(\tau),\tau) = 0.$$

Thus, we obtain

$$\frac{d}{d\tau}\mathcal{R}_0(\tau) = \frac{\beta}{\mu}\frac{d}{d\tau}S(\tau) = -\frac{\beta}{\mu}\frac{\frac{\partial\Phi}{\partial\tau}(S(\tau),\tau)}{\frac{\partial\Phi}{\partial S}(S(\tau),\tau)} < 0.$$

Then, the function $\tau \mapsto \mathcal{R}_0(\tau)$ is decreasing on $[0, +\infty)$. Furthermore, by taking $\tau = 0$ and $\tau \to +\infty$ in the equality:

$$\Phi(S,\tau) := S(\tau) + \frac{K(1-e^{-\mu\tau})}{\mu(1-\theta e^{-\mu\tau})}f(S(\tau)) = \frac{\sigma}{\mu},$$

we obtain that

$$\mathcal{R}_0(0) = \frac{\beta\sigma}{\mu^2} \quad \text{and} \quad \mathcal{R}_0(\infty) = \frac{\beta}{\mu}\Phi_\infty^{-1}\left(\frac{\sigma}{\mu}\right),$$

with

$$\Phi_\infty(S) := S + \frac{K}{\mu}f(S).$$

□

We conclude from Lemma 1 that $\mathcal{R}_0(\infty) < \mathcal{R}_0(\tau) < \mathcal{R}_0(0)$, for all $\tau \in (0, +\infty)$, and we immediately obtain the following result.

Proposition 2. *Suppose that $\tau \geq 0$. Then, we have three cases:*

- *If $\mathcal{R}_0(0) < 1$, then we have $\mathcal{R}_0(\tau) < 1$, for all $\tau \geq 0$.*
- *If $\mathcal{R}_0(\infty) > 1$, then we have $\mathcal{R}_0(\tau) > 1$, for all $\tau \geq 0$.*
- *If $\mathcal{R}_0(0) > 1$ and $\mathcal{R}_0(\infty) < 1$, then there exists a unique $\bar{\tau} > 0$ such that $\mathcal{R}_0(\tau) > 1$ for $0 \leq \tau < \bar{\tau}$ and $\mathcal{R}_0(\tau) < 1$ for $\tau > \bar{\tau}$, with $\mathcal{R}_0(\bar{\tau}) = 1$.*

We linearize System (4) around any equilibrium (S^*, I^*, u^*), and we obtain

$$\begin{cases} S'(t) &= -\beta I^* S(t) - \beta S^* I(t) - \mu S(t) - Kf'(S^*)S(t) + (1-\theta)e^{-\mu\tau}u(t-\tau), \\ I'(t) &= \beta I^* S(t) + \beta S^* I(t) - \mu I(t), \\ u(t) &= Kf'(S^*)S(t) + \theta e^{-\mu\tau}u(t-\tau). \end{cases}$$

We look for solutions of the form $S(t) = e^{-\lambda t}S_0$, $I(t) = e^{-\lambda t}I_0$ and $u(t) = e^{-\lambda t}u_0$, $t > 0$, and $\lambda \in \mathbb{C}$. Then, we obtain the following characteristic equation

$$\Delta(\lambda, \tau) := \begin{vmatrix} \lambda + \beta I^* + \mu + Kf'(S^*) & \beta S^* & -(1-\theta)e^{-\mu\tau}e^{-\lambda\tau} \\ -\beta I^* & \lambda - \beta S^* + \mu & 0 \\ -Kf'(S^*) & 0 & 1 - \theta e^{-\mu\tau}e^{-\lambda\tau} \end{vmatrix} = 0.$$

We develop the determinant and obtain

$$\begin{aligned} \Delta(\tau, \lambda) &= (\lambda - \beta S^* + \mu)\left[(\lambda + \mu)(1 - \theta e^{-\mu\tau}e^{-\lambda\tau}) + Kf'(S^*)(1 - e^{-\mu\tau}e^{-\lambda\tau})\right] \\ &\quad + (\lambda + \mu)\beta I^*(1 - \theta e^{-\mu\tau}e^{-\lambda\tau}), \\ &= 0. \end{aligned}$$

First, consider the disease-free equilibrium (9). Then, the characteristic equation becomes

$$[\lambda - \mu(\mathcal{R}_0 - 1)]\left[(\lambda + \mu)(1 - \theta e^{-\mu\tau}e^{-\lambda\tau}) + Kf'(\Phi^{-1}(\sigma/\mu))(1 - e^{-\mu\tau}e^{-\lambda\tau})\right] = 0.$$

We have an immediate real eigenvalue

$$\lambda_0 = \mu(\mathcal{R}_0 - 1).$$

The other eigenvalues are solutions of the transcendental equation:

$$\bar{\Delta}(\lambda) := P(\lambda) - Q(\lambda)e^{-\lambda\tau} = 0, \tag{11}$$

with

$$P(\lambda) := \lambda + \mu + Kf'(\Phi^{-1}(\sigma/\mu)) \quad \text{and} \quad Q(\lambda) := e^{-\mu\tau}[\theta\lambda + \theta\mu + Kf'(\Phi^{-1}(\sigma/\mu))].$$

We have the following properties:

Property 1.

(i) *The equation (11) has no purely imaginary root.*

(ii) *All roots λ_n, $n \in \mathbb{N}$, of (11) such that $|\lambda_n| \to +\infty$, have a negative real part for n large enough:*

Proof. (i) First, we seek for pure imaginary roots $\lambda = \pm i\omega$, $\omega > 0$, of (11). Splitting in (11) the real and the imaginary part, we obtain

$$\begin{cases} \gamma\cos(\omega\tau)e^{-\mu\tau} + \theta\omega\sin(\omega\tau)e^{-\mu\tau} &= \mu + Kf'(\Phi^{-1}(\sigma/\mu)), \\ -\theta\omega\cos(\omega\tau)e^{-\mu\tau} + \gamma\sin(\omega\tau)e^{-\mu\tau} &= -\omega, \end{cases}$$

where $\gamma := \theta\mu + Kf'(\Phi^{-1}(\sigma/\mu))$. Solving this system, we find that

$$\begin{cases} \cos(\omega\tau) &= \dfrac{1}{(\theta^2\omega^2 + \gamma^2)e^{-\mu\tau}}\left[\theta\omega^2 + \gamma(\mu + Kf'(\Phi^{-1}(\sigma/\mu)))\right], \\ \sin(\omega\tau) &= \dfrac{1}{(\theta^2\omega^2 + \gamma^2)e^{-\mu\tau}}\left[-\omega\gamma + \theta\omega(\mu + Kf'(\Phi^{-1}(\sigma/\mu)))\right]. \end{cases}$$

Using the trigonometric identity $\cos^2(\omega\tau) + \sin^2(\omega\tau) = 1$, we obtain that ω satisfies

$$(\theta^2\omega^2 + \gamma^2)(e^{-\mu\tau})^2 = \omega^2 + (\mu + Kf'(\Phi^{-1}(\sigma/\mu)))^2.$$

Then, we obtain

$$\omega^2 = \frac{(\gamma e^{-\mu\tau} - (\mu + Kf'(\Phi^{-1}(\sigma/\mu))))((\mu + Kf'(\Phi^{-1}(\sigma/\mu))) + \gamma e^{-\mu\tau})}{1 - \theta^2 e^{-2\mu\tau}}. \tag{12}$$

Notice that $1 - \theta^2 e^{-2\mu\tau} > 0$ and

$$\gamma e^{-\mu\tau} - (\mu + Kf'(\Phi^{-1}(\sigma/\mu))) = [\theta\mu + Kf'(\Phi^{-1}(\sigma/\mu))]e^{-\mu\tau} - [\mu + Kf'(\Phi^{-1}(\sigma/\mu))] < 0.$$

Thus, the right-hand side of (12) is negative, which is absurd. We conclude that the Equation (11) has no purely imaginary root.

(ii) As the function $\bar{\Delta}$ is entire, the set of its roots cannot have accumulation points. Furthermore, $\bar{\Delta}$ has at most countably many zeros. If $\bar{\Delta}$ has infinitely many different zeros, $\lambda_n \in \mathbb{C}$, $n \in \mathbb{N}$, then

$$\lim_{n \to +\infty} |\lambda_n| = +\infty.$$

The sequence λ_n, $n \in \mathbb{N}$, satisfies

$$e^{\lambda_n \tau}\left(\frac{P(\lambda_n)}{\lambda_n}\right) - \frac{Q(\lambda_n)}{\lambda_n} = 0.$$

It is clear that

$$\lim_{n \to \infty}\left|\frac{P(\lambda_n)}{\lambda_n} - 1\right| = 0 \text{ and } \lim_{n \to \infty}\left|\frac{Q(\lambda_n)}{\lambda_n} - \theta e^{-\mu\tau}\right| = 0.$$

Then, there is a sequence $(\lambda'_n)_{n \in \mathbb{N}}$ of roots of the equation

$$e^{\lambda\tau} - \theta e^{-\mu\tau} = 0$$

such that

$$\lim_{n \to \infty}(\lambda_n - \lambda'_n) = 0.$$

This means that the closed-forms of the roots λ_n are the complex numbers

$$\bar{\lambda}_p = \frac{1}{\tau}\ln(\theta) - \mu + \frac{2p\pi}{\tau}i, \quad p \in \mathbb{Z}.$$

Since $\theta \in (0,1)$, we have that $\mathcal{R}e(\bar{\lambda}_p) < 0$. Thus, all roots such that $|\lambda_n| \to +\infty$ have a negative real part for n large enough. □

We state the stability of the disease-free equilibrium (9):

Corollary 1.

(i) *Suppose that there exists $\tau_0 \geq 0$ such that $\mathcal{R}_0(\tau_0) > 1$. Then, the disease-free equilibrium (9) is unstable for $\tau = \tau_0$.*

(ii) *Suppose that there exists $\tau_1 \geq 0$ such that $\mathcal{R}_0(\tau_1) < 1$ and the disease-free equilibrium (9) is locally asymptotically stable for $\tau = \tau_1$. Then, it is locally asymptotically stable for all $\tau \geq \tau_1$.*

(iii) *Suppose that $\mathcal{R}_0(0) < 1$. Then, the disease-free equilibrium (9) is locally asymptotically stable for all $\tau \geq 0$.*

Proof. (i) The real eigenvalue

$$\lambda_0 = \mu(\mathcal{R}_0(\tau_0) - 1)$$

is positive because $\mathcal{R}_0(\tau_0) > 1$. Then, the disease-free equilibrium (9) is unstable for $\tau = \tau_0$.
(ii) Suppose that there exits $\tau_1 \geq 0$ such that $\mathcal{R}_0(\tau_1) < 1$ and the disease-free equilibrium (9) is locally asymptotically stable for $\tau = \tau_1$. As $\tau \mapsto \mathcal{R}_0(\tau)$ is decreasing, we have $\mathcal{R}_0(\tau) < 1$

for all $\tau \geq \tau_1$. Then, the real eigenvalue λ_0 is negative for all $\tau \geq \tau_1$. The other eigenvalues given by

$$\bar{\Delta}(\tau,\lambda) := P(\tau,\lambda) - Q(\tau,\lambda)e^{-\lambda\tau} = 0,$$

with

$$P(\tau,\lambda) := \lambda + \mu + Kf'(\Phi^{-1}(\sigma/\mu)) \quad \text{and} \quad Q(\tau,\lambda) := e^{-\mu\tau}[\theta\lambda + \theta\mu + Kf'(\Phi^{-1}(\sigma/\mu))],$$

which cannot cross the imaginary axis when we increase τ starting from τ_1. The disease-free equilibrium (9), thus, keeps the same stability as for $\tau = \tau_1$, i.e., it remains locally asymptotically stable for all $\tau \leq \tau_1$.

(iii) Let us consider the case $\tau = 0$. Then, Equation (11) becomes

$$(\lambda + \mu)(1 - \theta) = 0.$$

This means that $\lambda = -\mu < 0$. Then, the disease-free equilibrium (9) is locally asymptotically stable for $\tau = 0$. We use the previous property, (ii), to conclude that the disease-free equilibrium (9) is locally asymptotically stable for all $\tau \geq 0$.

One can prove this corollary directly by proving that Equation (11) has no root with a nonnegative real part, and therefore, the stability of the endemic equilibrium is determined by the sign of $\mathcal{R}_0 - 1$. Indeed, let us suppose by contradiction the existence of such a root $\lambda = \alpha + i\omega$, with $\alpha \geq 0$. Then, we obtain

$$\frac{|P(\alpha + i\omega)|}{|Q(\alpha + i\omega)|} = e^{-\alpha\tau} \leq 1.$$

This gives the following inequality:

$$[P(\alpha) - Q(\alpha)][P(\alpha) + Q(\alpha)] + \left(1 - e^{-2\mu\tau}\theta^2\right)\omega^2 \leq 0,$$

with

$$P(\alpha) - Q(\alpha) = (1 - e^{-\mu\tau}\theta)(\alpha + \mu) + (1 - e^{-\mu\tau})Kf'(\Phi^{-1}(\sigma/\mu)) > 0.$$

This leads to a contradiction. □

Now, we focus on the endemic equilibrium (10):

$$(S^*, I^*, u^*) = \left(\frac{\mu}{\beta}, \frac{\sigma}{\mu} - \Phi\left(\frac{\mu}{\beta}\right), \frac{Kf(\mu/\beta)}{1 - \theta e^{-\mu\tau}}\right).$$

Proposition 3. *Suppose that $\mathcal{R}_0(0) > 1$. Then, for all $\tau \geq 0$ such that $\mathcal{R}_0(\tau) > 1$, the endemic steady-state is locally asymptotically stable.*

Proof. We suppose that $\mathcal{R}_0(\tau) > 1$, and we consider the endemic equilibrium. The characteristic equation becomes

$$\Delta(\tau,\lambda) := \lambda^2 + A\lambda + \mu\beta I^* - e^{-\mu\tau}e^{-\lambda\tau}\left[\theta\lambda^2 + (\theta A + Kf'(S^*))\lambda + \theta\mu\beta I^*\right] = 0, \quad (13)$$

with $A := \mu + \beta I^* > 0$. We follow the same steps as in the proof of the stability of the disease-free equilibrium. First, we consider the case $\tau = 0$. Then, the endemic steady-state becomes

$$(S^*, I^*, u^*) = \left(\frac{\mu}{\beta}, \frac{\sigma}{\mu} - \frac{\mu}{\beta}, \frac{Kf(\mu/\beta)}{1 - \theta}\right),$$

with $\mathcal{R}_0(0) = \beta\sigma/\mu^2$, and the characteristic equation is reduced to

$$\Delta(\lambda,\tau) := (1 - \theta)\begin{vmatrix} \lambda + \beta I^* + \mu & \beta S^* \\ -\beta I^* & \lambda - \beta S^* + \mu \end{vmatrix} = 0.$$

We obtain two eigenvalues $\lambda_1 = -\mu < 0$ and $\lambda_2 = -\mu - \beta(I^* - S^*) = -\mu(\mathcal{R}_0(0) - 1) < 0$. Hence, the endemic steady-state is locally asymptotically stable for $\tau = 0$. We then look for pure imaginary roots $\lambda = \pm i\omega$, $\omega > 0$. Then, splitting the real and imaginary parts in (13), we have the following system:

$$\begin{cases} \omega\Gamma\cos(\omega\tau)e^{-\mu\tau} + \rho_\omega\sin(\omega\tau)e^{-\mu\tau} & = & \omega(A + \psi f'(\mu/\beta)), \\ \rho_\omega\cos(\omega\tau)e^{-\mu\tau} - \omega\Gamma\sin(\omega\tau)e^{-\mu\tau} & = & \omega^2 - \mu\beta I^*, \end{cases}$$

with $\rho_\omega := (\omega^2 - \mu\beta I^*)\theta e^{-\mu\tau}$ and $\Gamma = (\theta A + \psi f'(\mu/\beta))e^{-\mu\tau}$. Using the identity $\cos^2(\omega\tau) + \sin^2(\omega\tau) = 1$, we obtain the polynomial equation in ω:

$$\begin{aligned} [1 - (\theta e^{-\mu\tau})^2]\omega^4 + [2\mu\beta I^*(\theta e^{-\mu\tau})^2 - 2\mu\beta I^* + (A + \psi f'(\mu/\beta))^2 - \Gamma^2]\omega^2 & \\ + (\mu\beta I^*)^2(1 - (\theta e^{-\mu\tau})^2) & = 0. \end{aligned}$$

Let us set

$$N := \frac{1}{1 - (\theta e^{-\mu\tau})^2}[2\mu\beta I^*(\theta e^{-\mu\tau})^2 - 2\mu\beta I^* + (A + \psi f'(\mu/\beta))^2 - \Gamma^2] \quad \text{and} \quad X := \omega^2.$$

Then, we obtain the following polynomial:

$$X^2 + NX + (\mu\beta I^*)^2 = 0. \tag{14}$$

First, if $N > 0$, then the Routh–Hurwitz criterion implies that all roots of (14) have a negative real part. This leads to a contradiction.

Suppose now that $N \leq 0$. We compute the discriminant of Equation (14) to obtain

$$\Delta = N^2 - 4(\mu\beta I^*)^2 = (N + 2\mu\beta I^*)(N - 2\mu\beta I^*).$$

As we supposed that $N \leq 0$, we have that $N - \mu\beta I^* < 0$. On the other hand, we have that

$$(1 - (\theta e^{-\mu\tau})^2)(N + 2\mu\beta I^*) = (A + Kf'(\mu/\beta))^2 - \Gamma^2.$$

But, as $\theta < 1$ and $e^{-\mu\tau} < 1$, we obtain

$$\Gamma^2 = [(\theta A + Kf'(\mu/\beta))e^{-\mu\tau}]^2 < (A + Kf'(\mu/\beta))^2.$$

We conclude that $\Delta < 0$. Therefore, there is no positive real root of (14) and $\omega > 0$ cannot exist. Furthermore, as for the disease-free equilibrium, if Δ has infinitely many different zeros, $\lambda_n \in \mathbb{C}$, $n \in \mathbb{N}$, then

$$\lim_{n\to+\infty} |\lambda_n| = +\infty.$$

The sequence λ_n, $n \in \mathbb{N}$, satisfies

$$e^{\lambda_n\tau}\left(\frac{P(\lambda_n)}{\lambda_n^2}\right) - \frac{Q(\lambda_n)}{\lambda_n^2} = 0,$$

with

$$P(\lambda) := \lambda^2 + A\lambda + \mu\beta I^* \quad \text{and} \quad Q(\lambda) := e^{-\mu\tau}\left[\theta\lambda^2 + (\theta A + Kf'(S^*))\lambda + \theta\mu\beta I^*\right].$$

We have

$$\lim_{n\to\infty}\left|\frac{P(\lambda_n)}{\lambda_n^2} - 1\right| = 0 \quad \text{and} \quad \lim_{n\to\infty}\left|\frac{Q(\lambda_n)}{\lambda_n^2} - \theta e^{-\mu\tau}\right| = 0.$$

Then, as for the case of the disease-free steady-state, the closed forms of the roots λ_n are

$$\bar{\lambda}_p = \frac{1}{\tau}\ln(\theta) - \mu + \frac{2p\pi}{\tau}i, \quad p \in \mathbb{Z}.$$

Thus, all roots such that $|\lambda_n| \to +\infty$ have a negative real part for n large enough. We conclude that all roots of (13) have a negative real part, and then, the endemic equilibrium is locally asymptotically stable. □

Remark 1. *As for the proof of Corollary 1, we can also prove directly by contradiction that there is no root $\lambda = \alpha + i\omega$ of (13) with $\alpha \geq 0$.*

4. Global Stability Analysis

We consider in this section the case:

$$f(S) = S.$$

The model becomes

$$\begin{cases} S'(t) &= \sigma - \beta I(t)S(t) - \mu S(t) - KS(t) + (1-\theta)e^{-\mu\tau}u(t-\tau), \\ I'(t) &= \beta I(t)S(t) - \mu I(t), \\ u(t) &= KS(t) + \theta e^{-\mu\tau}u(t-\tau), \end{cases} \tag{15}$$

with the initial condition:

$$S(0) = S_0, \quad I(0) = I_0 \quad \text{and} \quad u(t) = \varphi(t), \; t \in [-\tau, 0].$$

The function Φ given by (8) becomes

$$\Phi(S^*) = \left[1 + \frac{K(1-e^{-\mu\tau})}{\mu(1-\theta e^{-\mu\tau})}\right]S^*.$$

The corresponding disease-free equilibrium is

$$(S^0, I^0, u^0) := \left(\frac{\sigma(1-\theta e^{-\mu\tau})}{\mu + K - (\mu\theta + K)e^{-\mu\tau}}, 0, \frac{K\sigma}{\mu + K - (\mu\theta + K)e^{-\mu\tau}}\right), \tag{16}$$

and the endemic steady-state is

$$(S^*, I^*, u^*) = \left(\frac{\mu}{\beta}, \frac{\sigma}{\mu} - \Phi\left(\frac{\mu}{\beta}\right), \frac{K\mu}{\beta(1-\theta e^{-\mu\tau})}\right). \tag{17}$$

The basic reproduction number becomes

$$\mathcal{R}_0 := \frac{\beta}{\mu}\Phi^{-1}\left(\frac{\sigma}{\mu}\right) = \frac{\beta}{\mu}S^0 = \frac{\beta\sigma(1-\theta e^{-\mu\tau})}{\mu^2(1-\theta e^{-\mu\tau}) + \mu K(1-e^{-\mu\tau})}. \tag{18}$$

A model similar to (15) was studied in [11] as a generalization of a Kermack–McKendrick SIR model with an age-structured protection phase. We established the global asymptotic stability of the two steady-states. We showed that if $\mathcal{R}_0 < 1$, then the disease-free steady-state is globally asymptotically stable, and if $\mathcal{R}_0 > 1$, then the endemic steady-state is globally asymptotically stable. We constructed quadratic and logarithmic Lyapunov functions to establish this global stability. In the following subsections, we also present results on the global asymptotic stability of the two steady-states. We used similar techniques as those used for the proofs of the global stability results in [11].

4.1. Global Asymptotic Stability of the Disease-Free Steady-State

In this subsection, we assumed that $\mathcal{R}_0 < 1$, and we show that the disease-free equilibrium (S^0, I^0, u^0) is globally asymptotically stable. The proof is based on the use of the following auxiliary differential–difference system, for $t > 0$:

$$\begin{cases} \dfrac{dS^+}{dt}(t) & = & \sigma - (\mu + K)S^+(t) + (1-\theta)e^{-\mu\tau}u^+(t-\tau), \\ u^+(t) & = & KS^+(t) + \theta e^{-\mu\tau}u^+(t-\tau), \end{cases} \tag{19}$$

with the same initial condition as the main system:

$$S^+(0) = S_0 \quad \text{and} \quad u^+(t) = \varphi(t), \;\; t \in [-\tau, 0].$$

By using a comparison principle, we obtain that $S(t) \le S^+(t)$ and $u(t) \le u^+(t)$ for all $t > 0$. Furthermore, the system (19) has a unique equilibrium that corresponds to the disease-free equilibrium of the system (15). The basic reproduction number associated with (19) is also given by (18). The global asymptotic stability of the auxiliary system (19) was established in [11]. Indeed, by setting

$$\hat{S}(t) := S^+(t) - S^0, \quad \hat{u}(t) := u^+(t) - u^0$$

and considering the Lyapunov function $V : \mathbb{R} \times C([-\tau, 0], \mathbb{R}) \longrightarrow \mathbb{R}^+$,

$$V(S_0, \varphi) = \frac{S_0^2}{2} + \xi \int_{-\tau}^{0} \varphi^2(s)ds, \quad \text{with } \xi = \frac{1}{2K^2}\left[\mu(1 - \theta^2 e^{-2\mu\tau}) + K\right] > 0,$$

we proved in [11] the following lemma.

Lemma 2. *Suppose that $\mathcal{R}_0 < 1$. Then, the unique steady-state (S^0, u^0) of the system (19) is globally asymptotically stable.*

Thanks to a comparison principle and the global attractivity of the set:

$$\begin{aligned} \Omega_\varepsilon \;:=\; & \{(S, I, u) \in \mathbb{R}^+ \times \mathbb{R}^+ \times C([-\tau, 0], \mathbb{R}^+) : \\ & \quad 0 \le S \le S^0 + \varepsilon,\; 0 \le u(s) \le u^0 + \varepsilon,\; s \in [-\tau, 0]\}, \end{aligned}$$

for $\varepsilon > 0$ small enough, we are able to obtain the global asymptotic stability of the disease-free equilibrium of (15). More precisely, the proof of the global asymptotic stability of the disease-free steady-state (16) is based on the following lemma.

Lemma 3. *Suppose that $\mathcal{R}_0 < 1$. Then, for any sufficiently small $\varepsilon > 0$, the subset Ω_ε of $\mathbb{R}^+ \times \mathbb{R}^+ \times C([-\tau, 0], \mathbb{R}^+)$ is a global attractor for the system (15).*

Proof. The solutions of (15) satisfy, for all $t > 0$, the system:

$$\begin{cases} S'(t) & \le & \sigma - (\mu + K)S(t) + (1-\theta)e^{-\mu\tau}u(t-\tau), \\ u(t) & = & KS(t) + \theta e^{-\mu\tau}u(t-\tau). \end{cases}$$

By the comparison principle and the positivity of the solutions, we have $0 \le S(t) \le S^+(t)$ and $0 \le u(t) \le u^+(t)$, for all $t > 0$, where (S^+, u^+) is the solution of the system (19). Lemma 2 implies that $(S^+(t), u^+(t)) \to (S^0, u^0)$ as $t \to +\infty$. This convergence means that the subset Ω_ε, with $\varepsilon > 0$ small enough, is a global attractor for the system (15). □

Lemma 3 allows us to restrict the analysis of the global stability of the disease-free steady-state (16) of (15) to the subset Ω_ε with $\varepsilon > 0$ small enough.

Theorem 1. *Suppose that $\mathcal{R}_0 < 1$. Then, the disease-free steady-state $(S^0, 0, u^0)$ given by (16) of the model (15) is globally asymptotically stable.*

Proof. We consider the solutions of System (15) in the subset Ω_ε, with $\varepsilon > 0$ small enough. It is clear that the second equation of (15) implies that

$$I'(t) \leq \beta(S^0 + \varepsilon)I(t) - \mu I(t) = -\mu\left(1 - \frac{\beta(S^0 + \varepsilon)}{\mu}\right)I(t).$$

Since $\mathcal{R}_0 = \frac{\beta}{\mu}S^0 < 1$, we can choose $\varepsilon > 0$ such that $\frac{\beta(S^0 + \varepsilon)}{\mu} < 1$. This implies that $\lim_{t\to+\infty} I(t) = 0$. Then, there exists $T_\varepsilon > 0$ such that $0 \leq I(t) \leq \varepsilon$, for all $t > T_\varepsilon$. We then have, for $t > T_\varepsilon$,

$$\begin{cases} S'(t) & \geq & \sigma - (\mu + K)S(t) - \varepsilon\beta S(t) + (1-\theta)e^{-\mu\tau}u(t-\tau), \\ u(t) & = & KS(t) + \theta e^{-\mu\tau}u(t-\tau). \end{cases}$$

We again use the comparison principle to obtain $S(t) \geq S_\varepsilon(t)$ and $u(t) \geq u_\varepsilon(t)$, for all $t > T_\varepsilon$, where $(S_\varepsilon, u_\varepsilon)$ is the solution of the problem, for $t > 0$,

$$\begin{cases} S_\varepsilon'(t) & = & \sigma - (\mu + K)S_\varepsilon(t) - \varepsilon\beta S_\varepsilon(t) + (1-\theta)e^{-\mu\tau}u_\varepsilon(t-\tau), \\ u_\varepsilon(t) & = & KS_\varepsilon(t) + \theta e^{-\mu\tau}u_\varepsilon(t-\tau), \\ S_\varepsilon(0) & = & S_0, \quad u_\varepsilon(s) \ = \ \varphi(s), \quad \text{for } -\tau \leq s \leq 0. \end{cases} \tag{20}$$

We use the same techniques as for the proof of the lemmas 2 and 3 to show that $(S_\varepsilon(t), u_\varepsilon(t)) \to (S_\varepsilon^0, u_\varepsilon^0)$ as $t \to +\infty$, with $(S_\varepsilon^0, u_\varepsilon^0)$ the steady-state of System (20). In fact, $(S_\varepsilon^0, u_\varepsilon^0)$ is given by the expression:

$$(S_\varepsilon^0, u_\varepsilon^0) := \left(\frac{\sigma(1 - \theta e^{-\mu\tau})}{\mu_\varepsilon + K - (\mu_\varepsilon\theta + K)e^{-\mu\tau}}, \frac{K\sigma}{\mu_\varepsilon + K - (\mu_\varepsilon\theta + K)e^{-\mu\tau}}\right),$$

with $\mu_\varepsilon := \mu + \varepsilon\beta$. Then, there exists $\tilde{T}_\varepsilon > T_\varepsilon > 0$ such that, for $t > \tilde{T}_\varepsilon$,

$$S_\varepsilon^0 - \varepsilon \leq S(t) \leq S^0 + \varepsilon \quad \text{and} \quad u_\varepsilon^0 - \varepsilon \leq u(t) \leq u^0 + \varepsilon.$$

As $\varepsilon \to 0$, we have $S_\varepsilon^0 \to S^0$ and $u_\varepsilon^0 \to u^0$. Then, we obtain

$$\lim_{t\to+\infty} S(t) = S^0 \quad \text{and} \quad \lim_{t\to+\infty} u(t) = u^0.$$

Recall that $(S^0, 0, u^0)$ is locally asymptotically stable. Then, it is globally asymptotically stable. □

4.2. Global Asymptotic Stability of the Endemic Equilibrium

In this subsection, we assumed that

$$\mathcal{R}_0 > 1,$$

where $\mathcal{R}_0$ is given by (18), and we studied the global asymptotic stability of the endemic steady-state (17). Let us define

$$\tilde{S}(t) := S(t) - S^* \quad \text{and} \quad \tilde{u}(t) := u(t) - u^*.$$

Then, the system (15) becomes, with $\beta S^* = \mu$,

$$\begin{cases} \tilde{S}'(t) & = & -(\mu + K)\tilde{S}(t) - \beta\tilde{S}(t)I(t) - \beta S^* I(t) + \beta S^* I^* + (1-\theta)e^{-\mu\tau}\tilde{u}(t-\tau), \\ I'(t) & = & \beta\tilde{S}(t)I(t), \\ \tilde{u}(t) & = & K\tilde{S}(t) + \theta e^{-\mu\tau}\tilde{u}(t-\tau). \end{cases} \tag{21}$$

The endemic steady-state (17) of the system (15) becomes $(0, I^*, 0)$ (as a steady-state of the system (21)). We then obtain the following result.

Theorem 2. *Let us suppose that $\mathcal{R}_0 > 1$. Then, the endemic steady-state (S^*, I^*, u^*) given by (17) of the model (15) is globally asymptotically stable.*

Proof. The proof of this theorem is based on the use of the following Lyapunov function $V : \mathbb{R} \times \mathbb{R}^+ \times \mathcal{C}([-\tau, 0], \mathbb{R}) \to \mathbb{R}^+$ defined by

$$V(S_0, I_0, \varphi) = \frac{S_0^2}{2} + \xi \int_{-\tau}^{0} \varphi^2(s)ds + S^*\left[I_0 - I^* - I^* \ln\left(\frac{I_0}{I^*}\right)\right],$$

with $\xi = \frac{1}{2K^2}\left[K + \mu(1 - (\theta^2 e^{-2\mu\tau})\right]$.
First, we note that the function $G : (0 + \infty) \to [0 + \infty)$ defined by

$$G(I_0) = I_0 - I^* - I^* \ln\left(\frac{I_0}{I^*}\right), \quad I_0 > 0,$$

satisfies $G(I_0) \geq 0$ for all $I_0 > 0$ and $G(I_0) = 0$ if and only if $I_0 = I^*$. Then, we have $V(S_0, I_0, u_0) = 0$ if and only if $(S_0, I_0, u_0) = (0, I^*, 0)$. We set

$$\tilde{V}(t) := V(\tilde{S}(t), I(t), \tilde{u}_t), \quad t \geq 0,$$

where $(\tilde{S}(t), I(t), \tilde{u}_t)$ is the solution of (21). Then, we obtain

$$\begin{aligned} \tilde{V}'(t) &= -a\tilde{S}^2(t) + b\tilde{S}(t)\tilde{u}(t-\tau) - c\tilde{u}^2(t-\tau) - \beta I(t)\tilde{S}^2(t), \\ &\leq \frac{b^2 - 4ac}{4c}\tilde{S}^2(t), \\ &= -\kappa\tilde{S}^2(t), \end{aligned} \tag{22}$$

with

$$\begin{cases} a &= \mu + K - \xi K^2, \\ b &= (1-\theta)e^{-\mu\tau} + 2\xi K\theta e^{-\mu\tau} > 0, \\ c &= \xi(1 - \theta e^{-\mu\tau})(1 + \theta e^{-\mu\tau}) > 0, \\ \kappa &= (4ac - b^2)/4c > 0. \end{cases}$$

We conclude that the function $t \mapsto V(\tilde{S}(t), I(t), \tilde{u}_t)$ is nonincreasing. Then, we obtain

$$\lim_{t \to +\infty} V(\tilde{S}(t), I(t), \tilde{u}_t) = \inf_{s \geq 0} V(\tilde{S}(s), I(s), \tilde{u}_s) =: V^* \geq 0.$$

By integrating (22) from 0 to $t > 0$, we obtain

$$\kappa \int_0^t \tilde{S}^2(s)ds \leq V(\tilde{S}(0), I(0), \tilde{u}_0) - V(\tilde{S}(t), I(t), \tilde{u}_t).$$

It is clear that the limits on both sides exist when $t \to +\infty$, and we have

$$\lim_{t \to +\infty} \int_0^t \tilde{S}^2(s)ds \leq \frac{1}{\kappa}\left[V(\tilde{S}(0), I(0), \tilde{u}_0) - V^*\right]. \tag{23}$$

Furthermore, the first equation of System (21) implies that $t \mapsto \tilde{S}'(t)$ is uniformly bounded. Then, the function $t \mapsto \tilde{S}(t)$ is uniformly continuous. We conclude from (23) that $\lim_{t \to +\infty} \tilde{S}(t) = 0$, and the fluctuations lemma implies that there exists a sequence $(t_k)_{k \in \mathbb{N}}$, $t_k \to +\infty$ such that $\lim_{k \to +\infty} \tilde{S}'(t_k) = 0$. On the other hand, using the difference equation satisfied by $\tilde{u}$, we also have $\lim_{t\to+\infty} \tilde{u}(t) = 0$. Then, the first equation of System (21) implies that $\lim_{k\to+\infty} I(t_k) = I^*$. We also have from the expression of V that

$$\lim_{t\to+\infty} G(I(t)) = \frac{V^*}{S^*}.$$

Furthermore, the continuity of the function G implies that $\lim_{k\to+\infty} G(I(t_k)) = G(I^*) = 0$. Then, $V^* = 0$. This means that $\lim_{t\to+\infty} G(I(t)) = 0$. The properties of the function G imply that $\lim_{t\to+\infty} I(t) = I^*$. We conclude that the endemic steady-state (S^*, I^*, u^*) is globally asymptotically stable. □

We assumed, for the first time, that the rate of the start of PrEP treatment was constant and that $f(S) = S$. Thus, the model admits two equilibrium points, the disease-free equilibrium and the endemic equilibrium. By considering $\mathcal{R}_0$ as a function of the delay, we showed that, if $\mathcal{R}_0 < 1$, the disease-free equilibrium is globally asymptotically stable and that, if $\mathcal{R}_0 > 1$, then it is the endemic equilibrium that becomes globally asymptotically stable.

5. Applications to French Clinical Data

In order to apply our model to real data, we chose the French MSM population, and later, we focused more specifically on the high-risk individuals within this group. We define here the high-risk MSM population as multi-partner gay men, as well as sexual intercourse while using drugs, usually called chemsex, or new generations not inclined to use any protection anymore (mainly condoms). Of course, this reduces our study to a small part of the population, but, because of their having the highest rate of infectivity, they belong to the target of PrEP treatments at the infectious disease center in France.

Furthermore , for a more realistic approach, ψ was considered time-dependent, and ψ is defined by the logistic equation for a more accurate data fit (details and parameters in the first subsection below). The PrEP users were collected between January 2016 (starting year of PrEP in France) and June 2019 (before the SARS-CoV-2 outbreak) (see [2]).

Section 5 is structured into three subsection: First, we introduce the data and the methods to approximate the parameters. Then, we propose a set of simulations adapted to the general French MSM population. The last subsection is focused on the so-called high-risk individuals as described previously.

It is important at this stage to remind that HIV is not curable and that PrEP does not have a direct influence on the decreasing number of the infected compartment over time, which is mainly due to natural death (with a life expectancy for treated persons as high as non-infected ones) or, more rarely now, thus neglected here for the French group, untreated AIDS individuals. However, PrEP policy in the population may have an important impact on the infectivity rate. Since PrEP's efficiency can be measured in a long-term range and using incidence, we simulated over 15 years (that is, 180 months) for a forecast of this prevention strategy over time.

5.1. Choice of the Parameters

In Table 1, we give the parameters used in Model (1), as well as their meaning and values for the general and high-risk MSM community in France estimated from [2], assuming that 60% of the the population considered in the dataset of the study are MSM.

PrEP treatment in France started in 2016, and since the SARS-CoV-2 epidemic drastically modified sexual habits (through successive lockdowns), we considered the population data until 2019 only. Then, after, we simulated our model based on the estimated parameter values for the following 15 years. Note here that we did not take the SARS-CoV-2 nor the monkey pox epidemic into account for three reasons: first, because these periods are a bias for our model and need to be carefully adjusted with updated parameter values; second, to the best of our knowledge, the official French data related to these past two years have not been released yet; finally, we preferred keeping our model as simple as possible for this present work. A more complex approach will be the object of a future work.

Table 1. Parameters used in Model (1) with values applied to the French population estimated from [2].

Symbols	Signification	Value for General MSM	Value for High-Risk MSM	Unity
θ	Probability to keep the PrEP treatment	0.83	0.83	
σ	Recruitment	3000	562	indiv.months^{-1}
μ	Removal rate from the compartments	0.000758333	0.0076	indiv.months^{-1}
β	HIV transmission rate per infected individual	1.821×10^{-10}	2.85×10^{-7}	(indiv.months)$^{-1}$
τ	Duration of the period of PrEP taking	3	3	months

In [2], information between 2016 and 2019 was collected every 6 months. We remind here that, at the end of a 3-month period, the patient decides whether to give up the treatment or to continue. This is the reason why our simulations below were computed on a monthly basis.

Initial conditions for functions $t \mapsto S(t)$, $t \mapsto I(t)$ and $t \mapsto u(t)$ were chosen to be January, the 1st of 2016, according to [2].

Because of the delay equation for u, the function $u_{\text{init}} : [-3, 0] \to \mathbb{R}^+$, $t \mapsto u_{\text{init}}(t)$ was adjusted with a cubic spline interpolation of 60% of each total number of the last column in Table 2. Note that u_{init} is the same for both populations' (general MSM and its high-risk subset) simulations because we assumed here that most of the French PrEP users belong to the high-risk MSM group.

Regarding the susceptible: based on an AVAC study (https://www.avac.org/sites/default/files/u3/MSM_in_Europe_Euro_Rave.pdf, page 5) (accessed on 13 September 2022), 4–10% of French males declare belonging to the MSM group. Assuming that France has about 65,000,000 inhabitants, it seems then reasonable to assume that $S(0) = 2{,}600{,}000$.

Furthermore, on the official website of UNAIDS (https://www.unaids.org/en/regionscountries/countries/france) (accessed on 13 September 2022), we obtained that 170,000 individuals were infected with HIV in France in 2016. We assumed that a majority belong to the MSM group, but not the entire number (indeed, a large portion of new cases was reported to be foreign heterosexuals, among other subcases). This is why we took $I(0) = 90{,}000$. It is important to remind here that this value may not be the exact one, since the number of HIV infections detected is always below the real number of HIV infections (HIV testing is not compulsory, and thus, several individuals may carry the virus for years without knowing it).

Table 2. Summary of initial conditions for susceptibles and infected among general MSM and MSM high-risk populations.

Initial Conditions	Value for MSM	Value for High-Risk MSM
$S(0)$	2,600,000	40,000
$I(0)$	90,000	9000

Finally, when simulating the MSM high-risk population, the estimated susceptible number would be between 3000 and 50,000 depending on the literature. Thus, we took $S(0) = 40{,}000$ according to [2]. According to French data (https://vih.org/20190328/stabilite-des-chiffres-du-vih-en-france/) (accessed on 13 September 2022), French infections have been stable since 2010. On average, there are 6500 contaminations per year, and infections within the MSM population represent 43%. Then, we chose $I(0) = 9000$.

According to the official French data (https://www.insee.fr/fr/statistiques/2383440) (accessed on 13 September 2022), $\mu = 0.000758333$ individuals.months^{-1} at the country scale. We chose this value for the French MSM removal rate (death, as well as removed from sexual life). For the high-risk MSM, μ is considered much larger because a high-risk sexual life style does not last longer than the average MSM one. Thus, $\mu = 0.0076$ individuals.months^{-1} in this subgroup.

The 2016–2019 semester official French datasets are given in Table 3.

Table 3. Total number of PrEP users in France since 2016, given by semester (see Table 3 in [2]).

Semester	Initiation of PrEP	Renewal of the Treatment	Total PrEP Users
S1—2016	1166	###	1166
S2—2016	1826	911	2737
S1—2017	2193	2273	4466
S2—2017	2564	3807	6371
S1—2018	3138	5413	8551
S2—2018	4488	7647	12,135
S1—2019	5103	10,398	15,501

Thanks to Tables 2 and 3, we are able to assess the values of functions θ and ψ for the years 2016–2019. Indeed, for each semester, we obtained a different θ by using the following formula coming from its definition:

$$\theta(\text{semester}) = \frac{\text{Number of renewal treatment of the current semester}}{\text{Total of PrEP users of the previous semester}}.$$

We assumed that this value is the same for every month of the semester. Then, we chose ψ, per month, as follows:

$$\psi(\text{months}) = \frac{\text{Number of individuals who begin the treatment}}{S(0) * 6},$$

where $S(0)$ is the initial condition for the susceptible compartment S.

These values are given in Table 4.

Table 4. Values of parameters ψ and θ per month according to each semester, computed according to Tables 2 and 3.

Semester	Values of ψ for General MSM	Values of $\psi$for High-Risk MSMS	Values of θ
S1—2016	0.0000747	0.0048583	###
S2—2016	0.000117	0.007608	0.7813
S1—2017	0.00014	0.00913	0.8305
S2—2017	0.000164	0.0106	0.8159
S1—2018	0.000201	0.0130	0.8496
S2—2018	0.00029	0.0187	0.8943
S1—2019	0.00033	0.0216	0.8569

We selected $\theta = 0.83$ as the average value of all the previous θ from Table 4.

As mentioned in Section 2, we assumed that ψ is the solution of a logistic equation given by:

$$\frac{d\psi}{dt} = r\psi\left(1 - \frac{\psi}{K}\right),$$

where K is the carrying capacity and r exponential growth. We remind that the explicit form of ψ is then written by the following expression:

$$\psi(t) = \frac{K}{1 + \left(\frac{K}{\psi_0} - 1\right)\exp(-rt)},$$

where ψ_0 is the initial condition depending on the population type. Using the data for ψ given in Table 4, we summarize our results in Table 5.

Table 5. Values of parameters K and r depending on the population.

Parameters	Values for General MSM	Values for High-Risk MSM
K	0.0007	0.072
r	0.0000222	0.000026

We assumed a Hill function for the dynamics of the function f:

$$f(S) = S_{sat}\frac{S^n}{\gamma^n + S^n},$$

with S_{sat} the saturation of the Hill function, γ the abscissa of the inflection point, and n the intensity of the slope. We summarize the values of these parameters in Table 6.

Table 6. Values of parameters S_{sat}, γ, and n depending on the general French MSM and the high-risk French MSM.

Parameters	Values for MSM	Values for High-Risk MSM
S_{sat}	5×10^6	230,000
γ	120	50
n	2	1.56

One of our goals was to estimate the HIV epidemic $\mathcal{R}_0$ for French MSM. We used the package in the R® language untitled R0 (https://www.rdocumentation.org/packages/R0/versions/1.2-6) (accessed on 13 September 2022) and, precisely, the function *est.R0.SB*, which estimates $\mathcal{R}_0$ using a Bayesian approach following the idea developed in [13]. Thanks to our data of new HIV infections ([14,15]), we obtained $\mathcal{R}_0 = 0.93$ for the normal MSM French population.

The two remaining parameters, β and σ, were estimated to keep $\mathcal{R}_0$ equal to 0.93. We decided to choose $\sigma = 3000$; in other words, each month, 3000 individuals might join the susceptible compartment (by reaching the sexual consent age or deciding to join the MSM group). Thus, $\beta = 1.821 \times 10^{-10}$(individuals.months)$^{-1}$ was estimated for the French general MSM group.

On the other hand, according to the official French data (https://solidarites-sante.gouv.fr/IMG/pdf/argumentaire_depistage_vih_HAS_2009-2.pdf) (accessed on 13 September 2022), the basic reproduction number related to the high-risk MSM ranges between 1.27 to 1.44. We took $\mathcal{R}_0 = 1.31$ and estimated $\beta = 2.85 \times 10^{-7}$(individuals.months)$^{-1}$, with $\mu = 0.0076$ months^{-1} and $\sigma = 562$ given by Table 1.

5.2. Numerical Simulations for the General French MSM

In Figure 2, protected (P) in green (graph on the right) keeps track of the exact data (crosses) for the first semesters, then reaches a threshold due to the French policy of regulating PrEP users. Indeed, the treatment is fully taken care of by the health insurance in France. Thus, a threshold needs to be set up (estimated at 60,000 MSM individuals here). With this threshold, it seems already that, within 15 years, the number of infected drops and keeps on decreasing. The number of susceptibles (blue curve on the left of the graph) keeps on growing with a lower slope between 50 and 100 months due to the increase of the protected and then the threshold. However, even with the increase of the susceptibles, the infected remain low. The protected compartment plays the role of a reservoir to prevent the HIV epidemic from growing back.

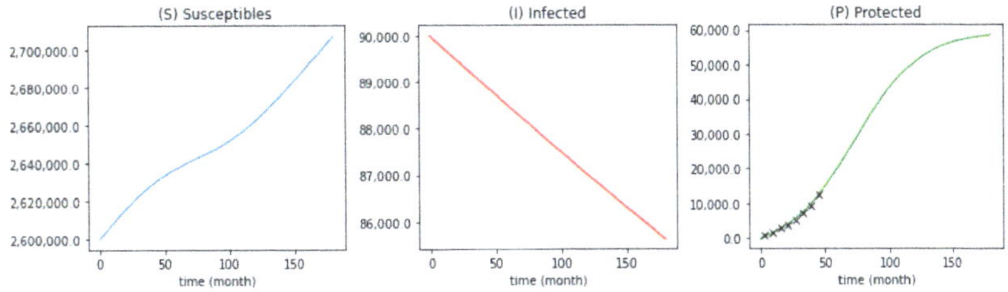

Figure 2. Plot of the evolution of the French MSM population (4) along the time (over 15 years). The crosses in the last plot represent the real values of PrEP users taken from Table 3. Function ψ verifies the logistic equation, and f is a Hill function.

Just as a comparison point, we simulated our model with a function f defined as identity (and not a Hill function anymore) (see Figure 3). We easily observed that the graph of the protected population does not fit the data in the first months with the same realistic parameter sets. Then, it seems that f needs to be more complex than identity for the case of French MSM, and the Hill function seems to be validated here.

In Figure 4, we plot the incidence with or without PrEP treatment. It seems obvious that without the PrEP reservoir (in blue), the incidence keeps on growing with no chance for the HIV epidemic to be controlled. On the other hand, with the PrEP compartment (in red), it is possible to keep the incidence at a low level (and even to decrease it significantly for the first years). The slight increase at the end (after Month 125) is due to the threshold of the number of PrEP users imposed in our model and likely used by the French health insurance policy.

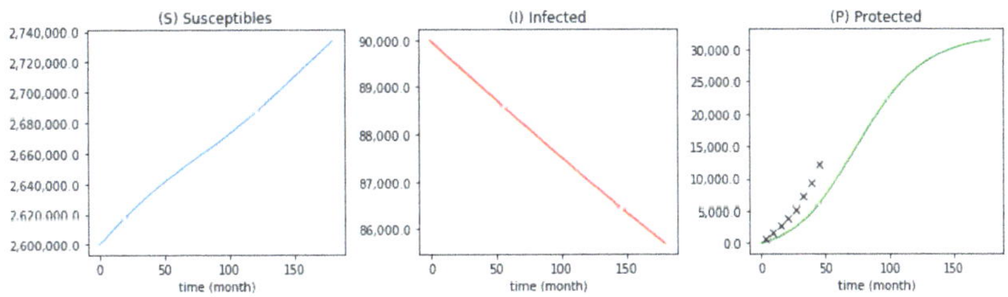

Figure 3. Plot of the evolution of the different compartments of the model (4) along time (over 15 years). The crosses in the last plot represent the real values of PrEP users taken from Table 3. ψ verifies the logistic equation, and f is identity.

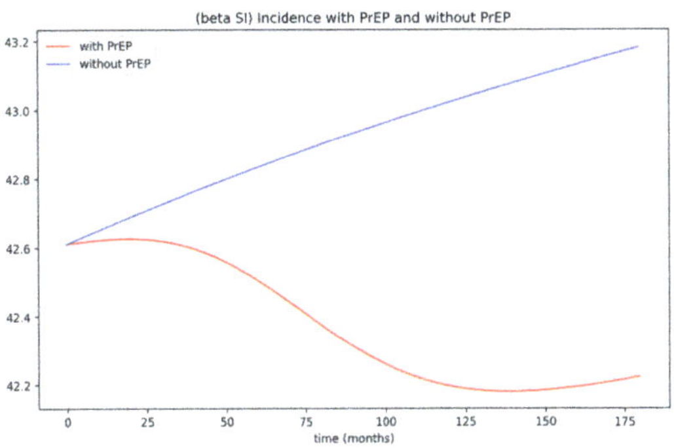

Figure 4. Plot of the evolution of the incidence with PrEP (in red) and without (in blue) from the system (4) over 15 years among the general French MSM.

In Figure 5, we depict the effect of the variation of $\mathcal{R}_0$ as a function of ψ. It appears clearly here that, as ψ increases (that is, the number of PrEP users rises), $\mathcal{R}_0$ declines drastically. This is, however, not linear, and a plateau may be reached after a certain threshold (above 0.2), which indicates that the flow of new PrEP users does not need to expand drastically. Indeed, even at ψ larger than 0.125, we obtain $\mathcal{R}_0$ already below 0.3, which is quite satisfactory. Augmenting ψ would decrease $\mathcal{R}_0$, but not as fast as the first values of ψ.

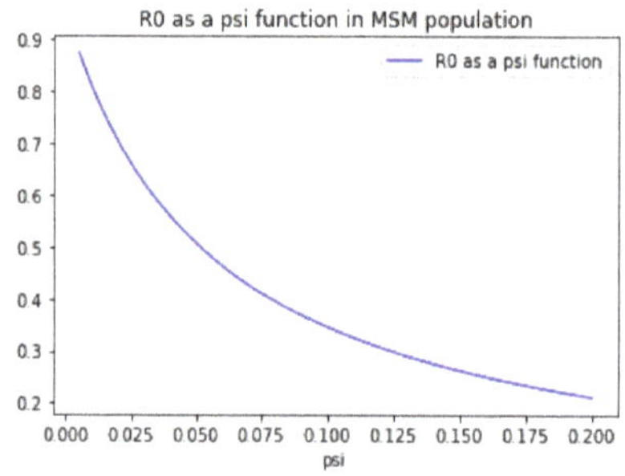

Figure 5. Plot of the $\mathcal{R}_0$ as a function of ψ.

5.3. Numerical Simulations for High-Risk Population

In this subsection, we focus our attention to the French MSM high-risk population. We remind that this MSM subgroup consists of individuals with multi-partner intercourse, sex relationships while using drugs (chemsex), etc. The HIV risk of infection is thus much higher than the rest of the MSM population. This is one of the reasons why this subgroup is the PrEP treatment target for the French health insurance. The protected compartment in this particular case plays a major role as a reservoir. This was clearly confirmed in our model simulations, as shown in Figure 6, where the number of susceptibles clearly drops as the number of protected individuals increases. Note that the infected population rises, but for the first time, reaches a threshold. This means that barely any new infected cases appear. We remind here that the model is an SI and not an SIR, that is no recovered individuals can appear since HIV is a disease with a lifetime treatment.

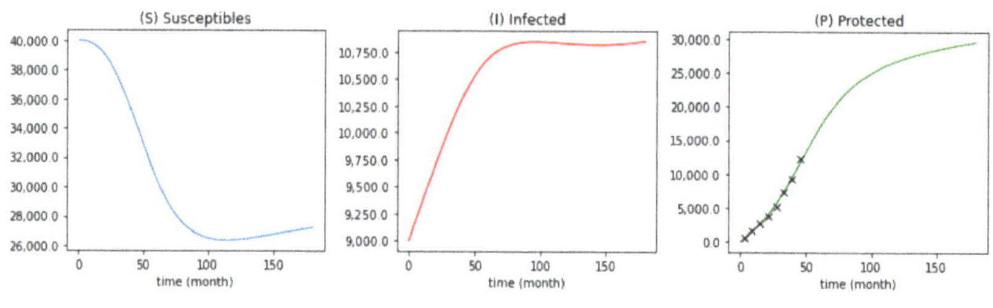

Figure 6. Plot of the evolution of the different compartments of the high-risk french population along time (over 15 years). The crosses in the last plot represent the real values of the number of PrEP users obtained from Table 4. ψ verifies the logistic equation, and f is a Hill function.

In Figure 7, the incidence evolution is plotted with or without PrEP treatment. The reservoir effect is even more explicit there in the sense that, with PrEP, the incidence declines to reach a low plateau, while without, it keeps on growing indefinitely.

Finally, as mentioned before, for the MSM high-risk population, the $\mathcal{R}_0$ in France is higher than 1. Figure 8 reveals that, as the number ψ of new PrEP users increases, $\mathcal{R}_0$ not only decreases below one, but also keeps on falling off. Here, the critical value of ψ, which keeps $\mathcal{R}_0$ below one, is $\psi_{critical} = 0.113$ person.months^{-1}. According to our data, $\psi = 0.071$ person.months^{-1}, as we assume the maximum threshold has been reached. The decay appears, however with a smaller slope, which means, as in the previous subsection, that, after a certain threshold (0.2 here), very large values of ψ do not influence the reduction of $\mathcal{R}_0$ much.

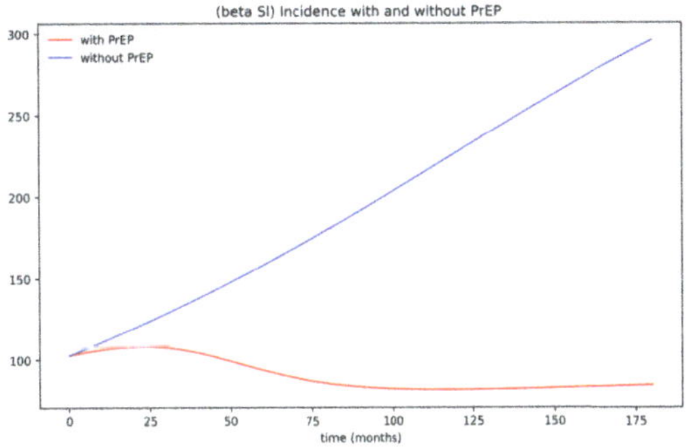

Figure 7. Plot of the evolution of the incidence with and without PrEP (4) over 15 years among French high-risk MSM.

This reservoir effect is so important that, if for any reason, there is the decision to stop PrEP treatment for this MSM group, the rise in new infected individuals would be inevitable, as shown in Figure 9.

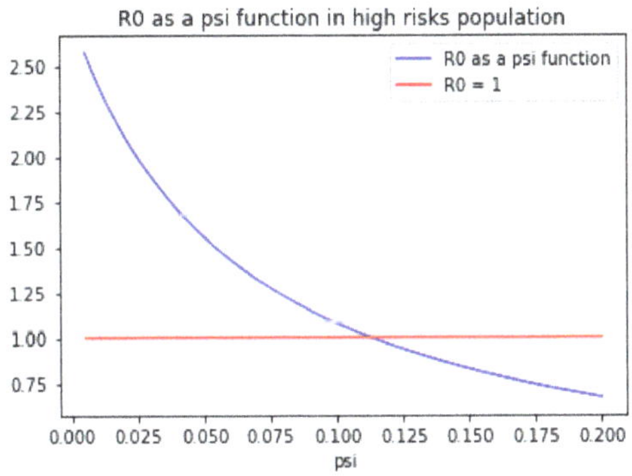

Figure 8. Plot of the $\mathcal{R}_0$ as a function of ψ.

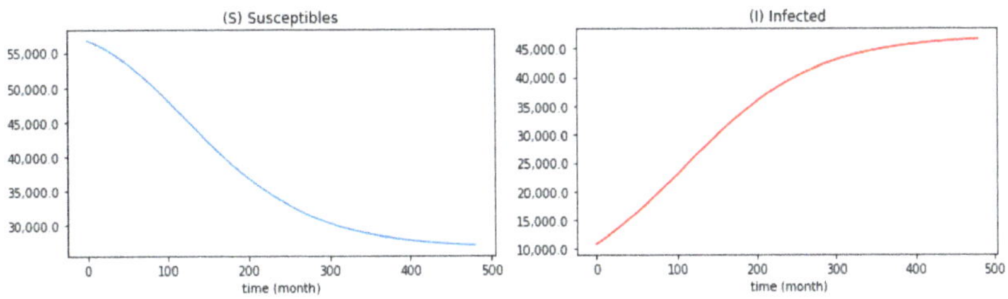

Figure 9. Plot of the susceptibles and infected if PrEP were stopped in 15 years. We considered that all the protected individuals become susceptibles again.

6. Conclusions and Discussion

The aim of this work was to propose a brand-new model for prescribing PrEP for 3 months, with the choice to continue treatment or to stop it at any time after this period.

This choice changes many things in the new modeling approach by introducing difference equations with delay and, thus, the possibility of describing the effect of inertia and the reservoir of protected individuals, not only analytically, but also numerically. This approach could also be generalized to other epidemiological models describing the effect of vaccine or booster doses for improved efficacy of protection.

Furthermore, the double insights of the MSM general and high-risk populations seemed very important to us, especially to depict the effect of PrEP treatment on the disease incidence of the disease and the French health insurance policy to target the high-risk subgroup. With our model and simulations, it appeared that these strategies are much more effective than random targeting of any MSM individual.

Our future work, in production, will take into account that the exponential growth of susceptibles is not realistic for a longer period of time, so it would be better to model it as a logistic growth and then numerically simulated on a longer period of time.

The data we worked on were from 2016 to 2019. It would be interesting to analyze the effect of the SARS-CoV-2 lockdown effect on the incidence and PrEP users. It would also be informative to analyze the booster effect of the non lockdown period (mid-2021 and after). For this purpose, it is necessary to wait a few more years to collect a sufficient amount of data.

A future model should also consider θ time dependent. Indeed, depending on certain periods (a lockdown, for example, or a seasonal effect), the number of PrEP users willing to take the treatment at the end of their 3-month prescription may vary over time. Some users may also take it for a short period of time (e.g., 2 years on average) and discontinue treatment after choosing a long-term closed relationship.

The addition of a compartment of the infected population under tritherapy should also be more realistic. Indeed, with tritherapy, HIV individuals can no longer be infectious and can be removed from the I compartment. The estimate of β would then be more accurate and reflect a more realistic situation.

Finally, it would be interesting to add the cost of treatment and the cost-efficient strategy with the threshold of PrEP users in the compartment for optimal disease control and, eventually, its disappearance. For this purpose, our next goal is to compare data and policies across multiple countries (some with full financial support for treatment, some with partial support, and some with no support).

Author Contributions: Supervision, M.A., L.P.-M. and J.W.; Writing—original draft, J.M.; Writing—review & editing, G.R. All authors have read and agreed to the published version of the manuscript.

Funding: G.R. was supported by the Natural Sciences and Engineering Research Council and the York Research Chairs program.

Institutional Review Board Statement: Not applicable.

Informed Consent Statement: Not applicable.

Data Availability Statement: Not applicable

Conflicts of Interest: The authors declare no conflict of interest.

References

1. Van Manen, D.; Delaneau, O.; Koostra, A.; Boeser-Nunnink, B.; Limou, S.; Bol, S.; Burger, J.; Zwinderman, A.; Moerland, P.; van't Slot, R.; et al. Genome-Wide Association Scan in HIV-1-Infected Individuals Identifying Variants Influencing Disease Course. *PLoS ONE* **2011**, *6*, e22208. doi: 10.1371/journal.pone.0022208. [CrossRef] [PubMed]
2. Billioti de Gage, S.; Le Tri, T.; Dray-Spira, R. Suivi de l'utilisation de Truvada® ou génériques pour une prophylaxie pré-exposition (PrEP) au VIH à partir des données du Système National des Données de Santé (SNDS)—Actualisation des données jusqu'au 30 Juin 2019 (27/11/2019). 2019. Available online: https://www.epi-phare.fr/app/uploads/2020/04/Billioti-de-Gage-et-al.-2019-Suivi-de-l-%E2%80%99utilisation-de-Truvada%C2%AE-ou-ge%CC%81ne%CC%81riques-p.pdf (accessed on 13 September 2022)
3. Silva, C.J.; Torres, D.F.M. A SICA compartmental model in epidemiology with application to HIV/AIDS in Cape Verde. *Ecol. Complex.* **2017**, *30*, 70–75. [CrossRef]

4. Akpa, O.; Oyejola, B. Modeling the transmission dynamics of HIV/AIDS epidemics: An introduction and a review. *J. Infect. Dev. Ctries.* **2010**, *4*, 597–608. doi: 10.3855/jidc.542. [CrossRef] [PubMed]
5. Rivadeneira, P.; Moog, C.; Stan, G.B.; Brunet, C.; Raffi, F.; Ferre, V.; Costanza, V.; Mhawej, M.J.; Biafore, F.; Ouattara, D.A.; et al. Mathematical Modeling of HIV Dynamics After Antiretroviral Therapy Initiation: A Review. *BioRes. Open Access* **2014**, *3*, 233–241. doi: 10.1089/biores.2014.0024. [CrossRef] [PubMed]
6. Liu, D.; Wang, B. A novel time delayed HIV/AIDS model with vaccination & antiretroviral therapy and its stability analysis. *Appl. Math. Model.* **2013**, *37*, 4608–4625. doi: 10.1016/j.apm.2012.09.065. [CrossRef]
7. Nsuami, M.U.; Witbooi, P.J. A model of HIV/AIDS population dynamics including ARV treatment and pre-exposure prophylaxis. *Adv. Differ. Equ.s* **2018**, *2018*, 1–12. doi: 10.1186/s13662-017-1458-x. [CrossRef]
8. Silva, C.J.; Torres, D.F.M. Modeling and optimal control of HIV/AIDS prevention through PrEP. *Discret. Contin. Dyn. Syst.* **2018**, *11*, 119–141. doi: 10.3934/dcdss.2018008. [CrossRef]
9. Simpson, L.; Gumel, A.B. Mathematical assessment of the role of pre-exposure prophylaxis on HIV transmission dynamics. *Appl. Math. Comput.* **2017**, *293*, 168–193. doi: 10.1016/j.amc.2016.07.043. [CrossRef]
10. Pinto, C.M.A.; Carvalho, A.R.M. The impact of pre-exposure prophylaxis (PrEP) and screening on the dynamics of HIV. *J. Comput. Appl. Math.* **2018**, *339*, 231–244. doi: 10.1016/j.cam.2017.10.019. [CrossRef]
11. Adimy, M.; Chekroun, A.; Ferreira, C. Global dynamics of a differential–difference system: A case of Kermack-McKendrick SIR model with age-structured protection phase. *Math. Biosci. Eng.* **2020**, *17*, 1329–1354. doi: 10.3934/mbe.2020067. [CrossRef] [PubMed]
12. Webb, G.F. *Theory of Nonlinear Age-Dependent Population Dynamics*; M. Dekker New York, CRC Press: Boca Raton, FL, USA, 1985; p. 294.
13. Bettencourt, L.; Ribeiro, R. Real Time Bayesian Estimation of the Epidemic Potential of Emerging Infectious Diseases. *PLoS ONE* **2008**, *3*, e2185. doi: 10.1371/journal.pone.0002185. [CrossRef] [PubMed]
14. Cazein, F.; Pillonel, J.; Le Strat, Y.; Pinget, R.; Le Vu, S.; Brunet, S.; Thierry, D.; Brand, D.; Leclerc, M.; Benyelles, L.; et al. Découvertes de séropositivité VIH et sida—France, 2003-2013. *Bull. Epidemiol. Hebd.* **2015**, *9–10*, 152–61.
15. Cazein, F.; Pillonel, J.; Sommen, C.; Bruyand, M.; Lydié, N.; Che, D.; Coignard, B.; Lot, F. Bulletin de Santé Publique. Découvertes de séropositivité VIH et diagnostique de SIDA—France, 2018. *Bull. Santé Publique Vih/Sida* **2019**.

mathematics

Article

Improved Properties of Positive Solutions of Higher Order Differential Equations and Their Applications in Oscillation Theory

Barakah Almarri [1] and Osama Moaaz [2,3,*]

[1] Department of Mathematical Sciences, College of Sciences, Princess Nourah Bint Abdulrahman University, P.O. Box 84428, Riyadh 11671, Saudi Arabia; bjalmarri@pnu.edu.sa
[2] Department of Mathematics, College of Science, Qassim University, P.O. Box 6644, Buraydah 51452, Saudi Arabia
[3] Department of Mathematics, Faculty of Science, Mansoura University, Mansoura 35516, Egypt
* Correspondence: o_moaaz@mans.edu.eg

Abstract: In this article, we present new criteria for testing the oscillation of solutions of higher-order neutral delay differential equation. By deriving new monotonic properties of a class of the positive solutions of the studied equation, we establish better criteria for oscillation. Furthermore, we improve these properties by giving them an iterative character, allowing us to apply the criteria more than once. The results obtained in this paper are characterized by the fact that they do not require the existence of unknown functions and do not need the commutation condition to composition of the delay functions, which are necessary conditions for the previous related results.

Keywords: neutral differential equations; higher-order; oscillation theory; monotonic properties; noncanonical case

MSC: 34C10; 34K11

Citation: Almarri, B.; Moaaz, O. Improved Properties of Positive Solutions of Higher Order Differential Equations and Their Applications in Oscillation Theory. *Mathematics* **2023**, *11*, 924. https://doi.org/10.3390/math11040924

Academic Editor: Alexandra Kashchenko

Received: 3 January 2023
Revised: 1 February 2023
Accepted: 8 February 2023
Published: 11 February 2023

1. Introduction

Delay differential equations (DDE) are differential equations (DE) that take into account the effect of different times. Therefore, they are a better way to model natural phenomena in engineering and physical problems. It is easy to note the recent increase in research into the qualitative theory of DDEs. This is not only due to their practical importance, but also because they are rich in analytical problems and interesting open issues.

One of the most important branches of qualitative theory is oscillation theory, which studies the asymptotic and oscillatory behavior of solutions of DEs. Finding adequate conditions to guarantee that all DE solutions oscillate is one of the main objectives of oscillation theory. Ladas et al. [1] is one of the earliest monographs addressing oscillation theory, including the findings up until 1984. The main objective of this monograph is to investigate the deviating arguments on the oscillation of solutions; neutral delay equations are not discussed in this monograph. The monograph by Gyori and Ladas [2], which made significant contributions to the creation of linearized oscillation theory and the relationship between the oscillation of all solutions and the distribution of the roots of characteristic equations, is one of the key works in the theory of oscillation. Additional topics that are crucial to the theory of oscillation are covered in [3], including determining the conditions for the existence of solutions with particular asymptotic properties and calculating the separation between zeros of oscillatory solutions. The monographs [4–9] covered and summarized many of the results known in the literature up to the past ten years for further results, approaches, and references.

In addition to the theoretical importance and many interesting analytical problems, delay differential equations have many vital applications in engineering and physics, as they appear when modeling many phenomena that are fundamentally time dependent. For example, we find that such equations appear in the modeling of electrical networks that contain lossless transmission lines (such as high-speed computers). Understanding the qualitative properties and behavior of equation solutions greatly helps in studying and developing the studied models.

It is easy to notice the research movement that aims to improve and develop the criteria for oscillation of solutions of DDEs, especially of the second-order, which is led by the Slovakian school; see, for example, the papers of Baculíková, Džurina and Jadlovská [10–13].

Mostly, we find that the study of the oscillation of solutions of DDEs of different orders adopts one of two approaches, either substituting Riccati or comparing with equations of lower orders, often first-order. In 1999, Koplatadze et al. [14], with a different approach than the traditional one, studied the asymptotic and oscillatory behavior of solutions to the DE

$$\frac{\mathrm{d}^n x}{\mathrm{d}u^n} + q \cdot [x \circ g] = 0, \tag{1}$$

where $u > 0$, $n \geq 2$, and $[x \circ g](u) = x(g(u))$. They considered the even- and odd-order of this equation. One of their results was to ensure that solutions of DDE (1) oscillate under the conditions $g(u) \leq u$, $g'(u) \geq 0$, and

$$\limsup_{u \to \infty} \left[g(u) \int_u^{\infty} g^{n-2}(v) q(v) \mathrm{d}v + \int_{g(u)}^{u} g^{n-1}(v) q(v) \mathrm{d}v + \frac{1}{g(u)} \int_0^{g(u)} v g^{n-1}(v) q(v) \mathrm{d}v \right] > (n-1)!.$$

Before and after that, many researchers also verified the oscillation of the higher order DDEs solutions in the canonical case by using traditional methods; see, for example, [15–20].

In the non-canonical case, the oscillation conditions for solutions of the DDE

$$\frac{\mathrm{d}}{\mathrm{d}u} \left(a \cdot \left(\frac{\mathrm{d}^{n-1} x}{\mathrm{d}u^{n-1}} \right)^{\alpha} \right) + q \cdot [f \circ x \circ g] = 0 \tag{2}$$

were established by Baculíková et al. [21] and Moaaz et al. [22] by using the comparison technique. Using the Riccati substitution, Zhang et al. [23] and Moaaz and Muhib [24] studied oscillation of the DDE

$$\frac{\mathrm{d}}{\mathrm{d}u} \left(a \cdot \left(\frac{\mathrm{d}^{n-1} x}{\mathrm{d}u^{n-1}} \right)^{\alpha} \right) + q \cdot \left[x^{\beta} \circ g \right] = 0.$$

The results of the second-order equation were most recently expanded to the even-order equations in the non-canonical case by Moaaz et al. [25]. In order to develop iteratively new oscillation criteria, they developed an approach that involved obtaining new monotonic properties for positive decreasing solutions.

For the neutral equations, which the higher derivative appears on the solution with and without delay, Li and Rogovchenko [26] related oscillation of solutions of the DDE

$$\frac{\mathrm{d}}{\mathrm{d}u} \left(a \cdot \left(\frac{\mathrm{d}^{n-1}}{\mathrm{d}u^{n-1}} (x + p \cdot [x \circ h]) \right)^{\alpha} \right) + q \cdot \left[x^{\beta} \circ g \right] = 0 \tag{3}$$

to three equations of the first-order by using comparison techniques. In [27], a criterion for ruling out the existence of so-called Kneser solutions to DDE (3) was developed. The results in [27] are more accurate and effective than those in [26] since they do not rely on unknown functions. Very recently, Elabbasy et al. [28] studied the asymptotic behavior of the solutions of the DDE (3). Let us review the following theorem, which gives the conditions ensuring that non-oscillatory solutions of (3) tend to zero.

On the other hand, for neutral equations of the second order, the study of oscillation of these equations has been developed with many improved techniques; see, for example, [29–31].

In this article, we consider the neutral DDE of the form

$$\frac{\mathrm{d}}{\mathrm{d}u}\left(a\cdot\frac{\mathrm{d}^{n-1}}{\mathrm{d}u^{n-1}}(x+p\cdot[x\circ h])\right)+q\cdot[F\circ x\circ g]=0, \tag{4}$$

where $u \geq u_0$, $n \geq 4$ is an even natural number. We also suppose the following:

(H1) $a,\ p,\ q \in C([u_0,\infty),[0,\infty))$, $a(u) > 0$, $p(u) \leq \mathcal{E}_0(u)/\mathcal{E}_0(h(u))$ and $\mathcal{E}_{n-2}(u_0) < \infty$, where

$$\mathcal{E}_0(u) := \int_u^\infty a^{-1}(v)\mathrm{d}v, \text{ and } \mathcal{E}_k(u) := \int_u^\infty \mathcal{E}_{k-1}(v)\mathrm{d}v,$$

for $k = 1,2,\ldots,n-2$.

(H2) $h,\ g \in C([u_0,\infty),\mathbb{R})$, $h(u) \leq u$, $g(u) \leq u$, $g'(u) > 0$, $\lim_{u\to\infty} h(u) = \infty$ and $\lim_{u\to\infty} g(u) = \infty$.

(H3) $F \in C(\mathbb{R},\mathbb{R})$, $F'(x) \geq 0$, $xF(x) > 0$ for $x \neq 0$, and $F(xy) \geq F(x)F(y)$ for $xy > 0$.

First, we define the corresponding function of solution x as $\omega := x + p\cdot[x\circ h]$. By a solution of (4), we mean a function $x \in C^{n-1}([u_x,\infty),\mathbb{R})$, for $u_x \geq u_0$, which $a\cdot\omega^{(n-1)} \in C^1([u_x,\infty),\mathbb{R})$ and x satisfies (4) for all $u_x \geq u_0$. We consider only those solutions of (4) that do not eventually vanish. A solution of DDE (4) is called oscillatory if it has arbitrarily large zeros; otherwise, it is said to be nonoscillatory. DDE (4) is called oscillatory if all its solutions are oscillatory.

The aim of the study is to provide new conditions for determining the oscillation parameters of all solutions of Equation (4) in the non-canonical case. We also aim to develop the oscillation theorems of higher-order neutral delay differential equations by deriving new oscillation parameters characterized by an iterative nature. The method employed is an extension of the method Koplatadze et al. [14] and, later, by Baculková [10].

2. Preliminary Lemmas

Notation 1. *The class of all eventually positive solutions of DDE (4) is denoted by the symbol* $\mathcal{P}_s$.

Notation 2. *To facilitate the presentation of the results, we define the function* $\mathcal{Q}$ *as*

$$\mathcal{Q} := q\cdot\left[F\circ\left(1-[p\circ g]\cdot\frac{[\mathcal{E}_{n-2}\circ h\circ g]}{[\mathcal{E}_{n-2}\circ g]}\right)\right].$$

Lemma 1 (Lemma 3, [32])**.** *Suppose that* $x \in \mathcal{P}_s$. *Then,*

$$\frac{\mathrm{d}}{\mathrm{d}u}\left(a\cdot\frac{\mathrm{d}^{n-1}}{\mathrm{d}u^{n-1}}\omega\right) \leq 0,$$

eventually. Moreover, one of the following conditions is satisfied eventually:

(D_1) ω, ω' *and* $\omega^{(n-1)}$ *are positive, and* $\omega^{(n)}$ *is negative;*

(D_2) ω, ω' *and* $\omega^{(n-2)}$ *are positive, and* $\omega^{(n-1)}$ *is negative;*

(D_3) $(-1)^m\omega^{(m)}$ *are positive, for* $m = 0,1,\ldots,n-1$.

Lemma 2. *Suppose that* $x \in \mathcal{P}_s$ *and* ω *satisfies case* (D_3) *in Lemma 1. Then, eventually,*

$$(-1)^{s+1}\frac{\mathrm{d}^s}{\mathrm{d}u^s}\omega \leq \left[a\cdot\frac{\mathrm{d}^{n-1}}{\mathrm{d}u^{n-1}}\omega\right]\cdot\mathcal{E}_{n-s-2}, \tag{5}$$

for $s = 0,1,\ldots,n-2$.

Proof. Since $\left(a \cdot \omega^{(n-1)}\right)' \leq 0$, $\omega^{(n-1)} \leq 0$ and $\omega^{(n-2)} > 0$ for all $u \geq u_1$, where $u_1 \geq u_0$, we conclude that

$$\omega^{(n-2)}(u) \geq -\int_u^\infty \left[a(v)\omega^{(n-1)}(v)\right] a^{-1}(v)\mathrm{d}v \geq -a(u)\omega^{(n-1)}(u)\mathcal{E}_0(u).$$

Integrating this inequality $n-2$ times from u to ∞, we obtain

$$\begin{aligned} \omega^{(n-3)}(u) &\leq \int_u^\infty \left[a(v)\omega^{(n-1)}(v)\right]\mathcal{E}_0(v)\mathrm{d}v \\ &\leq a(u)\omega^{(n-1)}(u)\int_u^\infty \mathcal{E}_0(v)\mathrm{d}v \\ &= a(u)\omega^{(n-1)}(u)\mathcal{E}_1(u), \end{aligned}$$

and so on until we get

$$(-1)^{s+1}\omega^{(s)} \leq \left[a \cdot \omega^{(n-1)}\right] \cdot \mathcal{E}_{n-s-2},$$

for $s = 0, 1, \ldots, n-2$. The proof is complete. □

Lemma 3. *Suppose that $x \in \mathcal{P}_s$ and ω satisfies case* (D_3) *in Lemma 1. Then,*

$$(-1)^s \frac{\mathrm{d}}{\mathrm{d}u}\left(\frac{1}{\mathcal{E}_{n-2}} \cdot \frac{\mathrm{d}^s}{\mathrm{d}u^s}\omega\right) \geq 0, \tag{6}$$

for $s = 0, 1, \ldots, n-2$.

Proof. From Lemma 2, we have that (5) holds. Using (5) with $s = n-2$, we find $\omega^{(n-2)} \geq -\left[a \cdot \omega^{(n-1)}\right] \cdot \mathcal{E}_0$. Thus,

$$\frac{\mathrm{d}}{\mathrm{d}u}\left(\frac{1}{\mathcal{E}_0} \cdot \omega^{(n-2)}\right) = \frac{1}{\mathcal{E}_0^2}\left[\mathcal{E}_0 \cdot \omega^{(n-1)} + a^{-1} \cdot \omega^{(n-2)}\right] \geq 0.$$

Furthermore, we find

$$-\omega^{(n-3)}(u) \geq \int_u^\infty \left[\frac{1}{\mathcal{E}_0(v)}\omega^{(n-2)}(v)\right]\mathcal{E}_0(v)\mathrm{d}v \geq \frac{1}{\mathcal{E}_0(u)}\omega^{(n-2)}(u)\mathcal{E}_1(u),$$

and so, $-\mathcal{E}_0 \cdot \omega^{(n-3)} \geq \mathcal{E}_1 \cdot \omega^{(n-2)}$. This implies

$$\frac{\mathrm{d}}{\mathrm{d}u}\left(\frac{1}{\mathcal{E}_1} \cdot \omega^{(n-3)}\right) = \frac{1}{\mathcal{E}_1^2}\left[\mathcal{E}_1 \cdot \omega^{(n-2)} + \mathcal{E}_0 \cdot \omega^{(n-3)}\right] \leq 0.$$

Proceeding in this manner, we arrive at

$$\frac{\mathrm{d}}{\mathrm{d}u}\left(\frac{1}{\mathcal{E}_{n-2}} \cdot \omega\right) \geq 0.$$

The proof is complete. □

Lemma 4. *Suppose that $x \in \mathcal{P}_s$ and ω satisfies case* (D_3) *in Lemma 1. Then,*

$$x \geq \left(1 - p \cdot \frac{[\mathcal{E}_{n-2} \circ h]}{\mathcal{E}_{n-2}}\right) \cdot \omega,$$

and

$$\frac{\mathrm{d}}{\mathrm{d}u}\left(a \cdot \frac{\mathrm{d}^{n-1}}{\mathrm{d}u^{n-1}}\omega\right) + \mathcal{Q} \cdot [F \circ \omega \circ g] \leq 0. \tag{7}$$

Proof. From Lemma 3, we have that (6) holds. Using (6) with $s = 0$, we obtain

$$[x \circ h] \le [\omega \circ h] \le \frac{[\mathcal{E}_{n-2} \circ h]}{\mathcal{E}_{n-2}} \cdot \omega.$$

This implies

$$\begin{aligned} x &\ge \left(1 - p \cdot \frac{[\omega \circ h]}{\omega}\right) \cdot \omega \\ &\ge \left(1 - p \cdot \frac{[\mathcal{E}_{n-2} \circ h]}{\mathcal{E}_{n-2}}\right) \cdot \omega. \end{aligned}$$

Thus, from (4) and (H3), we get

$$\frac{\mathrm{d}}{\mathrm{d}u}\left(a \cdot \frac{\mathrm{d}^{n-1}}{\mathrm{d}u^{n-1}}\omega\right) + q \cdot \left[F \circ \left(1 - [p \circ g] \cdot \frac{[\mathcal{E}_{n-2} \circ h \circ g]}{[\mathcal{E}_{n-2} \circ g]}\right)\right] \cdot [F \circ \omega \circ g] \le 0,$$

or

$$\frac{\mathrm{d}}{\mathrm{d}u}\left(a \cdot \frac{\mathrm{d}^{n-1}}{\mathrm{d}u^{n-1}}\omega\right) + \mathcal{Q} \cdot [F \circ \omega \circ g] \le 0.$$

The proof is complete. □

Lemma 5. *Suppose that $x \in \mathcal{P}_s$ and ω satisfies case (D_3) in Lemma 1. If there is a constant $\alpha > 0$ such that, eventually,*

$$\mathcal{Q} \cdot \mathcal{E}_{n-2}^2 \ge \alpha \mathcal{E}_{n-3}, \tag{8}$$

then ω converges to zero as $u \to \infty$.

Proof. Since ω is positive and decreasing (from case (D_3)), we have that $\omega(u) \to L$ as $u \to \infty$, where $L \ge 0$.

Suppose that $L > 0$. Then, there is $u_1 \ge u_0$ such that $[\omega \circ g] \ge L$ for $u \ge u_1$. Hence, from Lemma 4, we get

$$\frac{\mathrm{d}}{\mathrm{d}u}\left(a(u) \frac{\mathrm{d}^{n-1}}{\mathrm{d}u^{n-1}}\omega(u)\right) \le -\mathcal{Q}(u) F(L).$$

Integrating this inequality from u_1 to u and using (8), we find

$$\begin{aligned} a(u)\omega^{(n-1)}(u) &\le a(u_1)\omega^{(n-1)}(u_1) - F(L) \int_{u_1}^{u} \mathcal{Q}(v)\mathrm{d}v \\ &\le -\alpha F(L) \int_{u_1}^{u} \frac{\mathcal{E}_{n-3}(v)}{\mathcal{E}_{n-2}^2(v)}\mathrm{d}v \\ &= -\alpha F(L)\left(\frac{1}{\mathcal{E}_{n-2}(u)} - \frac{1}{\mathcal{E}_{n-2}(u_1)}\right). \end{aligned} \tag{9}$$

We note that $\mathcal{E}_{n-2}(u) \to 0$ as $u \to \infty$. Then, for all $\epsilon \in (0,1)$, we have that $\mathcal{E}_{n-2}^{-1}(u) - \mathcal{E}_{n-2}^{-1}(u_1) \ge \epsilon \mathcal{E}_{n-2}^{-1}(u)$, eventually. Therefore, (9) becomes

$$a \cdot \omega^{(n-1)} \le -\epsilon \alpha F(L) \frac{1}{\mathcal{E}_{n-2}}. \tag{10}$$

From Lemma 2, we have that (5) holds. Combining (5) at $s = 1$ and (10), we conclude that

$$\frac{\omega'}{\mathcal{E}_{n-3}} \le a \cdot \omega^{(n-1)} \le -\epsilon \alpha F(L) \frac{1}{\mathcal{E}_{n-2}},$$

or

$$\omega' \leq -\epsilon\alpha F(L)\frac{\mathcal{E}_{n-3}}{\mathcal{E}_{n-2}}.$$

Integrating this inequality from u_1 to u, we find

$$\omega(u) \leq \omega(u_1) - \epsilon\alpha F(L)\ln\frac{\mathcal{E}_{n-2}(u_1)}{\mathcal{E}_{n-2}(u)}.$$

Thus, $\omega(u) \to -\infty$ as $u \to \infty$, a contradiction. Then, $\omega(u) \to 0$ as $u \to \infty$. The proof is complete. □

3. Oscillation Criteria

In this section, we create a criterion that ensures that solutions to Equation (4) oscillate. The next theorem is a restatement of Theorem 2.1 in [28], when $\alpha = \beta$.

Theorem 1 ([28]). *Assume that*

$$\int_{u_0}^{\infty}\left(\int_{u}^{\infty}(\mu-u)^{n-3}\left(\frac{1}{a(\mu)}\int_{u_1}^{\mu}q(v)\mathrm{d}v\right)\mathrm{d}v\right)\mathrm{d}u = \infty$$

and

$$\limsup_{u\to\infty}\int_{u_0}^{u}\left(\mathcal{E}_0(v)q(v)(1-p(g(v)))\left(\frac{\eta_0 g^{n-2}(v)}{(n-2)!}\right)-\frac{1}{4a(v)\mathcal{E}_0(v)}\right)\mathrm{d}v = \infty, \qquad (11)$$

for some constant $\eta_0 \in (0,1)$. If the DDE

$$\frac{\mathrm{d}}{\mathrm{d}u}\psi + q\cdot\frac{\eta_1(1-[p\circ g])\cdot g^{n-1}(u)}{(n-1)!\,[a\circ g]]}\cdot[\psi\circ g] = 0 \qquad (12)$$

is oscillatory for some constant $\eta_1 \in (0,1)$, then every solution of (3), with $\alpha = \beta$, is either oscillatory or converges to zero as $u \to \infty$.

Lemma 6. *Assume that $\lim_{x\to 0}\frac{x}{F(x)} = K < \infty$, and (8) holds. If*

$$\limsup_{u\to\infty}\left[\mathcal{E}_{n-2}(g(u))\int_{u_0}^{g(u)}\mathcal{Q}(v)\mathrm{d}v + \int_{g(u)}^{u}\mathcal{E}_{n-2}(v)\mathcal{Q}(v)\mathrm{d}v \right.$$
$$\left. + F\left(\mathcal{E}_{n-2}^{-1}(g(u))\right)\int_{u}^{\infty}\mathcal{E}_{n-2}(v)\mathcal{Q}(v)F(\mathcal{E}_{n-2}(g(v)))\mathrm{d}v\right] > K, \qquad (13)$$

then ω satisfies case (D_2) in Lemma 1.

Proof. Assume the contrary that ω satisfies case (D_1) or (D_3).

Assume first that ω satisfies case (D_3) for $u \geq u_1 \geq u_0$. From Lemma 4, we obtain that (7) holds. Integrating (7) from u_1 to u, we find

$$\begin{aligned} -a(u)\omega^{(n-1)}(u) &\geq -a(u_1)\omega^{(n-1)}(u_1) + \int_{u_1}^{u}\mathcal{Q}(v)F(\omega(g(v)))\mathrm{d}v \\ &\geq \int_{u_1}^{u}\mathcal{Q}(v)F(\omega(g(v)))\mathrm{d}v. \end{aligned} \qquad (14)$$

Next, it follows from Lemma 2 that (5) holds. From (5) with $s = 0$, we note that the function

$$\omega + \left(a\cdot\frac{\mathrm{d}^{n-1}}{\mathrm{d}u^{n-1}}\omega\right)\cdot\mathcal{E}_{n-2}$$

is positive for $u \geq u_1$. Then, from (5) with $s = 1$,

$$\begin{aligned}\frac{\mathrm{d}}{\mathrm{d}u}\left(\omega + a \cdot \omega^{(n-1)} \cdot \mathcal{E}_{n-2}\right) &= \omega' - a \cdot \omega^{(n-1)} \cdot \mathcal{E}_{n-3} + \left(a \cdot \omega^{(n-1)}\right)' \cdot \mathcal{E}_{n-2} \\ &\leq \left(a \cdot \omega^{(n-1)}\right)' \cdot \mathcal{E}_{n-2},\end{aligned}$$

which, with (7), gives

$$\frac{\mathrm{d}}{\mathrm{d}u}\left(\omega + a \cdot \omega^{(n-1)} \cdot \mathcal{E}_{n-2}\right) \leq -\mathcal{E}_{n-2} \cdot \mathcal{Q} \cdot [F \circ \omega \circ g] \leq 0.$$

Integrating this inequality from u to ∞, we obtain

$$\omega(u) + a(u)\omega^{(n-1)}(u)\mathcal{E}_{n-2}(u) \geq \int_u^\infty \mathcal{E}_{n-2}(v)\mathcal{Q}(v)F(\omega(g(v)))\mathrm{d}v. \tag{15}$$

Combining (14) and (15), we find

$$\begin{aligned}\omega(u) &\geq -a(u)\omega^{(n-1)}(u)\mathcal{E}_{n-2}(u) + \int_u^\infty \mathcal{E}_{n-2}(v)\mathcal{Q}(v)F(\omega(g(v)))\mathrm{d}v \\ &\geq \mathcal{E}_{n-2}(u)\int_{u_1}^u \mathcal{Q}(v)F(\omega(g(v)))\mathrm{d}v + \int_u^\infty \mathcal{E}_{n-2}(v)\mathcal{Q}(v)F(\omega(g(v)))\mathrm{d}v,\end{aligned}$$

and hence,

$$\begin{aligned}\omega(g(u)) \geq\ & \mathcal{E}_{n-2}(g(u))\int_{u_1}^{g(u)} \mathcal{Q}(v)F(\omega(g(v)))\mathrm{d}v + \int_{g(u)}^u \mathcal{E}_{n-2}(v)\mathcal{Q}(v)F(\omega(g(v)))\mathrm{d}v \\ & + \int_u^\infty \mathcal{E}_{n-2}(v)\mathcal{Q}(v)F(\omega(g(v)))\mathrm{d}v.\end{aligned} \tag{16}$$

Using Lemma 3, we obtain that $\omega/\mathcal{E}_{n-2}$ is increasing, and so

$$F(\omega(g(v))) \geq F\left(\mathcal{E}_{n-2}^{-1}(g(u))\right)F(\mathcal{E}_{n-2}(g(v)))F(\omega(g(u))), \text{ for } u \leq v. \tag{17}$$

Thus, (16) reduces to

$$\begin{aligned}\frac{\omega(g(u))}{F(\omega(g(u)))} \geq\ & \mathcal{E}_{n-2}(g(u))\int_{u_1}^{g(u)} \mathcal{Q}(v)\mathrm{d}v + \int_{g(u)}^u \mathcal{E}_{n-2}(v)\mathcal{Q}(v)\mathrm{d}v \\ & + F\left(\mathcal{E}_{n-2}^{-1}(g(u))\right)\int_u^\infty \mathcal{E}_{n-2}(v)\mathcal{Q}(v)F(\mathcal{E}_{n-2}(g(v)))\mathrm{d}v,\end{aligned} \tag{18}$$

which contradicts (13).

Suppose that ω satisfies case (D_1) for $u \geq u_1 \geq u_0$. From (13), we can demonstrate that

$$\int_{u_1}^\infty \mathcal{E}_{n-2}(v)\mathcal{Q}(v)\mathrm{d}v = \infty,$$

by following the same procedure as in the proof of Theorem 1 in [10]. Further, it follows from (H1) that

$$\int_{u_1}^\infty \mathcal{Q}(v)\mathrm{d}v = \infty.$$

Since ω is positive and increasing, we get that $x \geq (1-p)\omega$, and there is $u_2 \geq u_1$ with $\omega(g(u)) \geq M$ for $u \geq u_2$. Integrating (4) from u_1 to u, we find

$$\begin{aligned} a(u_1)\omega^{(n-1)}(u_1) &\geq \int_{u_1}^{\infty} q(v)F(x(g(v)))\mathrm{d}v \\ &\geq \int_{u_1}^{\infty} q(v)F(1-p(g(v)))F(\omega(g(v)))\mathrm{d}v \\ &\geq F(M)\int_{u_1}^{\infty} q(v)F(1-p(g(v)))\mathrm{d}v. \end{aligned} \tag{19}$$

From the fact that $\frac{[\mathcal{E}_{n-2}\circ h]}{\mathcal{E}_{n-2}} \geq 1$, we find

$$q(u)F(1-p(g(u))) \geq \mathcal{Q}(u),$$

which with (19) gives

$$a(u_1)\omega^{(n-1)}(u_1) \geq F(M)\int_{u_1}^{\infty} \mathcal{Q}(v)\mathrm{d}v,$$

a contradiction. Therefore, ω satisfies case (D_2), eventually. The proof is complete. □

Theorem 2. *Assume that $F(x) = x$. If conditions (11) and (13) are satisfied, then Equation (4) becomes oscillatory.*

Proof. Assuming that there is a non-oscillatory solution to (4) necessarily means that there is a solution x of (4), in which $x \in \mathcal{P}_s$. From Lemma 1, the derivatives of the function ω have three possibilities. It follows from Lemma 6 that ω satisfies case (D_2), eventually. Following the same approach in Theorem 1, we can prove that if ω fulfills case (D_2), then we get a conflict with condition (11). The proof is complete. □

In addition to the above, we also present the following theorem, which provides a criterion for the oscillation of (4) based on the comparison principle. So, we need to review the following lemma.

Lemma 7 (Lemma 2.2.3, [33]). *Let $\Im \in C^s([u_0,\infty))$, $\Im(u) > 0$, $\lim_{u\to\infty}\Im(u) \neq 0$, $\Im^{(s)}(u)$ be of constant sign eventually, and $\Im^{(s)} \neq 0$ on a subray of $[u_0,\infty)$. If $\Im^{(s-1)}(u)\Im^{(s)}(u) < 0$ for $u \geq u_1$, then there is a $u_\mu \geq u_1$ such that*

$$\Im(u) \geq \frac{\mu}{(s-1)!}u^{s-1}\left|\Im^{(s-1)}(u)\right|,$$

for $0 < \mu < 1$ and $u \in [u_\mu,\infty)$.

Theorem 3. *Assume that $\lim_{x\to 0}\frac{x}{F(x)} = K < \infty$, and let (8) and (13) hold. The oscillation of the DDE*

$$\psi'(u) + F(\psi(g(u)))\frac{1}{a(u)}\int_{u_1}^{u} q(v)F(1-p(g(v)))F\left(\frac{\mu g^{n-2}(v)}{(n-2)!}\right)\mathrm{d}v = 0, \tag{20}$$

for some $\mu \in (0,1)$, ensures the oscillation of Equation (4).

Proof. Assuming that there is a non-oscillatory solution to (4) necessarily means that there is a solution x of (4), in which $x \in \mathcal{P}_s$. From Lemma 1, the derivatives of the function ω have three possibilities. It follows from Lemma 6 that ω satisfies case (D_2), eventually.

Using Lemma 7 with $\Im = \omega$ and $s = n-1$, we obtain

$$\omega(u) \geq \frac{\mu}{(n-2)!} u^{n-2} \omega^{(n-2)}(u), \tag{21}$$

eventually. Since ω is positive and increasing, we get that $x \geq (1-p)\omega$, and so, (4) becomes

$$\frac{\mathrm{d}}{\mathrm{d}u}\left(a \cdot \frac{\mathrm{d}^{n-1}}{\mathrm{d}u^{n-1}}\omega\right) + q \cdot [F \circ (1 - [p \circ g])] \cdot [F \circ \omega \circ g] \leq 0,$$

which, with (21), yields

$$\frac{\mathrm{d}}{\mathrm{d}u}\left(a \cdot \frac{\mathrm{d}^{n-1}}{\mathrm{d}u^{n-1}}\omega\right) + q \cdot [F \circ (1 - [p \circ g])] \cdot \left[F \circ \frac{\mu g^{n-2}}{(n-2)!}\right] \cdot \left[F \circ \omega^{(n-2)} \circ g\right] \leq 0.$$

Integrating this inequality from u_1 to u, we find

$$\begin{aligned} a(u)\omega^{(n-1)}(u) &\leq -\int_{u_1}^{u} q(v) F(1 - p(g(v))) F\left(\frac{\mu g^{n-2}(v)}{(n-2)!}\right) F\left(\omega^{(n-2)}(g(v))\right) \mathrm{d}v \\ &\leq -F\left(\omega^{(n-2)}(g(u))\right) \int_{u_1}^{u} q(v) F(1 - p(g(v))) F\left(\frac{\mu g^{n-2}(v)}{(n-2)!}\right) \mathrm{d}v. \end{aligned}$$

If we set $\psi = \omega^{(n-2)} > 0$, then we have that ψ is a positive solution of

$$\psi'(u) + F(\psi(g(u))) \frac{1}{a(u)} \int_{u_1}^{u} q(v) F(1 - p(g(v))) F\left(\frac{\mu g^{n-2}(v)}{(n-2)!}\right) \mathrm{d}v \leq 0.$$

From Theorem 1 in [34], Equation (20) also has a positive solution, which is a contradiction. The proof is complete. □

Corollary 1. *Assume that* $\lim_{x \to 0} \frac{x}{F(x)} = K < \infty$, $F(x)/x \geq 1$ *for* $|x| \in (0,1]$, *and let (8) and (13) hold. The fulfillment of the following condition ensures the oscillation of Equation (4):*

$$\liminf_{u \to \infty} \int_{g(u)}^{u} \frac{1}{a(s)} \left(\int_{u_1}^{s} q(v) F(1 - p(g(v))) F\left(\frac{s g^{n-2}(v)}{(n-2)!}\right) \mathrm{d}v \right) \mathrm{d}s > \frac{1}{\mathrm{e}}. \tag{22}$$

Proof. From Theorem 2.1.1 in [1], criterion (22) ensures the oscillation of Equation (20). □

4. Criterion of an Iterative Nature

In this section, we create a criterion of an iterative nature that ensures that the solutions to Equation (4) oscillate, when $F(x) = x$.

Lemma 8. *Suppose that* $x \in \mathcal{P}_s$ *and* ω *satisfies case* (D_3) *in Lemma 1. If (8) holds, then the function* $\omega / \mathcal{E}_{n-2}^{\alpha}$ *is decreasing and also converges to zero as* $u \to \infty$.

Proof. From Lemma 4, we have that (7) holds for $u \geq u_1 \geq u_0$. Integrating (7) from u_1 to u and using (8), we get

$$\begin{aligned} a(u)\omega^{(n-1)}(u) &\leq a(u_1)\omega^{(n-1)}(u_1) - \int_{u_1}^{u} \mathcal{Q}(v)\omega(g(v)) \mathrm{d}v \\ &\leq a(u_1)\omega^{(n-1)}(u_1) - \alpha\omega(u) \int_{u_1}^{u} \frac{\mathcal{E}_{n-3}(v)}{\mathcal{E}_{n-2}^2(v)} \mathrm{d}v \\ &= a(u_1)\omega^{(n-1)}(u_1) - \alpha\omega(u) \left(\frac{1}{\mathcal{E}_{n-2}(u)} - \frac{1}{\mathcal{E}_{n-2}(u_1)} \right). \end{aligned} \tag{23}$$

It follows from Lemma 5 that $\omega(u) \to 0$ as $u \to \infty$. Thus, there is a $u_2 \geq u_1$ such that $a(u_1)\omega^{(n-1)}(u_1) + \frac{\alpha\omega(u)}{\mathcal{E}_{n-2}(u_1)} \leq 0$ for $u \geq u_2$. Hence, (23) becomes

$$a(u)\omega^{(n-1)}(u) \leq -\frac{\alpha}{\mathcal{E}_{n-2}(u)}\omega(u). \tag{24}$$

Using Lemma 2 with $s = 1$, we get $\omega' \leq a \cdot \omega^{(n-1)} \cdot \mathcal{E}_{n-3}$, which with (24) yields

$$\frac{\omega'(u)}{\mathcal{E}_{n-3}(u)} \leq a(u)\omega^{(n-1)}(u) \leq -\frac{\alpha}{\mathcal{E}_{n-2}(u)}\omega(u). \tag{25}$$

Hence,

$$\frac{\mathrm{d}}{\mathrm{d}u}\left(\frac{\omega}{\mathcal{E}_{n-2}^{\alpha}}\right) = \frac{1}{\mathcal{E}_{n-2}^{\alpha+1}}\left[\mathcal{E}_{n-2}\omega' + \alpha\mathcal{E}_{n-3}\omega\right] \leq 0.$$

Now, we have that $\omega/\mathcal{E}_{n-2}^{\alpha}$ is positive and decreasing. Then, $\omega/\mathcal{E}_{n-2}^{\alpha} \to \ell$ as $u \to \infty$, where $\ell \geq 0$.

Suppose that $\ell > 0$. Hence,

$$\frac{\omega(u)}{\mathcal{E}_{n-2}^{\alpha}(u)} \geq \ell. \tag{26}$$

Next, we define

$$\phi := \frac{a \cdot \omega^{(n-1)} \cdot \mathcal{E}_{n-2} + \omega}{\mathcal{E}_{n-2}^{\alpha}},$$

and so

$$\begin{aligned}
\phi' &= \frac{\left(a \cdot \omega^{(n-1)}\right)'}{\mathcal{E}_{n-2}^{\alpha-1}} - \frac{1}{\mathcal{E}_{n-2}^{\alpha}}\left(a \cdot \omega^{(n-1)} \cdot \mathcal{E}_{n-3} - \omega'\right) + \alpha\frac{a \cdot \omega^{(n-1)} \cdot \mathcal{E}_{n-3}}{\mathcal{E}_{n-2}^{\alpha}} + \alpha\frac{\mathcal{E}_{n-3}}{\mathcal{E}_{n-2}^{\alpha+1}} \cdot \omega \\
&\leq -\frac{1}{\mathcal{E}_{n-2}^{\alpha-1}} \cdot \mathcal{Q} \cdot [\omega \circ g] + \alpha\frac{a \cdot \omega^{(n-1)} \cdot \mathcal{E}_{n-3}}{\mathcal{E}_{n-2}^{\alpha}} + \alpha\frac{\mathcal{E}_{n-3}}{\mathcal{E}_{n-2}^{\alpha+1}} \cdot \omega.
\end{aligned}$$

Thus, from (8), we get

$$\begin{aligned}
\phi' &\leq -\alpha\frac{\mathcal{E}_{n-3}}{\mathcal{E}_{n-2}^{\alpha+1}} \cdot [\omega \circ g] + \alpha\frac{a \cdot \omega^{(n-1)} \cdot \mathcal{E}_{n-3}}{\mathcal{E}_{n-2}^{\alpha}} + \alpha\frac{\mathcal{E}_{n-3}}{\mathcal{E}_{n-2}^{\alpha+1}} \cdot \omega \\
&\leq \alpha\frac{a \cdot \omega^{(n-1)} \cdot \mathcal{E}_{n-3}}{\mathcal{E}_{n-2}^{\alpha}}.
\end{aligned}$$

It follows from (25) and (26) that

$$\begin{aligned}
\phi' &\leq -\alpha^2\frac{\mathcal{E}_{n-3}}{\mathcal{E}_{n-2}^{\alpha+1}} \cdot \omega(u) \\
&\leq -\ell\alpha^2\frac{\mathcal{E}_{n-3}}{\mathcal{E}_{n-2}} < 0.
\end{aligned}$$

Integrating this inequality from u_1 to u, we find

$$\phi(u_1) \geq \ell\alpha^2 \ln\frac{\mathcal{E}_{n-2}(u_1)}{\mathcal{E}_{n-2}(u)},$$

which leads to a contradiction. Then, $\ell = 0$. The proof is complete. □

Lemma 9. *Assume that (8) holds. If*

$$\limsup_{u\to\infty}\left[\mathcal{E}_{n-2}(g(u))F(\mathcal{E}_{n-2}^{-\alpha}(g(u)))\int_{u_1}^{g(u)}\mathcal{Q}(v)F(\mathcal{E}_{n-2}^{\alpha}(g(v)))\mathrm{d}v\right.$$
$$+F(\mathcal{E}_{n-2}^{-\alpha}(g(u)))\int_{g(u)}^{u}\mathcal{E}_{n-2}(v)\mathcal{Q}(v)F(\mathcal{E}_{n-2}^{\alpha}(g(v)))\mathrm{d}v$$
$$\left.+F\left(\mathcal{E}_{n-2}^{-1}(g(u))\right)\int_{u}^{\infty}\mathcal{E}_{n-2}(v)\mathcal{Q}(v)F(\mathcal{E}_{n-2}(g(v)))\mathrm{d}v\right]>K, \quad (27)$$

then ω satisfies case (D_2) *in Lemma 1.*

Proof. Proceeding as in the proof of Lemma 6, we get that (16) and (17) hold. Using Lemma 8, we get

$$\omega(g(v))\geq\frac{\mathcal{E}_{n-2}^{\alpha}(g(v))}{\mathcal{E}_{n-2}^{\alpha}(g(u))}\omega(g(u))\text{ for }v\leq u. \quad (28)$$

From (17) and (28), (16) becomes

$$\frac{\omega(g(u))}{F(\omega(g(u)))}\geq\mathcal{E}_{n-2}(g(u))F(\mathcal{E}_{n-2}^{-\alpha}(g(u)))\int_{u_1}^{g(u)}\mathcal{Q}(v)F(\mathcal{E}_{n-2}^{\alpha}(g(v)))\mathrm{d}v$$
$$+F(\mathcal{E}_{n-2}^{-\alpha}(g(u)))\int_{g(u)}^{u}\mathcal{E}_{n-2}(v)\mathcal{Q}(v)F(\mathcal{E}_{n-2}^{\alpha}(g(v)))\mathrm{d}v$$
$$+F\left(\mathcal{E}_{n-2}^{-1}(g(u))\right)\int_{u}^{\infty}\mathcal{E}_{n-2}(v)\mathcal{Q}(v)F(\mathcal{E}_{n-2}(g(v)))\mathrm{d}v,$$

which contradicts (27). □

Theorem 4. *Assume that (8), (22) and (27) hold. Then, Equation (4) is oscillatory.*

It is also possible to continue to improve the monotonic property of the function $\omega/\mathcal{E}_{n-2}$ and then use it in the oscillation criteria.

Notation 3. *Since $\mathcal{E}_{n-2}(u)$ is decreasing, there is a $\epsilon>1$ such that*

$$\frac{[\mathcal{E}_{n-2}\circ g]}{\mathcal{E}_{n-2}}\geq\epsilon.$$

Let $\alpha_0\in(0,1)$, we define $\alpha_0=\alpha$

$$\alpha_{k+1}:=\alpha_0\frac{\epsilon^{\alpha_k}}{1-\alpha_k},$$

for $k=0,1,\ldots$.

Lemma 10. *Suppose that $x\in\mathcal{P}_s$ and ω satisfies case* (D_3) *in Lemma 1. Suppose also that there is $m\in\mathbb{N}$ such that $\alpha_k\in(0,1)$ and $\alpha_{k-1}<\alpha_k$ for $k=0,1,\ldots,m$. If (8) holds, then the function $\omega/\mathcal{E}_{n-2}^{m}$ is decreasing, and also converges to zero as $u\to\infty$.*

Proof. From Lemma 8, we have that $\omega/\mathcal{E}_{n-2}^{\alpha}$ is decreasing and also converges to zero as $u\to\infty$. We will prove the required when $m=1$.

From Lemma 4, we have that (7) holds for $u \geq u_1 \geq u_0$. Integrating (7) from u_1 to u and using the fact that $\omega / \mathcal{E}_{n-2}^{\alpha}$ is decreasing, we get

$$\begin{aligned}
a(u)\omega^{(n-1)}(u) &\leq a(u_1)\omega^{(n-1)}(u_1) - \int_{u_1}^{u} \mathcal{Q}(v)\omega(g(v))\mathrm{d}v \\
&\leq a(u_1)\omega^{(n-1)}(u_1) - \int_{u_1}^{u} \mathcal{Q}(v)\frac{\mathcal{E}_{n-2}^{\alpha}(g(v))}{\mathcal{E}_{n-2}^{\alpha}(v)}\omega(v)\mathrm{d}v \\
&\leq a(u_1)\omega^{(n-1)}(u_1) - \frac{\omega(u)}{\mathcal{E}_{n-2}^{\alpha}(u)}\int_{u_1}^{u} \mathcal{Q}(v)\mathcal{E}_{n-2}^{\alpha}(g(v))\mathrm{d}v \\
&\leq a(u_1)\omega^{(n-1)}(u_1) - \frac{\omega(u)}{\mathcal{E}_{n-2}^{\alpha}(u)}\int_{u_1}^{u} \frac{\alpha\mathcal{E}_{n-3}(v)}{\mathcal{E}_{n-2}^{2-\alpha}(v)}\frac{\mathcal{E}_{n-2}^{\alpha}(g(v))}{\mathcal{E}_{n-2}^{\alpha}(v)}\mathrm{d}v \\
&\leq a(u_1)\omega^{(n-1)}(u_1) - \alpha\epsilon^{\alpha}\frac{\omega(u)}{\mathcal{E}_{n-2}^{\alpha}(u)}\int_{u_1}^{u} \frac{\mathcal{E}_{n-3}(v)}{\mathcal{E}_{n-2}^{2-\alpha}(v)}\mathrm{d}v \\
&\leq a(u_1)\omega^{(n-1)}(u_1) - \frac{\alpha\epsilon^{\alpha}}{1-\alpha}\frac{\omega(u)}{\mathcal{E}_{n-2}^{\alpha}(u)}\left(\frac{1}{\mathcal{E}_{n-2}^{1-\alpha}(u)} - \frac{1}{\mathcal{E}_{n-2}^{1-\alpha}(u_1)}\right). \qquad (29)
\end{aligned}$$

It follows from Lemma 5 that $\frac{\omega(u)}{\mathcal{E}_{n-2}^{\alpha}(u)} \to 0$ as $u \to \infty$. Hence, (29) becomes

$$a(u)\omega^{(n-1)}(u) \leq -\frac{\alpha\epsilon^{\alpha}}{1-\alpha}\frac{\omega(u)}{\mathcal{E}_{n-2}(u)}.$$

The remainder of the proof has not been considered because it is identical to the proof of Lemma 8. □

Theorem 5. *Assume that (8) and (22) hold. If there is $m \in \mathbb{N}$ such that $\alpha_k \in (0,1)$ and $\alpha_{k-1} < \alpha_k$ for $k = 0, 1, \ldots, m$, and*

$$\begin{aligned}
\limsup_{u\to\infty} \Bigg[&\mathcal{E}_{n-2}(g(u))F\left(\mathcal{E}_{n-2}^{-\alpha_m}(g(u))\right)\int_{u_1}^{g(u)} \mathcal{Q}(v)F(\mathcal{E}_{n-2}^{\alpha_m}(g(v)))\mathrm{d}v \\
&+ F\left(\mathcal{E}_{n-2}^{-\alpha_m}(g(u))\right)\int_{g(u)}^{u} \mathcal{E}_{n-2}(v)\mathcal{Q}(v)F(\mathcal{E}_{n-2}^{\alpha_m}(g(v)))\mathrm{d}v \\
&+ F\left(\mathcal{E}_{n-2}^{-1}(g(u))\right)\int_{u}^{\infty} \mathcal{E}_{n-2}(v)\mathcal{Q}(v)F(\mathcal{E}_{n-2}(g(v)))\mathrm{d}v\Bigg] > K,
\end{aligned}$$

then Equation (4) is oscillatory.

5. Conclusions

Our aim in this article was to extend the approach taken in [14] to neutral equations and also to the non-canonical case. The study of the non-canonical case contains more analytical difficulties than the canonical case due to the possibility of the existence of positive decreasing solutions.

We deduced some asymptotic and monotonic properties of the positive solutions whose corresponding function is in class $\mathcal{P}_s$. Then, we created new oscillation parameters depending on the inferred characteristics. In addition, we iteratively derived these properties, so that it allows them to be applied more than once in the case of failure at the beginning. The results obtained in this article are characterized by the fact that they do not require the existence of unknown functions, unlike the results in [26] that require this. In addition, our results do not need the conditions $h \circ g = g \circ h$ and h is nondecreasing, which are necessary conditions for the results in [28].

Extending our results in this study to the nonlinear case of the investigated equation would be very interesting. This is due to many analytical difficulties that must be addressed to obtain improved monotonic properties in the nonlinear case.

Author Contributions: Conceptualization, B.A. and O.M.; methodology, B.A. and O.M.; investigation, B.A. and O.M.; writing—original draft preparation, B.A. and O.M.; writing—review and editing, B.A. and O.M. All authors have read and agreed to the published version of the manuscript.

Funding: This research received no external funding.

Data Availability Statement: Not applicable.

Acknowledgments: The authors extend their appreciation to the Deputyship for Research & Innovation, Ministry of Education in Saudi Arabia for funding this research work through the project number RI-44-0820.

Conflicts of Interest: The authors declare no conflict of interest.

References

1. Ladde, G.; Lakshmikantham, S.V.; Zhang, B.G. *Oscillation Theory of Differential Equations with Deviating Arguments*; Marcel Dekker: New York, NY, USA, 1987.
2. Gyori, I.; Ladas, G. *Oscillation Theory of Delay Differential Equations with Applications*; Clarendon Press: Oxford, UK, 1991.
3. Erbe, L.H.; Kong, Q.; Zhong, B.G. *Oscillation Theory for Functional Differential Equations*; Marcel Dekker: New York, NY, USA, 1995.
4. Agarwal, R.P.; Grace, S.R.; O'Regan, D. *Oscillation Theory for Second Order Linear, Half-Linear, Superlinear and Sublinear Dynamic Equations*; Kluwer Academic Publishers: Dordrecht, The Netherlands, 2002.
5. Agarwal, R.P.; Grace, S.R.; O'Regan, D. *Oscillation Theory for Second Order Dynamic Equations*; Series in Mathematical Analysis and Applications; Taylor & Francis Ltd.: London, UK, 2003; Volume 5.
6. Agarwal, R.P.; Bohner, M.; Li, W.-T. Nonoscillation and oscillation: Theory for functional differential equations. In *Monographs and Textbooks in Pure and Applied Mathematics*; Marcel Dekker, Inc.: New York, NY, USA, 2004; Volume 267.
7. Tunç, C.; Tunç, O. On the boundedness and integration of non-oscillatory solutions of certain linear differential equations of second order. *J. Adv. Res.* **2016**, *7*, 165–168. [CrossRef] [PubMed]
8. Graef, J.R.; Beldjerd, D.; Remili, M. Some New Stability, Boundedness, and Square Integrability Conditions for Third-Order Neutral Delay Differential Equations. *Commun. Math. Anal.* **2019**, *22*, 76–89.
9. Saker, S. *Oscillation Theory of Delay Differential and Difference Equations: Second and Third Orders*; LAP Lambert Academic Publishing: Saarbruecken, Germany, 2010.
10. Baculíková, B. Oscillation of second-order nonlinear noncanonical differential equations with deviating argument. *Appl. Math. Lett.* **2019**, *91*, 68–75. [CrossRef]
11. Baculíková, B. Oscillatory behavior of the second order noncanonical differential equations. *Electron. J. Qual. Theory Differ. Equ.* **2019**, *2019*, 1–11. [CrossRef]
12. Džurina, J.; Jadlovská, I. A note on oscillation of second-order delay differential equations. *Appl. Math. Lett.* **2017**, *69*, 126–132. [CrossRef]
13. Džurina, J.; Jadlovská, I. A sharp oscillation result for second-order half-linear noncanonical delay differential equations. *Electron. J. Qual. Theory Differ. Equ.* **2020**, 2020, 1–14. [CrossRef]
14. Koplatadze, R.; Kvinkadze, G.; Stavroulakis, I.P. Properties A and B of n-th order linear differential equations with deviating argument. *Georgian Math. J.* **1999**, *6*, 553–566. [CrossRef]
15. Agarwal, R.P.; Grace, S.R.; O'Regan, D. Oscillation criteria for certain nth order differential equations with deviating arguments. *J. Math. Appl. Anal.* **2001**, *262*, 601–622. [CrossRef]
16. Bazighifan, O.; Minhos, F.; Moaaz, O. Sufficient conditions for oscillation of fourth-order neutral differential equations with distributed deviating arguments. *Axioms* **2020**, *9*, 39. [CrossRef]
17. Grace, S.R. Oscillation theorems for nth-order differential equations with deviating arguments. *J. Math. Appl. Anal.* **1984**, *101*, 268–296. [CrossRef]
18. Moaaz, O.; Kumam, P.; Bazighifan, O. On the oscillatory behavior of a class of fourth-order nonlinear differential equation. *Symmetry* **2020**, *12*, 524. [CrossRef]
19. Xu, Z.; Xia, Y. Integral averaging technique and oscillation of certain even order delay differential equations. *J. Math. Appl. Anal.* **2004**, *292*, 238–246. [CrossRef]
20. Zhang, B. G. Oscillation of even order delay differential equations. *J. Math. Appl. Anal.* **1987**, *127*, 140–150. [CrossRef]
21. Baculíková, B.; Džurina, J.; Graef, J.R. On the oscillation of higher-order delay differential equations. *J. Math. Sci.* **2012**, *187*, 387–400. [CrossRef]
22. Moaaz, O.; Cesarano, C.; Askar, S. Asymptotic and oscillatory properties of noncanonical delay differential equations. *Fractal Fract.* **2021**, *5*, 259. [CrossRef]
23. Zhang, C.; Agarwal, R.P.; Bohner, M.; Li, T. New results for oscillatory behavior of even-order half-linear delay differential equations. *Appl. Math. Lett.* **2013**, *26*, 179–183. [CrossRef]
24. Moaaz, O.; Muhib, A. New oscillation criteria for nonlinear delay differential equations of fourth-order. *Appl. Math. Comput.* **2020**, *377*, 125192. [CrossRef]

25. Muhib, A.; Moaaz, O.; Cesarano, C.; Alsallami, S.A.M.; Abdel-Khalek, S.; Elamin, A.E.A.M.A. New monotonic properties of positive solutions of higher-order delay differential equations and their applications. *Mathematics* **2022**, *10*, 1786. [CrossRef]
26. Li, T.; Rogovchenko, Y.V. Asymptotic behavior of higher-order quasilinear neutral differential equations. *Abstr. Appl. Anal.* **2014**, *2014*, 395368. [CrossRef]
27. Ramos, H.; Moaaz, O.; Muhib, A.; Awrejcewicz, J. More Effective Results for Testing Oscillation of Non-Canonical NDDEs. *Mathematics* **2021**, *9*, 1114. [CrossRef]
28. Elabbasy, E.M.; Moaaz, O.; Ramos, H.; Muhib, A. Improved criteria for oscillation of noncanonical neutral differential equations of even order. *Adv. Differ. Equ.* **2021,** *2021*, 412. [CrossRef]
29. Bohner, M.; Grace, S.R.; Jadlovská, I. Sharp oscillation criteria for second-order neutral delay differential equations. *Math. Methods Appl. Sci.* **2020**, *43*, 10041–10053. [CrossRef]
30. Bohner, M.; Grace, S.R.; Jadlovská, I. Sharp results for oscillation of second-order neutral delay differential equations. *Electron. J. Qual. Theory Differ. Equ.* **2023**, 1–23. [CrossRef]
31. Džurina, J.; Grace, S.R.; Jadlovská, I.; Li, T. Oscillation criteria for second-order Emden–Fowler delay differential equations with a sublinear neutral term. *Math. Nachrichten* **2020**, *293*, 910–922. [CrossRef]
32. Moaaz, O.; Albalawi, W. Asymptotic behavior of solutions of even-order di§erential equations with several delays. *Fractal Fract .* **2022**, *6*, 87. [CrossRef]
33. Agarwal, R.P.; Grace, S.R.; O'Regan, D. *Oscillation Theory for Difference and Functional Differential Equations*; Kluwer Academic: Dordrecht, The Netherlands, 2000.
34. Philos, C.G. On the existence of nonoscillatory solutions tending to zero at ∞ for differential equations with positive delay. *Arch. Math.* **1981**, *36*, 168–178. [CrossRef]

mathematics

MDPI

Article

Relaxation Oscillations in the Logistic Equation with Delay and Modified Nonlinearity

Alexandra Kashchenko *,† and Sergey Kashchenko †

Regional Scientific and Educational Mathematical Center «Centre of Integrable Systems», P. G. Demidov Yaroslavl State University, 150003 Yaroslavl, Russia
* Correspondence: a.kashchenko@uniyar.ac.ru
† These authors contributed equally to this work.

Abstract: We consider the dynamics of a logistic equation with delays and modified nonlinearity, the role of which is to bound the values of solutions from above. First, the local dynamics in the neighborhood of the equilibrium state are studied using standard bifurcation methods. Most of the paper is devoted to the study of nonlocal dynamics for sufficiently large values of the 'Malthusian' coefficient. In this case, the initial equation is singularly perturbed. The research technique is based on the selection of special sets in the phase space and further study of the asymptotics of all solutions from these sets. We demonstrate that, for sufficiently large values of the Malthusian coefficient, a 'stepping' of periodic solutions is observed, and their asymptotics are constructed. In the case of two delays, it is established that there is attractor in the phase space of the initial equation, whose dynamics are described by special nonlinear finite-dimensional mapping.

Keywords: dynamics; delay; asymptotics; stability; Andronov–Hopf bifurcation; normal forms; relaxation oscillations

MSC: 34K25; 34K18

Citation: Kashchenko, A.; Kashchenko, S. Relaxation Oscillations in the Logistic Equation with Delay and Modified Nonlinearity. *Mathematics* **2023**, *11*, 1699. https://doi.org/10.3390/math11071699

Academic Editor: Carmen Chicone

Received: 28 February 2023
Revised: 27 March 2023
Accepted: 31 March 2023
Published: 2 April 2023

1. Introduction

The logistic equation with delay is the name given to the equation

$$\dot{u} = \lambda[1 - u(t-T)]u. \tag{1}$$

Being a natural extension of the classical logistic equation, it arises in many applied problems, but most of all it is used in problems of mathematical ecology (see, for example [1–15]). The value u describes the dynamics of changes in the number of specimens in the population or density of an isolated biological population living in a homogeneous environment. Therefore, it makes sense to consider only non-negative solutions of Equation (1). We note that the solution of Equation (1) with a non-negative initial function $\varphi(s) \in C_{[-T,0]}$ specified at some value t_0 (i.e., $u(t_0+s) = \varphi(s)$) remains non-negative for all $t > t_0$. The coefficient λ is called the Malthusian coefficient of linear growth and the parameter $T > 0$ is called the delay time. It is associated with the age of animal units capable of procreation in the corresponding population.

The dynamic properties of the solutions of Equation (1) are well understood. Under the condition $\lambda T \le \frac{\pi}{2}$, the equilibrium state $u_0 \equiv 1$ is asymptotically stable, while for $\lambda T > \frac{\pi}{2}$ it is unstable and the periodic solution $U_0(t,\lambda)$ is stable. Under the condition $0 < \lambda T - \frac{\pi}{2} \ll 1$, we obtain its asymptotics on the Andronov–Hopf bifurcation theory application basis (see, for example [16–18]). It is shown in [7] that for sufficiently large λ the periodic solution $U_0(t,\lambda)$ has a pronounced relaxation structure. There is a single wavelet of this function on the segment of the period $T_0(\lambda)$ length. The duration of the wavelet is close to the value of T and the period $T_0(\lambda)$ is equal to $(\lambda T)^{-1}\exp(\lambda T(1+o(1)))$. It is important to note the asymptotic equalities.

$$\max_t U_0(t,\lambda) = \exp(\lambda T(1+o(1))), \tag{2}$$

$$\min_t U_0(t,\lambda) = \exp(-\exp(\lambda T)(1+o(1))). \tag{3}$$

We also note results of [19,20], in which important results on the dynamics of logistic equations with delay and diffusion are obtained, [21], where a randomized non-autonomous logistic equation is discussed, and Ref. [22], where interesting results were obtained for an equation in which the delay itself is a function of u.

Due to the applied significance, it is of interest to study equations with various types of nonlinearity. By virtue of biological meaning, solutions must remain positive. Similar to this restriction, it is natural to require solutions to be bounded not only from below, but also from above. In addition, unlimited asymptotic growth, as in the case of Equation (1), is not always convenient, for example, for describing the dynamics of changes in the number of species.

In this paper we study the dynamics of the new model—the logistic equation with delay and modified nonlinearity

$$\dot{u} = \lambda[1-u(t-T)]u(A-u), \quad A>1. \tag{4}$$

The main difference between the solutions of Equation (4) and the solutions of Equation (1) is that under the condition $0 \le \varphi(s) \le A$ the inequalities

$$0 \le u(t,\varphi) \le A$$

hold for the solution $u(t,\varphi)$ of Equation (4) with the initial condition $u(t_0+s)=\varphi(s)$ as $t>t_0$. Thus, the use of the factor $(A-u)$ on the right-hand side of Equation (4) leads to the restriction $u(t,\varphi) \le A$ for the solutions of Equation (4). Therefore, the solutions of Equation (4) (in contrast to the solutions of Equation (1)) do not take asymptotically large values for large values of λ.

Model (4) is quite complex. At the moment, there are no analytical methods that would allow for absolutely any values of the parameters λ, T, and A to obtain results on the qualitative and quantitative behavior of all solutions of Equation (4) on the entire positive semiaxis $t \in [0,+\infty)$. In addition, numerical methods are also not very effective in the study of such models, since, firstly, it is impossible to enumerate all possible initial conditions in order to draw a qualitative conclusion about the dynamics of the model, and secondly, for some values of the model parameters, the solutions are very close will approach zero (see Sections 3 and 4), so a relatively small error in the calculations can lead to a completely wrong result.

Therefore, in the paper, the research is carried out by analytical (asymptotic) methods. At present, the most effective among them are the methods of the theory of bifurcations in the study in the neighbourhood of the equilibrium state and the methods of a large parameter (for $\lambda \gg 1$) in the study of nonlocal processes. Large parameter methods are based on the use of singular perturbation theory, but even in cases where the λ parameter (Malthusian coefficient in model Equation (4)) is not large enough, nevertheless, conclusions can be drawn about the trends in fluctuations with an increase in this parameter. In addition, we point out that the relaxation nature of the oscillations obtained for model Equation (4) in the case of sufficiently large values of parameter λ corresponds to ideas about the dynamic behavior of population density dynamics in mathematical ecology [4,11].

The paper is organized as follows. In Section 2, the conditions for the parameter λ are found using the methods of bifurcation analysis. Under them, the Andronov–Hopf bifurcation occurs in Equation (4) and a cycle arises from the equilibrium state.

The main content of Section 3 and all subsequent sections is devoted to the study of the solutions of Equation (4) on the interval $t \in [0, +\infty)$ provided that the parameter λ is sufficiently large:

$$\lambda \gg 1. \tag{5}$$

In this case, the equation under consideration is singularly perturbed. After dividing by the left-hand and right-hand parts of Equation (4) by λ, we obtain an equation with a small parameter at the derivative:

$$\lambda^{-1}\dot{u} = [1 - u(t-T)]u(A-u). \tag{6}$$

However, the reduced equation

$$0 = [1 - u(t-T)]u(A-u)$$

does not describe the behavior of the Equation (6) solutions (except the simplest equilibrium states) under the condition (5).

It is important to mention that from a computational point of view, this problem is difficult, since the relaxation solution approaches A and 0 very closely, so even a small error in the calculations will take us out of the class of solutions under consideration.

Therefore, a special analytical research method was developed. First, we briefly describe it for the simplest case, for studying slowly oscillating solutions. Recall that slowly oscillating solutions are those solutions for which the time distance between adjacent roots of the equation $u(t) = 1$ is greater than the delay time. Consider Equation (6). Denote by $S \subset C_{[-T,0]}$ the set of all such functions $\varphi(s) \in S \quad (s \in [-T, 0])$ that satisfy the conditions (see Figure 1).

$$\varphi(0) = 1; \quad 0 \leq \varphi(s) \leq \exp\left(\frac{\lambda}{2}s\right). \tag{7}$$

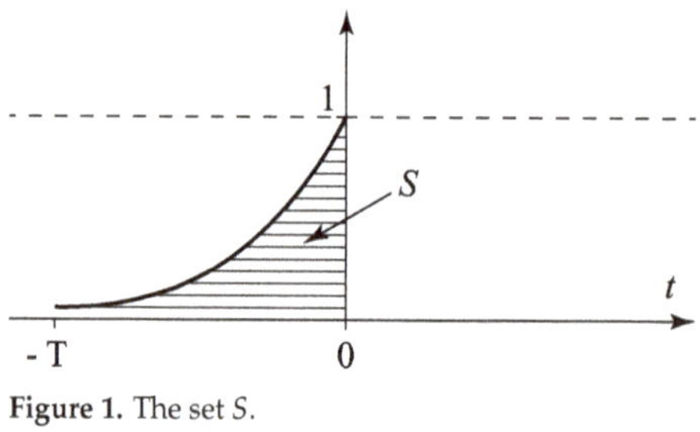

Figure 1. The set S.

Denote by $u(t, \varphi)$ a solution of (6) with initial condition $\varphi(s)$:$u(s, \varphi) = \varphi(s)$ $(s \in [-T, 0])$. The method of steps will be used: for $t \in [0, T]$, taking into account the initial function $\varphi(s)$, to determine $u(t, \varphi)$ we obtain an ordinary differential equation of the first order. It is easy to find the asymptotics of this solution as $\lambda \to \infty$ on the indicated interval. Then we consider $u(t, \varphi)$ on the interval $[T, 2T]$, on which we also obtain a first-order ordinary differential equation, and find the asymptotics of the solutions. After that, we will carry out the same actions on the segment $[2T, 3T]$, then on the segment $[3T, 4T]$, and so on.

In Section 3.1 we study the asymptotic behavior at $\lambda \to \infty$ of all solutions $u(t, \varphi)$ with initial conditions from S. In particular, the asymptotics of the first two positive roots $t_1(\varphi)$ and $t_2(\varphi)$ of the equation $u(t, \varphi) = 1$ will be found. The main conclusion is that after the time interval $t_2(\varphi)$ the solution $u(t, \varphi)$ will again fall on the set S:$u(s + t_2(\varphi), \varphi) \in S$. This gives reason to introduce the Π operator:

$$\Pi(\varphi(s)) = u(t_2(\varphi) + s, \varphi)$$

and justify the inclusion $\Pi S \subset S$. From this and the well-known results of functional analysis [23], we conclude that S has a fixed point $\varphi_0(s)$ of the operator Π: $\Pi(\varphi_0(s)) = \varphi_0(s)$.

Then the function $u_0(t) = u(t, \varphi_0)$ is periodic with period $t_2(\varphi_0)$. In Section 3.1, asymptotic formulas for $u_0(t)$ will be given.

In Section 3.2 we investigate the asymptotic behavior of rapidly oscillating solutions. As a set of initial functions, we consider the set $S(\tau_1, \tau_2)$ depending on two parameters τ_1 and τ_2. It is shown schematically in Figure 3. In Section 3.2, a rigorous description of this set is given and the asymptotic behavior of all solutions (6) with initial conditions from $S(\tau_1, \tau_2)$ is studied. Again, by $t_1(\varphi)$ and $t_2(\varphi)$ we denote the first and second positive roots of the equation $u(t, \varphi) = 1$. We again introduce the operator Π: $\Pi(\varphi(s)) = u(t_2(\varphi) + s, \varphi)$ and it will be shown that up to $o(1)$ the inclusion $\Pi(\varphi(s)) \in S(\bar{\tau}_1, \bar{\tau}_2)$, where $\bar{\tau}_{1,2}$ are explicitly expressed in terms of $\tau_{1,2}$. This gives grounds to take the function $u(s + t_2(\varphi), \varphi)$ as the initial one and pass to the iteration process. It is possible to find a fixed point (τ_1^0, τ_2^0) and a function $\varphi_0(s) \in S(\tau_1^0, \tau_2^0)$ such that the solution $u_0(t, \varphi_0)$ will be periodic with period $t_2(\varphi_0)$. It is important to note that the rapidly oscillating periodic solutions found in this way are unstable.

The results of Section 4 are more interesting. We consider equations with two delays

$$\dot{u} = \lambda[1 - \alpha u(t - T) - (1 - \alpha)u(t - h)]u(A - u), \tag{8}$$

where $\alpha \in (0, 1)$ and $h < T$.

It is commonly supposed that the use of two (or more) delays allows one to take into account the influence of the population age structure on the dynamics of population level changes [24–27].

One succeeded to clearly describe the nonlocal dynamic properties of Equation (8) under the condition (5). In contrast to the results of the Section 3, the relaxation step solutions for (8) can be stable.

We note that for the simpler logistic equation with two delays

$$\dot{u} = \lambda[1 - \alpha u(t - T) - (1 - \alpha)u(t - h)]u \quad (\alpha \in (0, 1), h < T) \tag{9}$$

the results were obtained in Refs. [7] as $\lambda \gg 1$. It follows from them that for sufficiently large λ in (9) there is an orbitally stable periodic solution which is similar in appearance to the solution of Equation (1) with the same initial conditions, and the asymptotic representation (2) holds for it.

2. Andronov–Hopf Bifurcations in Equations with One Delay

We shall fix the parameters λ_0, A_0 and T_0 so that the following equality is fulfilled:

$$\lambda_0(A_0 - 1)T_0 = \frac{\pi}{2}. \tag{10}$$

Lemma 1. *Suppose that in Equation* (4)

$$\lambda(A - 1)T < \frac{\pi}{2}. \tag{11}$$

Then the equilibrium state $u_0 \equiv 1$ *is asymptotically stable.*

Proof. To prove this statement we linearize (4) on u_0 and consider the characteristic quasi-polynomial

$$\mu = -\lambda(A - 1)\exp(-\mu T). \tag{12}$$

Under the condition (11) all its roots have negative real parts. From this, and from known results (see Ref. [5]) on the stability in the first approximation, the proof of Lemma 1 follows. □

Next we introduce a small positive parameter ε:

$$0 < \varepsilon \ll 1, \tag{13}$$

and assume that in Equation (4), for certain constant λ_1, A_1 and T_1, the following relations are fulfilled:

$$\lambda = \lambda_0 + \varepsilon\lambda_1, \quad A = A_0 + \varepsilon A_1, \quad T = T_0 + \varepsilon T_1. \tag{14}$$

We set

$$b = \left(1 + \frac{\pi^2}{4}\right)^{-1}\left[\left(\frac{\pi}{2} + i\right)(\lambda_1(A_0 - 1) + \lambda_0 A_1) + \lambda_0^2(A_0 - 1)^2 T_1\left(1 - i\frac{\pi}{2}\right)\right], \tag{15}$$

$$d = -\lambda_0\left(1 + \frac{\pi^2}{4}\right)^{-1}\left[\frac{\pi}{2} + i + \frac{3(A_0 - 2)^2}{5(A_0 - 1)}\left(\frac{\pi}{2} - 1 + i(\frac{\pi}{2} + 1)\right)\right], \tag{16}$$

$$\omega = \pi(2T_0)^{-1}, \tag{17}$$

$$\begin{aligned} \xi_0(\tau) &= \xi_0 \exp(i\psi\tau), \quad \psi = \operatorname{Im} b + \xi_0^2 \operatorname{Im} d, \\ \xi_0 &= \left[\left(\tfrac{\pi}{2}(\lambda_1(A_0 - 1) + \lambda_0 A_1) + \lambda_0^2(A_0 - 1)^2 T_1\right)\lambda_0^{-1}\left(\tfrac{\pi}{2} + \tfrac{3(A_0-2)^2}{5(A_0-1)}\left(\tfrac{\pi}{2} - 1\right)\right)^{-1}\right]^{\frac{1}{2}}. \end{aligned} \tag{18}$$

Theorem 1. *Let conditions (13)–(15), (17), and (18) hold.*

1. Let $\operatorname{Re} b < 0$. *Then all solutions of Equation (4) with initial conditions from a sufficiently small (and independent of* ε*) neighbourhood of the equilibrium state* $u \equiv 1$ *tend to 1 as* $t \to \infty$.

2. Let

$$\operatorname{Re} b > 0. \tag{19}$$

Then for all sufficiently small ε *Equation (4) has in the neighbourhood of the unit equilibrium state a stable periodic solution* $u_0(t, \varepsilon)$ *for which the following asymptotic equality is fulfilled:*

$$u_0(t, \varepsilon) = 1 + \varepsilon^{1/2}[\xi_0(\tau)\exp(i\omega t) + \bar{\xi}_0(\tau)\exp(-i\omega t)] + O(\varepsilon),$$

where $\tau = \varepsilon t$.

Proof. Under the condition (10) the quasi-polynomial (12) has a pair of purely imaginary roots $\mu_{1,2} = \pm i\omega$, where the value of ω is given in (17), and all its other roots have negative real parts. Then, under the condition (14), and for all sufficiently small ε, Equation (4) in the neighbourhood of $u \equiv 1$ has (see Refs. [16–18,28]) a two-dimensional stable local invariant integral manifold, on which this equation can be written, to within higher-order terms, in the form of a complex scalar equation—a normal form:

$$\frac{d\xi}{d\tau} = B\xi(\tau) + D\xi(\tau)|\xi(\tau)|^2, \tag{20}$$

where values B and D are to be determined.

In the case $\operatorname{Re} B \neq 0$ and $\operatorname{Re} D \neq 0$ normal form completely determines the behavior of all solutions in a neighbourhood of $u \equiv 1$ (see Refs. [16–18,28]). The solutions of (20) are connected with the solutions of (4) by the relation

$$\begin{aligned} u(t, \varepsilon) =& 1 + \varepsilon^{1/2}[\xi(\tau)\exp(i\omega t) + \bar{\xi}(\tau)\exp(-i\omega t)] + \\ &+ \varepsilon u_2(t, \tau) + \varepsilon^{3/2} u_3(t, \tau) + \ldots \end{aligned} \tag{21}$$

Here, $\tau = \varepsilon t$, the $u_j(t, \tau)$ are periodic in t with period $2\pi/\omega$. Substituting (21) into (4) and collecting coefficients of equal powers of ε, we successively find all the elements appearing there. At $\varepsilon^{1/2}$ we obtain true identity, and collecting coefficients of the first power of ε and taking into account (10), (12), and (17), we find equation for determining the function $u_2(t, \tau)$:

$$\frac{\partial u_2}{\partial t} = -\lambda_0(A_0-1)u_2(t-T_0,\tau) + i\lambda_0(A_0-2)\xi^2(\tau)\exp(2i\omega t) - i\lambda_0(A_0-2)\bar{\xi}^2(\tau)\exp(-2i\omega t).$$

Thus, taking into account that $u_2(t,\tau)$ is periodic in t with period $2\pi/\omega$, we find that

$$u_2(t,\tau) = \frac{(A_0-2)(2-i)}{5(A_0-1)}\xi^2(\tau)\exp(2i\omega t) + \frac{(A_0-2)(2+i)}{5(A_0-1)}\bar{\xi}^2(\tau)\exp(-2i\omega t).$$

Collecting coefficients of $\varepsilon^{3/2}$ we obtain an equation for $u_3(t,\tau)$:

$$\frac{\partial u_3}{\partial t} = -\lambda_0(A_0-1)u_3(t-T_0,\tau) + B_1\exp(i\omega t) + \bar{B}_1\exp(-i\omega t) + B_3\exp(3i\omega t) + \bar{B}_3\exp(-3i\omega t), \tag{22}$$

where B_1 and B_3 are complex values.

From the condition that Equation (22) be solvable in the class of functions periodic in t with period $2\pi/\omega$ (this condition is $B_1 = 0$) we arrive at Equation (20) for the unknown amplitude $\xi(\tau)$, in which $B = b$ and $D = d$ (coefficient b is defined in (15) and the coefficient d is defined in (16)).

Multiplying both sides of Equation (20) by $\bar{\xi}(\tau)$ and taking into account equalities $B = b$ and $D = d$ we obtain a scalar real ordinary differential equation

$$\frac{1}{2}\dot{\rho}(\tau) = \mathrm{Re}\, b\rho(\tau) + \mathrm{Re}\, d\rho^2(\tau), \tag{23}$$

where $\rho(\tau) = |\xi(\tau)|^2$.

We note that $\mathrm{Re}\, d < 0$.

That is why, if $\mathrm{Re}\, b < 0$, all solutions of (23) tend to zero as $t \to +\infty$. Thus, all solutions of (4) from the neighbourhood of $u \equiv 1$ tend to 1 as $t \to +\infty$. This completes the proof of the first part of the Theorem.

Under the condition (19) Equation (20) with $B = b$ and $D = d$ has a stable periodic solution $\xi_0(\tau)=\xi_0\exp(i\psi\tau)$, where the values ξ_0 and ψ are given in (18). Taking into account here the asymptotic equality (21) we have completed the proof of the Theorem. □

It is interesting to note that the bifurcation effect considered here can be realized for fixed $\lambda = \lambda_0$ and $T = T_0$, i.e., for $\lambda_1 = T_1 = 0$, and only upon variation of the parameter A.

3. Step-like Solutions of the Logistic Equation with Delay and with a Restriction on the Nonlinear Function

All statements below refer to the case of $\lambda \to +\infty$. For example, everywhere below $o(1)$ means that the function tends to zero as $\lambda \to +\infty$. Note that the phrase "for all sufficiently large λ" means the existence of a value λ_0 such that for all $\lambda > \lambda_0$ the corresponding assertion is true.

We separately consider questions about slowly and rapidly oscillating solutions of Equation (4).

3.1. Asymptotic Behavior of Slowly Oscillating Solutions

We shall consider the asymptotic behavior of a slowly oscillating relaxation periodic solution of Equation (4).

In (4) it is convenient to replace the time $t \to tT$ and to again denote the product λT by λ. Then Equation (4) takes the form

$$\dot{u} = \lambda[1 - u(t-1)]u(A-u). \tag{24}$$

Let us introduce some notation.

By S we denote the set of all functions $\varphi(s) \in C_{[-1,0]}$ that satisfy the conditions (7).

Let $u(t,\varphi)$ be the solution of (24) with an initial condition $\varphi(s)$ specified at $t=0$, i.e., $u(s,\varphi)=\varphi(s)$ for $s\in[-1,0]$. We shall construct the asymptotics for $\lambda\to\infty$ of all solutions $u(t,\varphi)$ with $\varphi(s)\in S$.

Theorem 2. *For all sufficiently large λ Equation (24) has an asymptotically orbitally stable periodic (with period $T(\lambda)$) solution $u_0(t,\lambda)$, for which $u_0(0,\lambda)=u_0(t_1(\lambda),\lambda)=u_0(t_2(\lambda),\lambda)=1$, where $t_j(\lambda)$ are successive positive roots of the equation $u_0(t,\lambda)=1$, and*

$$\begin{aligned} t_1(\lambda) &= 1+(A-1)^{-1}+o(1), \\ T(\lambda) &= t_2(\lambda)=A+1+(A-1)^{-1}+o(1). \end{aligned}$$

For every t from the intervals $(0,t_1(\lambda))$ and $(t_1(\lambda),t_2(\lambda))$, respectively, the following equalities are fulfilled:

$$u_0(t,\lambda)=\begin{cases} A+o(1), & t\in(0,t_1(\lambda)), \\ o(1), & t\in(t_1(\lambda),t_2(\lambda)). \end{cases}$$

Proof. We use the following formula for the solutions $u(t,\varphi)$ of Equation (24):

$$\begin{aligned} u(t,\varphi) =& Au(\tau,\varphi)\exp\left(\lambda A\int_\tau^t(1-u(s-1,\varphi))ds\right)\cdot \\ &\left[A-u(\tau,\varphi)+u(\tau,\varphi)\exp\left(\lambda A\int_\tau^t(1-u(s-1,\varphi))ds\right)\right]^{-1}, \end{aligned} \tag{25}$$

where t and τ are arbitrary values such that $0<\tau<t$.

We shall formulate some simple statements:

Lemma 2. *Let $t\in(0,1]$. Then*

$$u(t,\varphi)=A\Big[1+(A-1)\exp\Big(-\lambda A(1+o(1))t\Big)\Big]^{-1}. \tag{26}$$

The proof of (26) follows from (25) with $\tau=0$.

Setting $\tau=1$ in (25), we immediately arrive at the following statement:

Lemma 3. *Let $t\in(1,1+(A-1)^{-1}+\delta]$, where $\delta>0$ is some small but fixed value. Then*

$$u(t,\varphi)=A\Big[1+(A-1)\exp\Big(\lambda A\big[(A-1)(1+o(1))(t-1)-1\big]\Big)\Big]^{-1}. \tag{27}$$

Below, we denote by $t_1(\varphi),t_2(\varphi),\dots$ the first, second, ... positive roots of the equation $u(t,\varphi)=1$.

From (27) we arrive at the conclusion that the value $t_1(\varphi)$ exists and

$$\begin{aligned} t_1(\varphi) &= 1+(A-1)^{-1}+o(1), \\ u(t,\varphi) &= A+o(1) \text{ for every } t\in(0,t_1(\varphi)), \\ u(t,\varphi) &= o(1) \text{ for every } t\in(t_1(\varphi),t_1(\varphi)+1). \end{aligned}$$

The last equality is true, because formula (27) holds on the interval $(t_1(\varphi),t_1(\varphi)+1)$.

Then we construct asymptotics of solution on the interval $t>t_1(\varphi)+1$. We set $\tau=t_1(\varphi)$ and take into account that $u(s-1)=A+o(1)$ on the interval $s\in(t_1(\varphi),t_1(\varphi)+1)$. We use equality $u(s-1)=o(1)$ for $t_1(\varphi)+1<s<t$. It follows from formula (25) that this equality holds for all $t>t_1(\varphi)+1$ while

$$\int_{t_1(\varphi)}^t(1-u(s-1,\varphi))ds<0.$$

We obtain the following result:

Lemma 4. *For $t \in [2+(A-1)^{-1}, A+1+(A-1)^{-1}+\delta]$, where $\delta > 0$ is some small but fixed value*

$$u(t,\varphi) = A\exp\Big(\lambda A\Big(1-A+t-(2+(A-1)^{-1})+o(1)\Big)\Big)\cdot$$
$$\Big[A-1+\exp\Big(\lambda A\Big(1-A+t-(2+(A-1)^{-1}+o(1))\Big)\Big)\Big]^{-1}. \tag{28}$$

From (28) the existence of $t_2(\varphi)$ and the asymptotic equalities

$$t_2(\varphi) = A+1+(A-1)^{-1}+o(1)$$

and

$$u(t,\varphi) = o(1) \text{ for } t \in (t_1(\varphi), t_2(\varphi))$$

follow.

We introduce the translation along the trajectories operator Π, which links the function $u(s+t_2(\varphi),\varphi)$, $(s \in [-1,0])$ to a function $\varphi(s)$. From the formulas given above we arrive at the conclusion that

$$\Pi(\varphi(s)) = u(s+t_2(\varphi),\varphi) \in S,$$

meaning that $\Pi S \subset S$.

From this and from Ref. [23] it follows that this operator has in S a fixed point $\varphi_0(s)$, i.e.,

$$\Pi(\varphi_0(s)) = \varphi_0(s).$$

This means that the solution $u_0(t,\lambda) = u(t,\varphi_0(s))$ is periodic, with period $T(\lambda) = t_2(\varphi_0(s))$.

The proof of the stability of $u_0(t,\lambda)$ is rather cumbersome. In the more complicated situation discussed in Refs. [7,29] a detailed proof was given of the stability of the solution constructed there, and so we shall not give the proof here. □

It is possible to obtain the asymptotic expansion of $u_0(t,\lambda)$ to any degree of precision. Here we note only that

$$\max_t u_0(t,\lambda) = u_0(1,\lambda) = A[1+(A-1+o(1))\exp(-\lambda A))]^{-1},$$
$$\min_t u_0(t,\lambda) = u_0(t_1(\varphi_0)+1,\lambda) = A(A-1)^{-1}\exp(\lambda A(1-A))(1+o(1)).$$

It is interesting to compare the principal characteristics of $u_0(t,\lambda)$ with the corresponding characteristics of the stable periodic solution $U_0(t,\lambda)$ of Equation (1) for $\lambda \to \infty$. To obtain formulas for $\max_t U_0(t,\lambda)$ and $\min_t U_0(t,\lambda)$ one should replace T by 1 in formulas (2) and (3) (see introduction of this paper and Ref. [7]). In Figure 2 we give graphs of periodic functions $u_0(t,\lambda)$ and $U_0(t,\lambda)$.

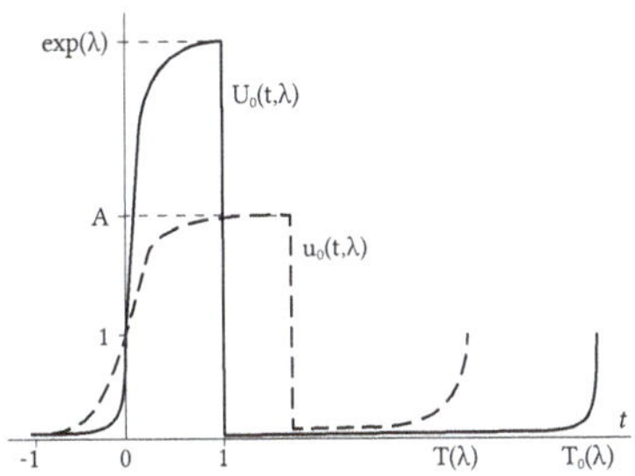

Figure 2. Form of the functions $u_0(t,\lambda)$, $U_0(t,\lambda)$.

3.2. Rapidly Oscillating Solutions of Equation (24)

We shall consider rapidly oscillating solutions of Equation (24).

These are the set of those solutions $u(t, \varphi)$ that become equal to 1 at $t = 0$, and have one "step" on the segment $[-1, 0]$, as shown in Figure 3.

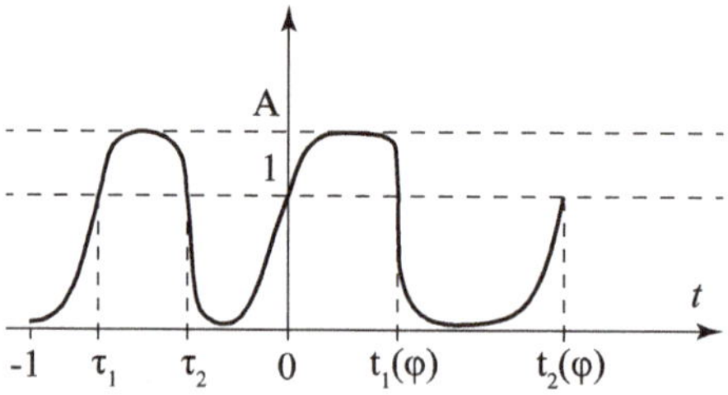

Figure 3. Graph of $\varphi(s) \in S(\tau_1, \tau_2)$ for $s \in [-1, 0]$ and $u(t, \varphi)$ for $t \geq 0$.

We shall describe the corresponding set of initial functions $\varphi(s)$. We arbitrarily fix values τ_1 and τ_2 for which

$$-1 < \tau_1 < \tau_2 < 0.$$

Below, we shall denote by $\delta > 0$ an arbitrary sufficiently small quantity that does not depend on λ and whose precise value is unimportant. We introduce into the analysis three functions $\kappa_{1,2,3}(s, \lambda)$:

$$\kappa_1(s,\lambda) = \exp\big(\lambda\delta(s-\tau_1)\big), \quad s \in [-1, \tau_1];$$
$$\kappa_2(s,\lambda) = \min\Big(A\big[1+(A-1)\exp\big(-\lambda\delta(s-\tau_1)\big)\big]^{-1}, A\big[1+(A-1)\exp(\lambda\delta(s-\tau_2))\big]^{-1}\Big),$$
$$s \in (\tau_1, \tau_2);$$
$$\kappa_3(s,\lambda) = \max\Big(\exp\big(-\lambda\delta(s-\tau_2)\big), \exp(\lambda\delta s)\Big), \quad s \in [\tau_2, 0].$$

Finally, by $S(\tau_1, \tau_2)$ we denote the set of functions $\varphi(s)$ from $C_{[-1,0]}$ that satisfy the conditions

$$\varphi(\tau_1) = \varphi(\tau_2) = \varphi(0) = 1;$$
$$0 \leq \varphi(s) \leq \kappa_1(s,\lambda), \text{ for } s \in [-1, \tau_1];$$
$$\kappa_2(s,\lambda) \leq \varphi(s,\lambda) \leq A, \text{ for } s \in (\tau_1, \tau_2);$$
$$0 \leq \varphi(s) \leq \kappa_3(s,\lambda) \text{ for } s \in [\tau_2, 0].$$

The first and the second positive roots of the equation $u(t, \varphi) = 1$ will be denoted by $t_1(\varphi)$ and $t_2(\varphi)$. We set $t_0 = A(A-1)^{-1}(\tau_1 + 1)$. Asymptotic analysis of $u(t, \varphi)$ for $t \in [0, \tau_2 + 1]$ leads to the following statement:

Lemma 5. *Suppose that the condition*

$$t_0 < \tau_2 + 1 \tag{29}$$

is fulfilled. Then for $t_1(\varphi)$ the following asymptotic (for $\lambda \to \infty$) equality holds:

$$t_1(\varphi) = t_0 + o(1).$$

Proof. As in Theorem 2, when constructing the asymptotics of the solution to Equation (24), we use the formula (25). It follows from (25), that on the segment $t \in [0, \tau_1 + 1]$ solution has form (26). It follows from (26), that on the interval $t \in (0, \tau_1 + 1]$ equality $u(t, \varphi) = A + o(1)$ holds.

On the segment $t \in [\tau_1 + 1, \tau_2 + 1]$ the function $u(t-1,\varphi) = A + o(1)$. That is why on this time segment the solution to Equation (24) satisfies the formula

$$u(t,\varphi) = A\left[1 + (A-1)\exp\left(\lambda A\left[-(\tau_1+1) + (A-1)(t-(\tau_1+1)) + o(1)\right]\right)\right]^{-1}. \quad (30)$$

While $\tau_1 + 1 < t < t_0$, the right-hand side in formula (30) is asymptotically close to A at $\lambda \to +\infty$, and for $t > t_0$ this expression is $o(1)$ at $\lambda \to +\infty$. Therefore, if $t_0 < \tau_2 + 1$, then the value t_0 is asymptotically close to $t_1(\varphi)$ at $\lambda \to +\infty$. □

We note that for every $t \in (0, t_1(\varphi))$ the relation

$$u(t,\varphi) = A + o(1)$$

is fulfilled. Next, for $t \in (t_1(\varphi), \tau_2 + 1)$, we have $u(t,\varphi) = o(1)$, with

$$u(\tau_2+1,\varphi) = A(A-1)^{-1}\exp(-\lambda A(A-1)(\tau_2 + 1 - t_0 + o(1))).$$

We set $t^0 = A(\tau_2 + 1) + (1-A)t_0$. If

$$t^0 < 1, \quad (31)$$

then for $t \in (\tau_2 + 1, t^0 + \delta_1)$ (where δ_1 is some sufficiently small quantity that does not depend on λ) we find that

$$u(t,\varphi) = A/\left[(A-1)\exp\left(-\lambda A\left(t - A(\tau_2+1) - (1-A)t_0 + o(1)\right)\right) + 1\right].$$

From this follow both the existence of $t_2(\varphi)$ and the asymptotic formula $t_2(\varphi) = t^0 + o(1)$.

It is easy to show, that if inequality $t^0 > 1$ holds, then $t_2(\varphi)$ exists, but $t_2(\varphi) - t_1(\varphi) > 1$. So, in the case $t^0 > 1$ we return to the case of the slowly oscillating solutions.

If inequality (31) holds, then as in the preceding section, we introduce into the analysis the operator Π, using the rule $\Pi(\varphi(s)) = u(s + t_2(\varphi), \varphi)$.

Note, that $t_2(\varphi)$ corresponds to 0, $t_1(\varphi)$ corresponds to τ_2, 0 corresponds to τ_1 (see Figure 3). That is why $\bar{\tau}_1 = 0 - t^0 + o(1)$ $\bar{\tau}_2 = t_0 - t^0 + o(1)$.

A consequence of the formulas given here is the following statement:

Theorem 3. *Let the conditions (29) and (31) are fulfilled. Then for all sufficiently large λ for the Equation (24) the following inclusion holds:*

$$\Pi(\varphi(s)) \in S(\bar{\tau}_1 + o(1), \bar{\tau}_2 + o(1)),$$

with

$$\begin{aligned} \bar{\tau}_1 &= A\tau_1 - A\tau_2, \\ \bar{\tau}_2 &= A^2(A-1)^{-1}\tau_1 - A\tau_2 + A(A-1)^{-1}. \end{aligned} \quad (32)$$

The system of Equation (32) is a linear inhomogeneous difference system of equations. After $\bar{\tau}_1$ and $\bar{\tau}_2$ have been determined, the situation is repeated, i.e., while for current values of $\bar{\tau}_1$ and $\bar{\tau}_2$ inequalities (29) and (31) are fulfilled, using (32) we calculate $\bar{\bar{\tau}}_1$ and $\bar{\bar{\tau}}_2$, and so on. This iteration process has a fixed point. By virtue of the fact that the determinant of the linear part in (32) is greater in modulus than 1 the iteration process is divergent, i.e., the equilibrium state in (32) is unstable.

We also remark that the number of periodic solutions of Equation (24) grows without limit as $\lambda \to \infty$. We shall show this. It was established above that for sufficiently large

λ Equation (24) has a slowly oscillating periodic solution $u_0(t,\lambda)$ with period $T(\lambda)$. This solution for each integer n satisfies the equation

$$\dot{u} = \lambda[1 - u(t - 1 - nT(\lambda))]u(A - u). \tag{33}$$

In (33) we replace the time $t \to (1 + nT(\lambda))t$. We then find that the function $u_n(t,\lambda) = u_0((1 + nT(\lambda))t, \lambda)$ is a solution of the equation

$$\dot{u} = \lambda(1 + nT(\lambda))[1 - u(t - 1)]u(A - u). \tag{34}$$

The period of the function $u_n(t,\lambda)$ is equal to $T(\lambda)[1 + nT(\lambda)]^{-1}$. In particular, the unstable periodic solution determinable from the fixed points τ_{10}, τ_{20} of the mapping (32) corresponds to the value $n = 1$ in (34), i.e., to the function $u_1(t,\lambda)$.

We shall consider the more general case when on the segment $[-1,0]$ the initial functions $\varphi(s)$ take the value 1 exactly $(2n+1)$ times:

$$-1 < \tau_1 < \tau_2 < \ldots < \tau_{2n} < 0, \quad \varphi(\tau_j) = \varphi(0) = 1 \quad (j = 1, \ldots, 2n). \tag{35}$$

Following the method proposed above, we arrive at the $2n$-dimensional map

$$\begin{aligned} &\bar{\tau}_1 = \tau_3 - t^0, \quad t^0 = A\tau_2 - A\tau_1, \\ &\bar{\tau}_2 = \tau_4 - t^0, \quad t_0 = A(A-1)^{-1}(\tau_1 + 1), \\ &\ldots \quad \ldots \\ &\bar{\tau}_{2n-1} = -t^0, \quad \bar{\tau}_{2n} = t_0 - t^0. \end{aligned} \tag{36}$$

While we are in the class of initial conditions (conditions (35) are satisfied), we iterate this map. It can be shown that if the equilibrium state in (36) exists, then it is unstable. Since solution $u_n(t, \lambda(1 + nT(\lambda)))$ corresponds to equilibrium state in map (36), then this periodic solution of (24) is unstable.

4. Step-like Solutions of the Equation with Two Delays

We normalize the time $t \to Tt$ and rename λT as λ and hT^{-1} as h $(h < 1)$ again in Equation (8) with two delays. As a result, we arrive at the equation

$$\dot{u} = \lambda[1 - \alpha u(t-1) - (1-\alpha)u(t-h)]u(A - u). \tag{37}$$

4.1. Construction of Slowly Oscillating Solutions

We shall consider the construction of slowly oscillating periodic solutions. We introduce into the analysis a set of initial conditions consisting of all those functions $\varphi(s) \in C_{[-1,0]}$ for which

$$\begin{aligned} &\varphi(0) = 1, \quad 0 \le \varphi(s) \le 1; \\ &\varphi(s) \le \exp(\lambda\delta s), \end{aligned}$$

where $\delta > 0$ is some sufficiently small but fixed value. We investigate the asymptotic form of all solutions $u(t,\varphi)$ with initial conditions from S. We denote by $t_1(\varphi)$ and $t_2(\varphi)$ the first and second positive roots of equation $u(t,\varphi) = 1$. In the case when

$$t_2(\varphi) - 1 > t_1(\varphi), \tag{38}$$

we can determine the translation along the trajectories operator Π: $\Pi(\varphi(s)) = u(s + t_2(\varphi), \varphi)$. From the inequality (38) we find that $\Pi(\varphi(s)) \in S$. If for all $\varphi(s) \in S$ we have $\Pi(\varphi(s)) \in S$, i.e., $\Pi S \subset S$, we can conclude that there exists an attractor with initial conditions from S and that there exists a fixed point $\varphi_0(s) \in S$. The solution $u_0(t,\lambda) = u(t, \varphi_0(s))$ is thereby periodic, with period $T(\lambda) = t_2(\varphi_0)$. For the expressions $t_{1,2}(\varphi)$ it is possible to obtain asymptotic formulas, and this means that we can formulate conditions on the parameters of the problem that ensure fulfilment of the inequality (38). We confine ourselves here to giving only sufficient conditions for fulfilment of this inequality.

Lemma 6. *Let*

$$1-(1-\alpha)A>0 \tag{39}$$

and

$$1-\alpha A<0. \tag{40}$$

Then for all sufficiently large λ for Equation (37) we have the following inclusion:

$$\Pi S\subset S.$$

Proof. For each $t\in(0,h]$ the asymptotic equality

$$u(t,\varphi)=A\big[1+(A-1)\exp\big(-\lambda A(t+o(1))\big)\big]^{-1}$$

holds. But if $t\in[h,1]$, then

$$u(t,\varphi)=A\Big[1+(A-1)\exp\Big(-\lambda A\big((1-(1-\alpha)A)t+h(1-\alpha)A+o(1)\big)\Big)\Big]^{-1}.$$

In particular,

$$u(1,\varphi)=A\Big[1+(A-1)\exp\Big(-\lambda A\big(1-(1-\alpha)A(1-h)+o(1)\big)\Big)\Big]^{-1}.$$

It follows from inequality (39) that $u(t,\varphi)=A+o(1)$ on the segment $t\in[h,1+\delta_1]$, where δ_1 is some positive and small (but independent on λ) constant.

Therefore, for $t>1$ while $u(t,\varphi)=A+o(1)$ formula

$$u(t,\varphi)=A\Big[1+(A-1)\exp\Big(-\lambda A\big(1-(1-\alpha)A(1-h)+(1-A)(t-1)+o(1)\big)\Big)\Big]^{-1}$$

holds. From this formula we find that $t_1(\varphi)$ exists and that

$$t_1(\varphi)=1+\big(1-(1-\alpha)A(1-h)\big)(A-1)^{-1}+o(1),\quad (t_1(\varphi)>1).$$

Starting from $\tau=t_1(\varphi)$ we obtain that on the interval $t\in(t_1(\varphi),t_1(\varphi)+h]$ equality $u(t,\varphi)=o(1)$ holds and that on the segment $t\in[t_1(\varphi)+h,t_1(\varphi)+1]$ formula

$$u(t,\varphi)=A\Big[1+(A-1)\exp\Big(-\lambda A\big((1-A)h+(1-\alpha A)(t-h-t_1(\varphi))+o(1)\big)\Big)\Big]^{-1}$$

is true. It follows from (40) that $u(t,\varphi)=o(1)$ on the segment $t\in[t_1(\varphi)+h,t_1(\varphi)+1]$. Then for $t>t_1(\varphi)+1$ while $u(t,\varphi)=o(1)$ we have the equality

$$u(t,\varphi)=A\Big[1+(A-1)\exp\Big(-\lambda A\big((1-A)h+(1-\alpha A)(1-h)+(t-1-t_1(\varphi))+o(1)\big)\Big)\Big]^{-1}. \tag{41}$$

From Formula (41) we obtain both the existence of $t_2(\varphi)$ and inequality $t_2(\varphi)-t_1(\varphi)>1$.

It follows from this that $\Pi(\varphi(s))\in S$ and $\Pi S\subset S$. The Lemma is proven. □

Theorem 4. *Let inequalities (39) and (40) hold. Then for all sufficiently large λ Equation (37) has an asymptotically orbitally stable slowly oscillating periodic (with period $T(\lambda)$) solution $u_0(t,\lambda)$,* *for which* $u_0(0,\lambda) = u_0(t_1(\lambda),\lambda) = u_0(t_2(\lambda),\lambda) = 1$, *where* $t_j(\lambda)$ *are successive positive roots of the equation* $u_0(t,\lambda) = 1$, *and*

$$t_1(\lambda) = 1 + \big(1 - (1-\alpha)A(1-h)\big)(A-1)^{-1} + o(1),$$
$$T(\lambda) = t_2(\lambda) = 2 + \big(1 - (1-\alpha)A(1-h)\big)(A-1)^{-1} + (A-1)h - (1-\alpha A)(1-h) + o(1).$$

For every t *from the intervals* $(0, t_1(\lambda))$ *and* $(t_1(\lambda), t_2(\lambda))$, *respectively, the following equalities are fulfilled:*

$$u_0(t,\lambda) = \begin{cases} A + o(1), & t \in (0, t_1(\lambda)), \\ o(1), & t \in (t_1(\lambda), t_2(\lambda)). \end{cases}$$

The proof of existence of the periodic solution in Theorem 4 follows from the proof of the Lemma 6, and proof of stability of this solution is rather cumbersome. In the more complicated situation discussed in Refs. [7,29] a detailed proof was given of the stability of the solution constructed there, and so we shall not give the proof here.

4.2. Construction of More Complicated Solutions

We shall consider the construction of rapidly oscillating periodic solutions. We arbitrarily fix τ, satisfying condition

$$\tau \in \Big(\max\big(h, 1 - h - h(1-\alpha A)(A-1)^{-1}\big), 1\Big) \tag{42}$$

and consider the set

$$\begin{aligned} S(\tau) = \{&\varphi(s) \in C_{[-1,0]} : 0 \le \varphi(s) \le A; \\ \varphi(-\tau) &= \varphi(0) = 1, \\ &\varphi(s) \le \max\Big(\exp\big(-\lambda\delta(s+\tau)\big), \exp(\lambda\delta s)\Big), \quad s \in [-\tau, 0]; \\ &\varphi(s) \ge \min\Big(A\big[1 + (A-1)\exp\big(-\lambda\delta(s+1)\big)\big]^{-1}, A\big[1 + (A-1)\exp(\lambda\delta(s+\tau))\big]^{-1}\Big), \\ &\quad s \in [-1, -\tau]\}. \end{aligned}$$

We shall give the final asymptotic formulas for $u(t,\varphi)$ $(\varphi \in S(\tau))$. In them we denote by $g(x)$ the function

$$g(x) = \begin{cases} x, & \text{if } x > 0; \\ 0, & \text{if } x \le 0. \end{cases}$$

We shall assume that the inequalities

$$1 - \alpha A > 0, \quad 1 - (1-\alpha)A < 0, \tag{43}$$

and

$$h < 1 - h \tag{44}$$

are fulfilled. Let $t \in (0, h]$. Then $u(t,\varphi) = A + o(1)$, and

$$u(h,\varphi) = A\Big[1 + (A-1)\exp\Big(-\lambda A\big[h - \alpha A\min(h, 1-\tau) + o(1)\big]\Big)\Big]^{-1}.$$

It follows from condition (42), that for $t \in [h, \max(h, 1-\tau)]$ we also have $u(t,\varphi) = A + o(1)$, and

$$u(\max(h,1-\tau),\varphi) = A\Big[1 + (A-1)\exp\Big(-\lambda A\big[\max(h,1-\tau) - \alpha A \min(h,1-\tau) - Ag(1-\tau-h) + o(1)\big]\Big)\Big]^{-1}.$$

We set

$$t_1^0 = \frac{\alpha A(1-\tau+h) - Ah}{1-(1-\alpha)A}.$$

From (42) and (43) we get that $t_1^0 > \max(h, 1-\tau)$. Then $t_1(\varphi) = t_1^0 + o(1)$, and for every $t \in (0, t_1(\varphi))$ we have the relation $u(t,\varphi) = A + o(1)$.

Suppose that the following inequality is fulfilled:

$$t_1^0 < 1 - h. \tag{45}$$

Then on the interval $(t_1(\varphi), t_1(\varphi) + h]$ we have the equality $u(t,\varphi) = o(1)$, and

$$u(t_1(\varphi)+h,\varphi) = A\Big[1 + (A-1)\exp\Big(-\lambda A\big[(1-(1-\alpha)A)h + o(1)\big]\Big)\Big]^{-1}.$$

If condition

$$(1-(1-\alpha)A)h + 1 - t_1^0 - h < 0 \tag{46}$$

is true, then on the interval $(t_1(\varphi)+h, 1]$ equality $u(t,\varphi) = o(1)$ holds, and

$$u(1,\varphi) = A\Big[1 + (A-1)\exp\Big(-\lambda A\big[(1-(1-\alpha)A)h + (1-t_1^0-h) + o(1)\big]\Big)\Big]^{-1}.$$

We set

$$t_2^0 = 1 + \Big((1-\alpha)Ah + t_1^0 - 1\Big)[1-\alpha A]^{-1}.$$

Suppose

$$t_2^0 < t_1^0 + 1, \tag{47}$$

then $t_2(\varphi) = t_2^0 + o(1)$, and for every $t \in [1, t_2(\varphi))$ the equality $u(t,\varphi) = o(1)$ is fulfilled. Finally, we introduce the quantity $\bar{\tau} = t_2(\varphi) - t_1(\varphi)$. Then, to order $o(1)$ (for $\lambda \to \infty$), we obtain the equality

$$\bar{\tau} = f(\tau), \tag{48}$$

where $f(\tau) = t_2^0 - t_1^0$.

After $\bar{\tau}$ has been determined, the situation is repeated, i.e., while for current value of $\bar{\tau}$ inequalities (42), (45)–(47) are fulfilled, using (48) we calculate $\bar{\bar{\tau}}$ and so on.

The one-dimensional mapping (48) plays a central role in the study of the solutions from $S(\tau)$. When the conditions (42)–(47) are fulfilled its attractors determine the structure of the periodic solutions from $S(\tau)$. For example, to the equilibrium state τ_0:

$$\tau_0 = f(\tau_0) \tag{49}$$

there corresponds, under the condition $|f'(\tau_0)| < 1$, a stable one-step periodic solution $u_0(t,\lambda)$ with the initial conditions in $S(\tau_0)$.

Lemma 7. *Let the inequality*

$$1 - A + A^2\alpha < 0 \tag{50}$$

hold. Then there exist values of h such that the map (48) has a stable fixed point $\tau = \tau_*$, where

$$\tau_* = \frac{A(A-1)(\alpha + (\alpha - 1)h)}{1 - A + A^2\alpha}, \tag{51}$$

such that inequalities (42)–(47) are fulfilled.

Proof. First, let us show, that if inequality (50) holds, then inequalities (43) are true.

It is easy to see, that inequalities (43) are equivalent to inequality $\alpha < \min(1/A, 1 - 1/A)$. Inequality (50) is equivalent to $\alpha < 1/A - 1/A^2$. This value is less than $\min(1/A, 1 - 1/A)$ (parameter $A > 1$), therefore, if (50) is true, then conditions (43) hold.

Second, let us substitute the values of t_1^0 and t_2^0 into the map (48):

$$\bar{\tau} = \frac{A^2\alpha^2}{(-1 + \alpha A)(1 - (1 - \alpha)A)}\tau + \frac{A(A-1)(h(1-\alpha) - \alpha)}{(-1 + \alpha A)(1 - (1 - \alpha)A)}. \tag{52}$$

This map has a fixed point τ_* satisfying formula (51). We should check whether this value τ_* satisfies conditions (42), (45)–(47), because map (52) corresponds to the initial equation only when all these inequalities hold, and we should study stability of the fixed point (51).

Let us begin with the study of stability. The fixed point τ_* is stable if and only if

$$-1 < \frac{A^2\alpha^2}{(-1 + \alpha A)(1 - (1 - \alpha)A)} < 1.$$

From the condition (43) we get that this value is greater than zero, and this value is less than 1 if and only if inequality (50) holds. Therefore, this fixed point is stable.

Now let us prove that if $\tau = \tau_*$ satisfies (51), then conditions (42), (45)–(47) hold.

Below, we always assume that inequalities (43) and (50) hold.

Substituting τ_* in inequality $\tau < 1$ from (42) we obtain, that this condition is equivalent to

$$h < \frac{(1-\alpha)A - 1}{A(A-1)(1-\alpha)} =: \gamma_1, \tag{53}$$

inequality $h < \tau$ from (42) is equivalent to

$$h > \frac{\alpha A(A-1)}{(A-1)^2 + \alpha A} =: \beta_1,$$

and condition $\tau > 1 - h - h(1 - \alpha A)(A-1)^{-1}$ from (42) is equivalent to

$$h > \frac{A-1}{A^2(1-\alpha)} =: \beta_2. \tag{54}$$

Condition (45) at $\tau = \tau_*$ can be rewritten in the form

$$h < \frac{(A-1)(1-\alpha A)}{(A(1-\alpha A) - (1 - (1-\alpha)A))} =: \gamma_2.$$

Condition (46) holds, if $\tau = \tau_*$ and (54) is true, and inequality (47) holds, if $\bar{\tau} = \tau_* < 1$ (the last inequality is equivalent to (53)).

Thus, at $\tau = \tau_*$ and under condition (50) the system of inequalities (42), (43), (45)–(47) is equivalent to

$$\max(\beta_1, \beta_2) < h < \min(\gamma_1, \gamma_2).$$

Parameter h must satisfy condition $h < 1/2$ (we obtain this inequality from condition (44)).

Let us prove that under condition (50) interval $(\max(\beta_1, \beta_2), \min(1/2, \gamma_1, \gamma_2))$ is not empty.

$$\beta_1 - \beta_2 = \frac{(A-1)(1-(1-\alpha)A)(1-A+A^2\alpha)}{A^2(-1+\alpha)((A-1)^2+\alpha A)} < 0,$$

therefore $\max(\beta_1, \beta_2) = \beta_2$. Let us estimate the values of $\gamma_1 - \beta_2, \gamma_2 - \beta_2, 1/2 - \beta_2$.

$$\gamma_1 - \beta_2 = \frac{1-A+A^2\alpha}{(A-1)A^2(-1+\alpha)} > 0,$$
$$\gamma_2 - \beta_2 = \frac{(A-1)(1-A+A\alpha)(1-A+A^2\alpha)}{A^2(1-\alpha)\big(A(1-\alpha A)-(1-(1-\alpha)A)\big)} > 0.$$

Inequality

$$1/2 - \beta_2 = \frac{2-2A+A^2-A^2\alpha}{2A^2(1-\alpha)} > 0$$

is equivalent to inequality $2-2A+A^2-A^2\alpha > 0$. Function $q(\alpha) = 2-2A+A^2-A^2\alpha$ is decreasing on the interval $\alpha \in (0, 1/A - 1/A^2)$. Therefore, $q(1/A-1/A^2) \le q(\alpha)$ for all $\alpha \in (0, 1/A-1/A^2)$.

$$q(1/A-1/A^2) = 2-2A+A^2-A^2(1/A-1/A^2) = A^2-3A+3 > 0,$$

thus inequality $1/2 - \beta_2 > 0$ holds for all $\alpha \in (0, 1/A-1/A^2)$. The Lemma is proven. □

From the constructions and the reasoning given above we obtain the following statement.

Theorem 5. *Let the inequality (50) hold. Then for all sufficiently large λ there exist h and $\tau = \tau_*$, satisfying (51), such that equation (37) has an asymptotically orbitally stable rapidly oscillating periodic (with period $T(\lambda)$) solution $u_*(t,\lambda)$, for which $u_*(0,\lambda) = u_*(t_1(\lambda),\lambda) = u_*(t_2(\lambda),\lambda) = 1$, where t_j are successive positive roots of the equation $u_*(t,\lambda) = 1$, and*

$$t_1(\lambda) = \frac{A(\alpha+(\alpha-1)h)}{1-A+A^2\alpha} + o(1),$$
$$T(\lambda) = t_2(\lambda) = \frac{A^2(\alpha+(\alpha-1)h)}{1-A+A^2\alpha} + o(1),$$
$$t_2(\lambda) - t_1(\lambda) = \tau_* + o(1) < 1.$$

For every t from intervals $(0, t_1(\lambda))$ and $(t_1(\lambda), t_2(\lambda))$, respectively, the following equalities are fulfilled:

$$u_*(t,\lambda) = \begin{cases} A + o(1), & t \in (0, t_1(\lambda)), \\ o(1), & t \in (t_1(\lambda), t_2(\lambda)). \end{cases}$$

In a similar way, one can determine the existence conditions and find the asymptotics of multi-step periodic solutions on the segment $[-1, 0]$ and obtain an n-dimensional (in terms of the number of steps on the segment $[-1, 0]$) mapping for their description.

5. Conclusions

The dynamics of the logistic equation with delays and with bounding modified nonlinearity are studied.

First, oscillations close to harmonic are studied. Using the methods of bifurcation analysis, we singled out the critical case in the problem of stability of stationary state and constructed the normal form. Its nonlocal dynamics determine the local behavior of the initial equation solutions in the neighborhood of the equilibrium state.

The solutions of the relaxation (step-like) type are studied for sufficiently large values of the parameter λ. We stress that, from a computational point of view, Equations (4) and (8) are difficult, since the relaxation solution approaches A and 0 very closely, so even a small error in the calculations will take us out of the class of solutions under consideration. Therefore, asymptotic methods play a special role. They not only allow one to find an approximation of the solution, but also reduce the problem of the dynamics of the original infinite-dimensional problem to the problem of the dynamics of the constructed finite-dimensional mapping (this object is much more simpler than the initial equation). Asymptotic formulas that couple the solutions of (4) and (8) with such mappings trajectories are obtained. The resulting formulas are suitable for engineering calculations. It is important to note that this method is applicable to equations with different types of nonlinearities [30,31] and to systems of two, three, and more singular perturbed equations with delay [30,32,33].

The use of the modified nonlinearity leads to the fact that the oscillations turn out to be 'safer' in comparison with Equation (1): their largest value A is significantly less than the value of $\exp(\lambda T)$ for Equation (1), and the smallest value of $\exp(-\lambda const)$ is significantly greater than the value of $\exp(-\exp \lambda T)$.

As a generalization of the obtained results, we note that they do not change if the function $(A-u)$ in (8) is replaced by a more general function $F_0(u)$ for which the conditions $F_0(u) > 0$ as $0 < u < A$, $F_0(0) = F_0(A) = 0$ and $F_0'(0) \neq 0$, $F_0'(A) \neq 0$ are satisfied. We also note that the proposed method allows extension to the case of more than two delays in Equation (8).

Author Contributions: Conceptualization, A.K. and S.K.; Methodology, A.K. and S.K.; Validation, A.K. and S.K.; Formal analysis, A.K. and S.K.; Investigation, A.K. and S.K.; Writing—original draft, A.K. and S.K.; Writing—review and editing, A.K. and S.K.; Visualization, A.K. and S.K. All authors have read and agreed to the published version of the manuscript.

Funding: This work was supported by the Russian Science Foundation (project No. 21-71-30011), https://rscf.ru/en/project/21-71-30011/, accessed on 28 February 2023.

Data Availability Statement: Not applicable.

Conflicts of Interest: The authors declare no conflict of interest. The funders had no role in the design of the study; in the collection, analyses, or interpretation of data; in the writing of the manuscript; or in the decision to publish the results.

References

1. Murray, J.D. *Mathematical Biology II*, 3rd ed.; Springer: New York, NY, USA, 2003. [CrossRef]
2. Okuba, A. Dynamical aspects of animal grouping: Swarms, schools, flocks, and herds. *Adv. Biophys.* **1986**, *22*, 1–94. [CrossRef] [PubMed]
3. Wu, J. *Theory and Applications of Partial Functional Differential Equations*; Springer: New York, NY, USA, 1996. [CrossRef]
4. Kuang, Y. *Delay Differential Equations: With Applications in Population Dynamics*; Academic Press: Boston, MA, USA, 1993. Available online: http://www.ams.org/mathscinet-getitem?mr=1218880 (accessed on 1 December 2022).
5. Wright, E.M. A non-linear difference-differential equation. *J. Reine Angew. Math.* **1955**, *194*, 66–87. [CrossRef]
6. Kashchenko, S.A.; Loginov, D.O. Estimation of the Region of Global Stability of the Equilibrium State of the Logistic Equation with Delay. *Russ. Math.* **2020**, *64*, 34–49. [CrossRef]
7. Kashchenko, S.A. Asymptotics of the Solutions of the Generalized Hutchinson Equation. *Autom. Control Comput. Sci.* **2013**, *47*, 470–494. [CrossRef]
8. May, R.M. *Stability and Complexity in Model Ecosystems*, 2nd ed.; Princeton University Press: Princeton, NJ, USA, 2001. [CrossRef]
9. Dorini, F.A.; Cecconello, M.S.; Dorini, L.B. On the logistic equation subject to uncertainties in the environmental carrying capacity and initial population density. *Commun. Nonlinear Sci. Numer. Simul.* **2016**, *33*, 160–173. [CrossRef]
10. Cushing, J.M. *Integrodifferential Equations and Delay Models in Population Dynamics*; Springer Science & Business Media: Berlin/Heidelberg, Germany, 2013.
11. Brauer, F.; Castillo-Chavez, C. *Mathematical Models in Population Biology and Epidemiology*; Springer: New York, NY, USA, 2012. [CrossRef]
12. Jin, Z.; Yuan, R. Hopf bifurcation in a reaction-diffusion-advection equation with nonlocal delay effect. *J. Differ. Equ.* **2021**, *271*, 533–562. [CrossRef]

13. Goryunov, V.E. Dynamics of solutions of logistic equation with delay and diffusion in a planar domain. *Theor. Math. Phys.* **2022**, *212*, 1092–1110. [CrossRef]
14. Sawada, Y.; Takeuchi, Y.; Dong, Y. Stability analysis of a single-species logistic model with time delay and constant inflow. *Appl. Math. Lett.* **2023**, *138*, 108514. [CrossRef]
15. Sorokin, V.G.; Vyazmin, A.V. Nonlinear Reaction–Diffusion Equations with Delay: Partial Survey, Exact Solutions, Test Problems, and Numerical Integration. *Mathematics* **2022**, *10*, 1886. [CrossRef]
16. Hale, J.K. *Theory of Functional Differential Equations*, 2nd ed.; Springer: New York, NY, USA, 1977. [CrossRef]
17. Oster, G.; Guckenheimer, J. Chapter Bifurcation Phenomena in Population Models. In *The Hopf Bifurcation and Its Applications*; Springer: New York, NY, USA, 1976; pp. 327–353. [CrossRef]
18. Marsden, J.E.; McCracken, M.F. *The Hopf Bifurcation and Its Applications*; Springer: New York, NY, USA, 1976. [CrossRef]
19. Gourley, S.A.; Sou, J.W.H.; Wu, J.H. Nonlocality of Reaction-Diffusion Equations Induced by Delay: Biological Modeling and Nonlinear Dynamics. *J. Math. Sci.* **2004**, *124*, 5119–5153. [CrossRef]
20. Kashchenko, S.A. Infinite-Dimensional Bifurcations in Spatially Distributed Delay Logistic Equation. *Mathematics* **2022**, *10*, 775. [CrossRef]
21. Jiang, D.; Shi, N. A note on nonautonomous logistic equation with random perturbation. *J. Math. Anal. Appl.* **2005**, *303*, 164–172. [CrossRef]
22. Golubenets, V.O. Relaxation oscillations in a logistic equation with nonconstant delay. *Math. Notes* **2020**, *107*, 920–932. [CrossRef]
23. Edwards, R.E. *Functional Analysis. Theory and Applications*; Holt, Rinehart and Winston: New York, NY, USA, 1965.
24. Chen, F.; Shi, J. Periodicity in a logistic type system with several delays. *Comput. Math. Appl.* **2004**, *48*, 35–44. [CrossRef]
25. Smith, H. *An Introduction to Delay Differential Equations with Applications to the Life Sciences*; Springer: Berlin/Heidelberg, Germany, 2011. [CrossRef]
26. Kashchenko, I.; Kaschenko, S. Infinite process of forward and backward bifurcations in the logistic equation with two delays. *Nonlinear Phenom. Complex Syst.* **2019**, *22*, 407–412. [CrossRef]
27. Yan, X.P.; Zhang, C.H. Bifurcation analysis in a diffusive Logistic population model with two delayed density-dependent feedback terms. *Nonlinear Anal. Real World Appl.* **2022**, *63*, 103394. [CrossRef]
28. Hartman, P. *Ordinary Differential Equations*, 2nd ed.; Society for Industrial and Applied Mathematics (SIAM): Philadelphia, PA, USA, 2002. [CrossRef]
29. Kashchenko, S.A. Relaxation oscillations in a system with delays modeling the predator–prey problem. *Autom. Control Comput. Sci.* **2015**, *49*, 547–581. [CrossRef]
30. Kashchenko, A.A. Relaxation modes of a system of diffusion coupled oscillators with delay. *Commun. Nonlinear. Sci. Numer. Simulat.* **2021**, *93*, 105488. [CrossRef]
31. Kashchenko, A. Asymptotics of Solutions to a Differential Equation with Delay and Nonlinearity Having Simple Behaviour at Infinity. *Mathematics* **2022**, *10*, 3360. [CrossRef]
32. Kashchenko, A.A. Influence of coupling on the dynamics of three delayed oscillators. *Izv. VUZ. Appl. Nonlinear Dyn.* **2021**, *29*, 869–891. [CrossRef]
33. Kashchenko, A.A. Dependence of the dynamics of a model of coupled oscillators on the number of oscillators. *Dokl. Math.* **2021**, *104*, 355–359. [CrossRef]

mathematics

Article

Kuramoto Model with Delay: The Role of the Frequency Distribution

Vladimir V. Klinshov [1,2,3,4,*] and Alexander A. Zlobin [1,2,3]

1 A. V. Gaponov-Grekhov Institute of Applied Physics of the Russian Academy of Sciences, 46 Ul'yanov Street, 603950 Nizhny Novgorod, Russia
2 Faculty of Radiophysics of Nizhny Novgorod, Lobachevsky State University, 23 Prospekt Gagarina, 603022 Nizhny Novgorod, Russia
3 Leonhard Euler International Mathematical Institute, Saint Petersburg University, 7-9 Universitetskaya Embankment, 199034 St. Petersburg, Russia
4 National Research University Higher School of Economics, 25/12 Bol'shaya Pecherskaya Street, 603155 Nizhny Novgorod, Russia
* Correspondence: vladimir.klinshov@ipfran.ru

Abstract: The Kuramoto model is a classical model used for the describing of synchronization in populations of oscillatory units. In the present paper we study the Kuramoto model with delay with a focus on the distribution of the oscillators' frequencies. We consider a series of rational distributions which allow us to reduce the population dynamics to a set of several delay differential equations. We use the bifurcation analysis of these equations to study the transition from the asynchronous to synchronous state. We demonstrate that the form of the frequency distribution may play a substantial role in synchronization. In particular, for Lorentzian distribution the delay prevents synchronization, while for other distributions the delay can facilitate synchronization.

Keywords: Kuramoto model; time delay; synchronization

MSC: 34K24

Citation: Klinshov, V.V.; Zlobin, A.A. . *Mathematics* **2023**, *11*, 2325. https://doi.org/10.3390/math11102325

Academic Editor: Alexandra Kashchenko

Received: 18 April 2023
Revised: 7 May 2023
Accepted: 10 May 2023
Published: 16 May 2023

1. Introduction

In many complex systems of various nature a similar pattern of collective behaviour can be observed: The adjustment of rhythms of oscillating systems due to their interaction. This phenomenon is called synchronization and is ubiquitous in the real world with examples ranging from the synchronous firing of pacemaker cells in the heart and neurons in the brain to the synchronous rotation of electric generators in power grids [1–3]. For a long time it was a mystery how the synchronization can emerge despite the inevitable diversity in the natural frequencies of different units. It was Kuramoto who introduced a mathematical model of coupled oscillators that allowed this problem to be solved [4–6]. Motivated by the behavior of chemical and biological oscillators, this model later turned out to be quite general and applicable to such systems as coupled arrays of Josephson junctions [7] or populations of of biological neurons [8,9].

What is now known as the "Kuramoto model" consists of N phase oscillators with the harmonic interaction function:

$$\dot{\theta}_j(t) = \omega_j - \frac{K}{N}\sum_k \sin(\theta_j - \theta_k), \tag{1}$$

where $j = 1, \dots, N$ is the unit number, $\theta_j \in S^1$ are the phase variables, ω_i are the natural frequencies, and K is the global coupling strength. In his pioneering work Kuramoto showed this model to be mathematically tractable and to demonstrate the phase transition from an asynchronous state to synchronization at the critical coupling strength.

In subsequent decades the Kuramoto model became a classical paradigm for studying synchronization phenomena and it found numerous applications (see reviews [10,11] for the examples). From the other side, the simplicity and generality of the Kuramoto model makes it perfect for various kinds of generalization and modification. One of the most natural ways to make the model more realistic is to include coupling delays which are inevitably in real world due to the finite speed of signal propagation [12–14]. To take into account coupling delays the phases $\theta_k(t)$ in the sum from the r.h.s. of (1) are replaced by their delayed versions $\theta_k(t-\tau)$. In the case of two coupled oscillators the delay causes multistabilty of synchronous solutions with different frequencies [15] (interestingly, multistability also emerges if the delay is introduced not into the coupling, but into the oscillators themselves [16]). The similar effect of multistability was found for globally coupled oscillators with time delays, which results in the possibility of discontinuous transitions between different regimes in addition to classical smooth transitions [17,18]. In the case of local coupling, the delays were shown to induce complex spatio-temporal patterns and clusters [19]. In the case of distant-dependant delays similar patterns emerge and become propagating structures [20,21]. The case of heterogeneous delays was also considered and the emergence of clusters with various phase relations was demonstrated [22]. In rings of oscillators with local coupling, the delay was shown to act differently depending on the network symmetry: It induces multistability for unidirectional coupling and stabilizes the most symmetric solution for bidirectional coupling [23]. In rings with nonlocal coupling, the delays give birth to travelling waves [24]. For networks of oscillators with complex connectivity, such as scale-free networks, coupling delays may induce explosive synchronization [25].

Another natural generalization of the Kuramoto model is the addition of external forces to the oscillator dynamics which results in the emergence of a phase-dependent and/or time-dependent term in the r.h.s. of (1). This term is often taken in the form $a\sin\theta_j$, in which case the phase oscillators turn into the so-called "active rotators". The dynamics of active rotators is much richer than that of phase oscillators since the former can demonstrate either oscillatory or excitatory behaviour depending on the relation between the individual frequency ω_j and the parameter a which is often called a "non-isochronicity parameter". Ensembles of globally coupled active rotators were first considered in Refs. [26,27], and two different collective regimes were found: Entrainment with the external force and mutual entrainment. The introduction of heterogeneous external forces leads to similar results [28]. The transition between locked and unlocked states can be similar to either a super-critical Andronov-Hopf bifurcation or a saddle-node bifurcation [29]. In the case of heterogeneous assemblies made up of excitable and oscillatory units, it has been demonstrated that the transition to synchrony may be classical or re-entrant, depending on the particular form of the frequency distribution [30]. In addition to the parameter regions with synchronous and asynchronous regimes, the regions of bistability between different regimes were found as well [31].

Other types of generalized Kuramoto models were studied as well, including time-dependent [8,32,33], adaptive [34–38] and memristive [39] coupling, including noise [26,27,40], non-harmonic coupling functions [41,42] and pulse coupling [43,44], systems on smooth manifolds [45–47], etc. Typically, the analytic study of the Kuramto model and its generalizations is performed in the thermodynamic limit when the number of units tends to infinity. In this case the microscopic equations (1) are replaced by the continuity equation, and the individual frequencies ω_j are replaced by the probability density $g(\omega)$. For the classical Kuramoto model the particular form of this distribution does not play any important role. First, the system is invariant under the change of variables $\omega_j \to \omega_j + \Omega$ for arbitrary Ω, which means that the mean frequency $\langle\omega\rangle$ can be always set to zero. Second, for unimodal symmetric distributions, the critical coupling at which the transition takes place equals $K_c = 2/(\pi g(0))$, i.e., it depends only on the height of the distribution peak but not on its particular shape. However, when coupling delays or non-isochronicity are included, the shape of the distribution comes into play because it becomes important how the typical frequencies ω relate to the delay τ and non-isochronicity parameter a.

In the present paper we study how the synchronization transition in the Kuramoto model with delay depends on the shape of the frequency distribution $g(\omega)$. For this sake we consider a series of rational distributions which are all unimodal and symmetric but are different in the flatness of the peak and decay rate of the tails. Using the Ott-Antonsen approach [48,49] we derive low-dimensional dynamical systems governing the collective dynamics of the population and perform its bifurcation analysis. We show that the shape of the frequency distribution can play a significant role for the system properties. For widely used Lorentzian distribution, the delay always prevents synchronization by raising the critical coupling strength. However, for distributions with lighter tails, the delay can also promote synchronization by lowering the critical coupling.

2. Model

We consider a heterogeneous assembly of N oscillators with delayed coupling

$$\dot{\theta}_j(t) = \omega_j - a\sin\theta_j(t) - \frac{K}{N}\sum_k \sin(\theta_j(t) - \theta_k(t-\tau)), \tag{2}$$

where $j = 1, \ldots, N$ is the unit number, $\theta_j \in S^1$ are the phase variables, ω_j are the natural frequencies, a is the non-isochronicity parameter, K is the global coupling strength and τ is the coupling delay. Strictly speaking, ω_i can be called "natural frequencies" only for $a = 0$. For non-zero a, the rotation becomes non-uniform with the frequency $\sqrt{\omega_j^2 - a^2}$ for $0 < a < |\omega_j|$. At $|\omega_j| = a$ an isolated unit undergoes a SNIPER bifurcation toward the excitatory regime. This very dependence of the local oscillatory dynamics on the parameter a allows us to call it a "non-isochronicity parameter".

In order to characterize the degree of synchrony in the population we introduce the Kuramoto complex order parameter

$$R(t) = \frac{1}{N}\sum_j e^{i\theta_j(t)}. \tag{3}$$

The absolute value of this parameter serves the main indicator of the system synchronization. When it is close to zero, the phases of the oscillators are not correlated, and the system is asynchronous. When the order parameter is sufficiently different from zero it indicates the emergence of a bunch of oscillators rotating with close phases, which means synchronization. Using the Kuramoto order parameter allows us to rewrite (2) as

$$\dot{\theta}_j = \omega_j - \frac{a}{2i}(e^{i\theta_j} - e^{-i\theta_j}) + \frac{K}{2i}(R_\tau e^{-i\theta_j} - R_\tau^* e^{i\theta_j}), \tag{4}$$

where $R_\tau \equiv R(t-\tau)$ and the asterisk denotes the complex conjugate. In the thermodynamic limit $N \to \infty$, the macroscopic state of the system is described by the probability density function $f(\theta, \omega, t)$, which obeys the continuity equation

$$\frac{\partial f}{\partial t} + \frac{\partial}{\partial \theta}(fv) = 0, \tag{5}$$

with the velocity v being the r.h.s. of Equation (4). The Kuramoto parameter in this case is evaluated as

$$R(t) = \int_{-\infty}^{\infty} d\omega \int_0^{2\pi} f(\theta, \omega, t) e^{i\theta} d\theta, \tag{6}$$

3. Reduction of the Collective Dynamics

Following the theory of Ott and Antonsen [48,49] we will look for the long-term dynamics of the continuity Equation (5) in the form

$$f(\theta,\omega,t) = \frac{g(\omega)}{2\pi}\left(1 + \sum_{n=1}^{\infty}\left[(z^*(\omega,t))^n e^{in\theta} + (z(\omega,t))^n e^{-in\theta}\right]\right), \tag{7}$$

where

$$g(\omega) = \int_0^{2\pi} f(\theta,\omega,t)d\theta \tag{8}$$

is the probability density function of the natural frequencies and

$$z(\omega,t) = \int_0^{2\pi} f(\theta,\omega,t)e^{i\theta}d\theta, \tag{9}$$

is the local complex order parameter of the subpopulation with the natural frequency ω. Obviously, the global and the local order parameter are connected by the self-consistency condition

$$R = \int_{-\infty}^{\infty} g(\omega)z(\omega)d\omega. \tag{10}$$

Substituting (7) into (5), one obtains the following equations for $z(\omega,t)$:

$$\dot{z}(\omega,t) = i\omega z + \frac{a}{2}(1 - z^2) + \frac{K}{2}(R_\tau - R_\tau^* z^2), \tag{11}$$

which together with (10) defines a delay integro-differential equation describing the collective dynamics of the population in the thermodynamic limit.

As the next step we consider a family of rational distributions $g(\omega)$, namely

$$g_n(\omega) = \frac{c_n}{(\omega - \Omega)^{2n} + \Delta^{2n}}, \tag{12}$$

where n is natural, Ω is the mean frequency, Δ is the distribution half-width, and

$$c_n = \frac{1}{\pi} n \sin\frac{\pi}{2n}\Delta^{2n-1} \tag{13}$$

is the normalization constant. For $n = 1$ this distribution turns into a classical Cauchy distribution, and for $n \to \infty$ it converges to a uniform distribution on the interval $\omega \in [\Omega - \Delta; \Omega + \Delta]$. Assuming the rational function $g(\omega)$ allows us to evaluate the integral (10) using the residue theorem. A similar approach was recently used for populations of quadratic integrate-and-fire neurons [50,51]. Consider the analytic extension of function $z(\omega,t)$ to complex ω, then the integration contour can be closed by an infinitely large arc in the upper complex half-plane. In this half-plane the function (12) has n simple poles

$$\omega_k = \Omega + \Delta e^{i\alpha_k}, \tag{14}$$

where $k = \overline{1,n}$ and $\alpha_k = \pi(k - 0.5)/n$. Thus, the integral (10) can be evaluated as

$$R(t) = -\frac{i}{\Delta}\sin\frac{\pi}{2n}\sum_{k=1}^{n}(\omega_k - \Omega)z(\omega_k,t). \tag{15}$$

Writing Equation (11) for $\omega_1, \omega_2, \ldots, \omega_n$ allows us to obtain a closed set of n delay differential equations for complex variables

$$\dot{z_k} = i(\Omega + \Delta e^{i\alpha_k})z_k + \frac{a}{2}(1 - z_k^2) + \frac{K}{2}(R_\tau - R_\tau^* z_k^2), \tag{16a}$$

$$R = -i \sin\frac{\pi}{2n} \sum_{k=1}^{n} e^{i\alpha_k} z_k, \tag{16b}$$

where $k = \overline{1,n}$ and $z_k(t) \equiv z(\omega_k, t)$. Introducing $z_k = x_k + iy_k$ and $R = X + iY$ allows us to rewrite these equations in the real form :

$$\dot{x_k} = -\Omega y_k - \Delta(y_k \cos\alpha_k + x_k \sin\alpha_k) + \dots$$

$$\frac{a}{2}(1 + y_k^2 - x_k^2) + \frac{K}{2}(X_\tau(1 + y_k^2 - x_k^2) - 2Y_\tau x_k y_k), \tag{17a}$$

$$\dot{y_k} = \Omega x_k + \Delta(x_k \cos\alpha_k - y_k \sin\alpha_k) - a x_k y_k + \dots$$

$$\frac{K}{2}(Y_\tau(1 + x_k^2 - y_k^2) - 2X_\tau x_k y_k), \tag{17b}$$

$$X = \sin\frac{\pi}{2n} \sum_{k=1}^{n} (x_k \sin\alpha_k + y_k \cos\alpha_k), \tag{17c}$$

$$Y = \sin\frac{\pi}{2n} \sum_{k=1}^{n} (y_k \sin\alpha_k - x_k \cos\alpha_k). \tag{17d}$$

This set of DDEs governs the collective dynamics of the population in the thermodynamic limit $N \to \infty$. The following analysis is based on system (17).

4. Studying the Role of the Coupling Delay

For the case of isochronous oscillations with $a = 0$, the system always has a trivial steady state $z_k = R = 0$ corresponding to asynchronous dynamics of the oscillators. This state is stable for weak coupling K and destabilizes via an Andronov-Hopf bifurcation when the coupling becomes sufficiently strong, which constitutes a classical Kuramoto scenario [5,10]. The stable limit cycle born in this bifurcation corresponds to a partial synchronization of the oscillators.

The dynamics of the system is illustrated in Figure 1 where the dynamics of the individual phases and the Kuramoto order parameter are shown for the synchronous and asynchronous regimes. In both cases, the system starts from random initial conditions. In the case of asynchronous dynamics, all the phases rotate incoherently, and the order parameter remains close to zero. When the synchronization is achieved, a bunch of oscillators quickly emerge whose phases rotate with the same frequency, and the order parameter reaches a sufficiently non-zero value.

In order to illustrate the transition from the asynchronous to the synchronous state we plot the dependence of the Kuramoto order parameter on the coupling strength in Figure 2. The order parameter is small for weak coupling and rapidly grows as the coupling strength exceeds the critical value. Note that the results obtained by the simulation of the reduced model (17) coincide with those obtained for the microscopic system up to the fluctuations induced by the finite size effects. Note also that adding of the coupling delay might sufficiently influence the system dynamics and shift the critical value of the coupling strength. Further, we will analyze the role of the delay in detail with the help of the reduced system.

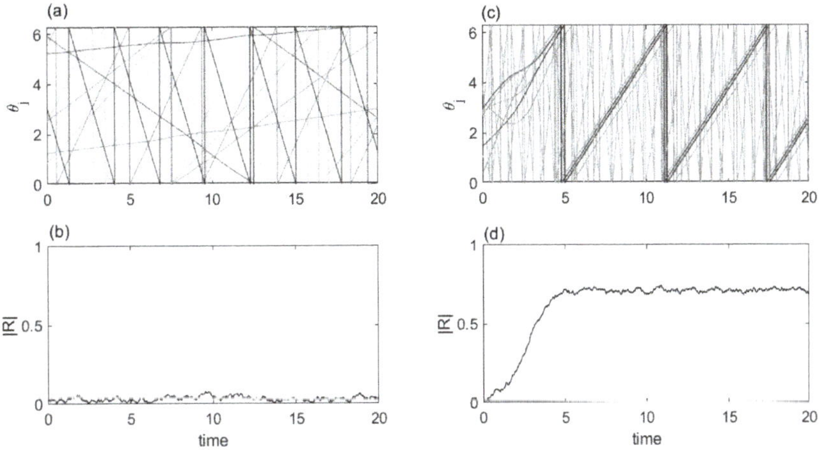

Figure 1. The dynamics of the system in the asynchronous (**a**,**b**) and synchronous (**c**,**d**) regimes. The top panels show the time traces of 10 randomly chosen phases θ_j, while the bottom panels show the time trace of the Kuramoto order parameter $|R|$. The coupling strength $K = 1$ for (**a**,**b**) and $K = 4$ for (**c**,**d**) The other parameters are $N = 1000$, $n = 1$, $\Omega = 1$, $\Delta = 1$, $\tau = 0$.

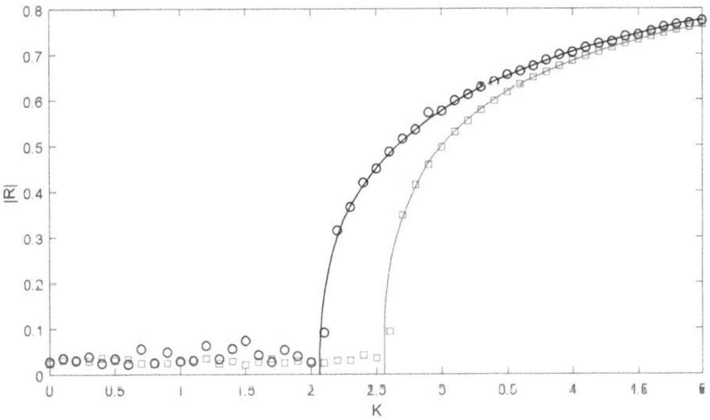

Figure 2. The dependence of the Kuramoto order parameter on the coupling strength. Black circles: $\tau = 0$, gray squares: $\tau = 1.5$. The other parameters: $N = 1000$, $n = 1$, $\Omega = 3$, $\Delta = 1$. Solid lines indicate the results obtained by the simulation of the reduced system (17).

In the case of zero delay $\tau = 0$ the critical coupling K_c depends on the distribution width Δ in a linear way. Indeed, according to the results of Kuramoto [52],

$$K_c = \frac{2}{\pi g(\Omega)} = \frac{2\Delta}{n \sin \frac{\pi}{2n}}. \tag{18}$$

For nonzero coupling delays the critical coupling becomes delay-dependent. In order to determine the bifurcation point it is necessary to write the characteristic equation for the trivial steady state which has the form $|D(\lambda)| = 0$, where D is $(2n) \times (2n)$ matrix

$$D = \begin{pmatrix} D^{xx} & D^{xy} \\ D^{yx} & D^{yy} \end{pmatrix}, \tag{19}$$

and D^{xx}, D^{xy}, D^{yx}, D^{yy} represent $n \times n$ matrices with the following elements:

$$D^{xx}_{km} = (-\lambda - \Delta \sin \alpha_k)\delta_{km} + \frac{K}{2} \sin \frac{\pi}{2n} e^{-\lambda\tau} \sin \alpha_k, \tag{20}$$

$$D^{xy}_{km} = (-\Omega - \Delta \cos \alpha_k)\delta_{km} + \frac{K}{2} \sin \frac{\pi}{2n} e^{-\lambda\tau} \cos \alpha_k, \tag{21}$$

$$D^{yx}_{km} = (\Omega + \Delta \cos \alpha_k)\delta_{km} - \frac{K}{2} \sin \frac{\pi}{2n} e^{-\lambda\tau} \cos \alpha_k, \tag{22}$$

$$D^{yy}_{km} = (-\lambda - \Delta \sin \alpha_k)\delta_{km} + \frac{K}{2} \sin \frac{\pi}{2n} e^{-\lambda\tau} \sin \alpha_k, \tag{23}$$

where δ_{km} equals one for $k = m$ and zero in other case.

At the Andronov-Hopf point a pair of roots $\lambda = \pm i\omega$ emerge, which allows us to determine the value of the coupling strength K_b at the bifurcation point by solving $|D(i\omega)| = 0$. For small delays, this equation can be solved numerically by taking (18) as the initial point, then the solution can be traced along the delay value as a parameter. The obtained dependence $K_b(\tau)$ is plotted in Figure 3a for the Lorentzian distribution of the oscillator frequencies ($n = 1$). The bifurcation coupling shows a minimum at $\tau = 0$ and grows rapidly and monotonically for non-zero delays. Note that we have calculated the bifurcation curve for both positive and negative delays. Although negative time delays are not physical, we use them in the bifurcation analysis for a reason that will become clear later. Namely, they will help us to find other bifurcation curves existing for positive delays.

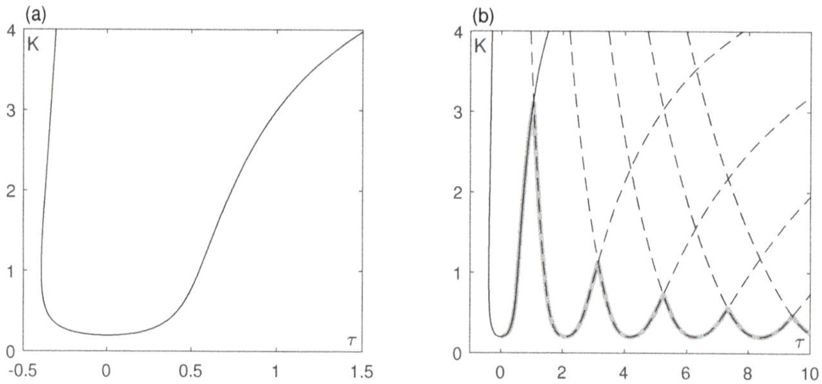

Figure 3. (**a**) The Andronov-Hopf bifurcation curve for system (17) with $n = 1$, $a = 0$, $\Omega = 3$ and $\Delta = 0.1$. (**b**) The same curve (black solid line) and its reappearing instances (black dashed lines). The gray thick line shows the synchronization border.

An important point is that the existence of one Andronov-Hopf bifurcation curve in a system with time delay implies the existence of other bifurcation curves at other delay values due to the so-called reappearance of periodic solutions [53]. Indeed, if the bifurcation takes place at the coupling strength K_b for the delay τ_0 this means the existence of a limit cycle with the period $T = 2\pi/\omega$ and vanishing amplitude. This implies the existence of the same limit cycle at the same coupling strength for the delays $\tau_k = \tau_0 + kT$, where k is an integer, which means that each of these points are also Andronov-Hopf points. Note, however, that the stability of the emergent limit cycle can change, which means that the bifurcation can be either supercritical or subcritical.

The bifurcation curve found by starting from the delay-less case reappears in the manner described above and leads to the emergence of other bifurcation curves as shown in Figure 3b. These curves demonstrate minimums at $\tau = kT_0$, where $T_0 = 2\pi/\omega_0$ and ω_0 is the frequency at which the collective oscillations emerge for $\tau = 0$. Obviously, it is the frequency of the distribution peak, i.e., $\omega_0 = \Omega$. For non-zero delays the frequency becomes different, therefore the different bifurcation curves do not exactly match each other in shape. However, they all still a single minimum at the multiples of T_0. The trivial steady state, i.e., the asynchronous regime is stable when the coupling strength is below all the bifurcation curves. Thus, the synchronization border is defined by the lowest point of the curve and has a saw-like shape. This border coincides completely with that obtained in Ref. [17] for the same setting which corroborates the validity of our analysis.

The obtained results suggest that introduction of the coupling delay prevents the system synchronization: For non-zero delays, the critical coupling at which the oscillators start to synchronize increases with respect to the delay-free case (at best, the critical coupling does not change if the delay is a multiple of T_0). This result seems to be obvious from the physical viewpoint: It is harder to adjust if one receives outdated information. However, it turns out that the coupling delay can in some cases promote synchronization. This surprising effect is observed when the distribution $g(\eta)$ is different from Lorentzian, i.e., $n > 1$.

In order to illustrate this effect we calculated the synchronization borders on the $\tau - K$ plane for different values of n. We adjust the distribution half-width as

$$\Delta = \frac{n}{2} \sin \frac{\pi}{2n}, \tag{24}$$

so that the critical coupling for the delay-free case equals unity for all n. The results are plotted in Figure 4 and show a significant difference between the Lorentzian distribution and distributions with $n > 1$. For the Lorentzian distribution the delay always prevents synchronization and the critical coupling is always not less than unity. For the distributions of higher order $n > 1$, some delay values can promote synchronization so that the critical coupling becomes less than unity. Another feature of high-order distributions is the complex form of the synchronization border with many peaks and valleys of different shapes.

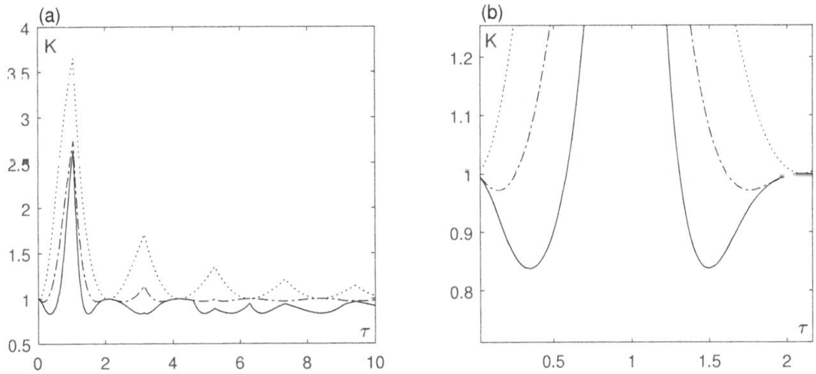

Figure 4. (**a**) The synchronization borders of system (17) for $n = 1$ (dotted line), $n = 2$ (dash-dotted line) and $n = 5$ (solid line). The mean frequency $\Omega = 3$, the half-width $\Delta = \frac{n}{2} \sin \frac{\pi}{2n}$. (**b**) Enlarged part of the panel (**a**).

5. Conclusions

In this paper we performed an analysis of the Kuramoto model with coupling delay paying special attention to the distribution of the oscillator frequencies ω. We used the method of Ott and Antonsen which allows one to reduce the system dynamics in the case of infinitely many oscillators. For the rational frequency distributions, the dynamics can be reduced to a set of delay-differential equations whose number equals the degree of the denominator. By the means of bifurcation analysis, we obtained the Andronov-Hopf bifurcation curves indicating a synchronization transition in the population and so constructed the synchronization border in the parameter plane. Our results have revealed the different role of the delay for different frequency distributions. Thus, for the Lorentzian distribution, the delay always prevents synchronization by increasing the critical coupling strength. In contrast, for the distributions different from Lorentzian, the delay can promote synchronization: For certain delay values, the critical coupling turns out to be lower than in the delay-less case.

In the studies of collective dynamics of heterogeneous populations, it is typical to consider a Lorentzian distribution of local parameters. The reason for this choice is the simplicity of analytical treatment: For example, in our study the Lorentzian distribution with $n = 1$ leads to the reduced system (9) of just a single differential equation for the complex variable z_1. The Lorentzian distribution is often treated as paradigmatic and qualitatively reflects the properties of an arbitrary unimodal distribution. However, our results show that the particular shape of the distribution can play a significant role in the system behaviour and synchronization. In particular, the role of the coupling delay turns out to be opposite for the Lorentzian and non-Lorentzian distributions.

In the end, we would like to emphasize that the present study is limited to the local stability analysis and does not consider the global stability of the asynchronous state. It means that the stable asynchronous state might coexist with a synchronous state in some parameter regions leading to bistability areas, as was demonstrated in Ref. [17] for the Lorentz frequency distribution. The emergence of bistability is associated with the subcritical Andronov-Hopf bifurcation, while the supercritical bifurcation supports monostability. The type of the bifurcation can be determined by the calculation of the first Lyapunov coefficient [54,55] which could be one of the directions of the further investigation. Other possibilities include consideration of a broader class of frequency distributions, including non-unimodal ones.

Author Contributions: Conceptualization, V.V.K.; Methodology, V.V.K.; Software, A.A.Z.; Formal analysis, V.V.K. and A.A.Z.; Investigation, V.V.K. and A.A.Z.; Writing—original draft, V.V.K.; Supervision, V.V.K.; Funding acquisition, V.V.K. All authors have read and agreed to the published version of the manuscript.

Funding: The derivation of the reduced system was supported by the Ministry of Science and Higher Education of the Russian Federation, agreement no. 075-15-2022-287. The bifurcation analysis of the reduced system and the numerical simulations were supported by the Russian Science Foundation, grant no. 19-72-10114.

Data Availability Statement: The data that support the findings of this study are available on request from the corresponding author.

Conflicts of Interest: The authors declare no conflict of interest.

References

1. Pikovsky, A.; Kurths, J.; Rosenblum, M.; Kurths, J. *Synchronization: A Universal Concept in Nonlinear Sciences*; Cambridge University Press: Cambridge, UK , 2003; Volume 12.
2. Strogatz, S.H. *Sync: How Order Emerges from Chaos in the Universe, Nature, and Daily Life*; Hachette: London, UK, 2012.
3. Winfree, A.T. *The Geometry of Biological Time*; Springer Science & Business Media: Berlin, Germany, 2013; Volume 12.
4. Kuramoto, Y. Self-entrainment of a population of coupled non-linear oscillators. In Proceedings of the International Symposium on Mathematical Problems in Theoretical Physics, Kyoto, Japan, 23–29 January 1975; Springer: Berlin/Heidelberg, Germany, 1975; pp. 420–422.
5. Kuramoto, Y. *Chemical Oscillations, Waves, and Turbulence*; Springer: Berlin, Germany; New York, NY, USA, 1984; Volume 19, p. 156.
6. Kuramoto, Y.; Nishikawa, I. Statistical macrodynamics of large dynamical systems. Case of a phase transition in oscillator communities. *J. Stat. Phys.* **1987**, *49*, 569–605. [CrossRef]
7. Wiesenfeld, K.; Colet, P.; Strogatz, S.H. Frequency locking in Josephson arrays: Connection with the Kuramoto model. *Phys. Rev. E* **1998**, *57*, 1563. [CrossRef]
8. Cumin, D.; Unsworth, C. Generalising the Kuramoto model for the study of neuronal synchronisation in the brain. *Phys. D Nonlinear Phenom.* **2007**, *226*, 181–196. [CrossRef]
9. Breakspear, M.; Heitmann, S.; Daffertshofer, A. Generative models of cortical oscillations: Neurobiological implications of the Kuramoto model. *Front. Hum. Neurosci.* **2010**, *4*, 190. [CrossRef] [PubMed]

10. Acebrón, J.A.; Bonilla, L.L.; Vicente, C.J.; Ritort, F.; Spigler, R. The Kuramoto model: A simple paradigm for synchronization phenomena. *Rev. Mod. Phys.* **2005**, *77*, 137–185. [CrossRef]
11. Rodrigues, F.A.; Peron, T.K.D.M.; Ji, P.; Kurths, J. The Kuramoto model in complex networks. *Phys. Rep.* **2016**, *610*, 1–98. [CrossRef]
12. Smith, H. *An Introduction to Delay Differential Equations with Applications to the Life Sciences*; Springer: Berlin/Heidelberg, Germany, 2011.
13. Erneux, T. *Applied Delay Differential Equations*; Surveys and Tutorials in the Applied Mathematical Sciences; Springer Science & Business Media: Berlin/Heidelberg, Germany, 2009; Volume 3, p. 204.
14. Kashchenko, S.; Maiorov, V.V. *Models of Wave Memory*; Springer: Berlin/Heidelberg, Germany, 2015.
15. Schuster, H.G.; Wagner, P. Mutual Entrainment of Two Limit Cycle Oscillators with Time Delayed Coupling. *Prog. Theor. Phys.* **1989**, *81*, 939–945. [CrossRef]
16. Kashchenko, A.A. Multistability in a system of two coupled oscillators with delayed feedback. *J. Differ. Eqs.* **2019**, *266*, 562–579. [CrossRef]
17. Yeung, M.K.S.; Strogatz, S.H. Time Delay in the Kuramoto Model of Coupled Oscillators. *Phys. Rev. Lett.* **1999**, *82*, 648–651. [CrossRef]
18. Choi, M.Y.; Kim, H.J.; Kim, D.; Hong, H. Synchronization in a system of globally coupled oscillators with time delay. *Phys. Rev E-Stat. Phys. Plasmas Fluids Relat. Interdiscip. Top.* **2000**, *61*, 371–381. [CrossRef]
19. Nakamura, Y.; Tominaga, F.; Munakata, T. Clustering behavior of time-delayed nearest-neighbor coupled oscillators. *Phys. Rev. E Stat. Phys. Plasmas Fluids Relat. Interdiscip. Top.* **1994**, *49*, 4849–4856. [CrossRef]
20. Zanette, D.H. Propagating structures in globally coupled systems with time delays. *Phys. Rev. E-Stat. Phys. Plasmas Fluids Relat. Interdiscip. Top.* **2000**, *62*, 3167–3172. [CrossRef] [PubMed]
21. Jeong, S.O.; Ko, T.W.; Moon, H.T. Time-delayed spatial patterns in a two-dimensional array of coupled oscillators. *Phys. Rev. Lett.* **2002**, *89*, 154104. [CrossRef] [PubMed]
22. Petkoski, S.; Spiegler, A.; Proix, T.; Aram, P.; Temprado, J.J.; Jirsa, V.K. Heterogeneity of time delays determines synchronization of coupled oscillators. *Phys. Rev. E* **2016**, *94*, 12209. [CrossRef] [PubMed]
23. D'Huys, O.; Vicente, R.; Erneux, T.; Danckaert, J.; Fischer, I. Synchronization properties of network motifs: Influence of coupling delay and symmetry. *Chaos* **2008**, *18*, 37116. [CrossRef] [PubMed]
24. Laing, C.R. Travelling waves in arrays of delay-coupled phase oscillators. *Chaos Interdiscip. J. Nonlinear Sci.* **2016**, *26*, 94802. [CrossRef]
25. Peron, T.K.D.; Rodrigues, F.A. Explosive synchronization enhanced by time-delayed coupling. *Phys. Rev. E* **2012**, *86*, 16102. [CrossRef]
26. Shinomoto, S.; Kuramoto, Y. Phase Transitions in Active Rotator Systems. *Prog. Theor. Phys.* **1986**, *75*, 1105. [CrossRef]
27. Sakaguchi, H.; Shinomoto, S.; Kuramoto, Y. Phase transitions and their bifurcation analysis in a large population of active rotators with mean-field coupling. *Prog. Theor. Phys.* **1988**, *79*, 600–607. [CrossRef]
28. Arenas, A.; Vicente, C.J.P. Exact long-time behavior of a network of phase oscillators under random fields. *Phys. Rev. E* **1994**, *50*, 949. [CrossRef]
29. Antonsen, T.M., Jr.; Faghih, R.T.; Girvan, M.; Ott, E.; Platig, J. External periodic driving of large systems of globally coupled phase oscillators. *Chaos Interdiscip. J. Nonlinear Sci.* **2008**, *18*, 37112. [CrossRef] [PubMed]
30. Lafuerza, L.F.; Colet, P.; Toral, R. Nonuniversal results induced by diversity distribution in coupled excitable systems. *Phys. Rev. Lett.* **2010**, *105*, 084101. [CrossRef] [PubMed]
31. Klinshov, V.; Franovic, I.; Franović, I. Two scenarios for the onset and suppression of collective oscillations in heterogeneous populations of active rotators. *Phys. Rev. E* **2019**, *100*, 062211. [CrossRef] [PubMed]
32. Petkoski, S.; Stefanovska, A. Kuramoto model with time-varying parameters. *Phys. Rev. E* **2012**, *86*, 46212. [CrossRef]
33. Khatiwada, D.R. Numerical Solution of Finite Kuramoto Model with Time-Dependent Coupling Strength: Addressing Synchronization Events of Nature. *Mathematics* **2022**, *10*, 3633. [CrossRef]
34. Timms, L.; English, L.Q. Synchronization in phase-coupled Kuramoto oscillator networks with axonal delay and synaptic plasticity. *Phys. Rev. E* **2014**, *89*, 32906. [CrossRef]
35. Ha, S.Y.; Noh, S.E.; Park, J. Synchronization of Kuramoto oscillators with adaptive couplings. *SIAM J. Appl. Dyn. Syst.* **2016**, *15*, 162–194. [CrossRef]
36. Kasatkin, D.V.; Nekorkin, V.I. Dynamics of the Phase Oscillators with Plastic Couplings. *Radiophys. Quantum Electron.* **2016**, *58*, 877–891. [CrossRef]
37. Kasatkin, D.V.; Yanchuk, S.; Schöll, E.; Nekorkin, V.I. Self-organized emergence of multilayer structure and chimera states in dynamical networks with adaptive couplings. *Phys. Rev. E* **2017**, *96*, 062211. [CrossRef]
38. Feketa, P.; Schaum, A.; Meurer, T. Stability of cluster formations in adaptive Kuramoto networks. *IFAC-Pap.* **2021**, *54*, 14–19. [CrossRef]
39. Xu, Q.; Liu, T.; Ding, S.; Bao, H.; Li, Z.; Chen, B. Extreme multistability and phase synchronization in a heterogeneous bi-neuron Rulkov network with memristive electromagnetic induction. *Cogn. Neurodyn.* **2022**, 1–12. [CrossRef]
40. Zaks, M.A.; Neiman, A.B.; Feistel, S.; Schimansky-Geier, L. Noise-controlled oscillations and their bifurcations in coupled phase oscillators. *Phys. Rev. E* **2003**, *68*, 66206. [CrossRef]

41. Komarov, M.; Pikovsky, A. The Kuramoto model of coupled oscillators with a bi-harmonic coupling function. *Phys. D Nonlinear Phenom.* **2014**, *289*, 18–31. [CrossRef]
42. O'Keeffe, K.P.; Strogatz, S.H. Dynamics of a population of oscillatory and excitable elements. *Phys. Rev. E* **2016**, *93*, 62203. [CrossRef] [PubMed]
43. Canavier, C.C.; Tikidji-Hamburyan, R.A. Globally attracting synchrony in a network of oscillators with all-to-all inhibitory pulse coupling. *Phys. Rev. E* **2017**, *95*, 032215. [CrossRef]
44. Klinshov, V.; Lücken, L.; Yanchuk, S. Desynchronization by phase slip patterns in networks of pulse-coupled oscillators with delays: Desynchronization by phase slip patterns. *Eur. Phys. J. Spec. Top.* **2018**, *227*, 1117–1128. [CrossRef]
45. Fiori, S. A control-theoretic approach to the synchronization of second-order continuous-time dynamical systems on real connected Riemannian manifolds. *SIAM J. Control Optim.* **2020**, *58*, 787–813. [CrossRef]
46. Markdahl, J.; Thunberg, J.; Goncalves, J. High-dimensional Kuramoto models on Stiefel manifolds synchronize complex networks almost globally. *Automatica* **2020**, *113*, 108736. [CrossRef]
47. Cafaro, A.D.; Fiori, S. Optimization of a control law to synchronize first-order dynamical systems on Riemannian manifolds by a transverse component. *Discret. Contin. Dyn.-Syst.-Ser. B* **2022**, *27*, 3947–3969. [CrossRef]
48. Ott, E.; Antonsen, T.M. Low dimensional behavior of large systems of globally coupled oscillators. *Chaos Interdiscip. J. Nonlinear Sci.* **2008**, *18*, 37113. [CrossRef]
49. Ott, E.; Antonsen, T.M. Long time evolution of phase oscillator systems. *Chaos Interdiscip. J. Nonlinear Sci.* **2009**, *19*, 23117. [CrossRef] [PubMed]
50. Klinshov, V.; Kirillov, S.; Nekorkin, V. Reduction of the collective dynamics of neural populations with realistic forms of heterogeneity. *Phys. Rev. E* **2021**, *103*, L040302. [CrossRef]
51. Pyragas, V.; Pyragas, K. Mean-field equations for neural populations with q -Gaussian heterogeneities. *Phys. Rev. E* **2022**, *105*, 044402. [CrossRef] [PubMed]
52. Kuramoto, Y. Proceedings of the International symposium on Mathematical Problems in Theoretical Physics. *Lect. Notes Phys.* **1975**, *30*, 420–422.
53. Yanchuk, S.; Perlikowski, P. Delay and periodicity. *Phys. Rev. E* **2009**, *79*, 1–9. [CrossRef] [PubMed]
54. Kuznetsov, Y.A. *Elements of Applied Bifurcation Theory*; Springer: New York, NY, USA, 2004.
55. Guckenheimer, J.; Holmes, P. *Nonlinear Oscillations, Dynamical Systems, and Bifurcations of Vector Fields*; Springer Science & Business Media: Berlin/Heidelberg, Germany, 2013; Volume 42.

MDPI
St. Alban-Anlage 66
4052 Basel
Switzerland
Tel. +41 61 683 77 34
Fax +41 61 302 89 18
www.mdpi.com

Mathematics Editorial Office
E-mail: mathematics@mdpi.com
www.mdpi.com/journal/mathematics

MDPI

www.ingramcontent.com/pod-product-compliance
Lightning Source LLC
Chambersburg PA
CBHW061453210926
51850CB00008B/1699
* 9 7 8 3 0 3 6 5 8 2 8 6 3 *